BUCKY HARRIS

BUCKY HARRIS

A Biography of
Baseball's Boy Wonder

Jack Smiles

McFarland & Company, Inc., Publishers
Jefferson, North Carolina, and London

LIBRARY OF CONGRESS CATALOGUING-IN-PUBLICATION DATA

Smiles, Jack, 1947–
    Bucky Harris: a biography of baseball's boy wonder / Jack
Smiles.
        p.   cm.
    Includes bibliographical references and index.

    ISBN 978-0-7864-4160-0
    softcover : 50# alkaline paper ∞

    1. Harris, Bucky, 1896–1977.   2. Baseball players — United
States — Biography.   3. Baseball player-managers — United
States — Biography.   4. Baseball managers — United States —
Biography.   I. Title.
GV865.H272S55 2011
796.357092 — dc22
[B]   2011015344

BRITISH LIBRARY CATALOGUING DATA ARE AVAILABLE

Front cover: Bucky Harris, October 7, 1924 (Library of
Congress); Background and bats © 2011 Shutterstock

Manufactured in the United States of America

McFarland & Company, Inc., Publishers
    Box 611, Jefferson, North Carolina 28640
    www.mcfarlandpub.com

Table of Contents

Preface

In 2005 when my book *Ee-Yah: The Life and Times of Hughie Jennings* was published, it wasn't considered to be the first book in a trilogy. But with the publication of this book about Bucky Harris, following the Jennings and Ed Walsh books, I have written three books about coal miners who grew up within a five-mile radius of each other in Pennsylvania and became baseball Hall of Famers, two of them great managers as well as players.

Hall of Fame manager Bucky Harris managed in the major leagues for 29 seasons, 18 with the Washington Senators. He played in 12 seasons, though in three of those he appeared in fewer than 10 games. The bulk of his playing career was from 1920 to 1928 as the Senators' regular second baseman.

In 1924 Senators owner Clark Griffith named Harris player-manager of the team. Only 27 years old, at the time, Harris was dubbed "The Boy Wonder"; the move was quickly dismissed in the press as "Griffith's Folly."

But Harris and the Senators proved the critics wrong in '24. They upset the New York Yankees to win the American League pennant and then the New York Giants to win the World Series. It remains the only World Series championship in Washington baseball history.

That amazing 1924 season — which is said to have inspired the book *The Year the Yankees Lost the Pennant*, the basis for the Broadway play "Damn Yankees" — is explored in depth, as is Harris's 1947 championship with the Yankees.

Among the other topics from Harris's life and career that, because of their interest or importance, come in for detailed coverage are his professional basketball career, four seasons as manager and general manager in the minor leagues at Buffalo and San Diego, his role in the racial integration of two major league teams, his enigmatic personality, and his relationship with Clark Griffith.

A note about the Washington ball club nickname: Bucky Harris managed the American League's original Washington team three different times for 18 seasons. Though sometimes called the "Nationals" or "Nats" in newspapers, the team was most commonly known as the "Senators." For clarity, "Senators" is used throughout the book except where "Nats" or "Nationals" is used in quotes from newspapers.

Thanks go to Bucky's sons Stanley and Dick and his great nephew Drew Smith for agreeing to interviews and other assistance. Thanks to SABR member Howard Henry of Buffalo, New York, for research assistance. Thanks to SABR member Stephen Wheeler and the San Diego Public Library for research assistance.

Special thanks to Phil White of Laramie, Wyoming, who proofread and edited the manuscript.

Thanks to my wife Diane and daughter Sadie for their love, patience and support.

Chapter 1

Bucky and Merle

It may have been the birthday of the Prince of Peace, but on Christmas night in 1917, 20-year-old Stanley Harris was not in a peaceful mood. When Scranton Miners player-coach Jimmy Kane hit him across the arms with a hard foul as he broke toward the basket during a Penn State League professional basketball game, Harris, a 5'9", 140-pound guard for the Pittston Pitts, turned and threw a punch at the 6'2", 225-pound 36-year-old Kane, a popular Scranton native who had played 55 games with the Pittsburgh Pirates in 1908.

With some 700 fans in Scranton's Town Hall screaming for Kane, the men exchanged punches until their teammates and referee Ward Brennan pulled them apart. Harris was unmarked, but Kane came away with a nasty cut over his eye. Harris was ejected from the game, while Kane, after the cut was closed, was allowed to continue. The Scranton writers said Harris started the fight and his conduct throughout the game led to the hard foul. It was further alleged that Pittston's Hoby Fyfe held Kane while Harris punched him. The doctor said the nasty cut over Kane's eye must have been caused by a ring on Harris's finger.[1] While Stanley Harris was mixing it up, his older and more levelheaded brother, Merle, considered the better athlete, stayed out of it.

Merle and Stanley had been born in Port Jervis, New York, but they were solid Pennsylvania hard coal-bred boys raised in the tiny borough of Hughestown in the northeastern part of the state, midway between the so-called "Twin Cities" of Scranton and Wilkes-Barre. When Stanley was 4 and Merle 11, their father, Tom Harris, moved the family to Hughestown for work. Hughestown bordered the city of Pittston, where Hugh Jennings was born. It was a lively, prosperous city, with Pittston at the center of a vast anthracite coal field that contained three-quarters of the world's known deposits. There were plenty of jobs with the mining companies and related industries, such as mine equipment supply and railroading, where Tom Harris found work.

Stanley always said he had no memory of Port Jervis. To him his life began in Hughestown, though there was an irony of being born in Port Jervis that Stanley, who from childhood was called "Bucky," liked to laugh about: He was born on Ball Street. It was an appropriate beginning for the future major league player and manager. Ironically, his climb up the baseball ladder almost didn't make it past the first rung.

Three things slowed Bucky's rise in baseball. One was a misadventure at Tigers training camp in Texas in 1916. Another was the effect of World War I on baseball. The third was a funny new game where men bounced a ball on the floor of a gymnasium and tried, oftentimes unsuccessfully, to throw it through 10-foot-high hoops. Basketball was the only one of the big three American team games to be invented by an individual at a specific time and place and for a specific purpose. Football and baseball evolved incrementally from old English games over decades. Basketball and its rules evolved, too, but the basic premise as developed by James Naismith in December of 1891 did not. Naismith was a physical education instructor at Springfield College in Massachusetts, teaching boxing and swimming. That winter the school was having a problem with a group of 18 young men who were studying to be YMCA secretaries. Their course required an hour of gym class every day. In the spring and fall they could play football and baseball outside, but they got bored with calisthenics in the gymnasium during the long, dark New England winter. The lack of activity caused the men to grow "incorrigible," as Naismith described them after he was given the assignment of finding something for them to do indoors during the winter.

Though Naismith's idea was to create a goal game, he didn't want simply an indoor version of soccer or football. He didn't want the goals on the floor, where players could easily surround them and block scores, and he didn't want a game dominated by brute force. But how else could goals be scored? Thinking about a game from his youth in Canada called "Duck on Rock," where a team of kids threw a rock in an attempt to knock the opponents' rock, the "duck," from its nest on a higher rock, Naismith recalled how he and his friends tossed their rock in a high arc to hit the duck.

He realized that a goal raised above the players' heads would prevent participants from blocking the goal. The next day he asked a janitor if he had two boxes about 18 inches square. The janitor didn't, but offered Naismith a pair of peach baskets. They got a ladder and nailed the baskets to the balcony on either end of the gym. It just so happened the balcony was 10 feet from the gym floor.

His next problem was how to reduce the use of force and rough play. He quickly drew up a list of rules that called for the use of a soccer ball and outlawed running with the ball so that it had to be thrown from player to player. He also wrote a rule penalizing "holding, pushing, tripping or striking in any way the person of an opponent." The rules also called for a center jump to start the game and after each basket.

This game came to Naismith overnight. The next morning he typed and posted the rules, and that afternoon, sometime in December of 1891, the first game of basketball was played.[2] Within a couple weeks lunchtime games in the Springfield gym were attracting 200 observers. The Springfield players demonstrated the game at other Y's later that winter. The game spread with incredible speed among YMCAs that had gymnasiums.

The next winter, on December 5, 1892, almost exactly a year after the first game in Springfield, a game was played between teams from the Scranton and Wilkes-Barre YMCAs in northeastern Pennsylvania coal country, 225 miles southwest of Springfield. The game was between teams of nine players whose positions were goal, home, right and left guard, right and left forward, and right and left centre. "A good sized crowd" watched the game, which ended in a 1–1 tie.[3]

By 1894 the game had spread to other YMCAs in northeastern Pennsylvania, and a four-team league was formed among the Y teams from Scranton, Wilkes-Barre, Pittston and Kingston, a nearby town. The next season, 1895-96, backboards were introduced, although not to help shooting. Since the baskets were mounted on balconies fans could easily reach out and interfere with shots. To stop this, 4' × 6' wood or wire backboards were constructed where needed.

Around that time players got the idea to bounce the ball off the floor to themselves and advance it with a series of bounces and catches, a technique called "dribbling" and "double-dribbling." Other players got the idea to tap the ball in the air to keep it alive while running down the court. That method did not catch on, of course, but dribbling did. In 1898 the YMCA rules outlawed double-dribbling because it encouraged brute force. A big, strong player could double-dribble with his back to the basket, push his way inside, and turn around and shoot.

Before 1898 the number of players recommended by Naismith was nine, though additional players or fewer could be used depending on the size of the playing area. The 1898 rule changes reduced teams to five participants. Though the new rules were only binding to YMCA teams, the teams that were increasingly being formed and sponsored by other organizations adopted most of the rules.[4]

By 1903 there were 15 teams in the Pittston/Wilkes-Barre area and several more in and around Scranton. One such team was a youth team sponsored by a volunteer fire company in Hughestown, Pennsylvania, a tiny borough adjacent to Pittston. In 1909 a new player joined the Hughestown Hose Company basketball team. He was only 13, four years younger than the game itself. He was 5'3" and 100 pounds and his name was Stanley Raymond "Bucky" Harris.

When Bucky joined the Hose Company basketball team, it was for the same reason the game had been invented in that it was something to do in the winter. He was more enamored with baseball, of which Hughestown, a town of about 2,000, was a local hotbed. The town had at least two first-class diamonds, at least by local standards, one of which bears Bucky's name today.

"Baseball always has been uppermost on my mind. I played during recess and after school and after work when I was at the colliery. I was always thinking and talking baseball and playing when I could," Bucky said in an interview years later.[5]

As early as age eight and during the springs and summers up through age 13 or 14, Bucky was the mascot for the Pittston Brothers, one of the top

Bucky Harris (back row, left), about age 13 or 14, with the Hughestown Hose Company basketball team, approximately 1910. Others are unidentified (courtesy Marguerite Ciannelli).

amateur adult teams in the local area. The Brothers played in northeastern Pennsylvania and upstate New York. Bucky practiced with the Brothers and the fungo hitters couldn't hit anything too hot for him to handle.

Pete Smaltz, the Brothers manager, said there were a lot of boys in the coal region who could play ball but none had the "fighting spirit" that Bucky had. Fighting was a literal description of Bucky. Members said that Bucky was always on the sidelines with a chip on his shoulder, ready to "take on the other team's kid rooters."

Bucky had a reputation around his Hughestown neighborhood, too, where the adults thought of Bucky as something of a Peck's bad boy. Peck's Bad Boy was the fictional star of newspaper stories and books who had a penchant for getting into trouble. Peck was created by George W. Peck in the late 1800s and played by George M. Cohan in an 1891 stage adaptation. An example of Bucky's Peck side is the story told about the day the Brothers came back to Hughestown after a Sunday road game and went to Smaltz's combination poolroom, cigar store, barbershop and general store. Bucky climbed into the attic of Smaltz's and dumped a pail of water on the backs of the crowd as they discussed that day's game.[6]

Bucky's shenanigans were tolerated in the sports-crazed Pittston area where athletics was one of the few diversions from mine work. Bucky, by the time he was 13, was considered the best young athlete in the area and one who could hold his own against older boys in just about any game. Playing basketball for the Hughestown Hose Company team was rough on the tiny floor in the hose house and Bucky roughed it up with the toughest of them. It was speculated that had he gone to college, he could have excelled in five sports. When he was 16 Bucky won the local pool contest with partner Ed Ruane. He was fast enough to be a sprinter and excelled in pickup football and handball. When he was in his late teens to early 20s, he often teamed with his mentor, Hughie Jennings, in handball games. They once defeated a team considered the champions of New York City.

Around the time he was emerging as an athlete and after finishing sixth grade, Bucky told his mother, Catherine, he wanted to quit school and go to work in the mines. He was good at play, but mine work was another matter. As an adult Bucky was not big — he was listed in the major leagues generously at 5'9", 156 pounds — and as a 13-year-old he was likely around 100 pounds. His mother worried that he was too frail for mine work. Unlike most mothers, she encouraged her boys' ball playing and she used Bucky's love of sports to discourage him from quitting school for the mines, saying it would leave him little time for baseball and basketball while reminding him he had just been named starting shortstop for the St. Peter's Lutheran Church Sunday School team.

But Bucky was adamant. "Merle did both and so can I," he'd say. Merle was Bucky's big brother, seven years Bucky's elder, but as an adult he was even smaller than Bucky. He was about 5' 6" but a lot thicker than Bucky and as tough as nails. Merle was the man of the house as their father, Tom Harris, had left the family, though why and exactly when is not known. It is known that Tom Harris was a fair baseball pitcher who played on Pittston area teams with Hugh Jennings as his catcher. While Jennings remained a family friend and would later help Bucky get his feet wet in professional baseball, Tom Harris seemingly disappeared. He would surface in 1924 during the World Series when he drew interest from newspapermen as the father of the Senators' manager. He was then a chief of detectives for the Lackawanna Railroad in Hoboken, New Jersey. He told a story saying he had walked Bucky to the railroad station when Bucky went to his first professional baseball tryout at age 16.

Bucky never wrote or talked about his father walking him to the train. Bucky felt abandoned by his father and never talked about him in any context. And it seems unlikely that Tom Harris was around the Pittston area when Bucky was 16. It is clear when Bucky was 13 and trying to convince his mother to let him quit school and go into the mines his father was already gone and Merle was the man of the house.

Bucky worshiped his big brother. Merle not only worked in the mines as the family breadwinner, he also had a five-year minor league baseball career and an even longer professional basketball career. For three years he played both. In his 1925 series of newspaper articles that later became the book *Mine Boy to Manager*, Bucky wrote about Merle.

> I finally earned the starting shortstop place on the St. Peter's Lutheran Church nine. It was in the Sunday school league. We played twilight baseball after work. That season Merle was with Charleston in the Atlantic League. Hughie Jennings had placed him there. Between working and playing baseball in the early evenings I was running home in the half-hour lunch period to get the Charleston paper to keep track of Merle. If the paper was delayed in the mail, I went back to work disappointed. Merle was an honest-to-goodness professional baseball player and my hero. I idolized him. The other boys looked up to me and I thought it was because of my baseball ability. I know better now. It was because of Merle.

Bucky continued working on his mother, and Merle to let him quit school and go to work. Finally, after exacting a promise from Bucky that he would go to night school, his mother and Merle relented. Getting a job was easy. Hughie Jennings' brother, W.P. Jennings, was the superintendent of the Pennsylvania Coal Company's no. 9 colliery in Hughestown. Jennings gave Bucky a job as a slate picker, or breaker boy, as the boys who separated slate and other waste from the coal were called. It was dirty and dangerous work, as the breaker boys had to pick slate from the coal as he roared down chutes from the top of the breaker. Pay was 12 cents an hour for a nine-hour workday, which came to $6.48 a week. Bucky so was proud of his first pay check he took the envelope unopened and gave it to his mother.

After six months Jennings offered Bucky a job as an office boy at the nearby Butler Colliery. As it paid less and came with a ribbing from his friends in the breaker, Bucky didn't want to take the office job. His mother and Merle insisted he take it. Merle suggested the office job would give Bucky more time and energy to play ball. The Butler Colliery was four miles from Pittston. In the office Bucky answered the phone, sorted mail, and ran errands for the mine bosses. He wore patched hand-me-downs that had belonged to Merle and he took a ribbing for them from other office workers.

Bucky made friends with a big Polish miner who had his name Americanized to Nick Stanley, probably from something such as Stankoski or Stankcowicz. Stanley protected Bucky and once beat up two miners who threw Bucky out of his seat onto the floor of a train. "He pulled me off the floor, put me in the seat and told me that when I grew up to never let a big man pick on a little one."

The No. 9 Breaker of the Pennsylvania Coal Company in Hughestown, Pennsylvania. Bucky went to work here at age 13.

In *Mine Boy to Manager*, Bucky explained what happened to Stanley. "We became good friends. He told me to keep my eyes and ears open and learn and someday I would be a mine boss. I told him I wanted to be a ballplayer and that some of them made $5,000 a year. He was stunned. I said, 'Maybe I won't ever make $5,000 a year, but I'll make a couple hundred a month.'

"'Don't aim low, aim high,' he said. 'Someday you'll be big and you'll do big things.' I wish he'd been around to see the world's series with the Giants, but he went to France to fight for his adopted country and never returned."

Bucky continued to play shortstop for the Sunday school team and scrub games, as the pickup games with the mine boys were called, during the week after work. After a year as office boy he was promoted to assistant weigh master at 18 cents an hour, boosting his weekly envelope to $9.72.

"I didn't tell my mother about the promotion until I brought home my first week wages. She was peeling onions at the time, whether the onions or my pay were to blame or not, tears ran down her cheeks and she smiled. She hugged me, praised me for being a big man and told me how much help and comfort I was to her. My eyes got wet too and it wasn't from the onions. That Sunday we had ice cream with dinner.

"As assistant weigh master I had to keep track of the coal leaving the colliery. I felt big bringing home $10 a week and not yet 15 years old."

Unlike a lot of the mothers of the mine boys, Bucky's mom did not discourage Bucky's baseball dreams. After all, she already had one son playing minor league ball thanks to Hughie Jennings, who had recommended Merle to Traverse City in the Michigan State League. Nobody had ever left the mines and gone further than Jennings, the one-time shortstop of the Baltimore Orioles "Big Four" and manager of the Detroit Tigers. And he wasn't just a famous name in the newspapers and magazines. He was a flesh-and-blood Pittston miner who more than once had sat in her kitchen.

Bucky not only followed his brother's career in the papers and magazines, he also kept up on Jennings, the O'Neill brothers from nearby Minooka, the Coveleski brothers and Chick Shorton, all former miners from the area. Bucky was the only one of the mine boys who could recite major league batting and fielding averages.

When Merle came home from Michigan after his first minor league season in 1912, he was hailed a hero in Hughestown. There was still a month or so left to play baseball. Merle, a shortstop, took Bucky in hand and worked with him. He taught him how to shift his feet and how to toss to second to start double plays. Merle ragged Bucky about his size. He couldn't do anything about his height, but Merle wanted him to get bigger and stronger. Bucky would cite Wee Willie Keeler and Donnie Bush as small players and Merle would say, "Yeah they're small, but at least they are in the bantam weight class; you're in the paperweight class."

Merle worked on Bucky's batting stance, trying to get Bucky, who was a pull hitter, to hit to all fields. Bucky was too weak to hit past an infielder on the right side but doggedly worked at it. As long as he could get somebody to throw and shag he stayed out until dark while trying to hit over first base. Merle's lessons weren't all about the mechanics of fielding and batting. "I was playing third in a scrub game and my brother was coaching third for the other team. With a runner on third the catcher threw to me to keep him close and my brother said to me, 'Let me see that ball.'

"I flipped it to him and he stepped out of the way and the ball rolled away and the run scored. I was mad enough to fight and hurt that my brother had pulled a trick on me and told him so. He just held my arms and laughed until I cooled down.

"Merle was testing me. 'If you want to play baseball for a living, you've got to keep your mind on the game every minute from start to finish.'"

That fall and winter Bucky tried to build himself up. He played basketball all winter and ate a lot of meat and potatoes. Bucky played basketball with the Hose Company team while Merle played with adults at the YMCA. Evenings when they weren't playing basketball, Merle and Bucky talked baseball. At the time Merle secretly believed Bucky had no chance of reaching the major leagues, and he admitted that to Bucky when Bucky did make it. But Merle never discouraged Bucky when he was a kid and gave him all the time he could spare.

After Merle left to report to the Pensacola Snappers in the Cotton State League in 1913, Bucky, now 16, continued to play shortstop for the Sunday school team and began to fill out. Before long he'd put on 25 pounds and received an offer to play for the Hamtown team in the Suburban League on Sundays for $2 a game. Hamtown was a nickname for Hughestown, so named for the swine that roamed the dirt streets. The Suburban League was a high-caliber adult Pittston-area league wherein there was an intense rivalry among teams from such towns as Browntown, Sebastapool, Avoca, Duryea and Exeter.

Bucky may have been a little out of his league with Hamtown, as he was the youngest player in a league of adults, many of them strapping ethnic miners in their 20s and 30s. In his first game he got a hit on a lucky bounce, walked twice and handled five routine plays at shortstop. Hamtown won 5–3. Bucky was paid two dollars in small change.

"I believed my foot was on the first rung of the ladder to the major leagues. I gave the $2 to my mother and told her there would be more coming.

She started a bank account for me. I have been fortunate to have added to it since."

Bucky got knocked down a peg a couple days later when he met Tony Walsh, one of the best semi-pro ballplayers around Pittston. Walsh had seen Bucky make his debut and, as Bucky recalled it, said, "If you are going to stay in there you better take out an insurance policy. You'll try to stop a fast one someday and be carried out to the outfield."

Walsh took an interest in Bucky and filled in where Merle had left off. He worked with Bucky on fielding and getting throws off quickly. He shortened Bucky's batting stance to draw more bases on balls. "He was most helpful," Bucky said, "but rarely offered praise. When he did compliment, it meant something."

Word got back to Jacob Kuschel, the Sunday school superintendent, that Bucky was rushing from Sunday school to make a few dollars playing Suburban League games. Kuschel headed Bucky off one Sunday after class. A big man, he stood blocking the doorway as Bucky tried to run out and gave Bucky an ultimatum: Hamtown or the Sunday school team. Kuschel wasn't going to have any paid players on his team.

Bucky blurted out "Hamtown" and dived between Kuschel's legs to escape. Bucky continued to go to Sunday school, but Kuschel never said a word about Bucky's decision until he signed with Washington. Then they had a good laugh about it. Kuschel sent Bucky a glowing letter when he signed and made a ring with his own hands for Hughestown fans to present to Bucky.

Bucky played shortstop for Hamtown on Sundays and holidays and in any scrub game he could find on weekdays. He improved steadily and gained more weight, but without competition for the shortstop job on the team Bucky got a little complacent. Walsh called him on it.

"You've got to come to life and keep on your toes every minute. Maybe if you keep plugging away you can make something of yourself. But kid, don't ever let up. You think Warner and Bush got where they are by lying down?"

It took a benching for Bucky to take Walsh's warning to heart. In a game against Avoca, Hughie Jennings's hometown, Bucky was jeered by the fans for failing to run out a grounder and pulled from the game. He sulked and blamed the manager and fans. When Walsh heard about Bucky's reaction he jumped all over him. "He bawled me out. I shifted from foot to foot on the verge of tears."

Walsh dragged Bucky to the ball field and hit him grounders until he calmed down. The next Hamtown game Bucky hit the first pitch of the contest for a double and received a big hand.

"Since then I never worried about the jeers. They hurt, but made me hustle all the more."

When Bucky wasn't playing and when he could scrape up a few nickels and dimes, he took the train to Scranton and Wilkes-Barre to watch the Miners and Barons play in the New York State League. Bucky saw former and future major leaguers in those games, including Monte Cross, who had been a shortstop with the American League champion A's in 1902.

The trips to Scranton and Wilkes-Barre games didn't do much for Bucky's confidence. Seeing a player like Cross made him doubt himself as major league material. The playing conditions in the Suburban League didn't help his attitude. The Suburban ball fields looked cheap and small compared to Scranton and the players had to do the work. The poorer teams used burlap feed bags filled with sand for bases. A few hand-made benches served as a grandstand.

Even so the Sunday Suburban League games were important events in the mining towns. It was about the only recreation for most of the miners. On Labor Day Hamtown played Browntown, a close rival. Hamtown had the lead in the ninth when Browntown rallied. They tied the game but Bucky started a double play to end the inning. As he ran off the field, a fan hit Bucky in the ear with a banana. Bucky wanted to fight and had to be restrained by his teammates. In the ninth Bucky walked, was bunted to second, and went to third on an infield out.

"I read of something that Cobb did and still steaming, I tried it. I picked up the third base bag and ran for home. The pitcher fired the ball to the catcher, Natsie Loftus. They had me dead until I hit Natsie in the face with the bag. He came after me spitting sand from his mouth and shaking it out of his hair. He dove on me and we rolled on the ground. Some of the players and fans mixed it up, too. I came out of it with a bloody nose, cut lip and black eye."

The next weekend Bucky scraped a big piece of skin off his hip while sliding. He treated it himself, as a lot of players did, by cleaning it and covering it with tissue paper. When the cut didn't heal, Bucky's mother called the doctor. He diagnosed blood poisoning, which we would call an infection today, and ordered Bucky to bed. He was bed-ridden for three weeks. Before he played again he made sliding pads out of towels and string.

If seeing Cross play shortstop had damaged Bucky's self-esteem, seeing another major leaguer later that summer was nearly a fatal blow. Hughey Jennings brought the Tigers to Wilkes-Barre for an exhibition game. Bucky and some of the other miners took the day off and went to the game. Bucky got a bleacher seat for 25 cents and kept his eyes on his favorite player, Tigers shortstop Donie Bush.

Bush was 5'6" and 140 pounds, a perfect fit for Bucky, and Bush was dazzling with his speed and quickness. He covered ground, impossibly it seemed to Bucky, getting to balls deep in back of third, charging slow rollers and covering second on double plays.

He was so good, he made Bucky doubt himself. "I was dazed and dazzled and couldn't imagine playing like that, yet within 10 years we were teammates in Washington."

On the train on the way home, Tony Walsh wouldn't let Bucky beat himself up. After all, Bush was a 27-year-old man in his fifth season as a major league shortstop. "You're a baby in baseball," Walsh said. "Keep plugging away. Even if you don't make it you'll have the satisfaction of knowing you tried."

"Tony was always there when I needed him," Bucky said. "He was killed in a mine accident in Pittston but lived long enough to see me reach the majors and become manager of the Senators."

Within three years after he marveled at Donie Bush, Bucky played against major leaguers himself. Bucky's reputation as a ball player grew over the next couple of summers, and in 1915 he was selected to play on a team of minor leaguers and semi-pros in an exhibition game against the Yankees in Scranton. The Yankees made the stop on their way home from a western swing. Bill Coughlin, a Scranton man and manager of the Scranton team in the New York State League, managed the Yankees' opponent. He was a veteran of the American League and had a pennant to prove it with Hughey Jennings and the Tigers in 1907. He was also a veteran of the mines and had a missing finger to prove it.

Jimmy O'Neill, who later was one of four O'Neill brothers to reach the major leagues, played short for Bucky's team. From the players' bench Bucky marveled at Yankees shortstop Roger Peckinpaugh. Little could Bucky have imagined that one day he and "Peck," as he was called, would be the best double play combination in the American League. In the sixth inning Coughlin put Bucky in to play third against the Yankees. "It was the most important day of my life. I've had my share of thrills like winning the starting berth with Washington, being named youngest big league manager, beating the Yankees in the pennant race and winning the series, but I can honestly say none of them touched the joy I felt that day in Scranton."

The game went 10 innings. Bucky admitted to being nervous as a cat and made clean plays on the balls hit to him, but made high throws. Once again Tony Walsh was there to help Bucky out. Playing first base he jumped for the throw and came down on the bag both times. Dazzy Vance, then an unknown who had just come up from the Nebraska League, pitched the last four innings for the Yankees. Bucky faced him twice. He struck out and hit a ground ball up the middle that Peckinpaugh turned into an out.

After the game Coughlin tried to sign Bucky to a Scranton contract on the back of an envelope for $125 a month. At the time Bucky was a weigh-master at the Butler colliery making 12 bucks a week and he was overwhelmed by the offer. But he was paralyzed to act, saying he wanted to talk it over with Merle and Tony Walsh. As the New York State League was in its final week, Coughlin agreed to give Bucky the winter to think it over and made the offer stand for the next season.

On the way home Walsh told Bucky it was a good thing he didn't sign with Coughlin on the spot because he'd heard Hughey Jennings had a scout there. Back home Bucky told his mother the good news about the scout and gave her the $20 he got for playing. She put the money away to save for him, though they did celebrate by going to the movies that night.

The scouting report on Bucky that got back to Jennings wasn't good: too small, too weak. Jennings decided to give Bucky a tryout anyway at the behest of mutual friends of the Harris and Jennings families, Pittston attorney A.T. Walsh, no relation to Tony, and Dr. Joseph Burke.

Walsh and Burke went to Bucky's house on a snowy Sunday in early March with a telegram containing the news that Bucky was to report to Wax-ahachie, Texas, immediately. Bucky and his mother were stunned. Waxahachie, Texas, was 1,000 miles from Hughestown. It was an unfathomable distance, and Bucky had never been further away than Wilkes-Barre or Scranton. Merle was already on his way to camp with the Columbia, South Carolina, Comers in the Sally League, and Bucky's mother, realizing she would be alone for the first time since Merle was born, cried. The next morning Bucky went to the mine asking for a leave and the superintendent, learning why, wished him well and told him a job would be waiting for him if things didn't work out.

In Texas Bucky expected Jennings to meet him at the station but he wasn't there. Bucky checked into the hotel and found his way to the ball field where he learned Jennings was hospitalized in a nearby city recovering from an injury he sustained while running a sliding drill. Coach Jimmy Burke got Bucky a uniform, and he joined practice. "Little attention was paid to me, as a stringy kid weighing 115 pounds. The veterans didn't even bother to play pranks on me. I was green enough for the cows to eat."

Bucky's early workouts proved the scouting report, small and weak, was right. Burke hit grounders and line drives at Bucky at third like nothing he'd seen back in Hughestown. He missed most of them, and the ones he did field he barely got across the diamond to first base. As luck would have it in his first intra-squad game on March 17, Bucky batted against Grover Cleveland Lowdermilk — a 6' 4", 190-pound major league veteran who had been second in walks, third in hit batsmen and fifth in strikeouts in the A.L. in 1915. Lowdermilk blew Bucky away with fastballs.

Though Bucky may not have looked like a professional prospect, his hard-headed, coal-country reckless hustle and running speed impressed the coaches. Once Jennings got back in camp he gave Bucky more of a shot than he likely deserved, probably because of his friendship with Bucky's family and maybe because he saw something of himself in Bucky. When the Tigers broke camp Bucky was sent on a barnstorming trip with the Yannigans, as teams of non-regular players were called, as their third baseman. Burke was the manager. Harry Heilman, Oscar Vitt, Frank Fuller, George Maisel, George Harper, catcher Red McKee and Ray Dauss and a couple of the other pitchers made up the lineup. McKee was Bucky's roommate and he and Dauss befriended him, taking him to the Texas towns after games to buy postcards and souvenirs.

Bucky caught up with the fielding but didn't hit a lick. The Yannigans rejoined Jennings and the regulars in Kansas City and Bucky was released. Jennings let him stay with the team to Chicago for the season opener and gave him a ticket for the game. Jennings promised to work on landing Bucky with a minor league team.

"That was my first major league game. I didn't enjoy it much. That night I took the train back to Pittston thinking my baseball career was over."[7]

Chapter 2

From the Diamond to the Cage

World Series victories in the early part of the twentieth century set off some wild celebrations in the winning cities. In 1906 thousands of fans roamed the streets hours after the White Sox beat the Cubs, setting bonfires and singing and chanting outside the players' homes and hotels. In 1919 when the Reds' train returned to Cincinnati after the clinching game in Chicago, the mayor proclaimed a holiday and thousands of raucous men, women and children swarmed the train station throwing confetti, hats and newspaper. A police gauntlet hustled the players into cabs as the throng grabbed at the players' hats and clothes.[1] In 1920 a celebration in Cleveland turned into a riot as a crowd of 30,000 broke through a police line, rushed a platform erected for the players, trampled chairs to bits and pinned fans against the platform until it collapsed. Children were handed over the crowd to save them from the crush.[2]

But all previous celebrations — in size and scope though not violence — were like garden parties in contrast to what happened in the nation's capital after the Washington Senators defeated the New York Giants in Game 7 on October 10, 1924.

The pandemonium in the streets lasted into the early morning. Hours after the game, Senators manager Bucky Harris, having earlier escaped from the throngs at Griffith Stadium, was in a cab after a visit to Judge Landis' hotel suite. His cab had a sticker on the windshield labeled "Bucky," but so did every cab Bucky saw looking out from the back seat. Bucky marveled at the mayhem and what had become of his life. After all, 10 years earlier he had been an obscure, small-town mine boy who had never been more than 10 miles from his home. He was having a hard time grasping the magnitude of it all and the fact that he was at the center of it.

The cab was stopped at an intersection by a police officer. The cop insisted to Bucky's driver that he couldn't let him through if the cab carried the president of the United States.

"Man," Bucky's driver said, "I've got Bucky Harris."

"Why didn't you say so in the first place?" the cop responded and stopped traffic to let Bucky's cab snake through.

"That's when I knew I had reached the top in the baseball world," Bucky thought.[3]

When Bucky returned home from Texas after being released by the Tigers in April of 1916, he thought he'd missed his chance to make it in professional baseball. Merle stuck with Columbia in the Sally League, leaving Bucky at home with his mom. She met him at the station and tried to console him, reminding him he was only 19 and making him his favorite meal for dinner, roast beef with onions.

That night Bucky went to Smaltz's cigar store to hang out with the guys. He expected they would rag on him for being cut by Jennings, but he was treated more like a hero than a bum. His friends besieged him with questions about the Tigers. What were Cobb, Crawford, Veach, Young, and Bush really like? How did they talk, what did they eat, how did they spend their spare time? Do they think they'll win the pennant? He had to admit he didn't meet Cobb, who reported after Bucky had gone home.

Encouraged by his mother and friends Bucky kept playing with Hamtown and wherever else he could find a game. Jennings had promised to land Bucky with a minor league team, but three weeks passed and Bucky heard nothing. Just when he despaired that Jennings was going to keep his promise, the telegram came ordering him to report to Muskegon, Michigan, in the Central League. As it happened the train lay over in Detroit, allowing Bucky to see a Tigers game and give his thanks to Jennings.

When he arrived in Muskegon the team was in Evansville, Indiana, for a pre-season game. By the time he got there he was nearly out of money. He signed a contract for $125 a month, but he didn't get paid for a couple of weeks. Until his first pay, he had to walk to the park while the other players took street cars. The Muskegon manager, Babe Myers, immediately put Bucky in the lineup at second base. That day Bucky handled a few chances, got a hit in three at-bats and stole second after misreading a sign for a hit and run. Though he stole the base, he got bawled out for misreading the sign.

Bucky played a lot of the exhibition games, and when the season opened at Terre Haute, he was a starter at second base. As always, nobody out-hustled him and he never backed down from a hard slide or a hard slider. Even so, the game was a little faster than he was used to. The Central League, with teams in Grand Rapids, Springfield, Evansville, Wheeling, Terre Haute and South Bend, was a high-caliber league, and even though nobody tried harder, the league was a little out of Bucky's reach. He was making errors and not hitting a lick. Within a week of Opening Day he was benched. After a few games on the bench they tried him at third, but he played even worse there.

Joe Evers, brother of Johnny of Tinker-to-Evers-to-Chance fame, replaced Bucky at second. John Coveleski, brother of Steve, was also a teammate. Ty Cobb's brother Paul Cobb played for Terre Haute. Bucky batted against Springfield pitcher Jesse Haines, who later pitched a no-hitter for the Cardinals and won 210 major league games. "I don't believe I got much more than a foul off him," Bucky said.

Bucky was released in June. As most of his pay had been sent home, he had $20 to his name and was 700 miles from home. He wired Jennings, who told him to stay in Muskegon until he heard from him. His room was $2 a week and dinner at the hotel was 35 cents, so he figured he could hold out for a while. He went to the games when the team was home. A player named Dowling, who was brought in to replace Bucky, proved to be in over his head

Bucky's mother, Catherine, encouraged his ball playing (Library of Congress Digital Collection).

deeper than Bucky had been. Myers cut Dowling and signed Bucky to another contract. His second trial lasted a month before he was released again. In 55 games he hit .166 (28-for-169) with eight runs and two stolen bases. His fielding average was .892, second worst in the league. He had 82 putouts, 91 assists and 21 errors in 55 games. Jennings tried to land him with another team, but he wired Bucky there were no takers and he would try again the next spring. There was nothing to do but go home. Bucky was back in Hughestown in mid–July. By mid–August Merle was home, too, from Columbia. What had been Bucky's first minor league season would prove to be Merle's last.[4]

Before he was back from Muskegon, a note in the Pittston section of the local daily newspaper revealed Bucky's plans. "Stanley Harris, who is yet under contract with Hughie Jennings' Detroit team and who has been playing a star game for Muskegon of the Michigan State League will be home tomorrow and play third base with his former teammates Hamtown against Browntown. Harris last season was one of the stars of the Suburban League being a splendid hitter, clever fielder and possessing all that goes with making a good player."[5]

Bucky didn't play anything near a "star game" at Muskegon and he knew it, but the paper was right about his impact in the Suburban League. Back at a level he was used to, he quickly established himself as the best player in the league. He was moved to shortstop and batted fourth.[6] On August 18 Hamtown agreed to play a three-game series with Hyde Park, the top amateur team in the Scranton area. The teams played the series for a side bet of $200 and gate receipts. Bucky and Merle Harris were in the Hamtown lineup; Merle batted first and Bucky fourth. Hamtown won all three games.

As he had in 1915, Scranton manager Bill Coughlin approached Bucky after the Hyde Park series and offered to sign him. Scranton was a Class B team in the New York State League. As he was technically still under contract with Jennings and the Tigers, Bucky was warned to get Jennings' approval before he played with Scranton. That didn't happen in time and the season ended without Bucky appearing in a game for Scranton, though he was listed on the team's roster for 1916.[7]

That October a well-heeled family friend named Jimmy Fitzpatrick took Bucky to the World Series in New York. They also took in a Broadway show and dinner at a fine restaurant. Bucky the coal cracker knew nothing of New York City dining etiquette. As he put it in *Mine Boy to Manager*, "I didn't know how to eat."

Bucky saw the third and fourth games from the left-field bleachers in Ebbets Field. He saw Carl Mays pitch Game 3 for the Red Sox. He missed Ruth, who pitched Game 2 in Boston. Chick Shorten, from Scranton, played center for Boston in Game 3 and went 3-for-4. Game 3 featured two uncanny future connections for Bucky. Mays would be the opposing pitcher in Bucky's first major league at-bat two years later and Boston second baseman Hal Jarvin was the man Bucky would replace in Washington.

"As I watched the final game in Brooklyn, I thought about the first series I was interested in 1909. I got returns of the final game shivering in a snowstorm on the streets of Pittston."[8]

That fall Merle decided to quit professional baseball. Though he'd had a decent season while batting .290 in 113 games at Columbia, he was 27 and ready to admit he wasn't going to make it to the major leagues. Besides, he could make more money working for the colliery by day and playing professional basketball by night in the Penn State League (PSL).

The Penn State League had been formed in 1914. Trenton, New Jersey, is considered the birthplace of professional basketball. Players on the Trenton YMCA team broke from the Y and were paid to play in the 1896-97 season. They organized independently, renting the large high-ceilinged room on the third floor of the Masonic Hall for a court and charging 15 and 25 cents for admission. In 1898 the first professional league was formed. Called the National Basketball League, it had teams in Trenton, Millville and Camden, New Jersey, two teams in Philadelphia, and one in Germantown, Pennsylvania, which today is a section of Philadelphia.

As other professional leagues developed in New England and New York, players jumped from league to league for more money, leading to the rise and fall of various leagues. The Penn State League was formed for the 1914-15 season.[9] Merle led Pittston to an 18–2 record and the first PSL championship as the consensus best forward in the league. Despite its name, the league's original six franchises were towns within 20 miles of each other in the Northeast coal country — Pittston, Wilkes-Barre, Hazleton, Nanticoke, Freeland and Tamaqua. Other than Wilkes-Barre, the towns were little known outside the local area; nonetheless Penn State evolved into a high-caliber league known for paying players well. Because the anthracite section of the state was a sports-crazed area where workers had a little fun money to spend, the PSL attracted fans and some of the biggest star players of the time. Crowds of 2,000 or more were common for important games. Gary Schmeelk, a 6-foot, 220-pound forward and navy veteran from New York, was one example of the star players who joined the PSL. He played with the Pittston team and was soon one of the Harris brothers' best friends. He was a well-known competitive swimmer who had finished third in the 440-yard swim at the Jamaica Bay Yacht Club at Rockaway Beach in August 1915.[10]

In the early 1920s Schmeelk played for the Original Celtics, and in 1926-27 Schmeelk would be the player-coach of Brooklyn Arcadians in the American Basketball League, a premier precursor to the NBA. Schmeelk was one of several players in the Penn State League who would go on to the ABL. It may have been Schmeelk who gave Bucky his nickname. In the summer of 1918 Bucky was playing baseball for the Baltimore Dry Docks club. Frank Schulte was one of the outfielders. Schulte asked Bucky, who was then known around baseball as Stanley, if he had a nickname. Bucky answered that Gary Schmeelk named him "Bucky" after he bucked a couple players off his back in a basketball game "like a tough little Bronco."

According to Bucky's son, Stanley, today a retired federal judge, the basketball nickname story "drifts a little bit from full truth." He said when

Bucky's family moved to Hughestown from Port Jervis where he was born, the house in which they inhabited had a kid named Bucky. So all the kids in the neighborhood starting calling him Bucky.[11]

Newspaper accounts of Penn State League games seem to strengthen the judge's story. Though most of the accounts refer to him as Stanley, a story about his debut game in the PSL in the *Wilkes-Barre Times Leader* in November of 1915 does refer to him as "Merle's brother Bucky."

Merle got Bucky on the Pittston Pitts team as a sub for the 1915-16 season, when the league expanded to eight teams. Scranton was added that season and the regular season was more than doubled to 42 games. The Pitts played in one of the best venues in the league, a relatively new military armory on Main Street. Huge lengths of wire mesh with hooks along the bottom edge were suspended from the ceiling. For games, the ends were pulled down to the large open main floor and fitted to recessed locks to create a wire mesh wall to surround the court. The idea had been developed in Trenton. The effect of the mesh was that of a cage, hence the origin of the nickname "cagers" for basketball players. The cages prevented the balls from flying into the crowd and reduced violence among the players, as under early rules the team that got to a loose ball out of bounds first won possession, leading to some wild scrums that often involved the fans.

At the Pittston Armory, nicknamed "The Castle" for its outside appearance, and other PSL venues, the cages were hoisted up after the games for dances featuring popular local orchestras. The armory still stands in Pittston. It was used for a dress factory until the mid–2000s, during which time the cage locks in the floor were visible. Today it is a spa with new floors and the locks are hidden.

The Pennsylvania State League suggested baskets be at least 10 feet high with 4-by-4 backboards and the rim extending 12 inches from the board. The backboards were usually wire framed with wood. The PSL courts were not uniform. In the bigger towns — Scranton, Wilkes-Barre and Pittston — where there were armories, courts could be as large as 65 feet long and 35 feet wide, two-thirds the size of an NBA court today. In the smaller towns teams made do in halls that were considerably smaller. Some towns had wooden framed wire fences, or ropes, for cages.

The late Joel S. (Shikey) Gotthoffer, who later played for the famed Philadelphia Sphas, also played for Nanticoke in the Penn State League. He once talked about the Nanticoke court and the general roughness of PSL play. "I played the first few games at Nanticoke in a rope cage, and I came home with the cage's markings on me. You could play tic-tac-toe on everybody after a game because the cage marked you up; sometimes you were bleeding and sometimes not. You were like a gladiator, and if you didn't get rid of the ball, you could get killed."[12]

It was rough outside the cages as well as in the PSL towns. Fans were known to heat nails with miners' lamps and toss them through tears in the cage at opposing foul shooters. At Nanticoke hot steam pipes lined one wall at courtside and players were burned when pushed into them.[13]

Balls that hit off the cages were in play. The balls had seams and laces, making them difficult to dribble. In the PSL there was a center jump after every basket and players shot their own free throws. Some other leagues used a designated free throw shooter. The 40-minute games could be completed in a little over an hour because the clock rarely stopped.

Crisp passing was a winning skill. There were only two ways to shoot, the under-hand layup near the basket and the long-range two-handed set shot, from the chest or underhanded from 25 to 30 feet out. The jump shot and dunk were unknown, though the center pivot and hook shot soon developed. Without 10-second, three-second and 24-second rules, scores were low because teams would hold the ball for several minutes while waiting for a player to break free for a layup or for a set shooter to get open.

Bucky's role on the team during the first two seasons was like that of a hockey enforcer. As an account in a local paper put it, "Although Stanley Harris is light for a guard, he is playing a bang up game for Pittston. He is covering close and makes his opponents travel some to score."[14]

He got a few starts when the team was in a pinch, but he was mainly used to harass the opponents' best players when the single referee was not looking and to goad them into fights. When it came to pure basketball playing, the Pitts were always looking for somebody more polished than Bucky.

From a *Times Leader* story in January of 1916: "Pittston beat Freeland 25–20. Bernie Dunn took Stanley Harris' position at forward and played a brilliant game."

And this from a few days later: "Pittston fans were pleased at the chance to get Freddy Sager, the Hazleton youngster. He will succeed Stanley Harris at forward, the latter being retained as a sub."

Injuries and defections were common as players often jumped leagues, and Bucky continually got chances to play. On February 5, 1916, Pittston's starting guard Bill Clarke was out and Bucky got the start against Scranton. This was his first go-round with Scranton's Jimmy Kane, who was considered one of the top centers in the East. Bucky helped double-team Kane and hold him to one field goal. Bucky scored one himself as Pittston won, 22–8. Schmeelk and Merle scored six each. This was the start of a fierce rivalry between Bucky and Kane that would culminate with the infamous fight two seasons later on Christmas night in 1917. Bucky's game improved the more he played in the 1915-16 season. With Merle out with "acute indigestion" for a key game with Wilkes-Barre on February 18, Bucky subbed for him and

Pittston won. On February 26 Pittston beat Hazleton, 20–19. "Bucky replaced Allie Fisher in the second half and there was a marked improvement in the play of the Pitts."[15]

Increasingly Bucky was seen more as a basketball player who played baseball in the summer than the other way around. When Bucky went to Texas to try out with the Tigers in March of 1916 the local paper said, "Stanley Harris, substitute forward of the Pittston basketball team, was told to report to Waxahachie, Texas, by Tigers manager Hughie Jennings."

Bucky still thought of himself as a baseball player, though basketball was good for the family's bottom line. Bucky was likely making $5–$10 a game and Merle, a starter and scorer, as much as $40. Over a 40-game season Merle could make $1,600 while living at home, considerably more than he made living on the road in a six-month low minor league baseball season.

The Eastern Basketball League — a rival league with teams in Reading, Pennsylvania, and Trenton and Camden, New Jersey — adopted new rules for the 1916-17 season that were adopted by the PSL. The rules called for two officials; one had worked games previously. Jumps balls were used to start the games and second halves, after baskets, and to decide possession after the ball was batted out of the cage. The jumpers were banned from touching the ball a second time until touched by another player. Jumpers were to have a hand behind their backs. Under three minutes the clock would be stopped for free throws, but a timeout was subtracted from the fouling team.

The Eastern League and PSL presidents met to negotiate peace pertaining to players jumping leagues. It didn't work and players continued to jump between leagues.[16] For the 1916–17 seasons, players from the defunct New York State League and the Eastern League jumped to the Penn State League. Kane, who held the Eastern League field goal record, went from Trenton back to Scranton, his hometown, where he was named captain. Kane, 6'2" and 225 pounds, jumped center for Scranton. Maurice Tome of Kingston in the NYSL joined Scranton to jump center. Pittston, the defending champs, got Jack Nugent from Utica to jump center. With a jump ball after each basket, a tall and strong center-jumper was crucial to a team's success.

For the 1916-17 season, the winter after his failure in baseball at Muskegon, Bucky again served as a sub for the Pitts. Whenever he got a chance to play, Bucky out-hustled everybody and won the grudging respect of the fans, who were dubious of Bucky when he first appeared on the court. In early January of 1917 Pittston beat the Wilkes-Barre Barons 35–17, holding the Barons to just two field goals and getting within a game of first place. Merle scored 11, Schmeelk 10 and Bucky nine. But in early February, after a 36–35 loss in Nanticoke, Pittston fell to third place. Schmeelk scored 15 and Bucky nine. The same five players played all 40 minutes for both teams. On February 5

Pittston beat Plymouth, 24–19, to stay in the race. A subhead on the local newspaper story read, "Bucky Harris stars. Clever young guard tallies two field goals."[17]

The Pitts finished in fourth place in the 1916-17 season with a 24–17 record. The Carbondale Pioneers, from a town bordering Scranton to the north, ran away with the title with a 33–7 record and had a 35-game winning streak over two seasons. The reason for the gaudy record was a 5'4" 120-pound guard from New York City named Barney Sedran (Sedransky). He was one of several players considered among the best in the country who jumped to the Penn State League. Lew Wachter, Dick Leary, Jack Inglis, Andy Suils and Johnny Beckman were some of the others. Calling these men the best players in the country was not hyperbole. Inglis, Beckman, Barney Sedran, Andy Suils and Ed Wachter, Lew's brother, made up the first team on Nate Holman's all-time team selected in 1922.[18]

Holman was an early innovative coach known as "Mr. Basketball," "Old Drill Master," and "the Old Professor," and whose line of succession goes through Red Holtzman to Phil Jackson. Leary, a jumping jack center, also pops up on early all-time teams, including Ed Wacther's all-time team. Lew Wachter and his brother Ed were two of the organizers of the Hudson River League. Brother Ed is credited with inventing the bounce pass and fast break. From 1924 to 1928 he coached Dartmouth College, leading them to a 59–26 record. Ed was selected to the AP top 50 basketball players of the first 50 years of the twentieth century. Lew Wachter was the manager and co-owner with baseball legend Johnny Evers, of the Troy, New York, baseball and basketball teams in the New York State League. Evers made trips to Pennsylvania to watch Penn State League games and saw Bucky play at Nanticoke a couple of times.

Inglis is considered one of the first players to dunk in a game and to dribble behind the back. Beckman, from Newark, was nicknamed "The Speed King" and "Babe Ruth of Basketball." He was considered the master of the fast break and one of the best shooters among early professionals.[19] Though precise records don't exist, Beckman was a likely a 90 percent free throw shooter when 60 percent was more the norm. He led Patterson to the 1916 Inter-State League title, and repeated the feat with the Bridgeport Blue Ribbons the following year. He spent two seasons in the PSL—1918-19 and 1919-20. The 1918-19 season was suspended because of World War I but teams scheduled games independently. In 1920, he was the leading scorer and led the Nanticoke Nans to the championship. Beckman signed with the Original Celtics, became one of that team's leading scorers, and helped the squad to the 1922 Eastern League title. He reputedly earned $10,000 barnstorming with the 1923-24 Celtics who won 134 of 140 games.

Beckman finished his career with several different teams, and won the 1929 American Basketball League championship with the Cleveland Rosenblums. Although an excellent individual scorer, Beckman was known as one of the best men to play with because of his devotion to teamwork, passing, and team defense.

Sedran learned at the feet of legendary coach Harry Baum at the University Settlement House in New York City. Baum placed emphasis on speed and short passes, and he was among the first to teach switching men on defense and pioneered the five-man fire-drill. Harry Baum deserves recognition as the father of fundamental basketball tactics.

In 1911-12 Sedran won a championship with Newburgh in the Hudson River League, leading the league in field goals. Sedran, who played in every professional league in the East and sometimes for three or four teams over the course of a season, said he once made $12,000 in a season playing every night of the week in three different leagues. In 1913-14, Sedran set a professional record when he scored 17 field goals in a game against the Cohoes Company B team in the New York State League in a basket without backboards, with most of the shots coming from 20 to 25 feet.

In addition to leading Carbondale to the 1916-17 PSL title, Sedran helped a number of teams capture championships, including Newburgh (Hudson River League) in 1911-12; Utica (New York State League) in 1912-13 and 1913-14; and Jaspers (Philadelphia Eastern League) and Albany (New York State League) in 1919-20 and 1920-21.

Sedran and Beckman played against each other many times in the PSL and other leagues. In 1918 Beckman joined the Original Celtics, which had its origins in 1914 as a team for teenagers in the settlement house in Manhattan. At the end of World War I in November of 1918, the Celtics were taken over by a promoter named James Furey. He couldn't use the New York name so he called them the Original Celtics. With Beckman as the high scorer, they went 65–4 and drew 5,600 to a game at the Opera House.

The Original Celtics played a best-of-three series against the New York Whirlwinds for the metro championship. The Whirlwinds' leading scorer was Sedran. The first game drew 11,000 to the Garden. Sedran led all scorers with 10 points and the Whirlwinds won, 40–24. The second game was won by the Celtics, 26–24. The third game was never played.[20]

In 1925 promoters and football owners, like George Halas of the Chicago Bears and George Marshall of the Washington Redskins, founded the American Basketball League, the first attempt at a national professional league. The ABL had teams in Chicago, New York, Washington, D.C., and Cleveland, among other cities. The Cleveland franchise was called the Rosenblums after Cleveland department store owner Max Rosenblum. With Sedran, the Rosenblums captured the ABL championship that first year with a 13–1 record and a 3–0 sweep of Brooklyn in the playoffs. Following the season, Sedran retired at the age of 34 and turned to coaching. In 1932, Sedran began to coach the Brooklyn Jewels, a group of five men who had played together at St. John's University and turned professional as a team. After his stint with the Jewels, Sedran coached Kate Smith's Celtics, the Wilmington Bombers, and the New York Gothams in the ABL. All three teams won league championships. He finally ended his coaching career in 1946, the same year the NBA was founded under the name Basketball Association of America.

Sedran is a member of the Basketball Hall of Fame, the International Jewish Sports Hall of Fame, the New York City Basketball Hall of Fame, and the CCNY Athletic Hall of Fame. Inglis, Beckman and Lew Watchman are also in the Basketball Hall of Fame. Beckman and Sedran were premier attractions in the PSL, especially when they played against Pittston and were guarded by Bucky Harris, the Pitts' tough-as-nails, take-no-prisoners guard.

Eddie Burke, who was known as "The Little Celt," also was a member of the Original Celtics with Beckman and Schmeelk. He said Bucky was less inhibited on the basketball court than the baseball field.

"He would claw you to pieces," Burke said. "When he and Johnny Beckman played each other it was always war to the death."[21]

Bucky was promoted to a starter for the 1917-18 season and developed into one of the fastest, and most controversial, guards in the league. He was routinely panned in the newspapers and by opposing fans for rough play. With only one referee before the 1917-18 season, there was a lot of rough play behind the referee's back, and Bucky was there to take advantage. Defenders were picked off with football-style blocks and pinned against the cage. Even when the ref was watching, fouls were not called as often as they are today. Free throws were awarded only when the player with the ball was fouled. Fouls away from the ball only changed possession and passers were fair game.

Bucky's fight with Kane on Christmas night was not his first big blow up. Just four days before, during and after a one-point, last-minute win over Plymouth, Bucky had to be rescued from the Plymouth fans by police after a fight with a Plymouth player named Berger.

Stanley Harris hit Berger and was thrown headforemost on the floor. Plymouth fans rushed from the bleachers and crowded on the floor surrounding the entire visiting team. The Plymouth players tried to pacify the fans but they made a rush for Harris and only the prompt arrival of the police saved him from being severely dealt with. Following the game hundreds of angry fans surged the dressing quarters and waited over an hour for Harris to leave the hall. The police took the Pittston guard through a door in the rear of the building and rushed him into an automobile.[22]

Four nights later, the Pitts pulled off a comeback on Christmas night in 1917, beating Scranton, 23–22, after being behind for the first 30 of the game's 40 minutes. Of the 45 points scored, 29 were free throws. Only nine baskets were made from the field. Scranton led, 16–9, at the half and maintained the lead until 10 minutes were left when Pittston went on a spurt. After the fight with Kane, Bucky was ejected and did not score in the game. Schmeelk and Merle scored six each. On January 30, 1918, Pittston played Nanticoke and Beckman. Bucky, who scored one point, concentrated on defending Beckman, who had a four-inch advantage on him. Beckman scored a team-high seven, but even without Schmeelk Pittston won, 30–20. Pittston's newest star, the 6'2" oddly-named Hoby Fyfe from New England, scored a whopping 16. The game drew 1,600, one of largest crowds of the season to that point.[23]

After the fight in Plymouth and the Christmas night fight in 1917, condemnation of Stanley Harris was universal around the league, especially as Kane was one of the most highly respected men in the circuit. Harris was fined $5, which probably wiped out half his pay for the night. League president B.J. Lewis ordered Harris to pay the referee the $5 on the court before the next game in order to be eligible to play. Given that Harris's ring had opened up a gash on the opposing manager's head in an on-court fight, the punishment seems light by today's standards. But such was life in the Penn State League in 1917.

Bucky must have been warned sternly after the Kane fight as he stayed out of trouble for the next month. On January 22, 1918, this note appeared in a local newspaper column called "Cage Shots": "Stanley Harris, the Benny Leonard of the State League, has not been in a mix up since the second half started." (Benny Leonard was a lightweight boxing star of the time who learned to fight on the streets of the Jewish ghetto in New York City.)

The Pitts won the first half of the PSL in 1917-18 with a 22–6 record. Hazleton won the second half, setting up a best-of-five series for the league championship. Nanticoke, despite having Beckman for most of the season, finished second in the second half.

Hazleton's 6'3" star center, Dick Leary, led the league in scoring with 80 field goals and 135 free throws in 46 games, beating out Merle in the final game by four points. Merle led in free throws. Schmeelk led in field goals with 93. Bucky was 16th in scoring with 197 points. The series with Hazleton began in Pittston on March 19. Bucky was under a baseball contract with Buffalo and was due in camp. He wired that he was a holdout and said he wouldn't play baseball unless Buffalo met his terms. That was a ploy. He wanted to finish the basketball season.

After the opener in Pittston on March 19, the teams were to play March 21 at Hazleton, March 26 at Pittston, and March 28 at Hazleton. The fifth game, if needed, would be in the Wilkes-Barre Armory. The deal was for each team to keep its home receipts, pay the referee and other expenses and divide up what was left as they saw fit. A special train car from Hazleton left at 6:30 to make a connection in Wilkes-Barre with the Laurel Line, the local commuter line, for the ride to Pittston. Fifty reserved seats were provided to Hazleton fans. Reserved seats were 35 cents and general admission 25 cents, 10 cents more than the regular season.

Leary, from New England, was clearly the star for Hazleton, backed by John Russell, William Miller, Harry Schaub, Herbert Pfaff, William MacCarter, Ralph Herman, and George "Butch" Schwab, who was matched against Bucky. Pittston had Garry Schmeelk, Bucky and Merle, Fyfe, center John Noll, Walter Margie, and Harry Bruch.

The series was seen as a toss-up, even money, though most of the fans around the league considered Pittston the better team. The key matchup was at center since there was a mid-court jump ball after every score. Leary was expected to get the tips and be tougher under the basket, but Noll was considered faster and a better scorer. Merle and Schmeelk were seen as superior at forward. Bucky and Hobby Fyfe were given the edge over the Hazleton guards.

Pittston won the first game at home before 1,800 fans, 18–14. That turned out to be the biggest crowd of the series, which was a disappointment. From the local newspaper account: "Pittston showed great teamwork in passing and the fast cutting of Bucky Harris kept the visitors on defense." And: "Harris' work on defense was especially brilliant and was the real star of the Pittston lineup."

Harris and Butch Schwab had a battle. In the second half they got in a fistfight after Bucky roughly fouled Schwab, who was running down the floor away from the ball. Schwab turned and raced at Harris. They exchanged punches briefly before their teammates separated them. Despite the rule change, only one official worked the games in the series, and the newspaper said the ref lost control in the first game. "He allowed players on both teams to use roughhouse tactics and players on both teams talked back to him. His work never looked as bad as it did last night."

In the first half Merle banked in a shot from underneath the basket with a minute and a half to go. Merle's shot was Pittston's only field goal of the first half. Even so, they led at the half, 10–6, making eight free throws.

Bucky started the second half by scoring on a layup and made it a three-point play. Schmeelk scored from near midcourt, "the ball going through the hoop without touching the sides. It was one of the best baskets ever scored by the solider boy."

Schaub scored two field goals for Hazleton. The ref called 27 fouls on each team but still heard complaints. Merle was Pittston's scoring leader with six. Bucky scored four. Hazleton won the second game, 24–18, in Hazleton. Leary scored 10 and won the center jumps. Bucky got in another fight. He threw a punch at Pfaff after the latter hit Bucky with an elbow while backing out of the corner of the cage with 1:30 left. After Bucky hit Pfaff, the two squared off but the referee and players jumped between them. The crowd wanted to see a fight and hollered for the players to go at it, yelling, "Get Harris. Get Bucky."

Bucky tied the game, 16–16, with seven minutes left but Hazleton closed with an 8–2 run. Fyfe didn't play due to a shoulder injury he suffered during the previous game in a collision with Ralph Herman, who received a black eye. Attendance was 1,210. The third game was in Pittston and it must have been an ugly one, as the teams scored only 28 points combined, with Pittston winning, 16–14. "The game was poorly played, neither team showing the fast article of ball they furnished in the two previous contests."

Leary didn't play. No reason was given though he may have gone somewhere else to play for more money. "Russell went into the game in Leary's place and jumping against Noll and put up a good battle, although the Pittston boy managed to get the majority of the bats at center. Schmeelk and Stanley Harris cut in for the ball, placing Hazleton on the defense from the start." The game drew 1,600.

Also from the newspaper account: "Schmeelk was the real star of the game. The sailor Dutchman was all over the floor and his sensational shooting from long range gave the home team the victory."

Schmeelk scored six on three long shots, Fyfe got five on a field goal and three free throws, and Merle made two free throws. Bucky played every second but did not score. Concentrating on defense, he helped Pittston hold Hazleton to just one field goal. They scored their other 12 points on free throws. Bucky didn't get into a fight but the fans did. A scrap broke out in the balcony and several policemen had to head off an all-out brawl.

Pittston won the fourth game, 21–18, clinching the series three games to one at Peeley Hall in Hazleton before a disappointing crowd of only 1,100. Pittston led, 15–10, at the half. Hazleton closed within a point at 18–17. Schmeelk was the star of the game scoring three baskets against MacCarter, considered one of the best guards in the league. Merle Harris "played a spectacular floor game" and Noll out-jumped Leary. Pittston's strategy was to foul when Hazleton was near the basket and it worked, as Hazleton made only 10 of 25 free throws. Pittston was worse, making five of 19. Merle scored three on a field goal and free throw, Schmeelk scored six on three field goals, and Bucky scored five on two field goals and a free throw.[24]

The PSL suspended play for the 1918-19 season because of the war. That didn't stop the available players from playing. They formed independent teams and scheduled best-of-series with each other. Players were free to play wherever they wanted. By this time Bucky had developed into a top-level player who held his own with the greatest in the game, and he was in demand. In mid–February Bucky played on a Monday with Pittston in Newark and was the high scorer in a win. When Bucky returned home, George Keller, the manager of the Wilkes-Barre Barons, lobbied hard to get him for a series against Nanticoke that was being billed as the championship of the Wyoming Valley. Keller must have had a sweet offer, because Bucky jumped to Wilkes-Barre, joining Roy Steele of the Eastern League and Chief Mueller of the New York State League. Merle went to Nanticoke, and for the first time the brothers were opponents in basketball. Before the series the Barons played a game against Downingtown, a Philadelphia suburb. Bucky scored more than half the Wilkes-Barre points, getting 15 in a 26–15 win. "The Pittston boy had a night on. He banged in three two-pointers from the center of the floor." The high scorer for Downingtown was none other than Schmeelk, who scored six.

In the lead up to the Nanticoke series, Wilkes-Barre was given the edge, unless Leary played for Nanticoke. He was the expert at the center tap and it was said that if he could get the tap to Beckman, Nanticoke would win. Beckman was said to be the best scorer on either team. Merle was one of the most reliable players in the league, rated a good passer and a long-range shooter. Bucky was described as one of the best scoring guards ever in the PSL and a great defensive player with plenty of endurance. Bucky had to come from Baltimore where he had a job in the shipyards.

Leary did not play for Nanticoke and Wilkes-Barre won the first game, 25–24, before 2,000. The local paper called it the greatest ever played locally. "It is safe to assume that not one single fan failed to feel his red blood tingle as 10 stalwart athletes fuming with perspiration fought desperately for the honor of victory. Men and woman stood throughout most of the game swinging coats and hats."

Bucky went against Beckman. "The real surprise came from Bucky Harris. He clearly outplayed and outscored Beckman."

Beckman did not score a field goal for only the third time in his career, and it was said Bucky had guarded him each of those three times. Bucky's strategy for stopping Beckman was simple — foul him at every turn. There was no disqualification rule, and Bucky fouled Beckman seven times when he went toward the basket. Bucky's teammates fouled Beckman another three times. Beckman did wind up as Nanticoke's leading scorer with seven free throws. Bucky made two shots from near midcourt and was the game-high scorer with 10. Merle scored five for Nanticoke.

Nanticoke won the second game, 19–16, without Leary. This time it was

Beckman stepping up on defense, as Bucky went scoreless. Beckman finally made a basket. "Beckman who was blanked Thursday by Stanley Harris tallied a two-pointer from the center of the floor. The ball struck eight inches from the hoop banking on an iron beam and dropping into the basket. The Nanticoke rooters went wild."

The Barons won the third game in overtime, 28–23. It was 21–21 after regulation. "Battling as if their lives depended on it the Barons had the ball in their possession for 3½ of the five minute extra period."

Joe Berger, a high school kid from nearby Newtown who played for the Barons, was "like a streak of lightning. He was all over the floor and though he dribbled the ball on every occasion he never missed an opportunity to make a pass. Twice he went under the basket at full speed and scored two-pointers."

Berger made six of nine free throws and scored 10 points. Bucky made two free throws. Merle scored four for Nanticoke. Ward Brennan, athletic director of the Camp Mills military installation on Long Island, New York, was the ref and kept the players under control.

The Barons won the fourth game, 39–28, to take a three-to-one series lead before 1,800 in Nanticoke. Leary still had not made an appearance for Nanticoke, and Beckman, after scoring six in the first half, retired in the second with a back injury. The brothers were the stars of their respective teams. Bucky scored 15 for Wilkes-Barre. Merle asserted himself for Nanticoke, scoring 11. "Merle Harris was easily the star for Nanticoke. The Pittston midget played a wonderful game and twice in the first 10 minutes he kept the team in the running by scoring from the middle of the floor."

With Nanticoke down 3–1, Leary played the fifth game and "was like a tonic" for Nanticoke, scoring 17 points in the 34–29 win. "He lived up to our prediction that he is the best centerman in the country." Beckman was nearly back to 100 percent and scored eight. Bucky scored one and Merle was shut out.

The seventh game was the event of the season in the Wyoming Valley, drawing 3,000 to the Wilkes-Barre Armory. Leary and Beckman both played the full game, but the Barons overcame two of the best players in the country to win, 26–18. Bucky scored only three points, all on free throws, but was seen as a big contributor. "Bucky Harris did not take more than two shots. Despite this Bucky was all over the floor and played one of the best defensive games ever in the local cages."

Leary scored seven, Beckman had six and Merle two. For Wilkes-Barre Chief Mueller, the star of the Troy Trojans in the New York State League, had been quiet but came through in the seventh game with 13. Berger scored six.

Having won the Wyoming Valley championship, Wilkes-Barre was challenged by Pittston to a best-of-three for the Luzerne County championship. With no league rules to control player movement, both Bucky and Merle jumped back to Pittston for the series, as did Schmeelk, remaking the Pittston 1918 championship team.

"Bucky is a sweet player. He showed wonderful form in the series just closed. He played Johnny Beckman to a standstill and in seven games outscored the speed marvel." Pittston swept the series convincingly in two games, 34–14 and 30–16. In the first game Merle, once again referred to as "the midget forward," scored nine. "He showed amazing speed. All his shots were from under the basket."

Bucky was described as "the best guard in the state" and scored six. Schmeelk scored six. A fight broke out in the second game. Bucky got involved, going against Barney Dreyfuss, who had been recruited from Newark to replace Bucky in the Barons' lineup. Cops had to rush into the cage to stop the melee. Brennan also worked the Pittston series, and he was quoted as saying he picked Pittston as the world championship team.[25]

As soon as the series and the season ended, speculation was rampant as to where Bucky would play in the 1919-20 season when the PSL officially reorganized. Keller was determined to keep him in Wilkes-Barre. Bucky remained undecided but an agreement was supposed to be reached that week.[26]

Bucky chose Pittston when the Penn State League regrouped with five teams — Nanticoke, Plymouth, Wilkes-Barre, Scranton and Pittston — in November of 1919. Three clubs were lost from the 1917-18 season. Carbondale lost its hall, which was sold to a silk company. Hazleton could not generate interest, and Providence was dropped for lack of attendance. The league was set up to play two 24-game halves, with the half winners playing a series for the championship.

Rules said no team was permitted to carry more that two players who played in six or more games in NY State, Eastern or Central leagues the previous two seasons. The roster limit was 10. The maximum salary was $150 a month, not including expenses. The better players were likely paid much more than that, getting under-the-table cash bonuses based on performance and attendance. The referees' salaries were $300 a month.[27]

In 1919 with basically the same lineup as the end of the previous season, when they beat Wilkes-Barre and were declared by Ward Brennan to be world champions, Pittston hardly looked like one of the better teams in the five-team PSL. On December 29 they were embarrassed by Scranton, 39–11, and knocked out of the first-half race. Bucky made Pittston's only field goal. Scranton won the taps. Attendance was 2,700, the largest crowd of the season in the league. Scranton was 14–4. Pittston was tied for third with Nanticoke at 9–7.

Bucky played as hard as ever on defense and developed as a scorer. After 15 games he was fifth in league scoring with 86 points on 26 field goals and 34 free throws. On January 13, 1920, Pittston beat the Barons, 33–22, in the Pittston Armory on "the sensational shooting of Bucky Harris." He scored 11. They played again the next day in Wilkes-Barre and the Barons won, 35–27. Bucky was the leading scorer with nine, including "two screamers from midfloor."

Pittston regained its form in the second half and beat Wilkes-Barre, 25–17, on January 28 to go into first place before the biggest home crowd of season —1,800. Bucky scored a basket "from a dribble" to "put the game on ice 23–16 late in the game," his only score of the game. Schmeelk scored 12, including 10 in the first half on sensational shooting. Merle had three.[28]

On February 2 the Eastern League agreed to permit players to play in the PSL as long as they showed up for all Eastern League games. Players playing in both leagues could make $80–$100 a week. That night Dave Kerr, a prominent Eastern League star, made his first appearance for the Barons, and a player named Clinton, also from the EL, replaced Merle in the Pittston lineup. Merle was 30 by then and was out with the flu.

That same day, and just days after he promised to stay with Pittston for the season, Bucky abruptly quit under orders from Clark Griffith, owner of the Washington Senators baseball club. The Pitts faded to third without him and did not make the playoffs. Though Bucky would flirt with basketball again over the next few years, his career as a professional cager was nearing a close.[29] He was a major league baseball player now.

The PSL lasted only one more season, disbanding after 1921. The war among the professional basketball leagues in the East took its toll. Smaller towns such as Scranton, Wilkes-Barre, Pittston, Hazleton and Freeland could not compete with bigger cities in the high-stakes bidding for players. Officials in the Eastern, New York and Penn State leagues considered a consolidation and the appointment of a national president, who would have czar-like power to ban players who jumped leagues or played in more that one league in the same season.

Hughie Jennings, who was a regular at Pittston and Scranton games in the winter, was offered the job as eastern professional basketball czar. At the time he was the "assistant manager" of the Giants for his friend John McGraw, but he said he would consider the offer. The job description said it would require legal work. Jennings was an attorney in Scranton, which was centrally located in the Philadelphia-New York corridor. Jennings was a perfect choice. "He is a natural born leader, a man of sterling character, a dyed-in-the-wool sport and a lover of basketball."

But he eventually turned down the offer.[30]

Chapter 3

The Telegram

Beating a throw into second base, Ty Cobb slid in spikes high, aiming for the Washington Senators rookie second baseman 10 years his junior, five inches shorter and 20 pounds lighter. Bucky Harris didn't back down. The play was over, but Bucky tagged Cobb hard on the head.

Cobb got in Bucky's face, snarling, "The next time you try that, busher, I'll carve you like a turkey."

"The next time, old man, I'll hit you right between the eyes with the ball," Bucky said.

Recalling the play many years later Cobb said, "I had to laugh at that spunky kid. I think he would have done what he said and I liked him for that. He was my kind of ballplayer and we always played hard against each other — hard but with respect."[1]

Back home in August after having been released twice by Muskegon in 1916, Bucky played as much baseball as he could find for the rest of the summer. On Sundays he played for Lehighton, a semi-pro team in the Pocono Mountains where Jennings had once played, and for Hamtown the rest of the week.

During the winter, Jennings finally sent him the release from Detroit, the lack of which had prevented him from playing with Scranton. Jennings included a note saying he would try to find Bucky a spot on a minor league team somewhere in the spring. It's not clear why Jennings didn't recommend Scranton, as he lived there and was friendly with manager Bill Coughlin, who had played for him with the Tigers and had tried to sign Bucky twice. In any case Jennings came through. In March, Bucky received a telegram from Arthur Devlin, manger of Norfolk in the Virginia League, offering a contract.

Bucky reported on April 3. Devlin had 10 seasons of major league experience, most of it with the Giants. In 1908 with the Giants he led all N.L. shortstops in assists, putouts and fielding average. He was 40 in 1917, but still played a mean third base. He put Bucky at shortstop. As it happened, the

Buffalo Bisons of the International League were training in Norfolk that April. Joe Engel was a Buffalo pitcher. Bucky faced him in his first spring at-bat and struck out. Two years later Engel would have a huge impact on Bucky's life and career.

After 15 games with Norfolk in the regular season Bucky was hitting .118, 6-for-51, all singles. Had he kept up that pace he was likely headed for another release; fortunately, he was saved that embarrassment. The United States declared war on Germany in April and entered World War I. On May 18 a conscription law for all men 21 to 31 went into effect. The Norfolk team disbanded a week later. Bucky hung around Norfolk for a while, sending out telegrams looking for another roster spot until he ran out of money. He received no replies, and once again there was nothing to do but go home. But his short stint with Norfolk wasn't a total bust. "In the short training period and a few weeks with Devlin I learned more than in all my previous career," he said.[2]

Back home Bucky went back to playing local ball in the Suburban and Pocono leagues. He resigned himself to waiting until the next spring for another minor league shot. Then came the locally legendary incident of "the telegram." To this day whenever Bucky's name comes up among old-timers or local history buffs in the Pittston area, the story is told of the intercepted telegram from Reading, Pennsylvania, that put Bucky on the path to the major leagues.

There are several versions of the telegram story, but what led up to it is fact. The Reading second baseman, a player named Breen, got into a fistfight with Wilkes-Barre Barons manager Red Calhoun during a New York State League game. When Breen drew an immediate suspension, Reading manager George "Hooks" Wiltse refused to pay him while he was out. This led to Breen having a blow-up with Wiltse, who suspended him permanently, leaving Reading in a bad way for a second baseman. Breen didn't play organized ball again until 1922 when he got in 14 games in the Nebraska League. The often-retold story says Reading manager George Wiltse, on the recommendation of pitcher Bill Donohue, who had played with Bucky's brother Merle, sent a telegram to the Harris home offering Merle a contract and asking him to report immediately. Bucky intercepted the telegram and went in his place.

There are other versions. In *Mine Boy to Manager* Bucky wrote he precipitated the telegram with a phone call.

> I telephoned Wiltse and asked for a chance, thereby probably changing the course of my life. The telephone booth was sweltering like a steam room. I waited 20 minutes before central finally plugged the Reading manager in. I told Wiltse I had been in Norfolk with Devlin when the Virginia League disbanded. He didn't seem interested, but said he would get back to me.

Two days later my brother Merle said he had a chance to get back into baseball. He showed me a telegram addressed to him telling him to report to Binghamton. The message was signed by Wiltse.

I congratulated him. But he insisted the telegram was meant for me as I was the one who talked to Wiltse. When I got to Binghamton I saw Wiltse in the hotel lobby talking to the Binghamton manager Chick Hartman. I introduced myself as Harris. He looked me over, seemed puzzled and told me to go register.

I did and waited in the lobby. When Wiltse was free he looked at the register, then said to me, "Is there a Merle Harris down your way?"

"He's my brother."

"I wired him and draw you."

I told him Detroit tried me out and that I played in Muskegon and Norfolk and asked for a chance.

"You'll do for a couple days until I dig somebody up."

In 1944 Bucky told the *Washington Post* something similar, saying he phoned George Wiltse immediately after hearing the Reading second baseman had been suspended for fighting an umpire in Wilkes-Barre. Over the phone Wiltse thought he was talking to Merle but didn't use a first name, asking, "Are you Harris?"

"That's right, I'm your second baseman."[3]

In another version it's Bucky who sends the telegram. Wiltse reads it and thinks it's from Merle. In yet another version, which was syndicated in various papers, including the *Waterville Daily Times* in 1937, Merle and Bucky conspire to fool Wiltse. In this one the telegram is addressed to Merle asking him to report to Reading in Syracuse rather than Binghamton. Merle was determined to stay retired and suggested Bucky go in his place.

"They'd catch on for sure," Bucky says.

"No they wouldn't. This guy has never seen me. It would be simple."

So Bucky goes to Syracuse. The next morning in the hotel lobby the bell hop points out the Reading manager and Bucky introduces himself.

"So you're Harris. You look green. I thought you were older, but I guess you'll have to do."

The manager looked over Bucky's shoulder as he registered and sees he signed Stanley Harris and confronts Bucky, saying he wired for Merle Harris. Bucky says, "My brother couldn't come. I thought it would be all right."

A similar version was told, among other places and times by Herb Armstrong at Bucky's memorial service after his death. Armstrong said the telegram came unsolicited and addressed to Merle, asking him to report to Syracuse the next day. Merle, insisting nobody on the Reading team would know him on sight, gave Bucky the telegram and told him to go. Once with the team Bucky played it as Merle and asked the players who did know Merle not to blow his cover until he proved himself.

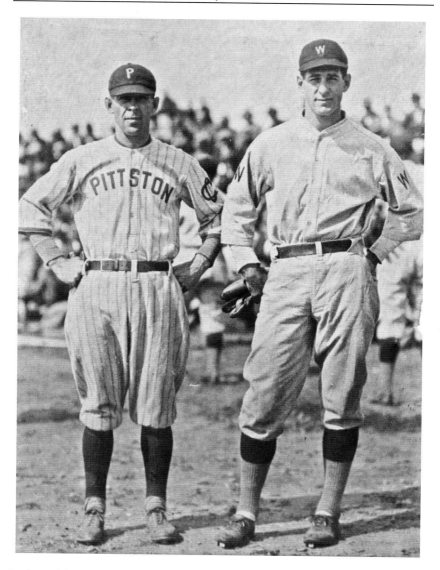

Bucky and his brother Merle at Exeter, Pennsylvania, near Pittston on September 12, 1924. Bucky brought the Senators to the Pittston area to play an exhibition game against a local squad that included Merle (courtesy of Drew Smith).

In one of his columns during the 1924 World Series, Billy Evans wrote it was Frank Brower who was playing first base for Reading who knew and recommended a Harris, with Brower saying he didn't remember the first name. The flaw in that version is Brower didn't play for Reading in 1918, though he was with Utica in the same league. In the Evans story the telegram read: "Harris, ballplayer, Pittston. Can you report at once. Need a second baseman badly."

The Wilkes-Barre paper carried a story about Bucky signing with Reading while recounting the Breen story but making no mention of a telegram. The oral version is likely apocryphal. Bucky worshiped Merle and it's hard to imagine him stealing a telegram meant for his brother. However, as it happened it seems likely that Wiltse was expecting Merle, but gave Bucky a shot out of desperation. After the doubleheader the day after Bucky reported, Wiltse found Bucky serviceable enough to offer him a contract for $125 a month. Under other circumstances Wiltse might have let Bucky go, but with the war on, managers took what they could get. Bucky signed the contract on the spot. He sent a telegram home explaining what happened and got one in return congratulating him from his basketball buddy Gary Schmeelk.

Reading was a railroad and agriculture center about 70 miles south of Pittston. The team was nicknamed the Pretzels, for the Reading area's signature product. In 1861 the first American commercial pretzel bakery was founded by Julius Sturgis in nearby Lititz, where the hard pretzel was developed. The Bachman and Unique bakeries are also Reading pretzel manufacturers that date to the nineteenth century and still operate in Reading.

So it was by chance that Bucky wound up at second base in Reading, a position he had played little in his life and not at all at Muskegon or Norfolk. Second base suited Bucky. He had a live arm if not a powerful one and a quick release. Just days after he joined Reading the Pretzels played a series in Wilkes-Barre. Hundreds of his fans came from Pittston and held what was described in the local paper as "a booster day."[4]

He played all but two games after joining the Pretzels, 75 in all. Though his fielding stats weren't great (.934 with 26 errors), they were better than six other second basemen in the league. His 153 putouts and 214 assists in 75 games and his chances-per-game average of five were likely among the league leaders at second. Batting was another matter. Slapping the ball around the infield, he hit .250 — 70-for-280 with 57 singles and only 85 total bases — against the best pitching he'd ever faced on a regular basis. After he struck out against Alex Ferguson, a big strapping right-hander for Utica, Bucky wondered why Ferguson wasn't in the majors. Bucky's assessment was right. Ferguson would spend 10 seasons in the majors, though with limited success. He had a 61–85 record with five different teams. Frank O'Rourke, who played in 14 seasons in the majors, was the Utica shortstop.

Oscar Tuero, an 18-year-old Cuban, was the leading pitcher in the league. He was 24–7 for pennant-winning Wilkes-Barre. He had a fastball and a mean breaking curve. Bucky couldn't touch him. In 1919 while pitching for the Cardinals, Tuero led the National League in appearances with 45. Mysteriously he twirled in just two games the next season and then disappeared. With the war on, the crowds were small in the New York State League as they were everywhere that season. Clubs carried a minimum number of players. When Bucky rolled his ankle while sliding, there was no trainer to treat it. Jack Fox, a pitcher, wrapped Bucky's foot and he continued to play. When the ankle was so bad that he couldn't put weight on it, a pitcher had to play second for two games.

Joe Birmingham, 32, who played outfield for Reading that season, had spent 10 seasons with the Cleveland Indians, four of them as manager. He invited an Indian scout to Reading, as bad luck would have it, the day Bucky injured his ankle. Birmingham told Bucky the slide was so ugly it turned off the scout. Bucky asked for help and Birmingham obliged. "Birmingham helped me with sliding more than he knows," Bucky said.[5]

The New York State League shut down on September 6, 1917. Back in Hughestown once again, Bucky returned to the mines as weighmaster and played basketball for the Pitts in the Penn State League. In October an odd story appeared in the Wilkes-Barre paper under a banner headline proclaiming, "Bucky Harris to go South with the Champion Giants."

The story said Hooks Wiltse, a friend to John McGraw, had arranged for Bucky to go to spring training with the Giants and that a contract to that effect was on the way. It was pure fantasy. Bucky was going to be lucky to be anywhere playing ball in April.[6] Early that spring Bucky learned the New York State League shutdown was permanent. The league, which had operated since 1894, was no more. Reading would not field a team. Baseball prospects were dim all over. Even the major leagues considered not operating, though they eventually did on a shortened schedule.

A businessman from Pittston named Ray Evans offered Bucky a job with an industrial team in North Canton, Ohio, for $175 a month. Out of options, Bucky took it. Bucky had done so well in basketball that winter that some fans and scribes wondered if he was chasing a ghost in baseball. He seemed stuck in the low minors in baseball while he was a major league basketball player who could hold his own with the best players in the world. When Bucky was mentioned in local newspaper stories about baseball, he was always referred to as "the basketball guard" or the "Pittston cager."

In Ohio, Bucky was given a token office job to play shortstop for the industrial company. He was there only two weeks when he received a telegram from Wiltse. The International League had decided to operate and Wiltse was named manager of the Buffalo Bisons. Wiltse wired Bucky an offer for $200 a month. He signed and headed to Easton, Pennsylvania, where the club was training at Lafayette College.

Wiltse saw something in Bucky despite his anemic hitting, and he installed him as the Bisons' regular second baseman. After an exhibition game in Allentown, Pennsylvania, Bucky joined other Bisons in a blackjack game in the train station to pass the time while they waited for a connection to Buffalo to open the season. Suddenly local police officers appeared and arrested the players. Joe Caset, the team's catcher, explained they were a ball team passing time, but it wasn't until men who had seen a couple games at Lafayette vouched for them that the cops let them go.

In 1917 and 1918 more than two million young American men were drafted into the military. The major leagues survived by taking most of the able-bodied men who were not subject to the draft. This had a devastating effect on the minor leagues, an effect compounded by raids by teams representing industries thought to be draft exempt. As the summer wore on, minor league teams and leagues collapsed all over the country. The International League hung on, though the crowds were small and the teams had trouble meeting payroll.

On August 6, 1918, the Wilkes-Barre paper reported, not approvingly, that Bucky had been taken in an industry raid.

> The baseball boll weevil had reached Buffalo. This insect of a man is of the ostensible scout brand or he may be a member of the team on which he is paid to play ball as it appears Sam Frock was in Binghamton.
>
> Manager Wiltse of Buffalo said yesterday that three members of his team had been approached but he didn't know who the approacher was. Result: Harris, the best second baseman in the league, has decamped for a ship building league under the apparent promise of draft immunity. Harris has a wife and two children, according to Wiltse, dependent on him. There is some excuse for him if he believed the dope handed out to him.
>
> Wiltse said that players are offered from $275 to $300 a month by the snaky scouts for the shipbuilding and other war industry managers for playing one or two games a week and a promised draft exemption.
>
> As a matter of fact, there is no such exemption. That has been specifically stated in official pronouncements. Manager Wiltse doesn't believe the government knows what is being done by the managers and scouts for the ship and munitions leagues under false representations.[7]

The story is wrong on one count. Bucky was not married and did not have two kids in 1918. He didn't get married until 1926 and his two sons were born in the 1930s. But the story was right on three counts. Sam Frock was the scout. Bucky did jump to a war industry team, but that did not exempt him from the draft. Bucky was approached by Frock in July. Whether Bucky thought the IL was about to suspend operations or believed he would get a draft exemption or was tempted by the money, he jumped to the Baltimore Dry Docks Club, a team representing a shipyard.

He played 86 games, including 66 at second, fielding .944, and 20 at short, fielding .904. He batted .241 with 11 doubles and seven triples. Bucky batted against some pitchers who later were stars in the major leagues, including Dazzy Vance, Ed Rommel and Waite Hoyt, who had jumped from Newark. Bucky and Hoyt were friends. When Bucky signed with the Dry Docks, Frock asked him to recommend a pitcher. Bucky told him to sign Hoyt and he did. Buffalo outfielder Johnny Bates also jumped to the Dry Docks.

As it turned out, the International League was the only minor league to finish its 1918 schedule. Toronto, managed by Nap Lajoie, won the pennant with an 88–39 record. Buffalo finished in the middle of the pack. Only one Bison player played more than 100 games, and Bucky's 85 games was the fourth highest on the team.

A possible draft exemption may have been the big attraction of the Dry Docks club for the players, but there were other perks, including money and competition. The Dry Docks were loaded. Every player was a future or former major leaguer. Senators Joe Judge, Frank "Wildfire" Schulte, and catcher Eddie Ainsmith joined the Dry Docks as soon as the American League season ended on September 2. Bucky played second. Fritz "Flash" Maisel was the third baseman and Chuck Wortman manned shortstop. Johnny Bates and Bobby Roth were outfielders. The pitchers included Scott Perry, Ed Rommel, Dave Danforth, and Alan Russell.

"We didn't lose a game that fall, "Bucky said. "I learned more in those few weeks than I had in all my previous career. The veterans went out of their way to help me. Ainsmith taught me how to take a throw from the catcher. Maisel and Judge worked with me on the pivot. Schulte gave me hitting pointers. I improved and played faster than ever."[8]

Schulte and Judge were still under contract with the Senators. They had manager/owner Clark Griffith's ear and urged him to buy Bucky from Buffalo for $5,000 but Griffith wasn't interested. After the Dry Docks season, the players were given time off. Bucky went back to Hughestown for a visit and found out he wasn't draft exempt after all. He got a draft notice and was ordered to report to Camp Crane at Allentown with a group of Pittston-area men. It was November 11, 1918, and Bucky and the men were at the train station in Wilkes-Barre waiting for an Allentown connection when news of the armistice arrived. They were sent home.

Having seen the Virginia and New York State leagues fold and the war end just as he got involved, Bucky had fodder for a joke he told for years. "I stopped two leagues and a world war."

Bucky went back to Baltimore in December and worked in the shipyard until March while going home on weekends to play basketball for the Pitts. Bucky had not burned his bridges with Buffalo by jumping to the Dry Docks. That winter he received a contract offer from Buffalo for $200 a month, a

$20-a-month cut. At the time the Buffalo franchise was owned by millionaire Joseph Lannin, a commodities and hotel magnate who had brought Babe Ruth to Boston as owner of the Red Sox before selling the team to Harry Frazee in 1917 for $200,000. Bucky wrote to Lannin asking for a raise and declared himself a holdout. It was a ploy to buy time to finish the basketball playoffs, which ended on April 14. To Bucky's surprise Lannin sent a new contract with an offer for $300. Bucky signed and returned the contract in April and reported to Easton for training camp.

Lannin also owned an interest in the Newark club, and he sent Bucky to Newark to play an exhibition game against the New York Yankees. Bucky filled in at shortstop. Ernie Shore and Pete Schneider pitched for the Yanks and Muddy Ruel, who would later be Bucky's teammate with the Senators, caught for the Yankees. Ed Rommel pitched for Newark. That season he won 22 in the International League and the next year went up to the A's.

With the war over, the IL was restocked for 1919. It was loaded with major leaguers on the way down and young players coming up. Among the IL players that season who would soon make their marks in the majors as Bucky would include George Kelly, Frank Bower, Frank Ellerbe, Frank O'Rourke, Ed Rommel, Socks Seibold, Charles See, Bill Ryan, Bennie Bengough (who was a back-up catcher for the Yankees for eight years, 1923–30), Al Schacht (who won 19 for Jersey City), and Wid "Spark Plug" Matthews. Schacht and Matthews would play for the Senators with Bucky.

Bucky was getting better with each game. Wiltse wasn't surprised. He knew Bucky had it in him and he continually encouraged him, telling Bucky and Bengough they were the best major league prospects on the team. In June the Bisons were in Newark for a series and had a day off. Wiltse arranged for Bucky and Bengough to try out at the Polo Grounds in front of John McGraw. The tryout consisted mostly of a fielding workout, and McGraw wasn't impressed. As Bucky put it, "He didn't rush for his checkbook." The next time Bucky would encounter McGraw, they were opposing World Series managers.

The Bisons were in Binghamton for a series in early August of 1919. Joe Casey, a 31-year-old catcher who had caught eight games for the Senators at the end of the 1918 season, leaned into Bucky on the field before the game. Nodding toward a box alongside the Bison dugout, he said, "Joe Engel's here to look you over."

Bucky remembered Engel, having batted against him in Norfolk. What Casey and Bucky didn't know was Engel was there on Griffith's orders to check out pitcher Pat Martin. Martin, a lefty from Brooklyn, was the Bisons' best pitcher that season and would get called up to the A's in September, but his entire major league career would consist of 10 appearances in 1919 and 1920.

Engel was young for a scout, just 26, only three years older than Bucky. He pitched four seasons for Griffith and the Senators from 1912 to 1915. Big and wild, the 6'3", 180-pound lefty walked 85 and hit 11 batters in 1913 while leading the league in balks.

The story was told that he was pitching in Minnesota and signaled he wanted manager Joe Cantillion to take him out of the game. Cantillion wouldn't budge, yelling that Engel had thrown the ball everywhere but over the fence. Engel promptly obliged, turning and throwing the ball over the outfield fence. He was tossed by the umpire. When Engel was released by Cleveland in 1919 after just one appearance, Griffith hired him as a full-time scout. His first assignment was Pat Martin. Watching the game that day in Binghamton, Engel saw Bucky get in a fight with a much bigger player after a play at second base. Engel was impressed by the tough little second baseman and in his report to Griffith recommended he consider buying Bucky. Griffith knew of Bucky from Joe Judge and the Dry Docks but didn't consider him a major league-caliber batter. Engel persisted and convinced Griffith to take a look at Bucky for himself.[9]

By the time Griffith got away, the Bisons were back in Buffalo. He left the Senators in Chicago on August 22, probably in the care of Nick Altrock, and caught a train to Buffalo. In the interim Bucky had taken a line drive to his right hand and injured his middle finger, though it wasn't known at the time just how bad the injury was. Bucky just taped the swollen digit to the next one and kept playing. A busted finger was a badge of honor to a mine boy. The day Griffith got to Buffalo, catcher Casey talked to Bucky on the field as he had when Engel was in Binghamton, saying, "There's the Old Fox himself."

Bucky stole a glance at Griffith. Though he was told Griffith was looking him over, he had a hard time buying it. Whether through luck or determination, or both, Bucky had the best day of his minor league career. He went 6-for-6 with a walk, was hit by a pitch, and handled 14 chances without an error in a double-header. After the game Griffith and Engel approached Bucky in the dugout just as he was unwrapping his fingers. Griffith complimented Bucky on his play that day and left.

That night Wiltse called Bucky to his room and told him Griffith offered to buy Bucky for $4,500. Although Lannin had $5,000 on Bucky's head, Wiltse expected Lannin to make the deal.[10] Later Engel said playing with that injured finger didn't hurt Bucky in Griffith's eyes. The Old Fox liked such gameness. The 6-for-6 day that raised his season average to .282, an all-time high for Bucky, couldn't have hurt. But there was a hitch. McGraw had an option on a Bison player due him. For a second time he passed on Bucky and chose pitcher Pat "Rosy" Ryan.

The sale went through. The mine boy was a major leaguer. Bucky sent a telegram to his mother and soon the word was all over the mining towns. The Wilkes-Barre papers ran the story on August 27 with the usual basketball reference.

> Buck Harris native of Pittston, a member of the Buffalo team of the International League, is to join the Washington club of the American League in a few days, according to word reaching this city last night. The exact day Harris will join the Senators or the terms of the agreement is not known. Harris is better known in Northeastern Pennsylvania as a star basket ball player, having been a leader of the Pittston quintet of the State League for some years.[11]

Bucky was on his way to New York to join the Senators the day that story appeared. He made his debut on August 28 against the Yankees. He had stayed in Buffalo a few days after the sale, clearing some affairs and treating his finger with a lemon poultice, a hot mushy concoction, to reduce the swelling. He also had a surprise visitor. Schmeelk came up from Pittston to congratulate him and to see him off.

That night he checked into the hotel in New York and reported to Griffith, who asked about the finger. Bucky shrugged that it was all right. Griffith told Bucky he might get some innings in the next day in the double-header against the Yankees. Griffith told the same thing to Frank Ellerbe, an infielder he bought from Binghamton on the same trip in which he purchased Bucky. Griffith also talked to J.V. Fitz Gerald, a writer for the *Washington Post*. "When the Senators take the field tomorrow in a double-header they may show two youngsters in the infield. They are Frank Ellerbe and Stanley Harris. Ellerbe will be at shortstop and Harris at second base according to the plans by Griffith tonight. Harris is the second baseman for whom the Senators gave Hal Janvrin and something of a bankroll according to Griffith."[12] In addition to the money, the Bisons also received Hal Janvrin for Bucky. Janvrin was hitting .178 in 61 games at second base for the Senators.

Bucky tossed and turned in his hotel room while running game scenarios through his head. What would he do if this happened or that? In the morning he was one of the first players out of his room. In the hotel lobby he ran into Joe Judge, a former teammate the previous summer with the Dry Docks. After taking the elevated train to the Polo Grounds, Judge introduced Bucky to Walter Johnson and the rest of team. Bucky watched Johnson warm up and thought his teammates back in Buffalo were right when they said he was lucky to be going to the Senators because he wouldn't have to bat against Johnson.

When the lineup was posted Bucky saw Griffith had bigger plans for him than playing a few innings in a double-header. He was starting at second base and batting seventh. He was thrilled to hear his name called when the

lineups were announced and a little confused when the crowd cheered Johnson's name. Attendance was 12,000, about twice what Bucky was used to, and
he was nervous. He calmed down after lining a single to center off Carl Mays
in his first major league at-bat and driving in the first two runs of the game.
He didn't get another hit, going 1-for-5, but he handled seven chances without
an error and was involved in one double play. Johnson wasn't sharp but was
still in there in the 14th inning when the Yankees beat him with a two-out
run. Bucky beat himself up over that run. From the *Washington Post* story:
"Pip doubled and Pratt's infield single sent him to third. He scored on Lewis'
Texas League single which either Rice, Milan or Harris should have caught."[13]

The story might as well have read "that Harris should have caught"
because it was Bucky's ball and everybody knew it. He expected to be called
on it, but Johnson said nothing. Griffith pulled him aside, likely figuring that
Bucky as a rookie had been reluctant to call off two veteran outfielders, and
calmly told him to take charge the next time. For the second game he wrote
Bucky in the lineup, again batting seventh and playing second. Bucky went
2-for-3 and made one error. "He was my friend and advisor from that day,"
Bucky said of Griffith.

Bucky didn't say anything but his finger was a mess. After 23 innings of
baseball, it was swollen and tender again. Senators trainer Mike Martin
checked the finger and told Bucky it might be broken but he couldn't tell for
sure until the swelling went down.

Writing in the *Post*, J.V. Fitz Gerald was impressed by Bucky and Ellerbe,
who played short in the second game. "The game marked the big league
debuts of Stanley Harris and Frank Ellerbe. The youngsters showed high
promise on their initial appearance in the big show and if they can play to
the standards of today, the Nationals will be vastly stronger another season.
They showed all the earmarks of being of big league caliber. Harris did almost
enough to win both games. He got three hits and drove in four runs. That
was stepping up considerably for a kid just up from the bushes."

Fitz Gerald couldn't resist taking a sarcastic shot at the Senators, who
were 43–70 after dropping the double-header for their 11th and 12th losses
out of their last 15 games. "The Senators varied their program somewhat
today. Instead of losing one game they lost two."[14]

The Senators varied their program again the next day by losing another
double-header to the Yankees. Bucky, having kept his hand in a bucket of ice
most of the night, played both ends of the double-header again. In the first
game he went hitless against Jack Quinn, a fellow hard coal country miner.
Quinn, who had been born in Austria-Hungary as Joannes Pajkos, was from
Pottsville in northeastern Pennsylvania. He was 36 in 1919, having reinvented
himself as a spitball pitcher. From New York the Senators went home for one

game against the Red Sox. Nervous before the home crowd, Bucky went hitless and made two errors. After the game the teams caught a train to Boston for a Labor Day double-header.

Bucky received his first look at Ruth in the first game. He limited the Senators to one run and won the game with a late triple. Bucky got a hit off Babe but jarred his finger when he made contact. This time he couldn't hide the pain and he watched the second game from the bench. He saw Ruth, who played right, hit his 24th home run high into the right-field bleachers. Bucky had never seen a ball hit farther.

Bucky played in only two more games in 1919. Martin ordered an x-ray of the finger, which was broken in three places, and Martin shut Bucky down. The Senators went on a western swing in September. Where another player with a mangled finger might have stayed behind or gone home, Bucky went on the trip. He sat next to Griffith and soaked up everything the Old Fox said and did. One day after watching Ray Chapman beat out two bunts down the first-base line when the pitcher covered first, Griffith ordered the second baseman to cover. Bucky took mental note of such things and didn't forget them.[15]

Back home after the season, Bucky returned to the mine weigh station and the basketball cage.

Chapter 4

.300 Hitter

Maxwell Marcus, a Pittston businessman who was the majority owner of the Pittston Pitts basketball team in the Penn State League, had no doubt who his starting guard would be when the 1919-20 season opened on November 10, 1919. As early as September 25 he said publicly that Bucky Harris would be anchoring his backcourt. Bucky returned to Hughestown on October 15, and a story in the Wilkes-Barre paper about his homecoming said he was returning to the cage. "Bucky will be seen in the local basketball lineup of the State League at the opening game at the State Armory in two weeks. He is rated as one of the fastest guards in the circuit."[1]

Another story claimed Bucky would be in a baseball lineup, too. Babe Ruth was due in Scranton two days later, October 17, to play an exhibition game to benefit the local Jewish Relief Fund. "Babe Ruth, who this year shattered the world's record for home run hitting, will positively be seen in action tomorrow afternoon in the big benefit baseball game in Athletic Park."[2]

Ruth sent a telegram to Mike McNally of Minooka, a Red Sox teammate, confirming he would play. The game was billed as a matchup between McNally's team of American League stars and an inter-county team of amateurs. Ruth was to play with the amateurs and Bucky was to play with the professional team. Hughie Jennings agreed to coach third base for the amateurs. Ruth showed but apparently Bucky did not. His name does not appear in the box score. Chick Shorten, a reserve infielder with the Tigers and a Scranton resident, and the O'Neill brothers from Minooka, Steve and Jimmy, played for the professionals, who won, 2–0. Ruth played first base for the amateurs and hit two doubles. Though it wasn't known then, Bucky and Jimmy O'Neill were to form a rookie double-play combination for the Senators the next spring.

Bucky was having his best season in the cage that winter. On January 6 after 15 games he was fifth in league scoring with 86 points on 26 field goals and 34 free throws and was the usual terror on defense. His buddy Schmeelk was fourth in scoring with 29 field goals and 30 free throws for 88 points. When Pittston beat Wilkes-Barre, 33–22, in the Pittston Armory on January 13, "the sensational shooting of Bucky gave Pittston a 5-point lead at the half." He led all scorers with 11.[3]

The next night the same teams played in Wilkes-Barre and the Barons beat Pittston, 35–27, overcoming Bucky's "two screamers from midfloor" early in the game. He was Pittston's leading scorer with nine. In January an all-star team picked by the fans was listed in the *Wilkes-Barre Times Leader*. Bucky was selected as a guard on the second team.

On January 28 against Wilkes-Barre Bucky "scored the basket from a dribble to put the game on ice." Pittston won, 25–17, to go into first place in second half of the season before 2,000 fans, the largest crowd of the season. Around this time rumors flew that Bucky was going to quit basketball because of baseball.

On February 2 Bucky promised to stay with Pittston for the season. After a game in Scranton, Bucky ran into Steve O'Neill, a catcher for Cleveland, O'Neill's brother Jimmy, and Mike McNally. They told Bucky that Washington had traded Harry Harper, Eddie Foster and Mike Menosky to Boston for Bobby Roth and Maurice "Red" Shannon.

Bucky was stunned. Shannon was a second baseman and a pretty good one at that. Bucky figured there wasn't much he could do about it. His signed contract with the Senators for 1920 was received by Griffith the first week of February, and until he heard otherwise he figured on reporting to spring training in Tampa. He told Schmeelk about the trade. Schmeelk wouldn't let him pout, saying anybody who worked his way up from the mines to the major leagues shouldn't be afraid of a little competition.[4]

The trade fueled speculation that Bucky might be sent back to Buffalo. "If Clark Griffith cannot find room for Stanley Harris as a regular it is on the cards that Stanley will rejoin the Bisons. Harris is a fine young ballplayer who will eventually shine in the fastest company."[5]

On February 20, despite his promise to the contrary a couple of weeks earlier, Bucky abruptly quit the Pitts. It was reported that Clark Griffith ordered him to quit basketball and get to Washington early for the trip to Tampa. Bucky caught a train with Jimmy O'Neill, whom Griffith had purchased from Shreveport of the Texas League after he hit .286 in 1919. It was February 23, O'Neill's 27th birthday; Bucky was 23.

When camp opened, Bucky and O'Neill, who was a shortstop, were under pressure. The consensus among the scribes was the Senators could be a first-division club if the infield came through. In the *Washington Post* on March 23, Fitz Gerald wrote about the team's prospects for improving upon 1919's seventh-place finish. He called Rice, Milan and Roth the best outfield trio the team ever had and predicted the pitching would be good. "Which brings us to the infield. It is here that the Senators will be made or broken."[6]

The rookies, pitchers and some early-bird veterans arrived in Tampa March 1. The veterans weren't due until March 7. Griffith had to be the only club president to don a uniform and practice with his team. He pitched batting practice and hit infield, beginning on March 3. Howard Shanks was the incumbent shortstop, but Griffith thought he was better suited for third and gave O'Neill a whirl at short. O'Neill and Bucky had been friends since they were kids. O'Neill's throwing arm was giving him trouble, something only Bucky knew and something he helped O'Neill hide. Bucky convinced Griffith that he and O'Neill needed to work on their double-play collaboration and continually yelled "Let's get two" during infield drills, hoping to shorten O'Neill's throws.[7] There was a side effect to the deception. Bucky was nailing the pivot play. He was getting to the base a stride quicker and getting the throw off to first base faster than he ever had. The scribes noted, "He can take the ball on either side of him equally well and has an arm like a sling shot."[8]

But for all Bucky's work, Shannon, who was bigger at 5'11" and 170 pounds and considered a better hitter, started the early exhibition games. The first game was March 11 against the Tampa Smokers of the Florida State League. Bucky, one of two rookies to play, pinch-hit and walked. Frank Ellerbe got the start with the regulars at short. Bucky and O'Neill were assigned to the Yannigans but they doubled up the regulars in the intrasquad games enough times to cause some embarrassment among the veteran and a change of mind for Griffith.

He started Bucky for the first time with the regulars in a 5–0 loss to the Havana Stars on March 16. Bucky had a busy day with mixed results. He made two wild throws for errors, one of which gave the Stars a run, but got in the middle of two double plays that were described as "lightning quick." He had two hits and brought home a run with a suicide squeeze bunt. He and Shannon alternated at second and Ellerbe and O'Neill alternated at short in the six-game series with the Cubans, who won four. Bucky and O'Neill started the last game and made an impression in a 3–0 win in which Walter Johnson pitched three innings. "The youngsters figured in two snappy double plays. Harris looked particularly good. Aside from his fast handling of the ball in double plays he made a great relay throw to come close to cutting down a Cuban at third and a gem of a stop and throw to cheat Almeda out of a hit in the seventh. He had to come in to pick up a slow bounder with one hand and throw to first while on the jump. It was by far the prettiest fielding play of the game." Bucky was 0-for-3 at the plate with a walk.[9]

Maybe assigning O'Neill and Bucky to the Yannigans was some kind of test. If it was, they passed. The day after the Cuban series ended, Griffith told Bucky and O'Neill they were going to be the starters for the 13-game traveling exhibition series with the Cincinnati Reds on the way north. "The Senators have uncovered a second baseman who as far as fielding goes is a real find. Harris is now booked to start the season at second.

"O'Neill also is a wonder at getting the ball away. He, too, has a fine pair of hands. He will open the campaign at short. He and Harris showed some fast work around the middle sack and it would be no surprise if they were doing duty there in the first league game."[10]

Bucky sent a special delivery letter home with the news. The folks in Pittston and Scranton were abuzz. One son of mine country making a big league lineup was exciting enough, but two comprising a double-play combo had them ecstatic.

In his column "The Round-Up" in the *Post* on March 28, Fitz Gerald wrote: "The Senators have picked up two of as likely rookies as have graced the training base in the last couple years. They are Stanley Harris and Jimmy O'Neill. As fielders they have shown they are of the big league type. It is too early to get a line on their hitting abilities. Harris and O'Neill will prove the finds of the season if they get the Senators out of their losing ways." The story was picked up and run in the papers back home.

Once Bucky was named the starter at second, Griffith made it his mission to fix Bucky's glaring fielding weakness — going back on fly balls. Griffith had seen Bucky have a few misadventures with Texas Leaguers at Buffalo and hadn't forgotten how Bucky, in his first major league start the previous September, had cost Johnson a game by not getting to a ball.

Twice a day in that last week in Tampa and once a day after the team hit the trail north, Griffith hit fungoes over Bucky's head as well as to his right and to his left down the right-field line. Griffith drilled him until they both were worn out. If Bucky failed to wave his arms, Griffith hit him a couple more.

"I stood out there for hours batting pops to Harris until the end of the day," Griffith said. "He could hardly drag himself to the shower. But he learned. I got the rap though. Bucky got the hang of catching pop flies and I got lumbago."[11]

The second base standard in the American League was Eddie Collins, and Bucky knew it. He called Collins "the king of second basemen." Bucky patterned himself after Collins, and before the season was out he would hear his name mentioned in the same sentence as the King. But there was one thing Collins could do that Bucky could not quite equal. Collins was the undisputed master of the swipe tag. Bucky got pretty good at it, but by his own admission he could never catch and swipe quite as fluidly as Collins.

Bucky also copied another strength of Collins by studying batters old and young and learning their tendencies.

Camp curfew was 10 o'clock but Bucky had no time for fun. He worked so hard he was usually in bed before 10. Being the starter on the trip north wasn't a guarantee of starting on Opening Day, but the scribes predicted Bucky would win the job. "Stanley Harris, who joined the Senators late last season and played with a broken finger, is in tiptop shape now and it is going to be a hard job for Shannon to run him out of the middle station. He has a great pair of hands and gets the ball away quicker than any of his infield rivals."[12]

James Crusinberry of the *Philadelphia Press*, who was covering training camps, said much the same. "Harris was a whirlwind at second base last season for Buffalo in the International League. He hit .278 and looks like he might do nearly as well in the big show."

The Senators' last game in Tampa was the first of their series with the Cincinnati Reds. O'Neill hit two doubles and Bucky hit a triple. The team left the next day to barnstorm north, but before they did a group of baseball fans in Saint Augustine sent a wire to Griffith asking for permission to fly Walter Johnson across the state to pitch a game there. Griffith sent a one-word reply: "No."

To make up for it, Griffith did take the Senators to Saint Augustine the next spring. Flying was a growing pastime in Florida. William Fleischmann, described as "a millionaire sportsman," landed his plane in a field alongside Plant Field to watch the Senators work out. He made the 200-mile flight from Miami in three hours, leaving the local newspaper to marvel, "He traveled at a rate better than a mile a minute."[13]

The Senators' barnstorming opponents were the defending World Series champions. Of course, the Reds' 1919 championship would become tainted later when the Black Sox scandal broke, but nobody was talking about that in the spring of 1920. Bucky was duly impressed by the Reds, especially their deep pitching, guys like Jimmy Ring, Dutch Ruether, Hod Eller, Dolf Luque, Ray Fisher, and Slim Sallee who had won 93 games among them the previous season.

In the first four or five games of the tour Bucky hit well, but as the games wore on the pitchers threw harder and with more stuff, causing Bucky to struggle. The Senators won eight of the 13 games on the tour, which stopped in Charleston, South Carolina; Greenville, North Carolina; Richmond, Danville, Portsmouth and Roanoke, Virginia; Clarksburg, West Virginia; and finally Cincinnati. By the end of the tour Bucky was hitting .196.

The low average didn't hurt Bucky in the eyes of the folks back home. On April 13, two days before the season opener in Boston, fans looking at the local paper read, "Bucky Harris, also of basketball fame, was with the Senators for a short time last season and in the spring down south he showed oodles of class and his position at second may be permanent. He'll start the season there and here's hoping that he sticks. Bucky is a likable boy, a solid mixer who knows how to live clean and he is of the scrappy type who is well-liked by a man like Griffith."[14]

The local paper was right. Griffith did like Bucky and wrote him into the starting lineup on Opening Day, playing second and batting eighth. O'Neill started at short and batted sixth. Bucky paid little attention as Calvin Coolidge, the governor of Massachusetts, threw out the first ball. Six years later, Coolidge, as president of the United States, would be a guest at Bucky's wedding. Bucky went 1-for-4 in a 7–6 loss. "The Big Train," Walter Johnson, was way off the tracks. He lasted only two innings, giving up four hits, three walks and five runs, a precursor of things to come. Even with Johnson diminished by the first sore arm of his career and knee tendonitis, the Senators played much better in April and May than they had at any time in 1919, when they finished in seventh place at 56–84. They were a game over .500 as June opened but fell back to even at 20–20 on June 1 after they were doubled up by the Yankees, 14–7. Bucky had his best game of the season to that point, going 3-for-5 with a single, double and his first major league home run. Babe Ruth started the game at pitcher and went four innings, his only four frames on the mound all season. He left the hill for right field in the fifth with the Yankees leading, 12–2. Bucky got the single and double off Ruth and the home run off Thormahlen in the sixth into the left-field bleachers. It was Bucky's only home run of the 1920 season, and he would not hit another until 1922. In the field he handled seven chances without an error. Griffith told the scribes he expected Bucky to develop into "one of the best in the country at the keystone sack."[15]

Back in Washington the next day against the Red Sox, Bucky came through with a clutch hit to pull one out for Johnson, 2–1. The Senators were losing, 1–0, in the bottom of the eighth with two outs when Bucky hit a triple to right-center, scoring Milan and Roth. Bucky was not in the lineup on June 11 for the first time in '20. His ailment, first said to be a sore arm, was a few days later described as a swollen neck gland. Both were true. A year earlier, Bucky got into a long-distance throwing contest with Jack Calvo, a reserve outfielder from Cuba. From the infield Calvo threw a ball over the right-field wall. Bucky tried to equal Calvo's throw and injured his biceps, which still bothered him in 1920. When a lump appeared under his right ear in June of 1920, Bucky believed it was related to his arm injury, but the doctor who examined him in Chicago disagreed. The lump grew and the right side of his face swelled. He was diagnosed with mumps or maybe a gland infection. He was out for more than two weeks, missing 14 games.[16]

Fully recovered, he returned on June 30, playing in both games of a dou-ble-header in Boston and going 2-for-8 while handling 13 chances without an error. The next day, Thursday, July 1, the Senators won a game in Boston that Bucky would talk about for the rest of his life — not because Walter Johnson pitched a no-hitter striking out 10 and not because Bucky knocked in the only run in the 1–0 win. The game stuck with Bucky because he made the error that cost Johnson a perfect game. Bucky muffed a routine ground ball hit by Harry Hooper leading off the seventh.

The Senators went to New York after the no-hitter where they beat the Yankees three straight. On the morning of July 5 the Senators were seven games over .500 at 36–29, in fourth place and only 7½ games behind the Yankees and Indians, who were tied for first. That day they lost the fourth game of the Yankee series, 17–0, precipitating a monstrous slide. They went 3–13 over their next 16 games on a western swing to Cleveland, Chicago and Detroit and limped into St. Louis three games under .500. They won two of three from the Browns, with the third game ending in a tie. They struggled back to .500 one more time at 44–44 with a 2–1 win in Detroit on July 29 before the bottom fell out on the season on another western swing. They went 2–14 in 16 games in Detroit, St. Louis, Cleveland and Chicago, losing 10 straight to end the trip. They played .367 ball the rest of the season, going 32–55, to finish in sixth place at 68–84. The biggest reason for the team's lack of success was Johnson's slump. After 10 consecutive 20-win seasons, he went 8–10 in only 21 appearances. Johnson had the flu early in the season and never really shook it. His arm was sore for the first time in his career, and he had pulled leg muscles. Pitcher Jim Shaw also had a down year. His wins dropped from 16 in '19 to 11 in '20 and his ERA jumped from 2.73 to 4.37. As it turned out, he was done. The rest of his major league career consisted of 15 games in 1921, when he was released with an ERA over 7.00 at age 28.

Joe Judge missed 20 games after getting spiked by Ty Cobb. Jimmy O'Neill missed half the season with a sore arm and a broken hand. The injured were lucky. Utility infielder Joe Leonard died in Washington May 1 of complications from surgery for appendicitis. The attack started in New York when the Senators played there from April 26 to April 29. He waited until he got back to Washington to have the operation. He was 25.

The Senators slumped, but their rookie second baseman didn't. On July 13 Bucky was rated nearly as well as 18-year-old golf phenom Bobby Jones, who the same day set a course record with a 69 at the Memphis Golf Club in the Western Amateur tournament. "Harris is one of the most sensational fielders to break into the American League in many a day. Eddie Collins is his only superior today. Barring the unexpected, Harris has a long and brilliant career ahead of him. Griff picked a winner last fall."

Two days later the Wilkes-Barre paper reported that the *Post* called Bucky the find of the 1920 season.

> Fewsler of the Yanks and Frisch of the Giants notwithstanding, the Senators little second sacker, playing in his first year in fast company is one of the most sensational infielders to break into the A.L. in many a day. Eddie Collins is his only superior in the league today.
>
> He is a tower of strength on the defensive and an aggressive and heady player. He has speed on the base paths and has every qualification a great player needs.

The story blamed an umpire for missing a call that would have been one of the greatest plays ever.

"He went back of second and made a diving stop, only the umpire thought he failed to force Johnston. That play in itself was enough to make Washington fans realize what a find the Senators have in Harris."[17]

Of the eight games Johnson won that season, Bucky was a central figure in three: the 2–1 win on June 3, when Bucky knocked in both runs in the eighth; the near-perfect no-hitter; and a 3–2 win on August 29. In the last one, Steve O'Neill was catching for Cleveland when he dropped a third strike for a passed ball with two outs. That loaded the bases for Bucky, who hit a two-run single and Johnson won, 3–2. Stan Coveleski, another hard coal miner and future Hall of Famer, was the loser. Bucky also made an outstanding fielding play of the type he and Griffith had practiced in the spring.

"Stanley Harris exemplified his 26th episode of how to play baseball according to Eddie Collins in the eighth when he travels fairly over behind first to rob Gardner of a hit following Speaker's single."[18]

Bucky batted in the .280s and .290s for most of the season, and he readily admitted batting .300 was a point of pride. Even though his best minor league average was .282, he liked to tell the folks back in Hughestown he would hit .300 in the major leagues some day. After the disastrous August and September, the Senators were playing out the string and Griffith was playing his new recruits in the final week. After going 0-for-4 on September 28, Bucky's average was .2917 with three games left. The next day he went 3-for-5, raising his average to .2948 with two games remaining. On the next-to-last day Bucky sat out a double-header while O'Rourke, whom Griffith had bought from Shreveport, played second.

Bucky must have done some math while he sat out. The next day he went to Griffith and said he wanted to play the last game against the A's. He figured that he needed to go 4-for-4 to finish the season at .300. He checked with Billy Evans, who was the umpire that day. Evans looked over the numbers and agreed. A 4-for-4 performance would do it.[19]

It was an ugly game. The A's had only nine players available. Connie

Mack's pitcher was Bob Hasty, who made his only start of the season and recorded his only win, 8–6. Griffith played 17 men.

"The closing number, which could be termed a fair farce-comedy, presented most everything in the baseball vocabulary, but was sadly lacking in real comedy stunts, as Chief Comedian Nick Altrock was among the missing, he having joined the Los Angeles troupe on the Pacific Coast League."[20]

Bucky got the last laugh in the farce. He got his 4-for-4, raising his average to .30039. Griffith pulled him before he got a fifth at-bat. Evans worried the official statistics might be different than what he and Bucky figured, but it turned out they were right on. Bucky Harris batted .300 in his rookie season, the only time he would achieve that mark in his career.

Bucky led the league in being hit by pitches with 21. No other player was in double figures. Though one scribe took a jab at Bucky by writing, "He appears as a hapless Wright who can not dodge pitched balls," Bucky was actually taking a cue from his old mentor, Jennings, who was hit 278 times in his career, including a record 51 times in 1896. Bucky patterned himself after Jennings in many ways off the field as well. Like Jennings, Bucky never forgot where he came from. He was always the mine boy. The 1920 census, taken during Bucky's rookie season, shows the full-time major league second baseman living at home with his mother. Under occupation it reads "weighmaster."

Chapter 5

Out of the Cage

Bucky went back to Hughestown after his rookie season in 1920, having promised Griffith he would not play basketball. Griffith believed a baseball player could have his legs crippled for life playing basketball. Harris notified Pittston secretary Max Marcus he wouldn't play. The *Post* reported on October 27 that he would manage the Pittston team because "due to his baseball contract he will not be permitted to play."[1]

Stories seemed to indicate Bucky was sticking with basketball management. By mid–November he had put together a team to represent Pittston. "Stanley Harris has gathered a fast bunch of basketball players four of the men coming from New York, while Merle Harris a Pittston boy fits in well with the combination."[2]

In a game against the Jersey Skeeters in mid–November, a headline called the Pittston basketball team "Bucky Harris' Ball Club." Bucky just couldn't stay out of the cage. Angered by a league decision in late November that awarded a player named Grimstead to Nanticoke after Bucky signed him for Pittston, Bucky agreed to don the Pitts uniform again. He informed Griffith he was going to play. The Grimstead incident was a convenient excuse, but three things likely swayed him to get back in the cage. One was money. Management only got paid if there was anything left after paying bills and the players' salaries. The lure of the competition was another. This was a high-caliber league and it must have pained Bucky to watch. Loyalty, to Pittston and the Penn State League, was a third. "He is acknowledged as one of the best guards in the PSL," wrote a local scribe, "and he would improve the league attendance and the Pittston team. From this distance it looks as if the Pittston boy will be just as successful in the cage as he was in baseball."[3]

The opinion among some of his friends and fans was that Griffith was right; Bucky was foolish to risk injury. There was also the suggestion that he was doing it more for the money than loyalty. "Harris like all other professionals wants to lay up a winter nest egg."[4]

Bucky also lent his name to one other basketball team that fall and winter. In November an amateur team called the Pittston Orioles formed and advertised for opponents in the local paper. Bucky Harris was listed on the roster. There's no indication he ever played for the Orioles, though he may have made token appearances to draw fans.

Wilkes-Barre and Pittston tied for the PSL first-half championship with 15–9 records. A best-of-three series was scheduled in late January to break the tie. Pittston won the first game, 28–26, on a late shot by Schmeelk, who scored 11. Merle scored six and Bucky, who played the entire game, three. "Not in years has so much interest been shown in a basketball game as evidenced by the fans last night. The 1,800 who braved the zero temperature were well repaid for their efforts. There was action and plenty of it in every second." Pittston won the second game to clinch the first half and 75 percent of the gate pot.

On February 1, when Nanticoke beat Pittston, 29–26, in a second-half game to move into first place, Bucky and Schmeelk did not play but were on the bench in uniform. No explanation was offered.[5]

Bucky was on the PSL statistics list on February 20 for having played in 12 games to this point, less than half the team's 28. Beckman led the league is scoring average at 8.5 points per game. It was noted that Joe Berger, a local school boy, was only 33 points behind the best basketball player in the world.

Scranton won the second-half title and in late March swept Pittston in two games in the playoff finals, which were the last two games ever in the Penn State League. The league disbanded, at least as a professional entity, after the 1920-21 season. Bucky did not play those last two games. He was in Washington under orders from Griffith. He met Joe Judge there and together they caught the train to Tampa to begin training for the 1921 season. O'Neill was not re-signed. Plagued by chronic arm problems, his career was all but over. He would appear in only 23 major league games after 1920.

In January of 1921 Griffith retired as field manager and appointed George McBride, a 40-year-old back-up infielder, as his replacement. McBride had been with Washington since 1908, four years before Griffith bought the team, and spent nine seasons as the starting shortstop. After 1916 his role as a player diminished each year to the point where he appeared in only 13 games in 1920. McBride was popular with the players and fans. The last week of February boosters threw a "Welcome Home" banquet for him at the Wardman Park Hotel. D.C. commissioners, congressmen and American League president Ban Johnson were among the guests.[6]

When Bucky and Judge arrived in Tampa, Judge was surprised to learn his failure to return his contract had caused him to be considered a holdout. He said he put the contract aside, intending to talk to the Old Fox about it later, and then went on an extended hunting and trapping trip to Maine where was out of touch. He said he was satisfied with the money Griffith offered but wanted three years while the contract called for one. He insisted he was happy in Washington and wanted to stay. He desired a multi-year contract because he wanted to buy a house in Washington. Bucky's contract, with the no-basketball clause that called for a $1,000 fine if he played, had been signed and returned weeks earlier.[7]

From Tampa the Senators went to Saint Augustine, as Griffith had promised the previous spring, to play the Florida amateur champions. The Senators were given a royal reception and received a tour of the country's oldest city and two banquets. Griffith skipped the tour to play a round of golf with the local country club pro. Bucky was hit over the eyebrow with a ball in batting practice. Martin closed the wound with stitches and Bucky played the game.[8]

The Senators opened at home against the Red Sox on April 13. President Harding signed a ball and threw it to starter Walter Johnson, who put it in his pocket. Later the ball would be added to Griffith's collection. General George "Blackjack" Pershing, the American commander in Europe during World War I, raised the American flag to a thunderous roar from the paid crowd of 18,212, an Opening Day record in the capital. Capacity at Georgia Avenue Park was 18,700.[9]

After the Red Sox won the opener, 6–3, knocking out Johnson in four innings, the Senators asserted themselves with 8–2 and 7–1 wins in the next two games. Bucky, after an 0-for-4 showing in the opener, was torrid in the next two games, going 4-for-7 with a sacrifice, hit batsman, two runs scored, three stolen bases and three double plays.

Bucky stayed hot in the early going and the scribes noticed.

> Bucky Harris is being groomed as the successor to Eddie Collins as the premier second sacker in the American League. The lightning-like stride of Harris in engineering double plays has given him a new first choice among sportswriters as the new Collins. Stan is a phenom and soon may be classed with Eddie Collins and Ross Barnes as the super second basemen of all time. Leading the league in stolen bases, batting around .500, and never failing to come through with a hit or near hits when men are on and contributing sensational plays in every game, his work is astonishing the most jaded.[10]

The story was picked up back home by the Wilkes-Barre and Scranton dailies.

An example of Bucky's Collins-like playing made it into the *New York Times*. "Harris dropped a drenched blanket on the crowd's hopes in the eighth inning of the game at the Polo Grounds when he made a glistening stop of Baker's hot shot off his right hand. His throw to first was wide and high, for he had no time to get set for it; but Judge came to the rescue with a neat one-handed nab. Spectacular, but very unjust."[11]

Bucky was hitting .263 after 37 games and leading the league in steals with 12. In July he plated seven runs in five games before the scoring streak was stopped on July 20. On August 20 he was still leading in steals with 24 and had boosted his average to .292.

The Senators' 1921 season was marred by what happened on July 27 in Chicago. Manager McBride was hit in the temple and knocked out by a ball thrown by outfielder Earl Smith during practice before a game. Trainer Martin revived him in short order, but he reported paralysis of the lower part of his face. At the time it was thought he would make a quick and full recovery. Though x-rays showed no signs of a concussion, he had recurring dizziness and fainting spells after returning to work on August 4. Even so, he refused to stop managing until doctors ordered him to go home to Milwaukee for an extended rest on August 18. He came back in September and finished the season, but his symptoms continued, and on December 6 he resigned as manager. Griffith offered him a job with the club as a scout, but McBride was not up for that either. McBride stayed out of baseball until 1925, when he returned as a coach with the Detroit Tigers, serving as Ty Cobb's "first lieutenant" during the 1925 and 1926 seasons. In 1929 Bucky, by that time managing the Tigers, hired McBride as a coach. The injury didn't hurt McBride's longevity. He lived to age 93.[12]

When George Mogridge shut out the White Sox in Chicago on August 21, 1921, the Senators peaked at 10 games over .500. They were 64–54 and in third place. The next day they lost in Chicago, the first of 13 losses over their next 14 games, to drop to 65–67. It took a torrid season-ending streak, when they won 11 of their last 12, to put the Senators back in the first division.

In mid–September Griffith learned from a golfing buddy that Jack Dunn, the owner of the International League Baltimore Orioles, was going to buy an outfielder for $5,000 who was tearing up the Sally League with a .390 average for the Columbia, South Carolina, club. Griffith immediately caught a train to Columbia and bought Leon "Goose" Goslin for $6,000. Goslin, a strapping 6', 180-pound 21-year-old farm boy from Jersey, got in only 14 games in '21, but was the next key piece of the 1924 championship team.[13]

Bucky didn't miss a game in '21. He led the American League in double plays by second basemen and was second in putouts and assists to the A's Jimmy Dykes. He batted .289 with a .367 on-base average, led the league in being hit by pitches again, was second in stolen bases, and scored 82 runs. Bucky started the season batting fifth. By August he was batting second regularly.

The return to form of Walter Johnson, who won 17 games, and Bucky's reliability at second helped the Senators rise to fourth place in 1921 with an 80–73 record, a 12-game improvement over 1920 when they were 68–84. Mogridge, a pitcher obtained in a trade by Griffith on New Year's Eve in 1920, was a huge contributor in 1921 and would prove to be an important piece of the team, which would rise to the top of the baseball world in 1924. Griffith got Mogridge from the Yankees for Braggo Roth and Duffy Lewis. In 1918 Mogridge had 16 wins and an ERA of 2.18 while leading the league in appearances and saves for the Yankees, but by 1920 he had fallen off to a 5–9 record with a 4.31 ERA in just 26 games. Griffith guessed the 6'2" left-hander who turned 32 on March 4, 1921, had something left, and he guessed right. Mogridge won 18 games for the Senators in 1921 and 65 over four seasons.

After the 1921 season the next pieces of the 1924 puzzle were plugged in via two multi-player trades. On December 20 the Yankees traded Jack Quinn, Rip Collins, Billy Piercy, shortstop Roger Peckinpaugh and $100,000 to the Red Sox for Everett Scott, Bullet Joe Bush and Sad Sam Jones. Three weeks later Griffith engineered a convoluted three-team trade in which the A's got Jose Acosta, Bing Miller and $50,000 from the Senators for Joe Dugan, who in turn was sent to Boston with Frank O'Rourke for Peckinpaugh. The Yankees had soured on Peckinpaugh's batting after he hit .179 in eight games in the 1921 World Series. But he was a tremendous fielder, having led the American League in assists in three and double plays in two of six seasons.

On New Year's Eve in 1921 news broke that Griffith was looking to trade Bucky to the Yankees for Home Run Baker and Bucky's friend, Mike McNally, the infielder from Scranton. Griffith had appointed Clyde Milan manager for 1922. The stories said Milan wanted the trade and was lobbying Griffith to make the move. Miller Huggins was high on Bucky, as were Yankee owners Rupert and Huston. Bucky was home in Pittston and didn't know anything until he read the Wilkes-Barre paper that morning. Bucky told the paper he liked Griffith and wanted to stay with the Senators but realized baseball was a business. Bucky expected to have a banner year in 1922 wherever he played and predicted he would hit .300.

"I'd like to play in New York, but somehow or other I'd hate to leave Washington. It's up to Griffith and if Washington gets Baker and McNally the club should be well fortified. If I go to New York or stay in Washington you can tell my friends that I'll be in there fighting every second for my employers."[14]

The *New York Evening Journal* reported the trade was all but official. "All that remains for the deal to become official is for Baker to consent to it, but early last spring he declared in unmistakable terms that he is against stepping out of a championship entourage to become one of the sights of the national capital."

When someone finally asked Griffith, he unequivocally denied everything. He told the *Post* he would not trade Harris for any three Yankees. "It is apparent New York sportswriters are again indulging in their favorite pastime of sending out bloomer stories on trades with the sole object of getting players disgruntled."[15]

Even with the demise of the Penn State League and the no-play clause in his contract, Bucky had a hard time letting go of basketball. After the 1921 season he was linked to a Catholic league sponsored by Lehigh University in Bethlehem, Pennsylvania. Bucky was listed on the roster of the St. Simon and Jude team, but there is no evidence he appeared in a game.

As he had when he hired McBride to manage in 1921, Griffith chose a veteran from his own roster to manage a year later. Clyde Milan had been an outfielder for the Senators since coming up late in 1907. From 1908 through 1921 he was the regular center fielder. He was a fair hitter, with a .286 career average. He had little power — only 17 career home runs — but he had plenty of speed. He had 495 career steals, leading the league with a then-record 88 in 1912.[16]

To avoid the temptation of the cage and a $1,000 fine if he gave in, Bucky left for Washington three weeks early. He spent several days golfing in the D.C. area before going south for spring training of his third major league season under his third different manager.[17] On March 4 Bucky, Griffith, pitcher Henry Courtney and former Washington commissioner John Hendrick were on a bus heading to play golf when the bus left the road and flipped over. The men were shaken up but not injured. They made their way to the golf course where Bucky beat Griffith by one stroke and Courtney by eight.[18]

This time Judge was a holdout. He was due in Tampa by March 13 for spring training. "Sure, I'm a holdout," he said, "and unless president Griffith comes across with a small raise, I don't intend to sign. It's his next move and I'm not even going to write him again. Of course, I'm not scheduled to leave for Tampa until March 11 and a lot can happen before then. However, I will not report until I get the salary I feel I am entitled to."[19]

Among the rookies in camp was a third baseman named Oswald "Ossie" Bluege. He didn't make the team in the spring, but later in the year Griffith bought him from Minneapolis, where he was hitting .315 for the Millers. He was another piece of the puzzle for 1924, as Griffith predicted. "We have a kid named Bluege to call on. This boy will be one of the infield stars of the league in a year or so."[20] The Senators looked strong in March, and as Opening Day approached the scribes rated them as serious contenders. "So wise a diagnostician as Babe Ruth predicts more trouble for his champions [the Yankees] from the Capital City, strange to say. Tris Speaker, manager of the Indians, and Lee Fohl of the St. Louis Browns, both of whom have high pennant hopes, figure Old Fox Griffith's club and not New York the one that must be headed in order to annex the laurel crown."[21]

From another story that same day: "The acquisition of Peck [Peckinpaugh] just about made the ballclub. The Senators were weak at short for years. He fits in nice and pretty and the team is all ready to go. The players feel they have a good chance to win the pennant and we are inclined to string along with them."[22]

The infield with Bucky at second, Judge at first, Howard Shanks at third and Peckinpaugh at short was rated the best in the league. Johnson, Mogridge and Tom Zachary were seen as a strong pitching front with Eric Erickson, Tom Phillips (25–7 at New Orleans) and Harry Courtney expected to fortify that group. The catchers, veteran Ed Gharrity and Walter Johnson's "caddy" Val Picinich, were considered more than adequate. Johnson could not find his fastball early that spring and Mogridge got the call on Opening Day.

With the Georgia Avenue Park sold out days in advance, Griffith arranged for capacity to be increased by 14,000, if need be, by selling 2,000 standing-room admissions in the grandstand, 4,000 in the pavilion, 5,000 on the field, and places for 3,000 to 5,000 in temporary circus seats erected in the outfield. As it turned out, Griffith didn't need all that added capacity, but another new attendance record was set as more than 25,000 saw the Senators open with a 6–5 win over the Yankees. The crowd was loud, animated and colorful. President Harding was seen to clap his secretary of state heartily on the back during the Senators' seventh-inning rally. The president kept a scorecard even with Walter Johnson Jr. sitting on his knee for the first three innings. The first lady wore out a pair of white gloves with her clapping. The crowd was "made up almost one-half of women in gayly decked hats and clothing, the mass took on the appearance of the spectrum. A splotch of gay red, a mass of green, somber black, grays in abundance, the peculiar mixture of colors which the flapper fan will wear to games this year all blend into a living, moving panorama of lights and shades."

Babe Ruth, under suspension for three days, walked into the stands alone in "spitter clothes to cheers and he smiled grimly as he took his seat." Ban Johnson entered later and sat next to the Babe.[23]

Bucky was 2-for-4 with two doubles and two runs scored in the opener and the Senators were off and running to nowhere. The spring analysis was way off. After that Opening Day win, the Senators lost eight of their next nine, giving up 59 runs, an average of over six per nine innings. They never recovered from that disastrous start. They got above .500 just once during the season, on June 8 when they completed a three-game sweep in Cleveland to improve to 26–25.

When they pitched well, they didn't score. In a 14-game stretch between

August 25 and September 10 they were 3–11, scoring only 21 runs in the losses. In the end they were 69–85, 14 games worse than 1921 and just one game better than 1920, a season Griffith, the players, scribes and fans thought they had left far behind. As a team the Senators were seventh in average and runs scored. Only the Indians hit fewer home runs. Though Walter Johnson was 16–17, his ERA was 2.99, good enough for fifth in the league. The overall pitching seemed adequate, with the team ERA ranking fourth in the league, but the second-tier pitchers were hideous flops. Ray Francis was 7–18 with a 4.28 ERA. Eric Erickson was 4–12 and 4.96; Phillips appeared in only 17 games and was 3–7. Courtney pitched only five innings.

Surprisingly, the fielding, at least by error count, was disappointing. The Senators were second in errors in the A.L. with 199. Sam Rice led all center fielders with 21 miscues. Only one second baseman had more errors than Bucky's 30, but Bucky got to far more balls than most. He led in putouts and total chances per game with 6.4. He, Peckinpaugh and Judge all led in double plays at their positions.

Rumors about trades with the Yankees for Bucky wouldn't die. On June 20 the *Post* reported Griffith turned down a $40,000 offer from the Yankees for Bucky. Terms were not made public, but the *Times Leader* cited a reliable source saying it was $40,000 for his outright release. The offer was made to manager McBride, who notified Clark Griffith. The offer was held under advisement for several days and then tuned down. The *Times Leader* had a letter Bucky wrote to his brother Merle in Pittston.

> Bucky confirms the story. He said he likes playing in Washington and if he was traded to New York his friends in Pittston and this city can depend on him giving the club his best effort as always.
>
>   Harris is an aggressive young fellow who has considerable fight in his system. He is a great team worker and is always in the game coaching his pitcher and calling for his teammates to get in the game. He goes after everything that comes out back of second base, is daring in his efforts to steal bases, and does not back from the plate for the best pitchers in the league.[24]

It was noted that Bucky's friend Mike McNally of Minooka was playing second base for the Yankees at the time and Bucky would have taken his place had the sale gone through.

In September the *Times Leader* stirred up more Bucky trade talk in an exclusive story.

> Bucky Harris, the Pittston boy, is dissatisfied with berth in Capital city. Has had several tilts with Clark Griffith and at the end of the season will be traded or placed on the market. There is nothing wrong with Bucky's playing. Bucky is just temperamental. Griffith was touting Bucky early, but when Peckinpaugh came to the team, the Judge-Peckinpaugh-Harris clique formed and they found fault with

the management and it has been intimated that they have not been giving their best efforts. Anybody who knows Harris will take this with a grain of salt, but he wants to be traded. Two weeks ago when Washington played in New York Harris and Joe Judge went to Brookline links to play golf. Because they left the hotel without getting Griff's permission he plastered them with a $50 fine.

The story did not cite any sources and it did not appear anywhere else.[25]

The Senators' dive to sixth place in 1922 affected Clyde Milan's health. He developed ulcers and didn't protest when Griffith fired him. Among the complaints about him was that he was "too easy-going," a label that would be stuck on Bucky in the future. After the 1922 season Bucky didn't get home to Hughestown until December. He wanted to spend the holidays with his legion of friends and family. Interviewed by a local paper, Bucky refused to discuss his contract. He did predict that Donie Bush would be named Senators manager for 1923. "Asked about leading the league in fielding percentage, he just smiled."

No wonder he just smiled. Bucky did not lead the league in fielding percentage in 1922. He was second to Eddie Collins. And he was right about Donie Bush. For a third consecutive season Griffith picked a veteran player from his roster to manage. But Bush was a veteran not of the Senators, but of Detroit, where he had been the starting shortstop under Hughie Jennings from 1908 to 1920. Griffith claimed him on waivers in August 1921, and he was Bucky's roommate for the rest of that season. He was also one of Bucky's boyhood idols. As a teenager Bucky saw Bush play when Hughie Jennings brought the Tigers to Wilkes-Barre for an exhibition game and Bucky was dazzled by Bush's quickness. The appointment of Bush was a surprise to the scribes who expected Griffith to hire Mike Kelley, the pennant-winning manager of St. Paul in the American Association. Griffith had met with Kelley in October.

Bucky told the *Times Leader*, "Bush is well liked by every player and has more baseball brains than men who have led teams to pennants." Bucky predicted Washington would be pennant contenders in 1923.

Griffith spent $100,000 on young players in the offseason and for 1923 had the largest crop of young players in camp in club history with 13. Among them were six pitchers, only two of which, Cy Warmoth and Bonnie Hollingsworth, would go north. They didn't do much pitching, only 177 innings between them with a combined 10–12 record. Of the position players Pinky Hargrave stuck as a back-up catcher and Ossie Bluege took over at third base. On February 10 the final pieces of the team to come in 1924 were put in place when Griffith traded Howard Shanks, Val Picinich and Ed Goebel to the Red Sox for catcher Muddy Ruel and pitcher Allen Russell.

On the opening day of camp Griffith named Bucky captain of the Senators. Being captain got Bucky a banner headline in the *Post* but not much power. It was largely a ceremonial position, but he took it to heart. "The responsibility, as I took it, was more intense study of the players and the game."[26]

There were personal highlights and low lights during the 1923 season. On May 30 Bucky made errors in consecutive losses to the Yanks. A misplay led to three runs in the first game. He bobbled a grounder and threw the ball away in a 4–2 loss in the second game. On June 5, again against the Yankees, he was 3-for-4 with a double and three double plays in a 5–2 win in Paul Zahniser's first major league start. Griffith bought Zahniser from the Memphis Chickasaws in the Southern Association in May.

On June 18 Bucky tripled in the 13th inning and scored the winning run on a single by O'Neill, who was filling in for Bluege at third, as Johnson beat Cleveland, 4–3. On July 3 Bucky was 3-for-5 in a 2–1 loss to the Yankees in their new home, Yankee Stadium. Ruth hit a home run in the 15th inning, his 16th of the season, to win the game, and 5,000 fans rushed the field. Ruth had to fight his way through the crowd to touch home plate.[27] On September 19 the Senators executed their 169th double play, breaking the record they set in 1922.

On September 25 Bucky helped rookie pitcher Fredrick "Firpo" Marberry win his first start, 5–3, over the White Sox. Bucky knocked in three of the Senators' five runs and made a "brilliant catch of Blankenship's liner doubling up Crouse to end the game."[28] Marberry, an obscure 24-year-old Texan, got in 11 games in 1923 and was little noticed. But in 1924 Bucky, as the Senators' manager, would use Marberry in an unprecedented way. Decades ahead of his time, Bucky turned Marberry into a closer who was as vital to the Senators' pennant and World Series triumphs as Walter Johnson.

On September 21, with the Senators owning a 68–71 record and residing in fifth place, a game out of fourth and 3½ out of third, *Washington Post* writer Frank Young wrote that Bush was out at the end of the season. "Despite the fact that President Griffith persists in denying the report that Donie Bush would be deposed as a manager of Washington at the end of the season, word has percolated from here to the effect that Lee Fohl, recently let out by the Browns, has already been decided upon for the 1924 berth, he and Griffith having reached an informal if not formal agreement. This information comes from a Mound City man high up in big league circles."[29]

Young said Griffith met with Fohl for two hours the last time the Senators were in St. Louis. Fohl was there to get St. Louis president Phil Ball to explain what he meant when he said Fohl was let out "for the good of the game." It was speculated that Fohl was fired because he wouldn't stand up for pitcher Dave Danforth, who was accused of doctoring the ball.

Bush had his supporters who noted that even with the Senators pitching their worst in years and the team batting average ranking seventh in the league, the team was within a few games of third place. Injuries and suspensions didn't help Bush. Johnson, Mogridge, Rice, Judge, Bluege and Bucky missed time. Judge sat out 40 games with a variety of injuries and illnesses. Bluege missed 44 with a knee sprain. After playing in every one of the Senators' 358 games in 1921 and 1922, Bucky had his consecutive-game streak, which went back to the end of 1920, stopped at 400 on July 15, after being spiked by Harry Heilmann the day before. Bucky missed nine games, returning to the lineup on July 24. Jimmy O'Neill, back with the Senators for the first time since 1920, filled in for Bucky while playing 23 games that season, the last of his career.

With the exception of a seven-game losing streak in late May and early June, during which Bucky was 6-for-25 with three runs, the Senators didn't go through dramatic hot and cold stretches in 1923. They played most of the season like what they were, a .500 team. They finished the season in fourth place at 75–78.

Muddy Ruel led the team in batting average, hitting .316. Bucky batted .282 with 36 extra-base hits, the most of his career. Two were home runs, his first since 1921. He readily attributed his power surge to the live ball. Bucky again led second basemen in putouts with 418, 71 more than Collins; double plays with 120, 43 more than Collins; and total chances per game. Bucky and Peckinpaugh became the first shortstop-second base tandem in which both took part in 100 double plays. Peckinpaugh made 100 exactly. Babe Ruth was selected American League MVP with 64 votes. Ruel got seven votes, and Bucky received three.

Chapter 6

Boy Wonder

Clark Calvin Griffith wasn't called "the Old Fox" because he was old, but rather because he was sly. He was born in 1869 in Missouri, along what was then the frontier. He was six when America celebrated her centennial, the National League was formed, and Custer made his last stand at Little Big Horn. Griffith got his professional start as a baseball pitcher with Milwaukee in the Western Association in the late 1880s. He starred for Milwaukee for three seasons and attracted the attention of Charlie Comiskey, who convinced him to jump to the St. Louis Browns in the American Association in 1891. When the association disbanded after the 1891 season, Griffith pitched in various backwaters, finally landing in Oakland, California, in 1893 where he won 30 games before the league disbanded in August. In September he was signed by Cap Anson's Chicago National League club. This was the first season of the 6' 6" pitching distance. At 5' 7" and only 150 pounds, Griffith didn't have much power from that distance, forcing him to use his smarts and wiles to get batters out and earn his nickname. He mastered control, changes of speed and tricks, such as his favorite — the quick pitch. He scuffed balls with his spikes and doctored them with tobacco juice. Over the next eight seasons Griffith won 152 games, six consecutive times winning more than 20.

In 1900 Griffith met with his old friend Comiskey and Comiskey's friend Ban Johnson, the president of the American League, who wanted to challenge the National League with a new major circuit. Griffith embraced the idea and over the winter convinced a approximately 40 N.L. stars to sign A.L. contracts. Comiskey, in turn, signed Clark to pitch for and manage his Chicago White Sox. Griffith won 24 games and the first A.L. pennant in 1901. For the 1902 season, Johnson moved the Baltimore franchise to New York, and named the Old Fox as manager of the New York A.L. team known as the Highlanders. After several years in New York and a return to the National League with the Reds, Griffith bought a one-tenth interest in the Washington club in 1911, becoming its largest stockholder, and signed a contract to manage the Senators in 1912. In 1919 Griffith and William M. Richardson, a Philadelphia grain futures broker, bought 80 percent of the Washington team's stock.

Griffith was the author of many bold plans. He mortgaged his family's farm to buy the Senators and raised money to buy baseball equipment for U.S. military training camps in World War I. Some credit him with inventing the squeeze play, and he was a pioneer of relief pitching specialists.

But his boldest move may have been appointing a manager in 1924.[1]

⁂

When Bucky was late returning home to Hughestown after the 1922 season, it was because, according to the *Times Leader*, he'd been on a barnstorming tour with an all-star basketball team. If that was the case, Bucky was taking a potentially expensive chance. His 1922 contract called for a $1,000 fine if he played basketball after the baseball season. The 1923 contract did not contain the no-basketball clause. As Bucky hadn't played, at least regularly or professionally, since 1920, Griffith may have figured there was no need for the clause. After all, by the end of the 1923 season Bucky was considered by many to be the top second baseman in the American League. Griffith thought only a fool would jeopardize a top-flight major league career by playing the winter game.

Bucky was no fool, but, as always, the lure of the cage was strong, as was Bucky's loyalty to his friend Garry Schmeelk, who was running a team in the New York State League named after him, the Glen Falls Garries. Bucky went to Glen Falls and joined the Garries in December of 1923. But Bucky didn't agree to play simply out of loyalty or for money, which may have been $100 a game. He liked the competition, and he believed basketball kept him in shape, kept his weight down, and was one of the reasons he was considered one of the fastest players in the major leagues in foot speed and reflexes. Between basketball games Bucky slipped into Washington in January of 1924 to attend a party. Unexpectedly, Griffith was there and noticed that Bucky had a black eye. Griffith guessed, correctly, it was from playing basketball and ordered Bucky to quit the damn game once and for all and to go immediately to Tampa with trainer Mike Martin. When he quit in January, Bucky was fourth in New York League scoring at 9.5 points per game.[2]

On January 27 Griffith made his training schedule public. All 32 candidates were due in Tampa no later than March 10. The first contingent of 13 pitcher and catcher candidates were to ship out February 16 with Nick Altrock in charge. On February 21 eight were due in Hot Springs, Arkansas, to get the kinks worked out, including Johnson, Mogridge, Judge, Peckinpaugh, Prothro, Ruel, Zachary and Zahniser. On February 24 Bluege was expected to be in a party of five to leave from Washington. Goslin, Evans, Rice, and

Leibold were traveling from their homes. Bucky was way ahead of them all. "Capt. Bucky Harris is already there, resting up and fishing while waiting for the season to roll around." And, unsaid but implied, staying away from basketball.[3]

A spring training schedule was fine, but something was missing — a manager. The Senators had been without one since Bush was let go in October. Speculation was rampant and *Washington Post* scribe Frank H. Young made a game of it. "Guessing the identity of the Senators manager is fast becoming the District's greatest indoor sport. It started just after Donie Bush was given his walking papers last October. One of the features on the new sport is that competitors may make as many guesses as they desire so there will be close to 500,000 winners when the answer is finally announced. The Old Fox is enjoying this game just as much as all the thousands of guessers who have entered the contest. Not less than 14 major candidates have been wished on the job."[4]

In January Griffith, saying he was through with short-term managers, made a strong pitch to get Jack Barry, the shortstop of Connie Mack's famous $100,000 infield with the A's who won three World Series titles in 1910, 1911, and 1913. Barry managed the Red Sox in 1917, winning 92 games and finishing second. By choice he had been out of major league baseball since then. Barry considered Griffith's offer, reportedly for multiple years at $10,000 per, but on January 24 politely refused, citing business interests and his job as baseball coach at Holy Cross.[5]

Griffith talked to the White Sox about a deal for Eddie Collins, he too of the $100,000 infield, with the intention of making him the Senators' player-manager. Griffith asked Bucky if he would switch to third base if a Collins deal was made. But the White Sox insisted any trade would have to include Bucky, and Griffith wouldn't consider that. On February 4 Griffith went to meet Barry at his home in Worchester, Massachusetts, and tried to get him to change his mind but to no avail.[6] Meanwhile, Bucky was telling friends he hoped Griffith would go back to being field manager. On February 6 at the American League meeting in Boston, Griffith said, "No manager yet," when asked. The next day, as the meeting broke up, Griffith, out of the blue, hinted that Bucky was a serious candidate. Griffith, according to the *Post*, "returned to Washington leaving the impression that he had about decided on Harris. The Washington boss has always been sweet on Harris." But then the next day back in Washington, Griffith denied Bucky was his choice. Two days later that was what came to pass.[7]

The news broke on February 10 in the *Washington Post* under the headline "Bucky Offered Pilot Berth For As Long As Desired." It is likely the Washington fans who were up early knew before Bucky did. "Harris himself probably did not get the letter announcing his selection until today," Griffith said, "and consequently we have not had a chance of talking terms. I wrote him, however, that he could sign for any period he desired and that we would get together as to this feature, as well as the salary, when I see him in Tampa shortly."[8]

Griffith said he saw Bucky as manager material back in 1921 but was hoping to wait another couple years to make the move. With the season approaching and the failure to get Barry or Collins, he decided to give Bucky a chance sooner than he expected. Griffith's only trepidation was that being manager might affect Bucky's playing negatively. Otherwise, Griffith believed Bucky would have a positive effect on a team some people saw as being a little lackadaisical. "He is full of that fighting spirit that makes for success on the ballfield. I believe Harris will instill the same in his teammates. I consider him a hard and willing worker; a smart player with a thorough knowledge of the game and I believe that his aggressiveness cannot help but bring results."[9]

Meanwhile down in Tampa, the day before Griffith's announcement, Bucky received a telegram from George Marshall — one of Washington's leading sports fans who would in 1937 bring the NFL's Redskins to Washington. The telegram contained one word: "Congratulations."

Bucky thought the telegram meant he had finally been dealt to the Yankees. When Bucky read the special delivery letter the next day and learned the real reason for Marshall's congratulations, he was stunned. "My hand shook and I had to sit down. I knew how a man feels when an unknown relative has left him a fortune."[10]

In Wilkes-Barre, the city's Sunday newspaper, the *Sunday Independent*, ran a huge two-line head across page one of section three: "Bucky Harris, Local Star of Baseball, Named Manager of the Washington Senators."

From the story: "A trait in his favor has been the fact that he is a gamester of the first water with pep and ginger. He is particularly known in this section as a basketball star having played the forward position at Pittston when the team won several championships in the Penn State League."

In Washington the reaction to the hiring of a 27-year-old player with only three full seasons of playing experience as the youngest major league manager ever was less enthusiastic. One scribe suggested one only needed to follow the money to understand why the tight-fisted Griffith hired Bucky. "The elimination of Donie Bush's name from the payroll and the failure to add one to replace his represents a saving to the club of at least $20,000 a year and possibly another $10,000 had Griffith been able to negotiate a deal for Eddie Collins. By the elevation of his second baseman to player-manager, Griffith has obviated the necessity of increasing his payroll by more than the amount of the increase that went to Harris."[11]

Then there was the opinion that Bucky would be a figurehead while Griffith ran the team on the field. In the *New York Times* Arthur Daley wrote, "Harris is almost sure to be a manager in name only. Clark Griffith is unable to overcome the habits of long years as a manager himself."

Bucky said that was "bunk." As captain he roomed with Bush and never saw or heard Griffith interfere with the manager's decisions. At the same time, Bucky said he'd have the benefit of Griffith's advice when he sought it.[12]

Some didn't think Bucky was ready. "Under the circumstances it is impossible to say the appointment of Harris is the best that could have been made. Griffith showed in his efforts to get Eddie Collins and Jack Barry and other men under the veiled heading of 'possibilities' that Harris was not his first choice. Since the big problem with the club is development of the existing team into a pennant-winning nine the baseball public would have preferred a man in whom it could have sighted fulfillment more immediately."[13]

That was mild compared to the "Boy Wonder" and "Griffith's Folly" monikers given to Bucky's hiring. Though the nickname "Boy Wonder" can be construed as derisive or laudatory, Bucky considered it the former and didn't like it. "Griffith's Folly" has appeared in books and articles over the years and comes up in conversations to this day. Its original attribution isn't known. Bucky was young and inexperienced compared to men like Collins and Barry, but Griffith's selection of him to manage the 1924 Senators was no "folly." Unlike a lot of players of his generation, Bucky was a serious student of the game and had been since he was a little boy worshiping his minor league brother. Remember, he was a boy for whom Hughey Jennings was practically a surrogate father; a boy who poured over newspaper sports pages and recited major league statistics to his friends at the cigar store in Hughes-town. He was a boy who was the mascot at age nine to one of the top amateur teams in the hard coal region. He was a boy who scraped together nickels and dimes to watch major leaguers play whenever they stopped in Scranton or Wilkes-Barre for exhibition games. And he didn't just watch the games as a fan. He "studied" the shortstops and second basemen, to use his own word, as he did when a benefactor took him to the 1916 World Series in New York.

In his the five seasons in the minors as well as with the Baltimore Dry Docks and his rookie season with the Senators, whenever he did not play he sat at his manager's elbow and absorbed all he could. In 1923 he even roomed with manager Donie Bush. Baseball-wise Bucky was intellectually suited to be manager at 27. And Bucky attracted both men and women — who said he resembled 1920s singer Rudy Vallee — as ticket-buyers. As player-manager he would sell even more tickets. Competitively, Bucky was, as Griffith suggested, inspirational. He was a good bunter and base runner. He had no peer at turn-ing the double play, and he had the instincts for batted balls that gave him great range at second. He played with a swagger. "I never saw a competitive spirit the equal of his, not even Cobb's. He was the gamest ballplayer I ever saw in 50 years of baseball. He was the smartest player I ever saw," Griffith said of Bucky years later.

Though much was made of Bucky's youth and status as a full-time player, his supporters said he compared favorably to Tris Speaker, who led Cleveland to the pennant in 1920 in his first full year as manager when he was 31 and a full-time outfielder. He batted .388 and led the league with 50 doubles.

Bucky's reaction to being named manager was well scripted. "In being appointed manager of the Washington baseball club, I was furnished with the greatest thrill of my life. Matching wits against Huggins, Cobb and Speaker will keep anyone busy, so I will start at once in an effort to get the very best results possible. In order to be on the job all the time, I have decided to make Washington my permanent home. My great hope is that I do not disappoint the fans or the scribes."[14]

When Griffith got to Tampa he signed Bucky to a two-year deal. The salary wasn't disclosed but it had to have been in the $10,000 a season range Griffith had offered Barry. That would nearly double Bucky's salary from 1923. Bucky's first official act as manager was to sign Mogridge and outfielder Carr "Spark Plug" Smith to contracts. Smith was described as a "fence buster" from Raleigh of the Piedmont League. Smith didn't bust any fences in Washington; he got in only five games in 1924, the last of his career. On February 19, 1924, Bucky watched the rookies and recruits work out in Tampa in the morning, then caught a noon train for Hot Springs to huddle with the regulars, leaving Jack Chesbro in charge in Tampa. Bucky asserted himself as boss early. In Tampa he fined rookie Byron Speece $50 for breaking discipline. In Hot Springs he vetoed a plan to have the Senators take part in a Wild West show. He called out Goose Goslin for loafing, giving him a deadline to shape up. Privately, though, Bucky worried about how the veterans, especially 36-year-old Walter Johnson, would react to having one of the youngest among them suddenly and unexpectedly appointed their boss.

"I didn't know how men like Johnson, Peckinpaugh, Judge, Zachary, Mogridge and Ruel would feel about my appointment as manager. They left no room for doubt when I arrived in Hot Springs. Every one of them congratulated me and said they would work their heads off for me and I knew they meant it, too."[15]

Even so, it took Bucky some time before he could make decisions involving Johnson.

> I wondered how I would handle Walter Johnson. I was hesitant in taking Walter out of a ball game when he got hit hard. Every time I would talk to him he would say, "Stanley, let me pitch to one more batter. I know I can get him out."

I found out what every young manager finds out. That one more batter can kill you. But Walter had such a great heart, he was so competitive he just didn't believe he could lose.

Eventually, I put sentiment aside and when I walked to the mound I'd say, "I'm sorry, Walter, but it's for the good of the club." He never went into a tantrum or sulked. I never saw anyone like him.[16]

One advantage to being a 27-year-old player-manager was Bucky could and did do everything he asked his players to do physically. In Hot Springs he got up every morning at 7 o'clock and had breakfast with them. Then they went on a six- or seven-mile jog in the hills around town. After the run they limbered up their arms with long toss and then took to the natural mineral baths. They had the afternoons off, and a lot of the players used their break to play golf. Bucky played right along with them, but once the season started he banned golf. "I don't believe playing golf is good for a ballplayer during the season. His job is baseball. His mind should not be diverted by another game. But as a means of relaxation in the off season, golf cannot be improved on."[17]

Bucky marveled at Walter Johnson's condition at Hot Springs. He had been hunting most of the offseason and the morning jaunts in the hills were nothing to him. He was starting his 18th season yet was as well conditioned as any of the younger guys. Best of all, the lump that popped out on his arm in 1923 was gone and the strength had returned.

"Johnson was our hike master," Bucky said. "We called him Mountain Goat. He set a fast pace on our daily jaunts. He had most of us staggering until we became accustomed to uphill going. I was groggy many times but I kept on going. I wouldn't expect any ballplayer to do anything I wouldn't do myself. Right there we laid the foundation for the club spirit which later helped us in the pennant race and World Series."[18]

Once they shaped up, Bucky and the veterans went back to Tampa to combine with the rest of the team. Bucky issued new training rules for the rookies but trusted the veterans to do their work and stay out of trouble. Bucky likened his managerial style to that of a football head coach. He admitted he couldn't be responsible for 25 or more players all the time. He trusted his coaches, Jack Chesbro, Al Schacht and Nick Altrock. He gave them authority and listened to their advice. Since Bucky and trainer Mike Martin had been living together since Griffith ordered them to Tampa in January, Bucky decided to make Martin his permanent roommate. They got along well, and Bucky considered Martin an ideal conduit to the players, whom Martin knew as well or better than the coaches. "He told me things about athletes I never knew. We stayed up late discussing the physical condition of players. He told me his plans to get better results."[19]

Despite the belief among the scribes that Bucky was a figurehead for Griffith, Bucky insisted that wasn't the case. Sure, he went to the Old Fox for advice and counsel, but Griffith didn't interfere or second-guess strategic decisions. Griffith did order a different approach to spring training in 1924. With a club of veteran players who were for the most part in shape, Griffith told Bucky to limit workouts to one a day and not to stage Yannigan-Regulars contests when outside games were not scheduled.[20]

But Bucky's handling of Johnson that spring was his idea. Recalling the poor season Johnson had in 1920 after the long spring barnstorming trip, Bucky sent Johnson ahead to Washington on April 1 when the Nationals started north on a barnstorming trip with the Boston Braves. He had different plans for Johnson once the season started, too. Bucky was determined to use Johnson only in turn and not in relief. In 1922 and 1923 combined, Johnson had appeared in 18 games in relief. Though Bucky was tempted during the season to change his plan, the only game Johnson worked out of the bullpen in 1924 was the last one.[21]

When Bucky called Goslin out early in the spring for "loafing," it wasn't just a way for Bucky to show early on he was the boss. Something was wrong with Goslin. He lacked energy but couldn't account for it. Martin couldn't find anything wrong with him and told him to see the team doctor in Washington. As the season approached and Goslin didn't improve, Bucky figured Goose's problems were in his head and sent him to Washington with Johnson to get himself ready by Opening Day or be suspended without pay. The club doctor's report said Goslin's lack of energy was caused by tonsillitis, which was affecting his whole system.[22] The doctor started treatment and said he hoped to avoid surgery until after the season. Whatever the doctor did must have worked. Goslin played on Opening Day and every day thereafter and wound up leading the league in RBIs.

Pitcher Alan Russell also went to Washington with Johnson, where they worked with newly hired pitching coach Arthur "Ben" Egan, a 41-year-old former back-up catcher who in 1914 had been sold to Boston by Baltimore with Babe Ruth.

The pre-season prognosticators did not give the Senators much of chance to contend. N. W. Baxter, the *Washington Post* sports editor, wrote, "The Washington team is in all of its essential features the team of 1923. The writers' guess is the Senators are due for a second division finish."

That was the consensus of many baseball writers. The Senators weren't considered a bad team, rather one that didn't improve itself, while the rest of the American League teams did. The Tigers, Indians, Browns and Athletics were deemed improved, but not enough to stop the Yankees. No matter how much other A.L. teams improved, the Yankees were still the Yankees. They

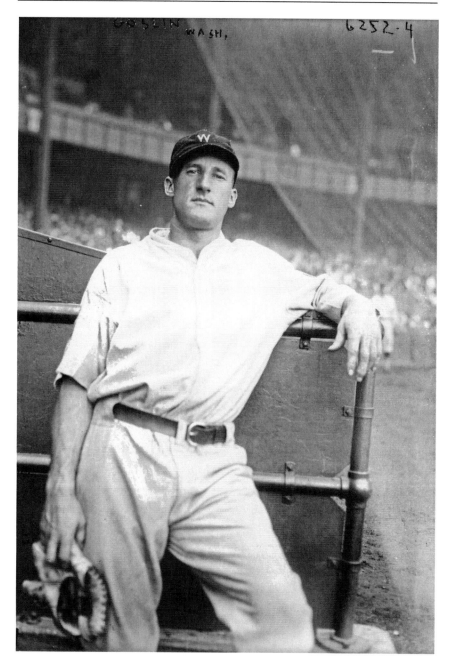

Griffith bought Leon "Goose" Goslin from Columbia in the South Atlantic League in 1921 for $7,000. In 1924, as Bucky's every day left fielder, he batted .344 and led the A.L. with 129 RBIs (Library of Congress Digital Collection).

had won the last three A.L. pennants, finishing on top in 1923 by 16 games. Everyone expected them to make it four consecutive A.L. pennants. Even Bucky, as optimistic as he was, didn't predict the Senators would unseat the Yankees. "I don't say we will win the pennant, but we will be up in the race right from the start to the finish."[23]

Why would he think otherwise? After all, no Washington team in the A.L., N.L., AA or Union Association had ever won a pennant. The perception was that Walter Johnson was washed up and was "a great heroic pathetic figure."[24] Johnson was 37 and coming off a season with his highest career ERA, 3.48, and 18 complete games, the lowest since his rookie year. He hadn't won 20 since 1918.

Once the season started the players quickly bought into Bucky's managerial style. On the field he let players play, a style he would carry throughout his career. With the veterans he didn't call pitches or position fielders. He let certain players bunt and run on their own. He believed as a general rule that players should think for themselves. He did, however, have one hard and fast on-field rule: Nobody was allowed to take any pop flies Bucky could reach. Bucky's 1924 Opening Day lineup had two differences from the regular lineup the Senators had used for most of 1923. On April 15 in Washington, Peckinpaugh, Bucky and Judge were around from short to first, Ruel was the catcher, and Rice and Goslin were in center and left. The two differences were at third, where James "Doc" Prothro supplanted Bluege, and right field, where George "Showboat" Fisher started over Nemo Leibold. Prothro was a 31-year-old practicing dentist from Tennessee. Fisher, from Iowa, was 25. Though both players had come up to the Senators at the end of 1923, they were technically rookies.

Fisher was a bust and, after having played in only 11 games, was traded to Milwaukee on June 3 with "a bunch of coin" for Wid Matthews, an outfielder who had set the A.L. on fire early in 1923 for the Athletics before he flamed out and was released to Milwaukee. Prothro lasted into June. It was something of a surprise when Bucky sent him to Memphis on June 27, as he was batting .333. Bucky put a premium on fielding, and Prothro had made 10 errors in 44 games and showed little range. On June 13 Prothro had been hit in the eye with a ground ball in fielding practice before a game at St. Louis. Bluege replaced him and was the regular at third for the remainder of the 1924 season and beyond.

"Bands blared, peanut and popcorn boys shrilled their vendors' cries, red-capped ushers tried frantically to find seats for dignified and pompous officials, shouts of 'ya can't tell the playas without a sco' cawd' rose and the crowd gathered." So began the 1924 Washington Senators baseball season on the sunny but brisk afternoon of April 15 at Griffith Stadium.[25]

President Coolidge congratulated Bucky, threw out the first ball, and shook hands with Johnson. Secretary of the Navy Curtis D. Wilbur headed the parade across the park to the flag raising. The paid attendance of 25,581 was the largest at the stadium since it opened as National Park in 1911. It had been renamed Griffith Stadium in 1921. Standing room went for $1. Walter Johnson pitched a four-hit shutout while walking two and striking out eight, as the Senators beat the Philadelphia A's, 4–0. It was Johnson's 104th shutout. Bucky's biggest concern early in the season was the third outfield position and relief pitching. In the outfield he tried Lance Richbourg, Carr Smith, Showboat Fisher, Wid Matthews and Nemo Leibold as the third with Goslin and Rice, finally settling on a Leibold–Matthews platoon until August when Earl McNeeley burst onto the scene.[26]

In 1923 Alan Russell pitched 52 games for the Senators, only five as a starter, and led the league in games finished and saves. With Russell out with a sore arm early in 1924, Bucky tried Slim McGraw, Ted Wingfield and By Speece in relief, but they were unreliable.

The Senators were 9–12 when they headed for home and a 12-game stand following a 4–2 loss in Boston on May 8. There were some highlights in those early game despite the losing record. A bright one was four wins over the Yankees in seven games. (In 1923, the Senators went 6–16 against the Yankees.) On April 20 Johnson beat the Yankees, 13–3, giving up a harmless home run to Ruth, the first of what would be a league-leading 46. On April 24 Joe Martina beat Philadelphia, 4–3. Sam Rice scored the winning run in the 10th on a passed ball. On April 27 the Senators beat Boston, 9–6, despite hitting into a triple play. Johnson and the Senators beat the Yankees, 3–2, on May 1 in New York. Bucky scored twice, including what proved to be the game winner in the fifth when he singled to left and scored on a double by Rice. In the first Bucky doubled down the third-base line and scored on a single by Judge. Johnson gave up only two singles through the first six innings.

In the seventh, after Ward and Scott led off the inning with back-to-back triples, Bucky pulled Johnson and brought in Fred Marberry with Scott on third and no outs. Previously, Bucky had used Marberry as other young pitchers were often used: as a spot starter against weak teams and to mop up blow-out losses. Here he brought Marberry in to save a game, an unheard of concept at the time. Marberry got a ground out but the run scored to make it 3–2. After a single and a bunt single, Marberry fanned Dugan for the second out. He walked Ruth to load the bases and then got Meusel to pop up. Marberry finished the game, striking out three in three innings. The next day Sam Rice hit a two-run homer in the ninth as the Senators beat the Yankees again, 6–4, beating Herb Pennock. Bucky was 1-for-4 with a triple and a run scored. Mogridge pitched the complete game, giving up 10 hits and striking out four.

On May 4 the Senators beat the A's, 3–2. Bucky knocked in the only earned run of the game with a single in the second. Again Marberry finished the game for Johnson. In the eighth Johnson walked Welch with one out, but Ruel picked him off. Then a walk to Hauser and a single by Simmons prompted Bucky to call on Marberry, who struck out Miller to end the inning. He walked a batter in the ninth with one out but struck out Bruggy and got Bishop to pop up.

From the *Post*: "Time was when many a ball game was lost simply because the manager for sentimental reasons hesitated in yanking Walter and some of the other veterans. Harris was taking no chances and as the relieving pitcher held the game safe. And also last Thursday in New York, the boy manager will have to be given credit for having guessed right, twice, anyway."[27] Many more correct guesses were coming.

The 1924 Senators pose for a photograph in April of 1924 just before the opening of the season. Walter Johnson and Bucky are front and center, fifth and sixth from the left in the front row. Clark Griffith is on the left of the last row. Other players, not in order, are Muddy Ruel, Roger Peckinpaugh, Joe Judge, Sam Rice, Goose Goslin, Showboat Fisher, Carr Smith, Doc Prothro, George Mogridge, Allen Russell, Paul Zanhiser, Pinky Hargrave, Bennie Tate, Tom Zachary, Slim McGrew, Firpo Marberry, John Martina, By Speece, Ted Wingfield, Nemo Leibold, Lance Richbourg, Chick Gagnon, Mule Shirley (Library of Congress Digital Collection).

The Senators were seventh in team batting when they started their home-stand on May 10, with Peckinpaugh the worst offender. He was hitting .220. The starting pitching was decent, especially Johnson, who was 4–2, but the defense was a disappointment to Bucky, who put a premium on fielding. The Senators made 25 errors in their first 13 games. Ruel had five and Peck six.

Being already 9–12 when Detroit arrived in Washington, the Senators were in danger of falling out of the race early. Western teams had wrecked the season of many an eastern club over the seasons. The 12-game homestand started with a 3–2 win over Detroit. Cobb scored one in the first on a wild pick-off attempt by Ruel and one more in the second. Joe Martina shut out the Tigers the rest of the way while striking out seven. Prothro, playing third, stroked the winning hit and started a double play with Bucky in the middle.

Mogridge beat the Tigers, 6–3, in the second game. In the sixth, Goslin, "tottering up to the plate with his big fat bat and big fat tonsils," as the *Post* put it, hit a triple off the right-field fence to start a three-run rally. In the seventh Bucky tripled in a run when Fothergill fell down chasing his fly ball. The Tigers won the last of the three games, beating Johnson, 5–3, in an eight-inning rain-shortened game. On May 12 Bucky recalled outfielder Carr Smith, who was batting .687 (19-for-28) at Chattanooga. Goslin was still bothered by tonsillitis and Bucky thought he needed another outfielder. Again Goslin proved him wrong by recovering and playing well. Smith was useful for a couple of games while subbing for Rice, who had a bum knee, but was gone for good by mid–June.

On May 23 in the first of a three-game set with the White Sox, Johnson pitched one of the best games of his career, a one-hitter with one walk and 14 strikeouts. He struck out six straight in the second, third and fourth innings. Harry Hooper, who singled and walked, was the only Sox batter to reach base. After the walk, Bucky wiped him out with a double play, touching the bag himself and throwing to Judge. Johnson faced one over the minimum.

That same day Bucky and Griffith claimed Warren "Curley" Ogden on waivers from the Philadelphia A's. Mack released Ogden after he started the season 0–3 with a 4.97 ERA. Ogden, 25, was a 6'1", 185-pound righty from a town of the same name, Ogden, Pennsylvania. On Monday he beat the Sox, 8–2, getting 16 infield ground outs and allowing only seven scattered hits. Bucky was 2-for-5 and stole a base. The Senators barely held their own on the homestand, going 6–6, then hit the rails for Boston to play a Memorial Day double-header, the start of a 30-day, 25-game road trip during which they would play the seven other A.L. teams. They won the get-away game, 6–1, the second of a double-header against the Yankees on May 28. They were 15–18 against the league when they left for Boston and 5–3 against the Yankees.

It looked like a daunting road trip and the Senators could have been expected to wilt. Instead they went 18–8 and closed the trip with a nine-game winning streak, the last four of those in New York. In Boston for Memorial Day a record Fenway crowd of 35,000, including A.L. president Ban Johnson and 1,000 newsboys who were given tickets, saw a split. The Senators lost, 9–4, and won, 10–5. With the stands filled, ropes were stretched across the outfield to accommodate the overflow and three mounted policemen kept order.

Sam Rice was 34 in 1924 when he led the A.L. in hits with 216 (Library of Congress Digital Collection).

Martina was hit hard for seven runs in the fourth inning of game one. The Sox's Ike Boone hit a home run high into the right-field bleachers, a spot only reached previously by Ruth. Rice was 7-for-10; Bucky was 3-for-10 with two doubles. Bucky sprained his ankle sliding during the double-header and took the next day off while watching the Senators and Ogden beat Boston, 12–0. Bluege played second. Rice was 4-for-5 in the game and 11-for-15 in the series.

On June 1 comedy ruled the day. The Senators signed Al Schacht as a coach, reuniting the famous baseball clown team of Schacht and Altrock, who was already on staff. Schacht must have come with a pretty fair salary, as both Chesbro and Egan were released to make room for him. No doubt Griffith wanted the team reunited to sell tickets. That was fine with Bucky, as long as their comedy antics were limited to pregame. "Stanley Harris' intention is to use him, as well as Altrock, on the coaching lines in place of the veterans who were let out. While the pair makes up a great brother team and the news of their combining will be welcomed throughout the whole Ban Johnson circuit, Harris made it clear that life will not be all fun for them and that, after the game actually starts, they will be just as serious as the players on the team."[28]

The Senators weren't due in Detroit until June 3 after the May 31 game in Boston. With two days off the Senators went to Philadelphia to sneak in a make-up game with the A's, only to have the game rained out again, the

Baseball clowns Nick Altrock and Al Schacht entertain the fans before the first game of the 1924 World Series. Bucky insisted they turn into serious coaches once the game began (Library of Congress Digital Collection).

12th postponement of the season. Determined to get the game in, the Senators stayed overnight and played the next day, June 2, then rushed to the station for the 11-hour trip to Detroit.

In the make-up game in Philadelphia, Bucky sat again and Johnson beat the A's, 8–3. At bat Johnson was 2-for-5 with a run scored. He was 11-for-33 batting for the season. Four hundred orphans from the St. Elizabeth Orphanage were the guests of the Shibes and Mack. Altrock (Schacht hadn't arrived yet) put on a comedy show for them.

Through June 2 Rice was hitting .336, Judge .345, and Prothro .298. Bucky was hitting .292 and leading the team with 10 sacrifices. Griffith made another deal around this time. He traded outfielder George Fisher and cash to Milwaukee for W.C. "Wid" Matthews, who was hitting .350 in the minors. Matthews, like Ogden, had been released by Mack.

In Detroit the Senators opened their western swing with Zachary pitching a two-hitter in an 11–1 win, played in a cold rain. Bucky was still off the ankle. Bluege played second, going 2-for-4. Players slipped and fell, but the Tigers would not call the game. The Senators won three of four against the Tigers while getting a little help from Umpire Moriarity in the first inning of the third game. Peckinpaugh had apparently made the third out on an easy tapper to short in the first with only one run in. The Tigers started off the field, but Moriarity said Tiger catcher Bassler had ticked Peck's bat with his mitt. The Senators scored five more in the first after the call and won, 9–7. Ogden won his third consecutive game, more than he had won in 1922 and 1923 combined for Mack, and hit a two-run triple in the six-run first. Bluege, still in for Bucky, was 2-for-5. Matthews got his first start in center and went 2-for-4 with a triple and a run scored. The next day the Senators went over the .500 mark for the first time in 1924 when Johnson shut out the Tigers, 2–0, for his seventh win. Matthews was in center again and asked Johnson where to play. Johnson told him to shade to left. Later in the game he moved him toward right. The last batter for the Browns, catcher John Bassler, lined out to end the game right where Matthews was standing.

The Senators stumbled in Cleveland, losing three of four. Bucky got back in the lineup on June 8 in an 11–3 loss to Coveleski. On June 11 in St. Louis, Zahniser, in his first start in more than a month, beat the Browns, 12–1, for his first win of the season. The Senators recorded 18 hits. Bucky was 2-for-5 with a double. Goslin was 2-for-6 with a home run. The bad news was Judge's knee was swollen and tender, and he was sent home to treat and rest it.

Ernest "Mule" Shirley filled in at first. In the three games in St. Louis, the lack of Judge didn't hurt. Shirley was on fire, going 6-for-10 with four runs scored and six RBIs. But Shirley fell off a cliff after that, going 0-for-20 over the next six games in Chicago and Philadelphia, where Judge returned to the lineup. The Senators lost the first two of four in Chicago, including a wild one, 9–8, on June 16. Thirteen runs were scored in the seventh and eighth innings. In the fourth Goslin hit a home run with Bucky on base. Johnson seemed a sure winner, leading, 3–1, through six. But in the seventh he loaded the bases on two walks and a bunt single and Harry Hooper hit a grand slam. The Senators scored five in the eighth. The Sox got four in bottom of the eighth. After that loss the Senators were 24–26 and in sixth place.

The next day the Senators started that nine-game winning streak with a 12–6 win in the third game of the series with the White Sox. Bucky was 2-for-3 with four RBIs and his league-leading 14th and 15th sacrifices. The Senators were leading, 7–0, in the third when Zachary blew up. After a walk with one out, he gave up a triple, double, single, walk and single, consecutively. Bucky pulled him and brought in Marberry, who got a strikeout to end the inning. Marberry stayed in the game and was the winner, pitching the last 6⅓ innings and allowing just two runs. Bucky called on Marberry to close out one-run games in the bottom of the ninth and 12th in the next two games against the White Sox and A's. In the first instance, Bucky called him in with

In 1924, Bucky turned Frederick Firpo Marberry into the first true relief pitcher (Library of Congress Digital Collection).

the bases loaded and one out. The Senators had scored two in the top of the ninth with two out to take a 5–4 lead. Peckinpaugh knocked in the two runs scoring Bucky, who had singled and stole second, and Ruel, who reached on a fielder's choice. In the bottom Mogridge loaded the bases with one out on a single, his own error and a walk. Marberry came in and got Kamm and Archdeacon to ground to Shirley at first.

After a travel day the Senators won in Philadelphia, 3–2, in 12 innings, with Marberry again being called on to get the final two outs with the winning runs on base. A subplot to the game was Wid Matthews. Playing in center field against his former team, he was 2-for-6 and threw a runner out at third in the second and at the plate in the eighth. In the first inning after Bucky struck out trying to sacrifice him to second, Matthews stole second on the throw back to the pitcher from catcher Cy Perkins. Ruel drove him in with a single. Bucky was 0-for-5 but was in on three double plays.

It was in this stretch of three consecutive games that Marberry, with a win and two saves, defined his role for 1924. Griffith and Bucky were decades ahead of their time with the way they used Marberry to close games in 1924. Griffith, who had been both a starter and reliever in his pitching career, had experimented with relief specialists. In 1923 Washington sportswriters called Allan Russell "the King of Finishers" after he appeared in 52 games, a record 47 in relief, and finished 26 games.

Marberry, like Bucky, was scouted and signed by Joe Engel, who found him with Little Rock in the Southern Association. A 6'1" and 190-pound Texan, Marberry was almost exclusively a fastball pitcher. He was nicknamed "Firpo" due to his resemblance to Luis Firpo, a heavyweight boxer from Argentina who had knocked Jack Dempsey out of the ring in a championship fight in September of 1923, though Dempsey recovered and won the fight. Schacht recalled how Marberry was always anxious to get into a game. "Sometimes Bucky would go to the pitcher's mound just to talk to the pitcher, unsure about whether to take him out. But he'd no sooner get to the mound, and there would be Marberry, out of the bullpen coming in."[29]

Throwing nothing but fastballs with a high leg kick and a rock-and-fire style, Marberry never tried to finesse batters, but he did try to intimidate them. Warming up, he would stomp around the mound while kicking up dirt. Muddy Ruel played along. He caught every pitch in the center of his mitt to maximize the sound of the glove pop and staggered back as he caught each pitch.

"We had a great relief pitcher in Fred Marberry," Bucky said after the season. "I doubt there has ever been a better one. He had a great fastball and the heart of a lion. He relieved Johnson in nine games and saved seven. He relieved other pitchers 36 times and finished 31 games."[30]

The word "saves" was not used then, but author Bill James believes Bucky's use of Marberry in 1924 was unprecedented. In his book *Bill James Guide to Baseball Managers*, James wrote: "Marberry was the first pitcher aggressively used to protect leads rather than being brought in when the starter was knocked out. Thus, Marberry is in my opinion the first true reliever."[31]

Marberry got a break in the second contest of the three-game sweep of the A's as Johnson went the distance for an easy 11–3 win to raise his record to 8–3. Bucky was 2-for-3 with a walk, three runs scored and an RBI double. Johnson walked two and stuck out four.

That same day in St. Louis there was a near-riot after Browns manager Dick Sisler and player Pat Collins were tossed by Umpire Holmes for arguing balls and strikes. Sisler was headed to the shower when a bottle nearly hit Holmes. He called Sisler back on the field and several more bottles were thrown that just missed Holmes. As plain-clothes policemen rushed onto the field, fans broke down the right-field gate and swarmed the field.

Before going to New York to wind up their long road trip with four against the Yankees, the Senators stopped at home for one make-up game on Sunday, June 22, against the A's. More than 18,000 fans saw Altrock and Schacht do their classic skit, a spoof of a bullfighting scene from a Rudolf Valentino movie using a goat as a bull and Altrock dressed as the girlfriend of Schacht's matador.[32]

There was a game and Matthews tormented his old team once again, going 2-for-4 with an RBI triple in a 5–4 win. At the end of the day the Senators were three games over .500 at 29–26 for the first time that season. The Yankees lost, 6–2, to Boston that day, and as the Senators boarded the train for New York, the A.L. standings looked like this:

New York	38–20	–
Detroit	34–28	.5
Boston	28–25	2
Washington	29–26	2

The four-game series in New York opened with a double-header on Monday, June 24. The Yankee brass was expecting a crowd of 20,000, but only half that many showed up to see the Senators sweep the twin bill. Lefties Mogridge and Zachary pitched complete games in the 5–3 and 4–2 wins. Matthews stayed hot, going 3-for-8 with three runs and an RBI.

This was the series, as told in the preface, during which Schacht said Bucky retaliated against knock-down pitches by Shawkey by bunting for a hit, sliding into second with intent to spike, and by knocking down Ruth when the Babe attempted to steal. Schacht said, "I believe Bucky single-handedly won the pennant for us that day."

It's a nice story, but there are a couple problems with it. The second game of the double-header was the only game Shawkey started that season against the Senators. Mogridge did not pitch in that game, though he did pitch the first one. Bucky did not bunt for a hit or steal second. He did reach on a fielder's choice, and he did score on a double by Judge. There is no evidence that Ruth was caught stealing. Of course, Schacht told the story 40 years after the fact. He likely mixed and matched facts from more than one game, but the story does illustrate the way Bucky played and energized his teammates.

The Senators won the next two games in New York, 4–3 in 10 and 3–2 in a seven-inning, rain-shortened game to go into first place for the first time since 1913. In the 10-inning game, after Yankee first baseman Wally Pipp and catcher Wally Schang collided and let his foul pop drop, Peckinpaugh hit an inside-the-park home run that rolled all the way to the bleachers in right-center. Russell, in relief of Zahniser, struck out Ruth for the second out in the 10th with the tying run on third, and Goslin made a running shoestring catch of a hit by Meusel to end it.

Bucky was 0-for-4 with a sacrifice and a double play. Matthews scored in the first after turning a bunt into a double when Ernie Johnson overran the ball while trying to field it. He also knocked in the winning run with a long sac fly in the 10th, bringing home pitcher Russell, who was carried back to the dugout by his teammates. The Senators made it a four-game sweep with the 3–2 win in seven innings. Marberry, getting a rare start, pitched the seven innings, giving up only two hits and no runs after Ruth hit a two-run homer in the first for the Yankee runs. Bucky scored the winning run in the third. He singled, stole second, went to third on a fielder's choice grounder to first, and scored on a sac fly by Judge. Officially, he was 1-for-1 with a sacrifice and a base on balls. It was so dark as the Yankees batted in the seventh that lights on the elevated train station and in the apartments around the stadium came on. Umpire Red Ormsby let the Yankees bat even though the ball was hard to see in the exchange from the catcher to the pitcher. Ormsby stopped play after the seventh because of the darkness and moments later a downpour started.

Not only did the Senators sweep the four games in Yankee Stadium, they did it without Walter Johnson, who was with his wife as she recovered from surgery for appendicitis. Matthews was hitting .389 since his call-up without an error in center field and was wowing Bucky, his teammates and the fans with burning speed and hit-the-wall hustle.

Though the party line in Philadelphia was Matthews had been sent to Milwaukee because he slumped after a torrid start in 1923, there was more to the story. Matthews had a hot-head reputation and an aversion to authority, traits the taciturn Mack wouldn't put up with. When Matthews joined the Senators in Detroit, Bucky had a heart-to-heart meeting with the newcomer, reminding Matthews this might be his last shot to stick in the majors.[33] In the *Post*'s "In the Press Box" column the day the Senators finished off the four-game sweep of the Yankees, sports editor N.W. Baxter said Matthews was one reason the Senators were in first place with the same team that finished fourth the season before but cautioned against giving him too much credit.

> Undoubtedly the greatest factor in the success of the Senators has been that the veterans on the team have worked like Trojans for the youngest leader in baseball. It might not have been surprising to have found the Washington team slightly out of line because of refusal of some players to take the boy manager seriously. There has been none of this evidently. The veterans rather seem to have become infected with the enthusiasm of the manager. Johnson, Mogridge, Peckinpaugh and Judge have given themselves valiantly to the task of putting Harris and the ball club across.[34]

After sweeping the Yankees, the Senators boarded a train for home in first place on the latest date in their history, having gone 17–8 on a three-week road trip and 33–26 on the season. Bucky was stunned to find several hundred fans waiting when the train arrived at Union Station in D.C. that night. Called upon to speak, he told to the fans, "We're happy and we're tough to beat. We had the breaks, but we made 'em. We have a real ball club and fear no team in the league. We are at the top and mean to stay there."

Bucky deflected the credit from himself. "Those two left-handers south-pawed the champs to death," he said of Mogridge and Zachary.[35]

Chapter 7
Yankees Be Damned

At 2:47 on the morning of August 3, 1923, while visiting in Vermont, Calvin Coolidge received word that he was president. President Warren G. Harding had died of a heart attack in San Francisco. By the light of a kerosene lamp, his father, who was a notary public, administered the oath of office as Vice President Coolidge placed his hand on the family Bible. His conservative pro-business policies rapidly became popular. The political genius of President Coolidge, Walter Lippmann pointed out in 1926, was his talent for effectively doing nothing: "This active inactivity suits the mood and certain of the needs of the country admirably. It suits all the business interests which want to be let alone.... And it suits all those who have become convinced that government in this country has become dangerously complicated and top-heavy."

Coolidge was famous for being a man of few but well-chosen words. Despite his reputation, "Silent Cal," as he was called, had a keen sense of humor. His wit was displayed in a characteristic exchange with a Washington, D.C., hostess, who told him, "You must talk to me, Mr. President. I made a bet today that I could get more than two words out of you." Coolidge famously replied, "You lose."

Coolidge captured the prevailing sentiment of the American people in the 1920s when he said, "The chief business of the American people is business." The essence of the Coolidge presidency was its noninterference in and bolstering of American business and industry. He staffed government regulatory agencies, such as the Federal Trade Commission, with people who sought to assist business expansion rather than to police business practices. Most Americans, identifying their own prosperity with the growth of corporate profits, welcomed this reversal of progressive reforms.

In 1924, as the beneficiary of what was becoming known as "Coolidge prosperity," he polled more than 54 percent of the popular vote. His 25.2-point victory margin in the popular vote is one of the largest ever.[1]

Coolidge was nearly as popular as the capital's baseball team, which he went to see on Thursday, June 26, 1924, as the first-place Washington Senators began a 34-game, 29-day homestand that would include 11 double-headers. The stand opened with a double-header against the A's. Griffith Stadium took on a festive atmosphere to rival a World Series opening. Fans lined up at the box office beginning at 7 o'clock that morning. The gates opened at 11 A.M. to get the crowd, which would reach 23,000, off the streets. "Men, women, children, government officials, military officers, congressmen, and ambassadors alike all filed through the gates."

At 1 P.M. the navy band led the Senators onto the field to a tremendous ovation. "A bevy of beautiful girls from the Pemberton Dancing school wearing nothing you couldn't write home about on a postcard, but probably wouldn't, glided onto the field strewing garlands in the path of the players. Some of the fathers on the club thought the girls ought to go home and put something on. The younger members thought it was good stuff."

The crowd was in holiday humor and whistled and sang as the band played "Hail, Hail the Gang's All Here."

Before the game Bucky was called to the plate to receive a floral piece from Washington, D.C., Commissioner Oyster on behalf of the fans. Bucky also received a floral horseshoe when he came to bat in the second inning and he showed his thanks by hitting a double down the third-base line.

Approximately 20,000 fans turned out for the first game and 3,000 more for the second, including President Coolidge and four secret servicemen. The presidential box behind the Senators' dugout was empty until the First Lady and her children arrived in the seventh inning of the first game. The president arrived just before the second game. The band played the national anthem as he entered the box. The crowd gave him a mighty cheer and he acknowledged them with a big smile and wave of his straw hat. He threw out the ceremonial first ball underhanded, prompting *Washington Post* scribe Harry Stringer to write he learned the underhand motion "pitching horseshoes at his father's farm in Vermont."

Altrock and Schacht went through their repertoire of comedy acts, dancing with the dance school girls, rowing and fishing in front of the president's box, and performing their famous slow-motion pitching and batting act. Stringer seemed to be obsessed with the dancing girls' attire, writing, "First the clowns participated in athletic dancing with the girls, though their uniforms seemed to hamper their movements, while the fair ones were under no such handicap. The president applauded vigorously."[2]

Johnson, who hadn't pitched in five days, won the first game, 5–0. It was the team's 10th straight win. Bucky was 2-for-4 with two doubles and three runs scored. Rommel put a damper on the celebratory mood by beating the Senators, 1–0, in the second game with a three-hitter, but they were still in first place by a full game over the Tigers at the end of the day. The Washington area was hit with thunderstorms the next day, washing out another game. They made it up the following afternoon with a double-header on a day when a tornado killed 350 people and injured 2,000 in Ohio. The Senators swept, beating the A's 4–1 and 4–0. Zahniser pitched the first game but was pulled for Russell in the ninth after the first two batters singled. Russell coaxed two strikeouts and a ground out to Bucky.

Mogridge pitched a complete game in the second contest. Bluege was 4-for-6 with a double and a stolen base and two RBIs. Bucky was 2-for-8 with three runs scored and made a double play in each game. The Senators, reheated by the sweep, won five of their next six, three of them shutouts by Mogridge, Ogden and Zahniser. The only loss in the span came in the first game of a June 30 double-header when the Red Sox's Ehmke beat Johnson, 2–1, in 11 innings. With the double-headers adding up, Bucky started Marberry in the second game and he pitched a complete game, winning 3–1. Bucky was 2-for-3 with a double, RBI and run. June ended with the Senators in first place with a 56–43 record and a 2½-game lead over both the Yankees and Tigers.

The Yankees made short work of that lead. They came to the capital on Independence Day and promptly swept a double-header, beating Zachary and Mogridge, 4–2 and 2–0. The Yankees made it three straight the next day, winning the first of two before 24,000. Pennock beat Johnson with a shutout in the first game, 2–0. In the fourth inning, Ruth ran into the concrete wall in foul territory while chasing a ball hit by Judge. He was unconscious for five minutes and had a bruised hip but finished the game and started the second game.[3]

In the second contest, the Senators broke a 22-inning scoreless streak with a four-run first, staking Marberry, who pitched a complete game, to an early lead in the 7–2 win. The Senators made two double plays, both reading "Peckinpaugh-Harris-Judge."

The Yankees made it four of five on July 6 with a four-run ninth to win, 7–4, aided by a boot by Bucky. The Senators led, 4–2, in the top of the eighth when Ruth hit his 22nd home run. In the ninth the Yankees' Schang singled and was forced at second. Ward hit a drive into left-center that Matthews tracked down at the base of the wall for the second out. Harvey, batting for Shawkey, hit to right and tried to stretch it into a double. Rice pegged to Peckinpaugh, who appeared to have Harvey for the game-ending out, but Harvey kicked the ball out on the slide, allowing the tying run to score. Martina walked Whitey Witt, prompting Bucky to bring in Marberry. Dugan grounded to Bucky, who muffed it. Peckinpaugh retrieved the ball and threw home as Harvey tried to score the go-ahead run. Again the ball beat him, but he crashed into Ruel with a football-style hit, knocking Ruel head over heels and dislodging the ball. Marberry ran the ball down but Ruel was so dazed he didn't cover home and Witt scored to make it 6–4. Ruth doubled in the seventh run. The Senators' lead in the A.L. was down to a game over the Yankees.[4]

After a scheduled day off and still another rainout, the Senators played consecutive double-headers against the Tigers, who were only three games back, on July 9 and 10. The Senators won the first game, 5–2. The second game was stopped for two minutes at 4 P.M. as the players and fans stood silently with heads bowed out of respect for Calvin Coolidge Jr., the president's 16-year-old son. At that moment services were being held over his casket in the East Room of the White House. The president's son died of blood poisoning set off by a toe blister caused by a barefoot game of tennis with his brother John in June. Modern antibiotics, which could have easily cured the boy, did not exist in 1924.[5]

In the first game Ty Cobb, the Tiger manager, had Rip Collins, a left-handed batter, starting at second base. Bucky started a lefty. Cobb, using the reverse of the cover pitcher ploy Bucky would make famous in the World Series, batted Detrill Pratt, a righty, in the first inning for Collins. The Senators went into a little slump beginning in the second game of the July 9 double-header. They lost that one, 4–2, and the first game of two the next day, 12–10, in 13 innings. Bucky was 4-for-4 with a double, a triple, a run scored and an RBI. He also walked and was hit by a pitch. He was just as busy with his scorecard, using 20 players, including five pitchers. The game took four hours. The second game, which didn't start until 6:05 P.M., was halted by darkness after five innings with the score tied, 3–3.

The Tigers won a single game the next day, 4–3, with Hooks Dauss beating Johnson. Cleveland followed the Tigers to town for still another double-header. The Indians won the first game, 7–1. Zachary, with a bandage on his thumb, won the second game, 9–2, the Senators' first win in six games. Scribe Young had an idea. "If someone would humanely fracture the thumbs of some of the other pitchers on the Harris staff it might help the Senators to get back in winning-ways for it was none other than old Jezebel Tecumseh Zachary, thumb in splints, and all, who hurled his team to a 9 to 2 win in game two."[6]

Bucky was glad to be playing single games for the next few days after having played six double-headers in 11 days. "Thank goodness there are no more double-headers until Thursday," said Harris after the battles were over, "as we're about all in. Not only are the regulars pretty well worn out but the strain has been too great on the veteran hurling staff."[7]

Single games were a tonic. The Senators beat Cleveland the next three days, scoring 26 runs in the first two and winning, 15–11 and 12–0. Goslin hit two doubles. In the 15–11 win Judge was 4-for-5 with two doubles. Bucky was 2-for-5 with a double and made a great one-handed stop in back of first to take away a sure hit. The Senators had 18 hits, but not all the fans were happy. After the last out a fan went onto the field and attacked umpire Ducky Holmes. He punched him once, but Cleveland second baseman Chick Fewster and Umpire Moriarity stopped him. Cops took him toward the exit between the grandstand and right-field pavilion, but he jerked himself loose and escaped into the crowd. Hundreds of fans hung around for a half hour but nothing more happened. A half-dozen police officers came in and ordered the fans to leave.

The fan was probably irate over what happened in the ninth inning. With two outs, Zahniser walked two and had a 2–0 count on the next batter when Bucky walked in from second base to talk to his catcher, Bennie Tate. He asked Tate if Zahniser was off or was it the umpire Holmes who was "off color." Holmes thought Bucky was pulling a stunt to show him up and threw him out of the game.[8] Normally Harris wouldn't have drawn a suspension for what he said, but because of what happened with the fans it was expected that league president Ban Johnson would suspend him. Just before the next game, on July 14, Bucky got a telegram from Ban Johnson suspending him indefinitely for the run-in with Umpire Holmes before the fracas. Bucky was in the stands under suspension.

"Stanley Harris has been suspended," wrote Young, "because he intimated that Umpire Holmes weighed more from the shoulders up than in the other direction."[9]

Peckinpaugh managed. Bluege played second and was 2-for-4 as the Senators won, 12–0, over Cleveland. On the 15th the Senators made it four straight over the Indians as Johnson beat Coveleski, 4–2. Bluege again played second base. Bucky's suspension was lifted for the next game. In standings at the end of the day on July 15, the Yankees were 48–33; the Senators, 47–36; and Detroit, 45–38.

The Browns came in next and won three of five. The second game was lost in 16 innings, 10–9. Bucky hit a ball in the 14th that Griffith argued should have been a home run. It bounced back onto the field, and Umpire Dick Nallin said it hit the wall a few inches below the stands. Umpire Bill Dinnen said he was watching Bucky touch the bases and didn't see where the ball hit. Griffith protested, but the home run and the game were lost.

The White Sox were the last team in for the homestand and the Senators won four of five. In a Nationals win in the opener on July 21, Sox manager Johnny Evers left his pitcher, Ted Lyons, in for the entire game, all 18 hits and 16 runs of it. On the last day of the homestand while the Senators beat Chicago, 7–5, the Tigers beat the Yankees in a game called after eight innings so the Yankees could catch a train. Detroit went into first place by ½ game over the Yankees and Washington.

The Senators were 20–14 on the homestand and 11–10–1 in the double-headers. Bucky took it easy on Marberry during that period. He appeared in relief only four times but started four games, all wins, completing three. Curly Ogden won all four of his starts in the homestand and was 7–1 since the Senators picked him up after Mack gave up on him. That was a puzzle in Philadelphia as the *Philadelphia Ledger* opined:

> Warren Ogden, commonly called Curley for no good reason since he puts the patent leather finish on his hair nowadays, was winless with the A's. It was generally believed he had a lame arm. He was honest about it when he joined the Senators — told Bucky Harris he feared his curving sinews would not respond to his commands. The Washington board of strategy told him to forget his hook for a while.
>
> That doesn't explain why he has won seven games against teams that regularly clubbed him when he was wearing the white elephant. It would be unkind to suggest that Connie Mack did not know how to get the best out of Ogden. That would be like saying that the whispered reports that McGillicuddy is through are true.[10]

The Senators went on a 17-game western swing starting July 26 in Cleveland where they lost three of four. They lost the opener, 2–0. Ogden then proved Mack wrong once again, winning the next day, 4–3, to raise his record to 8–4, 8–1 with the Senators. The Senators got only six hits off Coveleski in the third game of the series and Shute beat Marberry, 4–2, in the fourth game to drop the Senators to third place, a game behind second-place Detroit and 1½ behind the Yankees.

Bucky was on the bench for the opening of the series in Detroit, "the victim of ptomaine poisoning," and watched the Senators win, 1–0, on a three-hit shutout by Zachary. With the win they pulled within ½ game of the Yankees, who lost a double-header to St. Louis. Ruth hit his 33rd home run and 17th in July, breaking his own record for a month.

The Senators split the next two with the Tigers and then went to St. Louis. The Yankees had just left without their "Doodle Dandy," having lost three of four. The Browns treated the Senators even harsher, sweeping five, including a double-header on August 5. Suddenly the Senators found themselves in third place and only 1½ games ahead of the fourth-place Browns.

Shell-shocked, the Senators went to Chicago on August 7 where Bucky gave the ball to Johnson, who did not pitch in St. Louis, for one of the most pivotal games of the season. The game went to the tenth inning tied, 3–3. The Senators loaded the bases in the top of the 10th and Sox catcher Buck Crouse saved the day, and maybe the season, for the Senators. On a ground ball in the infield the Sox had a play at the plate, but Crouse failed to touch home and then threw the ball into center field while trying to get an out at second base. Two runs scored and the Senators won, 6–3. Johnson went the distance. Though they lost their next game, the Senators won 13 of 16, starting with that 6–3 gift from Crouse. Marberry finished with four of the wins.

The day after that 10-inning game a thunderstorm that had unleashed a tornado on Cedar Rapids a day earlier reached Chicago and washed out the scheduled game. But the day was not without news. Griffith stunned the base-ball world by parting with $50,000 and Wid Matthews and two players to be named at the end of the season for a 26-year-old Sacramento outfielder with no major league experience by the name of Earl McNeely. Bucky lobbied for the deal. This was the same Griffith who declared after the Red Sox had paid $50,000 for Dudley Lee during the winter meetings that no minor leaguer was worth that kind of money.

Matthews had gone through a mini 3-for-18 slump in mid–July and Bucky went back to Nemo Liebold, who had started the season in center before being supplanted by Matthews. Leibold went wild with his chance, hitting .564 (22-for-38) in a 10-game stretch and keeping Matthews on the bench. McNeely was batting .333 and slugging .474 at Sacramento. For the record, Bucky and Griffith had nothing but praise for Matthews as he left, explaining that Sacramento insisted on getting the outfielder in the deal. It was also noted that the Senators retained the right to recall Matthews (and did so on September 29, though he did not get in another game in 1924). He started 1925 with the Senators but was sold to Indianapolis in June after 10 games and never played in the major leagues again. Griffith and Bucky guessed right on McNeely. He hit .330 with five doubles, six triples and 15 RBIs, playing in 43 of last 47 games, mostly in center field, and batting leadoff in front of Bucky.

Of those 13 of 16 the Senators won from August 7 to August 25, Johnson won five. On August 12 he shut out Cleveland, 4–0, and struck out eight in the first game of a homestand. Bucky was charged with an error but handled four chances safely and started a double play. He was batting only .255 at this point but was the runaway league leader in sacrifices with 38 and led the team in steals with 16. The next day Mogridge pitched a two-hitter in a 1–0 win. Bucky singled and scored the only run in the bottom of the sixth. Rice sacrificed him to second and Goslin knocked him in with a single. On August 17 Johnson beat the Tigers, 8–1, on a four-hitter. There was a half-hour rain delay in the second inning. It took O'Day and the grounds crew so long to get the infield covered the game was nearly called. Johnson then beat Chicago, 2–1, on the 21st. When he shut out the Browns, 2–0, in Washington on August 25, he was 17–6 and the Senators were 70–52, one percentage point behind the Yankees, who were 69–51.

Bucky insisted that Griffith buy unknown Earl McNeely for the 1924 stretch drive. McNeely hit .330 in 43 games in August and September and was 3-for-5 in the fifth game of the World Series (Library of Congress Digital Collection).

On August 18 against Detroit, Bucky pulled Zahniser with two outs in the third after he'd given up three runs. Marberry came in, recorded the third out in the third and pitched shutout ball through the eighth. Russell pitched a one, two, three ninth and the Senators won, 6–3. Bucky started three double plays and threw O'Rourke out at home after making a running catch behind first base and a spectacular throw while falling backward.

Bucky was all over a double-header win over the Tigers, 4–3 and 5–3, on August 19 as a player and manager. Bucky knocked in the winning run in the ninth inning of the first game with a one-out double. He stole a base in each game, stealing home in the seventh inning of the second contest. He also made the turn on a 6-4-3 double play and laid down his league-leading 37th sacrifice. In the sixth inning of the second game Bucky brought Alan Russell in to replace Zachary with the tying run on third and no outs. Russell got out of it and pitched shutout innings in the seventh, eighth and ninth. Bucky was 5-for-7 in the double-header as the Senators moved into second place, only two behind the Yankees.

On August 21 Walter Johnson beat the White Sox and Michelangelo Cvengros, 2–1. Both pitchers went seven innings. Johnson left with indigestion and Cvengros was removed for a pinch-hitter. Umpire Ducky Holmes threw Joe Judge out of the game and Judge had to be escorted off the field by two policemen after he called Holmes a "fat head" and pushed him. Judge insisted he didn't call Holmes a "fat head" but admitted he did push him.[11] The Sox scored a run in the ninth and had two on base with one out when pinch-hitter Bucky Grouse lined to Shirley, who replaced Judge at first. Marberry pitched the eighth and ninth innings.

On August 23 Earl McNeely, the $50,000 investment, scored both runs in a 2–1 win over the White Sox. McNeeley reached on a throwing error and scored when the ball was thrown away on a bunt by Bucky. In the fifth McNeeley doubled and scored on a Rice single. Before the game Bucky gave a tryout to a Gressan Grazzini, a Dominican who had pitched a no-hitter against Quantico Marines. It was reported he showed some good speed and nice curves but was never heard from again.[12]

On August 24 the Senators and Zachary beat the White Sox, 4–1. Bucky was in the middle of four of five double plays, three from Peckinpaugh and one from Bluege. Bucky had seven putouts and four assists, a hit and a run scored. The screams heard coming from the Senators' clubhouse after the game emitted from utility infielder Tom Taylor as trainer Martin opened a boil on his chest. It took most of the team to hold Taylor down.

On August 25 Johnson pitched a seven-inning no-hitter against the Browns in the first game of a scheduled double-header. The game was stopped by rain. Johnson had such tremendous stuff the Browns had nothing close to

Joe Judge, pictured with his father at the 1924 World Series, was low key and quietly batted .324 in 1924. Acting out of character, he was tossed from a game on August 21 (Library of Congress Digital Collection).

a hit. He faced only 23 batters, walking two. Johnson went to Keith's, a popular nightspot, that evening. When he was recognized, the cheering didn't stop until he rose from his seat and acknowledged the fans. Headliner Julia Sanderson "after a dainty wind up" hurled a bouquet straight into Johnson's lap. He turned red with embarrassment. Sanderson was a Broadway and radio star with a star on the Hollywood Walk of Fame.[13]

After the Johnson no-hitter the Yankees could feel the Senators at their backs, just .001 point behind. The Yankees were 69–51–1, a .575 mark. Washington was 70–52–2, or .574. In Washington it was sinking in there might be a World Series in town, and some of the Senators' fans were determined not to miss it.

Despite the fact that the season still has over a month to go and the Washington team is only in second place aside, Secretary Eddie Eynon and his office force are being rushed handling requests for world's series reservations. Washington has never had one of these big sets of games and hundreds of fans are getting in requests for seats now while the getting is good. While, of course, it is not impossible for their efforts to be wasted and that either the Yankees or Tigers will win the pennant, nevertheless the fact that so many are making applications for reservations indicates that some, at least, are confident of the Harrismen's ability to stand the long, hard drive to come.

According to Secretary Eynon over 500 applications have been received to date with more coming in every day. They first started to arrive when the team returned from its last Western trip and each day the mail has been bringing them in larger and larger numbers. Seventy five were received yesterday Eynon said and at least this many are looked for daily from now on unless the Nats unexpectedly slump. Secretary Eynon lets it be known that those who had enough confidence in the Nats to make requests for seats so early will certainly be well taken care of.

Griffith was talking to the team scribes, getting their ideas on how to expand the press box to accommodate the 400 newspapermen and telegraphers expected to request badges.[14]

On the eve of a crucial four-game series with the Yankees in New York, the Senators lost the last game of a Browns series, 8–6, in 11 innings and the Yankees split a double-header with Cleveland. As the Senators arrived in New York on August 28, they were 71–54–2 and ½ game behind the Yankees, who were 70–52–1. Back in Washington, two pennants, white for Washington and blue for New York, fluttered from the big flag pole atop the Mills Building at 17th and Pennsylvania Avenue during the series. When Washington led, the white pennant flew above the blue; the opposite was true when the Yankees led. The pennants were visible for miles around. Senators fans saw a lot of white. At Walter Reed Hospital, 1,500 war veterans followed the games on radio.[15]

In the opener at the Stadium on August 28, 25,000 saw the Senators come from behind with an eight-run eighth inning and win, 11–6. They trailed, 6–3, at the start of the inning. In the eighth three Yankees pitchers were knocked out of the box, thirteen Nats came to bat, seven of them got hits and eight scored. In that inning, with the bases loaded, Yankee center fielder Whitey Witt lost Goslin's fly that went for a three-run triple. Goslin was 4-for-5. He hit for the cycle, walked once, and had six RBIs. Rice was

5-for-5 with two doubles. Ruth hit his 41st and 42nd home runs. Marberry finished the game, shutting out the Yankees in the eighth and ninth.

Johnson beat the Yanks the next day, 5–1. It was his 18th win against six losses. With one out in the Yankee eighth, Bucky nearly turned white when Johnson was hit on the hand by a line drive. "The Big Train crumpled like an accordion after Schang's wicked drive almost tore his hand off, but not until he picked the ball up and threw the batter out at first."

The game was stopped for five minutes as the Senators gathered around the mound. Johnson insisted he was all right and threw three warm-up pitches, but Bucky waved Marberry in. The injury was painful, but nothing was broken as an x-ray confirmed.[16] Johnson did not miss a turn. The Yankees won the third game, beating Ogden, 2–1, in the bottom of the ninth on a single by Meusel, who drove in both runs.

That day Browns manager George Sisler said Washington would win the pennant, with the infield defense being the biggest reason. "In Bluege, Peck, Harris and Judge they have as fine a double play quartet as I have ever seen. Harris has a rifle-shot arm that helps very wonderfully in completing double plays."[17]

The Senators made three double plays in the first two games of the series, with making Bucky the pivot on two. The fourth game was on a Sunday and 45,000 fans saw the Senators make it three of four, winning, 4–2, in 10. Bucky had another run–in with Umpire Holmes after Mogridge walked Ruth on a 3–2 count in the eighth with the Senators leading, 2–1. Mogridge yelled to Holmes that the ball had cut the plate in half. Bucky and Schacht picked up the argument to shield Mogridge but Holmes ran all three of them out of the game.[18] Miller subbed for Bucky. Marberry came in to pitch and walked in the tying run before he recorded a strikeout to end the inning. The Senators won it on a two-run double by Rice with two outs in the tenth. Marberry pitched a one-two-three tenth.

The fact that the Senators led the Yankees by 1½ games on September 1 was more than their fans could bear. The team's train didn't get in until 11:25 P.M., but more than 8,000 were jammed into Union Station to welcome them back. Long before the train was due, several hundred were gathered in front of the grating facing track no. 8, pushing to get near the exit the players were expected to use. Bucky was grateful for the support but worried about the size and overzealousness of the crowd. He wanted the players to get to bed since they had a morning-afternoon double-header the next day, Labor Day. He led the players through the train to the east end of the station where a passage had been roped off. It was a futile attempt. An official reception committee greeted them as they stepped from the train. Among the committee were Mrs. Walter Johnson; Mrs. Joe Judge; Griffith's sister, Mrs. Eugene

Robinson; Mae Nolan of California, the only female member of Congress; park police captain W. I. McMorris; and Loew's Theaters manager Larry Keatus.

The players greeted the committee and tried to get away, but before they could reach the waiting taxis the crowd surrounded them in the small passage. A detachment of police from the sixth precinct tried to hold the fans back, but the players couldn't escape until they had been patted on the back and shaken hands with everybody who could reach them.

Walter Johnson was greeted like the general of a returning victorious army. Over and over he was asked, "Walter how's your hand?" and he answered, "It's fine." Finally they let him go and he drove his car carefully through the crowd.[19]

If the Senators were bothered by the late arrival and reception, it didn't show. They swept the Labor Day double-header from the A's, 5–3 in the morning before 18,000 and 4–3 before 22,000 in the afternoon. Before the first game, some of Bucky's fans presented him with an oriental rug. A's outfielder Bill Lamar received a gold watch from his fan club from Rockville, Maryland, where he lived.

Both games featured action in the ninth innings. In the morning game, the A's, trailing 5–0, got five singles in the ninth off Tom Zachary, but Bucky stuck with him and he got out of it. In the second game, with a right-handed pitcher going for the A's, Bucky put left-handed batter Leibold in center instead of McNeeley, a righty. Leibold pulled up lame with a Charlie horse and McNeeley replaced him in the fifth. That worked fine as McNeeley was 3-for-3, including the game-winner in the ninth after a pinch-hit by Shirley.

The Senators scored two in the ninth with two outs and the bases empty. Peck hit a hard line drive that A's shortstop Chapman dropped. Shirley's pinch-hit brought him in with the tying run and McNeely's third hit won it. Bucky and Peck pulled off double plays in the eighth and ninth.

A's third baseman Sammy Hale ripped his uniform in the second game. In a show of sportsmanship 1924 style, Bucky agreed to let Hale go back in the game after getting the uniform fixed. By gentlemen's agreement Riconda played third for ⅔ of an inning. Bucky used three pitchers — Martina, Allan Russell and Marberry. Marberry, who was making his fifth appearance in seven games, pitched two innings and was the winner. During the seventh-inning stretch of the second game the fans rained straw hats on the field.

The wet and wild weather that plagued the country that spring and summer revved up again on September 2. It was a scheduled day off, which was good as a tremendous storm, described as a squall, hit Washington. A child was killed, several people were injured, roofs were blown off and 500 trees were downed. A table blown from the roof of the Powhatan Hotel landed on a huckster wagon. Downtown was a pandemonium of flying papers and blown-out windows.[20]

Walter Johnson's hand, hit by that Schang line drive in the Yankee series, was fine. After two days off, except for pitching a little batting practice the day after the storm, Johnson started on September 4 in the first game of a three-game series with the Red Sox. In what the *Post* described as a "lecture," Bucky urged the players to go at top speed no matter who the opponent was. He was afraid they would view the Red Sox, who came in 59–73, as an easy mark. The Red Sox provided little competition in the first two games as the Senators won, 12–5 and 8–2. The Senators pounded three Sox pitchers for 20 hits in the first game. The Sox scored runs in the sixth and seventh and had the bases full when Johnson recorded the third out. Bucky brought in Russell for the last two innings. Bucky was 3-for-5 with three runs scored. Johnson gave up nine hits in the seven innings and struck out seven.

In the second game with the Red Sox, the Senators beat Ehmke, 8–2, before 20,000. Bucky was 2-for-5 with two triples, one hit to the center-field wall, and three RBIs. He also had a double play. Mogridge pitched a complete game, giving up 11 hits. Bucky faked out a runner, turning a hit into an out. Standing still at second as though no play was being made, he caught a throw from the outfield and made his best Eddie Collins swipe tag on Ike Boone.

On Friday, September 5, Commissioner Landis visited Griffith to discuss World Series plans. Griffith announced an expansion of seating at the stadium would start on Monday morning when the Senators began a road trip. The plan was to move the scoreboard to right field and build a double-deck grand-stand in right-center to seat 6,000, raising capacity to 35,500. He also announced World Series tickets were to be reserved by mail order only. He was trying to avoid walk-up sales.[21]

A morning workout was attended by as many fans as attended games in lean seasons. Several photographers took pictures of the players in anticipation of the World Series. Clubhouse boy Frank Baxter didn't want to be photographed, but Goslin and Altrock carried him onto the field to face the photographers. Leibold wore a wad of chewing gum on the button of his cap. After the workout the team visited the White House. President Coolidge shook hands with each player and predicted the team would be in the Series. Bucky received a telegram from the Washington Monarch club of the Negro League. "We wish you continued success upon the invasion of the West."[22]

Judge was injured, limping badly on a swollen left ankle, and was expected to be out at least until the Philadelphia series started on Monday. Mule Shirley was his backup. For the last game of the homestand on September 7, 4,000 were waiting when the ticket office opened at noon. An hour later another 7,000 were in line. A record crowd of 30,000 attended only to see the Senators lose, 6–2. Bucky was 2-for-4, scored a run, and made two sparkling plays in the field. In the third he charged a slow roller by Veech, bare-handing it and pegging to first in one motion. Later he went out into short center to catch Clarke's Texas Leaguer.

The World Series preparations seemed a little premature. When the Senators boarded a train for Philadelphia the next morning at 9 o'clock, they were 79–56 and only two games ahead of the Yankees, who were 77–58. Detroit was third, five back.

Only 6,000 were in Philadelphia as Johnson beat the A's, 8–4, in the first game of the road trip for his 20th win of the season. He hadn't won 20 since 1919. Bucky stayed hot, going 2-for-4 with two RBIs and a run. Given an early lead, 7–1 in the third, Johnson took it easy according to the *Post* and didn't throw his hardest except when he needed a third out with runner on. He gave up two home runs and struck out three. Johnson was 2-for-4 at the plate with two runs and an RBI.

More rain the next day meant the 20th double-header of the season for the Senators on September 10. Lefties Zachary and Mogridge were Bucky's starters. The players didn't like double-headers as they often ended in splits and the Senators needed to win. The players were right. The double-header was split. The A's won the opener, 2–1. The Senators won the second, 6–5, but nearly blew it. They led, 6–1, in the third and had to pull it out, 6–5. It was 6–4 in the bottom of ninth and the A's had the bases loaded with one out when Bucky brought Marberry in to replace Mogridge. A sac fly made it 6–5, but Dykes flew out to McNeely to end it. Bucky hit his 25th double, knocked in a run and scored one.

Marberry was back on the mound the next day as a starter and went the distance, winning, 7–4, surviving 11 hits by the A's. The big news was a home run by Bucky, a three-run job in the first inning into the left-field bleachers at Shibe Park. It was his first and only home run of the regular season and the fifth in his career in more than 1,600 at-bats. He also had a double, walked and scored three runs. Rice and Goslin hit doubles, for each his 35th of the season. Judge tried to go but Shirley pinch-hit for him and finished the game.

Having seen Firpo Marberry win that afternoon, Bucky went to see the real Firpo that evening. Luis Firpo fought Henry Wills, a 6'3" black man from New Orleans known as the "The Black Panther." The fight drew 80,000 fans to Boyle's 30 Acres, an outdoor venue in Jersey City built in 1921 for a Dempsey fight. Wills floored Firpo once and got the better of the fight for 12 rounds, but by New Jersey rules it was declared a no decision because there was no knockout. By going to the fight, Bucky missed a parade for him in Pittston the next morning, where the Senators were scheduled to play an exhibition game. Bucky did arrive in time for the noon Rotary luncheon in his honor and the game. It was Friday, September 12, a travel day. Bucky sent Leibold, Marberry, Mogridge, Zachary, Johnson, Ogden, and Ruel on to Detroit and took the rest of the team to Pittston for a game against a local semi-pro team. Al Schacht pitched for the Pittston team. More than 3,000 came to the game with contingents representing local towns like West Pittston, Exeter, Wyoming, Forty Fort and, of course, Hughestown.

The Senators defeated the local team, called the Craftsmen, 15–3. Bucky's brother Merle played second base for the Craftsmen. Joe Martina, Byron Speece and Altrock played for both teams. Judge played to test his ankle and hit a home run. Before his first at-bat Bucky was given a diamond ring and then struck out. The fans also presented Bucky with a goat named "Melty" that was said to be a descendant from the goat that gave Bucky his nickname. "There is a long story connected with it in which Harris was called Bucky because of some characteristics he and the grandfather of the animal had in common."[23]

The Pittston Craftsmen team that played Senators on September 12, 1924. Merle Harris is fourth from the left in the front row. Others are unidentified (courtesy of Ruth Haynes).

On September 13 Johnson beat the Tigers, 6–4. It was his 21st win and 11th consecutive. He was relieved by Marberry in the eighth. Bucky was 3-for-5 with a triple, his ninth, and a double, his 26th, and scored twice. Judge did not play.

The next day Johnson was named American League MVP. Told of the honor in Detroit, he said, "It's a honor I never dreamed of. It's particularly gratifying in view of the fact that I am just about at the end of my career and all I need to make my happiness complete is for the Senators to get into the World Series." Johnson received 55 of 64 votes from the selection committee as well as a telegram of congratulation from the Chamber of Commerce in Coffeyville, Kansas, his hometown.[24] Eddie Collins was second in the MVP voting.

The Yankees also won that day, blasting the White Sox, 16–1. Ruth hit his 46th home run. The Senators' lead was one. The Senators lost the next two days in Detroit while the Yankees split in Chicago to pick up a game. It was September 15 and the teams were tied atop the A.L. at 82–59 with 13 games left to play.

The next day the Senators won in Cleveland, 6–2, behind Zachary for the team's 83rd win. The Yankees had the day off and were stuck at 82. Bucky had things figured out.

> The same teams which beat us will also give the Huggmen trouble. The Yankees gained on us while they were playing easy teams and we were playing hard ones. Don't let anyone tell you that the Athletics will be any softer picking for New York than they were for us. I look for the Tigers to hand them two lickings, maybe three. A double header with the Browns tomorrow won't help the Yankees either. I figure the team that wins 90 games this season will be declared the winner and that will be easier for us to win seven against our opponents than it will be for the Yanks to take eight. If we haven't already sewed things up by the time we tackle Boston in the last series we'll certainly do it then, for the Foggmen are our meat, while the Athletics who will be entertaining the New Yorkers are rank poison for them and are sure of handing them at least one setback and it wouldn't surprise me if they didn't break even in the four-game series.[25]

Bucky wanted to use his top four pitchers — Johnson, Mogridge, Zachary and Marberry — exclusively in the stretch run, with the first three starting and Marberry relieving and spot starting. Zachary and Johnson beat Cleveland on September 16 and 17. It was Johnson's 22nd win against six losses. He struck out six and walked one. Rice hit in his 24th consecutive game. In the sixth Bucky short-hopped a throw from Ruel, dived for Burns and tagged him out attempting to steal.

Bucky's exclusive pitching plan went by the wayside, but with a good result, in the third game of a series in Cleveland on September 18. Bucky started Marberry, but he didn't like what he saw and pulled him after the pitcher gave up five hits and three runs in two innings. Bucky brought in Russell but then pinch-hit for Russell in the fourth with the Senators behind, 4–0. Bucky then called on By Speece, a little-used mop-up man who had pitched only 49 innings all season. Speece allowed just one harmless run in six innings and the Senators rallied to win, 9–5. In the fourth Wade Lefler tied the game at four with a hit in his first at-bat as a Senator. Uhle pitched the full nine innings for the Indians, giving up 17 hits. It was 4–4 into the ninth when the Senators scored five on four hits, two hit batsmen, a suicide squeeze and an error. Bucky was hitless but dropped down his 44th sacrifice.

In St. Louis the Yankees swept the Browns, 7–3 and 8–7, to regain the tie. Both teams were 84–59. In Washington, the *Post* megaphoned the play-by-play of the Yankees-Browns double-header and showed the progress of the Senators-Cleveland game on the magnetic scoreboard. As the Yankees left St. Louis the Senators arrived. The last time the Senators were in St. Louis, the Browns swept five from them.

That same day, John Davis, the Democratic presidential nominee, spoke to 14,000 in Chicago and said he was taking the gloves off to fight the Republican Party on its record. He attacked the Republicans without attacking Coolidge directly, though he did mention Coolidge's vetoes of the veterans' bonus bill, the postal employees' bill, and his support of the Melon tax reduction. Back in Washington nobody was paying attention to Davis or the presidential race. Everybody was consumed by baseball. The excitement was so great that downtown streets were impassable as great crowds gathered to watch play-by-play on elaborate scoreboards and hear the games called on megaphones.

Most of the South was rooting for the Senators. The Baltimore papers were following the team with front-page stories. WRC radio, an RCA station, was broadcasting the play-by-play by way of a direct line from the *Post*. Mae Nolan, a congresswoman from California, promised to support ways to honor Walter Johnson. "Permit me to contribute in money and service to the Walter Johnson testimonial. He deserves all we can give him. If Washington wins the world's series I will introduce a resolution to make Walter's birthday a legal holiday in the District."[26]

Griffith announced the stadium was ready for the Series. The infield was resodded, and the pavilion and bleacher seats were renumbered and widened from 16 to 17 inches. The final configuration was 34,245 reserved and 3,000 standing room for a total of 37,245. A press holding room was readied for 400. A train was planned to bring 125 fans from Tampa to Washington for the Series. Plans were in the works for a special Pennsylvania Railroad car to take the Senators directly from Boston to New York for the first game of the Series.[27]

The plans seemed a bit premature if one were to look at the standings. In St. Louis the Senators scored 29 runs in the first two games but won only one. They won the opener, 15–9, and lost the second game, 15–14, in 10. In the first game the Senators scored nine in the first inning. Of the first five batters, three singled, one walked and one was hit by a pitch. McNeely had two hits leading off and was 4-for-6. Bucky was 2-for-6 and scored three times, and he and Peck were involved in three double plays. But Bucky also made three errors.

Nine pitchers were used in the 15–14 loss. Goslin was 4-for-6 with two home runs and a double. The Senators made six errors. After Goslin's homer in the top of the 10th had given the Senators a 14–13 lead, the Browns loaded the bases against Marberry in the bottom. The batter hit a high hopper back to the mound. Marberry jumped to field it cleanly, and with an easy play at the plate in front of him inexplicably turned toward second, hoping to get a double play to end the game. He did end the game — by throwing the ball into right-center. The Browns' winning runs scored without a play. The Yankees lost in Detroit, 6–5, and the Senators' lead remained one game.

Bucky's prediction a few days earlier ("I look for the Tigers to hand them two lickings") was right on. While the Senators wrapped up their three-game set in St. Louis with a 6–4 win, the Yankees lost another one-run game in Detroit, 4–3. It was September 21 and the lead was two games with seven left to play.

The Senators went into that last game in St. Louis knowing they had a chance to increase their lead to two. Rain delayed the start of their game to 4 P.M. and by then they knew the Yankees had lost. Zachary won the game, 6–4, which was called due to darkness after seven innings. Goslin hit another home run and Bucky took part in two double plays, a strike 'em out-throw 'em out from Ruel and a 4–6–3 to Peck and Judge, who was 3-for-4 with his 37th double.

The next day in Chicago, Johnson won his 13th straight decision and Peck hit in his 29th straight game as the Senators won, 8–3. Peck hit two doubles. Johnson struck out five and walked one. The Yankees stayed within two, winning in Cleveland, 10–4. Neither team wilted. The Senators completed a three-game sweep in Chicago, with Mogridge and Zachary winning, 7–6 and 3–2, while the Yankees completed their sweep in Cleveland. In that 7–6 win Bucky made things closer than they needed to be. The Senators had a 7–3 lead in the seventh, but Bucky's error led to two runs to make it 7–6. He brought in Marberry to bail him out, and it worked. Marberry got out of the seventh and pitched shutout innings in the eight and ninth.

Meanwhile in Washington, a grand parade was being planned for the Senators, win or lose the pennant, but nobody thought they were going to lose. The board of commissioners of the District appointed a committee headed by Melvin Hazen, the district surveyor, to plan the celebration. President Coolidge was expected to review the parade from the back of the White House, where Bucky would receive the key to the city from Commissioner Rudolph. After the parade a banquet at Occidental Hotel was planned by Gus Buchholz. The parade was to begin at the ball park at 3:30 P.M. There the players were to be taken by a squad of automobiles to Peace Monument, from where the parade up the avenue was to begin at 4:30 P.M.

At the Treasury the parade route was to swing toward the Ellipse. General Rockenbach, who played a leading part in the Defense Day parade, was the parade marshal. Scheduled to lead the parade were mounted police, scarlet-coated members of the Riding and Hunt Club, and the automobiles with the players. The route was mapped out by Lt. Col. Sherrill, in charge of public buildings and grounds.[28]

The Senators were just too hot for the Yankees to overtake. They made it four straight in Chicago over the White Sox and eight of nine wins overall with a 6–3 victory in the last of the four-game set on September 24. Zachary got the win. Rice hit in his 31st consecutive game. The Yankees won again and the lead stayed at two with four to play. Both teams headed back east for their final stops of the season, the Senators to Boston and the Yankees to Philadelphia, 25-hour train rides for each.

Again one of Bucky's predictions came true. "If we haven't already sewed things up by the time we tackle Boston in the last series we'll certainly do it then, for the Foggmen are our meat, while the Athletics who will be entertaining the New Yorkers are rank poison for them."

But the clinch in Boston had to wait one more agonizing day. Boston won the first game of the series, 2–1. The Yankees won in Philadelphia, 7–1, and the lead was down to one with three to go. Johnson was hit in the elbow by a pitch in the seventh. He was all right, but Bucky pulled him as a precaution. The ball caught Johnson on the crazy bone, causing excruciating pain but no injury. Ferguson pitched a complete game for the Red Sox for his 15th win and struck out five.

The Boston fans loudly rooted for Johnson and the Senators. A biographer of Johnson described it this way: "Upwards of 10,000 fans turned out ... yesterday and no visiting club was ever given more encouragement to go in and win. Walter Johnson was given an ovation when he went into the pitcher's box and each time he came to bat. When the Senators were coming to bat in the seventh inning it seemed as if everybody in the grandstand, the pavilion and the bleachers stood up showing that they desired to bring luck to the Senators."

And this from a newspaper account: "Ask any school child today to describe Washington and he will tell you it is the capital of the American League, located on the Potomac directly behind first base."[29]

The next day with the Boston fans on their side again, the Senators won, 7–5, and the Yankees took their poison, losing, 4–3, in Philadelphia. The Senators had clinched a tie with two to go. Bucky used four pitchers — Mogridge, Marberry, Russell and Zachary — who came in with two outs in the eighth after Russell walked the bases full. Schacht lay on the bench with a towel on his face as Russell walked the batters. Zachary got the last out in the eighth and pitched a one-two-three ninth. He got the save; Russell was the winner.

A player who started the season with the Red Sox was the unlikely and virtually unknown hero. Lefler was picked up on September 18 from Worcester in the Eastern League to which he had been banished by the Red Sox in April. Lefler, a lefty, batted .370 in Worcester with 14 home runs. Bucky sent him to pinch-hit four times in late-September games and he got three hits, none bigger than his three-RBI double in the 7–5 win at Boston. Thanks to Lefler, who never appeared in another major league game, a win in the next game would complete the impossible dream.

But that was going to have to wait a day. September 28 was a Sunday and there was no Sunday baseball in Massachusetts. Bucky, Peck and Bluege, seemingly relaxed as could be, went fishing and returned with their stringers full. That evening they sat around the hotel lobby and "swapped lies." Other players visited Boston historical points. Bucky talked to reporters and exuded confidence.

"We are going to put every ounce of strength into tomorrow's game and pack away the old American League pennant. We are not depending on the Athletics beating the Yankees in Philadelphia tomorrow or Tuesday, for I feel positive that we will experience little difficulty in disposing of the Red Sox in one of the two remaining games."[30]

The Yankees were rained out in Philadelphia on Monday, and that was fine with the Senators, who didn't want to back into the pennant. Back in D.C. fans gathered around radios. WRC, the big broadcasting plant of the Radio Corporation of America, had been broadcasting Washington games for three weeks. No one could remember seeing anything like what happened that afternoon in Boston with 20,000 fans rooting against their own team. It wasn't that the Boston fans were down on their hometown boys, they were just anxious to see the Yankees dethroned. Bucky was given one of the greatest ovations of his life when he came up to bat in the first inning. Following his usual custom, he didn't react. The Senators scored in the first when catcher Steve O'Neill, trying to catch Rice stealing, hit him and the ball bounced away into left-center field. The Sox got one in their half to tie the score at 1–

1. With two outs in the second, Peck singled and went to third on a single by Ruel. Zachary singled Peck home and Leibold singled Ruel home, making it 3–1 Senators. In the Sox third Veach singled and Zachary hit Boone. Red Sox first baseman Joe Harris sacrificed them to second and third. Ezzell lined back to Zachary, almost tearing his glove off. He recorded the out at first but a run scored, making the score 3–2 Senators.

In three innings, Zachary had hit three batters, walked two, and given up five hits. Bucky saw enough and brought in Marberry to start the fourth. He pitched shutout ball for the last six innings. In the eighth Bucky doubled to left and scored on a Rice single, giving the Senators a 4–2 pennant-clinching win. That would be the final score. Fittingly, Marberry was on the mound and Bucky was on the ball, turning a double play to end it. "Harris picked up Williams' grounder, tagged second and with a quick pivot and throw almost without looking got the ball to Judge in time."

Pandemonium broke loose as the game ended. Straw hats covered the field. The dugout went into hysteria. The players smashed the water coolers to pieces and threw every bat and glove onto the field. Fans rushed on the field by the hundreds to surround the Senators. Many of them ran next to Joe Judge and reached for his mitt. They wanted the ball. Judge pulled his glove away and stuck it into his chest with his left arm wrapped around it. He hung on to the ball and gave it to Walter Johnson, who in turn gave it to President Griffith. "I wouldn't take a million for it," the Old Fox said.[31]

Walter Johnson was in the bullpen warming up when the game ended. As he walked across the field, tears steamed down his cheeks. Fans ran up to him, patting him on the back and extending hands to congratulate him. But Walter didn't notice them. Irving Vaughn described the touching moment.

> As the great Walter Johnson neared the stand, 15,000 folks rose and gave him a cheer right from the hearts of a nation. Walter didn't look up. Life's greatest moment was too much for him.
>
> A few hours later, the moon was high over Fenway Park. Several fans remained for one reason. Walter Johnson was at the ballpark signing autograph books, and accepting the fans' congratulations and best wishes in the World Series.[32]

Chapter 8

Serious About the Series

Tens of thousands gathered around radios or in front of scoreboards and thrilled to the news of each play as it arrived from Boston. Breathlessly thousands of pairs of eyes followed the little red and white lights scampering around the electric boards. With and without umbrellas the crowd stood in the pouring rain. Water poured in torrents off dripping umbrellas, coursed along the folds of dripping raincoats and penetrated to the skins of those who had no protection against the weather. Many sought the protecting shelter of automobiles or got relief they could under the Avenue's shade trees, but in spirit they were in Boston where the Nationals were putting the finishing touches of what has been the ambition of many men.[1]

Meanwhile in a crowded theater in Washington, the game was shown play-by-play on an elaborate board that depicted the players in motion by a system called the shawdowgraph. Then at 4:42 on the afternoon of September 29, 1924, time seemed to stop in the nation's capital. The Washington baseball club had defeated Boston and won the pennant of the American League. The Senators were going to the World Series for the first time.

The avenue became a turbulent mass of humanity, with pedestrians, automobile and street cars thrown together in indescribable confusion. Sirens tried to drown the vocal enthusiasm and the clangor of bells beat an anvil tattoo. A wild outburst of cheering and shouting greeted the news that Washington had won. Umbrellas were tossed in the air, traffic cops forgot traffic and the White House stopped the wheels of government to send the telegram of congratulations.

Offices and stores were deserted. Thousands of automobiles horns blared. Admirals, generals, Bishops, jurists, legislators and high government officials are vying with the butcher, baker and candle stick maker in a celebration. In the cabaret, around the home fireside, wherever men and women gather, the one topic of conversation tonight, the source of unwonted elation is the unparalleled feat of Bucky Harris and the ball tossers.[2]

Mrs. Coolidge heard the result over the radio and carried the news to the president, who was working in his office. C. Bascom Slemp, secretary to the president, telegraphed Bucky at his hotel in Boston. "Heartiest congratulations to you and your great work in bringing Washington its first pennant. We of Washington are proud of you and behind you."

In Boston Bucky, Griffith, Johnson, Rice and Goslin left for D.C. after the clinching game. Reporters caught up with Bucky outside the hotel. "I knew we'd win just as soon as we caught the Yankees in June. You know how happy I am? I'm really too happy to talk. All I can say is we did what I expected to do and that we will do the same thing in the world's series. And you can't make that last any too strong," he said as he jumped into a taxi bound for the station.[3]

Edward Eynon, the team secretary, a handful of fans and reporters were at the train station at 7:39 the next morning, as the early vanguard of Senators tried to sneak in to Washington, except for Goslin, who got off in Philadelphia to see his family. Rice and Griffith talked to the fans and press, but Bucky and Johnson somehow got away, at least initially. "Harris and Johnson mysteriously disappeared. It seemed to the fans there that they had flown away."[4]

When found working a lollypop, Johnson said,

> I am anxiously waiting for Saturday's game to come. It will be one of the greatest days for me. I realize that I cannot go much farther. My arm is still good. I know I don't have the stuff I used to have. When the season started I fully made up my mind to retire at the end of the year. Now it all depends what comes up this winter. If I could get located in baseball somewhere in the West, that would suit me perfectly. I want to get settled. I have four children and I want to get out of baseball before I get useless. If I can help Washington win a world pennant that would certainly be the time to quit.

Bucky was reticent and deflected credit. "I just have the fightingest bunch of ball players ever assembled. That's what won the pennant. Everyone of them simply bent backwards helping. They deserve the credit."[5]

Griffith talked to reporters from the *New York Times* who were at the station. "The victory vindicates my faith in Bucky Harris. This team has been through the mill. A dozen times they were in a position where they had to win, not win just a game but a whole series, and they did. Harris is idolized by his men. Why when the game was over yesterday they picked him up and carried him off the field."[6]

Back in Boston there were no rules for the players the night the Senators clinched and it showed the next day in the last game, a meaningless and comedic affair with Peckinpaugh as manager. Fifteen Senators played in the game the *Boston Globe* described as "an affair which is highly complimented by being called a ball game."

Altrock pitched the last three innings. He had umpires Connolly and Owens cracking up when he threw his glove to the plate with the ball in it and fell to his knees and prayed every time a ball was hit. When he batted, the infield played in and the outfield came onto the fringe of the grass, allowing Altrock to hit a triple and drive in the Senators' only run in a 13–1 loss.[7]

There were four days between the clinching game and the start of the World Series on October 4. The pitching staff was looking forward to the time off. Of the last 18 games, only nine were completed by the starters. Mogridge did not complete any of his last five starts. "He seemed to have lost his control of his stuff," said the *Post* of Mogridge. "He had repeatedly gotten himself into holes and when forced to put the ball over he has been knocked all over the lot."

Marberry appeared in five of six games leading to the clinching contest. On the season he appeared in 50 games, starting 14.

Bucky was a huge star now that the Senators had won, and in the few days before the Series the fans clamored for information about him. The *Post* tracked down his long-lost father. He was 52 and a chief of the Lackawanna Railroad Police in New Jersey. He was interviewed in a story billed as a special to the *Washington Post*. Little was revealed that wasn't already known. Tom, as had Bucky, played with the Pittston Brothers. He was a pitcher for a team called the Ewings with Hughie Jennings as his batterymate. In a game against Inkerman, another small town adjacent to Pittston, he struck out 19 batters with Hughie catching.

At his office in Hoboken Bucky's father told a story about Bucky's first trip away from home. His father claimed he took Bucky to the train. This would have to have been in 1915 when Bucky went to the Tigers' camp in Texas.

As Tom told it, he had this exchange with Bucky:

"Have enough money son?"

"Just $2, Dad."

Then a few minutes before the train pulled out, this from young Stanley. "Howinell do you get into an upper berth?"[8]

If it was a true story, it's one Bucky never acknowledged. Bucky almost never talked about his father. In *Mine Boy to Manager*, he detailed his youth with barely a mention of his father, except a line about his having played with Jennings. Census records from 1910 when Bucky would have been 14 show no father in the household and listed his mother as head of the household in Hughestown. Bucky's older son, Stanley Jr., a retired federal judge living in Maryland, said he never heard Bucky talk about his father. It appears Bucky never forgave him for walking out. One day Bucky would do the same, leave his wife and two sons, though he stayed in their lives.

During the break before the Series, a victory song, "Bucky Harris and his Team," sung to the tune of "When Johnny Comes Marching Home," was sent to Cuno Rudolph, president of the board of commissioners, by an old friend. He made it public. The first two lines were:

> We've won the pennant and we're glad hurrah, hurrah.
> New York tried hard but it got bad, hurrah, hurrah.[9]

Washington Post scribe Baxter compared Bucky and John McGraw, the manager of the Giants, the Senators' World Series opponents.

There will be a sort of father-son complex about the world's series between New York and Washington. John McGraw, who counted by his baseball alone, is old enough to be the father of his opponent Stanley Harris.

It would seem that McGraw who had undoubtedly encountered every situation that baseball can present would be quicker to sense what is about to happen and what should be done to meet such a contingency than his younger rival.

There is no reason to think any such thing. Harris knows the game. He may not have the weight of years but he has the fire and enthusiasm of youth. McGraw is a driver. Harris is a leader.

This column does not believe that the lash of McGraw's tongue will have the effect in carrying his team through the rough spots and through the tense moments that the encouragement and advice of Stanley Harris will. A whispered word or a pat on the back on the diamond will accomplish much more that words of criticism delivered on the bench in the hearing of the entire team.

Another human interest touch is that Giants assistant manager Hughey Jennings stands in a sort of parental relationship to Harris. It was Jennings who first discovered in Harris the spark that has now burst into the full flame of an illustrious baseball career. The then manager of the Detroit Tigers was not wrong, only ahead of his time in his judgment of Harris.[10]

Asked for one big factor to success, Griffith heaped praise on Bucky.

Stanley Harris. I remember when I was in Boston for the meeting of the American League owners last spring, I had to tell reporters I didn't know who was going to manage my club.

That was a few weeks before the season opened. But I did know, but didn't want to announce the fact at the time. Stanley Harris is one of the hardest fighters and best leaders of men I have ever met. Coupled with that he knows how to direct his men on the field. It is one thing to be a great ballplayer yourself, and another to be able to tell others how and what should be done.[11]

Post scribe Frank H. Young leaped on the Bucky bandwagon.

I count the example that Harris has set for his men and his general good fellowship with them as the greatest asset to the team this season. He never asked one of them to do anything he would not do himself. What Bucky lacked in experience he made up for in fight and, when the going got rough and it looked like his ship would be swamped, instead of taking sail, he added on more and simply forced his men to bring the old boat through to her ultimate destination. It was largely his "do-the-thing-that-can't be done" spirit that kept his ship in the race and

Bucky meets Giants managerial legend John McGraw before the 1924 World Series. Their ages and styles were in stark contrast (Library of Congress Digital Collection).

brought it home first. Tonight the young pilot could be the president of the United States if he wanted to.[12]

The celebrity perks kept coming for Bucky. The *Post* reported he received a telegram from a theatrical firm offering him a three-week contract in vaudeville for $5,000. That sounded like an offer too good to be true, as it was more than his salary as a player-manager of a championship baseball team. It may have been, because there is no record of his ever having appeared on the vaudeville circuit.

Another telegram from R.H. Carley of the Portner Apartment was for real: "Congratulations and best wishes on the world's series, have named son, born this morning, after you."

For as bright a star as Bucky was, Walter Johnson was even brighter. A notice in the *Post* asked the throngs of fans besieging him for a handshake to shake his left hand for fear of an injury, "such as the one that incapacitated Olympian Bob Legendre." Legendre, an American, won a bronze medal in the pentathlon in the 1924 Olympics that July in Paris, breaking the world's long jump record along the way.[13]

Will Rogers wrote about Walter Johnson in the *Hartford Courant*, intimating that rooting against the Big Train was downright unpatriotic.

> He was just a big, strong healthy country boy. Now what could a boy like that do to have the eyes and interest and the good wishes of the entire one hundred and ten million people of our whole country focused on him and have his every move watched and reported to every little paper in the farthest corners of our land?
>
> He is still just a big country boy yet as I am writing this there is more genuine interest in him than there is in the Presidential election. How is it that one single individual can have the sincere good wishes of the President of the Untied States, the Congress, the Senate, the Judges of our supreme court, even the sincere wishes of the other two Presidential candidates (I suppose the only time in political history that three candidates ever so heartily agreed on one thing)? Now what had he done to arrive on such a pedestal? What no man ever did, no man in civil life, no philanthropist ever did. So what has he done? Nothing else in the world but play. But he has played so fair and so good and given his all to the game that the man, woman or child in the United States that don't love Walter Johnson and admire him as a man is not a good American.[14]

The *Post* solicited some comments from government officials:

Secretary Wilbur: "I became a Washington supporter when I saw the first game of the season. I will see some of the world series games at least."

Dwight F. Davis, assistant secretary of war: "I am thrilled. I am simply overjoyed. I regret I will miss the homecoming on Wednesday, but I hope to be back to see the home games and will add my portion to the noise of the dyed-in-the-wool fans."

General John J. Pershing: "As a Washingtonian I am delighted and will be on hand to celebrate when the boys return Wednesday."

Monsignor James Mackin of St. Paul's Catholic Church: "A victory for a fighting team with a clean record."

Daniel E. Garges, the D.C. board of commissioner secretary: "If the race had lasted another day I would be ready for the undertaker."

Fire chief George Watson took the opportunity to lobby for new equipment. "I suppose every man who can be spared will be on sick leave the end of the week, but I don't care. If you'll guarantee not to have any fires they can all go to the world series. You can't even worry me today about the antiquated worn out apparatus we've got to depend on."

Other dignitaries who said they would attend the Series were Admiral Edward Eberle; Director of Veterans Bureau Brig. General Hines; Postmaster General Harry S. New, who was a former sportswriter; and Supreme Court Justice Joseph McKenna and Chief Justice William Howard Taft, who was in Canada. He was due back in time for the Series. "His smiling rotund countenance will be prominent in the stands."

D.C. Commissioner Oyster wouldn't dare miss a game. He was a sandlot player of the Bucky Harris type. Playing ball as a youth he injured his finger, which never healed. The story was he made a bare-handed shoestring catch that won a championship game in extra innings. As it was getting dark, there was controversy about whether or not he caught it. He showed his broken finger and that decided the catch had ended the game.[15]

The players who had remained in Boston for the final game arrived back in D.C. at 9 o'clock the next morning. A crowd of 2,000 packed the station and platform. Each player was welcomed and cheered by name and had to battle his way through the frenzied crowd to reach the taxi cabs, which took them to the ballpark. Later the arriving players reassembled with the rest of the team at the Peace Monument to begin the elaborate parade and ceremony arranged by Melvin C. Hazen of the Washington Riding and Hunt Club. Leaving the Peace Monument at the foot of Capitol Avenue at 4:30 P.M., the parade went along Pennsylvania Avenue. The Senators were escorted by mounted police, the United States Cavalry band from Fort Myer, the Riding and Hunting Club attired in scarlet hunting coats, the city's most beautiful girls dressed in white on white horses, and a train of automobiles carrying the players. Students from McKinley High School acted as cheerleaders along the avenue amid a din of cheers, whistles, sirens, and automobile horns. The parade was headed to the Ellipse, where President Coolidge waited on a reception stand. The Ellipse is a 52-acre circular park located just south of the White House fence. The previous December Coolidge had started a tradition by lighting the first National Christmas Tree in the park.

The chaotic parade was described thusly in the *New York Times*: "Pennsylvania Avenue has seen many parades but none to vie for the nature and spirit of the one held today. Most of the other spectacles were of national import, but today's was Washington's own."

The crowd estimated at 100,000 stretched across the Ellipse toward the Washington Monument. Some of the crowd broke through, as the players' cars arrived at the reviewing stand. The police were overwhelmed and the crowd surrounded the automobiles. After a few tense moments, the police

Autos carrying the Senator players snake through a gauntlet of fans during a celebration of the 1924 A.L. pennant (Library of Congress Digital Collection).

and guardsmen regained control and parted the fans. When players emerged from the cars at the reviewing stand, many were in tears. Bucky and Johnson were escorted to the platform where the president was. They were visibly affected. Johnson blushed when he was greeted by Coolidge.

From the text of the president's talk:

> As the head of an enterprise which transacts some business and maintains a considerable staff in this town I have double the satisfaction of welcoming home the victorious Washington baseball team.
>
> I feel hopeful that with this happy result now assured it will be possible for the people of Washington gradually to resume the interest in the ordinary concerns of life. So long as we could be satisfied with a prompt report of the score by innings, a reasonable attention to business was still possible. But when the entire population reached the point of requiring play-by-play descriptions, I began to doubt whether the highest efficiency was being promoted.
>
> On Tuesday morning when I had finished reading details of the decisive battle at Boston and turned to the affairs of government, I found on top of everything else on my desk a telegram from Congressman John F. Miller of Seattle which I shall read. "Respectfully suggest it is your patriotic duty to call a special session of congress on Saturday so members of the Congress may have the opportunity to sneak out to see Walter Johnson make baseball history. Can't speak for the New York delegation but hereby pledge all others to root for Washington and serve without pay or traveling expenses."
>
> Mr. Miller has such judgment and his sense of public psychology is so accurate that I do not need to say what party he represents.

We are all agreed, at least in theory to the sentiment, "may the best team win." But I want to add that your fellow townsmen of Washington do not need to be told which they regard as the best team. They hold firm convictions about it.

Manager Harris, I am directed by a group of your Washington fellow citizens to present to you for the club this loving cup. It is a symbol of deep and genuine sentiment.

There is a place in both present and future America for true clean sport. We do not rank it above business, the occupations of our lives, and we do not look with approval upon those who, not being concerned in its performance, spend all their thought energy and time upon its observance. We recognize however that there is something more in life than the grinding routine of daily toil and that we can develop a better manhood and more attractive youth and a wiser maturity by rounding out our existence with wholesome interest in sport.

The training, the energy, the intelligence which these men lavish upon their profession ought to be an inspiration for a like effort in every walk of life.

Bucky smiled and thanked the president as Coolidge handed him the cup, but Bucky made no speech. President Rudolph of the board of commissioners presented Bucky the key to the national capital, a golden key in a blue plush case appropriately engraved.[16]

That evening the team was feted at Gus Buchholz's Occidental Hotel. As the players were introduced, alphabetically called by Bucky, 200 officials, business, civic and professional leaders stood and cheered each player. Bucky introduced Bluege as the best third baseman in the league. He said of Johnson, "He was the ace-in-the-hole, or rather, aces back to back." Introducing Marberry, he said, "In five or six years when Walter begins to slip we will have a real guy to take his place." Rice was introduced as the Man-of-War of the league, referring to the legendary thoroughbred race horse. The crowd disrupted the program by insistent demands that Walter Johnson speak, but he would not.

Bucky did, saying, "My blood is tingling and to say I am proud is putting it awfully mild. About six times this last season we were beaten and out of the race unless we came through and we did. Commissioner Bell has told you that in Pittsburgh, where he came from, New York is anathema. When we see anything New York we laugh. It's ours and we know it. No team in the world can beat us and we're going to win the world's series."

The dinner was "dry" and even pocket flasks were banned by Mr. Buchholz, who said, "The world series will not be lost here tonight."[17]

Amid the celebration, serious preparations for the Series opener in Washington on Wednesday were underway. The Potomac Telephone Company installed radio apparatus at Griffith Stadium so that two radio stations, WCA and WEAF, could broadcast play-by-play. The announcers were Graham McNamee, a nationally known radio star, and Stuart B. Hayes, who had broadcast Senators games during the season and was a player in the International, Virginia and Blue Ridge leagues. McNamee had broadcast the Republican and Democratic conventions.

Entrepreneurs used the Washington stars' celebrity as marketing tools. A car to be presented to Walter Johnson by the Walter Johnson Testimonial Committee before the first game was on display for public viewing at a car dealership on Connecticut Avenue and thousands filed by to look at it. Men's stores advertised hats and suit coats of the type worn by Clark Griffith, Walter Johnson and Bucky Harris.

Thousands of fans holding certificates for seats mailed to them after they had written for reservations swarmed the ticket booths in the days before the first game. More than 10,000 with the pink certificates were at the box office at 7 A.M. on October 1, three days before the first game. The box office did not open until 11:15 A.M. All 30,000 reserved seats for the first two games of the Series were sold out, leaving only about 5,000 bleachers seats for day-off walk-up sales.

A lot of fans who ordered ticket certificates were angry. Hundreds who

Miss Elsie Tydings had the distinction of purchasing the first ticket sold for a World Series in the nation's capital (Library of Congress Digital Collection).

ordered as early as August were expecting reserved seats at $3.50 but were given tickets in the center-field pavilion at $3.30, or no tickets at all. Some of the fans who had been following the team for years when the Senators were in last place went to the office for an explanation. The only explanation was that club management could do nothing because the National Commission and Judge Landis had charge of handling the reservations.

Pressed on the ticket situation, Griffith said no favoritism had been shown in distributing tickets and that orders were being handled in the order in which they were received with a limit of four. But the fans argued that applications made just two weeks earlier were getting tickets while those who applied earlier were not. Prominent businessmen who had regularly attended games in boxes were sent to the pavilion where seats are uncovered with no backs. Even calls and telegrams from the White House about tickets were not being answered.[18]

It was clear by looking at travel arrangements that many times more fans were going to descend on Washington than there were tickets for the first two games. New York aside, thousands of fans were coming from Norfolk and Richmond and other Southern cities. A lot of the Southern fans took steamers from Norfolk. When the direct boats to Washington sold out, they took the steamers from Norfolk to Baltimore and then the train to Washington.

Special trains with 29 extra sleepers were coming from Buffalo, Baltimore, Philadelphia and as far south as Tampa. One of the happiest fans on the Florida train was Cliff Blankenship, the old Washington catcher who was considered the discoverer of Walter Johnson. Johnson's mother and two brothers, coming from Kansas, made a connection to Washington from Cincinnati. The New Jersey Central Railroad had a special excursion train going to the first game in Washington, leaving from Liberty Street in New York City at noon.[19] On it was J.W. Coombs, Princeton baseball coach who picked the Senators to win.

Well-healed fans who were determined to get in one of the games and didn't mind getting scalped had options. The price on the streets ran up to "fabulous sums," according to the *Washington Post*. One broker said tickets were bringing as much as $50 for grandstand seats and $30 for pavilion seats, for which he had paid $5.50 and $3.30. Two scalpers, or brokers, from New York City whose names were known at every race track or prize fight set up for business in Washington. Ruby Weller put out his sign at a storefront at 112 Pennsylvania and Larry Russell set up two doors down. "These men dress flashily and step jauntily. They speak in terms of big money and produce it."[20]

In New York, tickets for the games in Washington and New York were being bought, sold and exchanged at Sussman's Theater Ticket agency on Broadway and at The Misses Waters, a milliners, in the Hotel Alamac in New

Walter Johnson with his mother and wife at the 1924 World Series. His mother came from Kansas to see him pitch in the major leagues for the first time (Library of Congress Digital Collection).

York at Broadway and 71st, where the Senators stayed when they were in the city. Under the revenue law, brokers registered with the IRS were permitted to resell tickets with the provision that half the profit in excess of 50 cents would go to the government. Though IRS agents were said to be on the street watching scalpers, enforcing the revenue law was next to impossible.

There were options, too, for fans without tickets. In Washington Loew's Palace and Loew's Columbia, where *Sinners from Heaven* and *Covered Wagon* were playing, advertised that scores would be announced after each inning from the stage. In New York City Jackson's Baseball Manikins promised to reproduce plays within 10 seconds at the Armory at 25th and Lexington, the Kismet Temple at 92 Herkimer Street, and in Brooklyn. Tickets were 50 cents.

At the Presidents' Theater in Washington, the games were being reproduced with a new invention that promised a moving picture reproduction of every play as fast as it came over the wire. Orchestra seats were $1.10 and balcony seats were 80 cents.

A select group of football fans had a way to follow the first World Series game. Catholic University scheduled October 4 as the day to dedicate a new football stadium with a game against the United States Marines team. Arrangements were made to broadcast the game between periods of the game. The telephone company connected wires carrying the game broadcast to an amplifier and speakers on a platform constructed just for the occasion. The platform was rolled to the center of the field during timeouts and between periods. It was estimated that 20,000 would see the dedication of the stadium and the football game.

Among the diplomats in the crowd of 20,000 at the football game were the ambassadors from Britain, Finland, Estonia, Lithuania, Haiti, France, Japan, Belgium, Austria, Italy, Brazil, Salvador and the Dominican Republic.[21]

Radios were on sale at the Radio Sales Studio at Dupont Circle, located at 1506 Connecticut Avenue. Sales were brisk for the sets, which cost from $35 to $425 and could be taken home with as little as $7.15 in cash down, which, a newspaper ad bragged, was less than the price of a ticket.

Despite the radio and the reproduction options, the telephone company put on 200 temporary operators to take the expected calls — as many as 25,000 — to the five daily newspapers for reports on the games. Plans were laid to send reports of the games throughout the world. Ninety extra wires for telegraph operators were installed in the upper tier of the grandstand behind home plate to send game reports throughout the Untied States, Canada and Mexico. From New York the stories would be sent to London and Europe, from San Francisco they went to Japan, China and the Philippines, and from New Orleans to South America.

In the Georgetown section, a young boy named Billy Roberts became a neighborhood sensation with his home-improvised scoreboard made of translucent paper, a flashlight and a chalkboard. He planned to follow the games on radio and create a reproduction of the contest for his neighbors from his front porch.[22] For those who just couldn't follow the games as they happened, more than 300 American newspapers were credentialed as were reporters from as far away as Tokyo and Sydney, Australia.

Ban Johnson caused a furor when he said the World Series should be called off just two days before the first game because of a game-fixing scandal. Giants coach Cozy Dolan and outfielder Jimmy O'Connell were accused of offering Philadelphia Phillies shortstop Heinie Sand $500 to throw the N. L. pennant-deciding game on September 27. The Giants won the game, 5–1. O'Connell was a 21-year-old back-up outfielder who had been a sensation in the PCL as a starter for San Francisco for two seasons. He said it was Dolan's idea. He also said High Pockets Kelly, Ross Youngs, Frank Snyder, and Frankie

Frisch knew of the plan and encouraged him to make the offer. Dolan was known as McGraw's right-hand man even before he was hired by the Giants. He had variously been described as his body guard, stool pigeon and door-keeper.

Rumors swirled that the Series would be canceled or that the Dodgers would be declared N.L. pennant winners and play the Senators. Because of that, betting was way off. At John Doyle's, a popular betting place on Broadway, only one wager was made that day and that was $2,000 that the Giants would not take part in the Series.

Landis defended his decision not to cancel. "An abortive attempt was made to bribe a ballplayer to throw a game. It did not succeed; why call off the World Series?"

Landis said flatly he would have nothing more to say, even after Johnson vowed not to attend the Series and threatened to send his attorney to Washington to call for a federal investigation. Griffith, who was a Johnson ally in starting the A.L., was livid. "Johnson's statement was extremely ill-advised and would have been better left unsaid. Johnson has no more to say about the world's series than the man on the next corner. Johnson is playing politics and is taking advantage of an unpleasant situation to put Judge Landis in a bad light. It is all right to play politics, but it should be played fairly. Washington is innocent of any connection with the scandal and the rest of the Giants are innocent, too. We have waited years for this world's series and now Johnson wants to call it off."[23]

Betting increased at even odds after the scandal talk died down, though many were holding out to take Washington as an underdog at 7-to-5.

The Giants party of 50 arrived on the Pennsylvania Railroad's crack Congressional Limited at 8:40 in the evening on October 2 and went immediately to the Wardman Park Hotel. McGraw and Jennings were not with them and were expected on a later train. Police formed a lane for the players to get to their cabs, and the arrival was an orderly one. The players speaking for the team said they were not affected by the scandal. "Every player resents the implication the whole team has been taking part in that fixing business. If people think the New York Giants have to be crooked to win, the only way to show them otherwise is to go out and lick the Washington club."[24]

Bucky wrote a series of byline stories for the *Post*. In the first he wrote about his players.

"While other teams have won pennants, there was never a champion in any league, big or bush, welcomed home by the president of the United States," he wrote the day after the parade. "As the manager of Washington's first pennant winner I am the happiest man in the world and I am mighty proud of those boys."

He likened his team to a college team. "The spirit that rules the collegians playing always for the love of the game this year took hold of the Washington club."

He talked about individual players and himself as a player. "Walter will be there for the opener. I believe he is now in as fine physical condition as he has been all season. He goes against a team that doesn't know him."

On Bluege: "Two months ago he was just an ordinary ballplayer. Today, because he had caught the spirit of the Washington baseball club, the idea that you're never up until you get up, he is in a class by himself."

He called Goslin the most dangerous batter in the league next to Babe and including Speaker and Heilmann. He said Rice exceeded expectations. "I never saw Sam play such ball. I didn't think he could as a matter of fact, but he has dazzled them all."

About himself he said, "Many followers of the game honestly believed that managerial duties would handicap my playing. On the contrary, I've played the best ball of my career and I hope there are better days ahead especially in the world's series. So far I'd much rather be directing from the field than sitting pretty on a bench watching others do the work."[25]

On the eve of the first game Bucky wrote about the Giants' brain trust.

> One thing is certain — John McGraw is the game's greatest manager. Ten pennants speak for themselves. It will be a great pleasure to play the New York Giants. Washington in its first baptism of fire is especially privileged.
>
> There's never much use in making predictions, for dope never goes when it comes to a world's series. Statistics show on paper the Giants have a slight edge in pitching. To be fair that's a hard question to decide. The pitchers on both teams come from different leagues and are up against different batters, all that sort of thing. It's difficult to say what might happen when two strange teams meet. Nehf is the best pitcher the Giants have, yet Johnson to my way of thinking is one of the greatest who ever wore a glove, if not the greatest. And Johnson at this moment is like a kid at Christmas waiting and raring to go. My one wish is that Frisch and Groh are able to play. If we are returned victors we shall have the added pleasure in having beaten the Giants intact with no substitutes.
>
> The Giants have one of the greatest coaches who ever did duty on a base line — Hughey Jennings, my mentor. He is an outstanding figure in baseball. Strange to say he gave me my first big league training. He took me down south with the Tigers in 1916.

McGraw cited his team's experience. "Don't overlook the fact that my team has been in three other world's series. The team knows what it can do and will not be flighty or nervous. The mental strain is more likely to affect the Nats than us."[26]

Walter Johnson's wife was commissioned by the *Post* to write a series of articles on the world's series. Her first appeared the day before the first game.

Bucky's mentor Hughie Jennings, left, was McGraw's assistant manager with the Giants in 1924. He's with the Senators' Muddy Ruel (Library of Congress Digital Collection).

"Walter is placidity itself—eats well, sleeps well and apparently he and excitement are utter strangers. But he has always been that way as long as I have known him. I guess he knows I'll do enough worrying for the two of us."

Up until the evening before the first game Walter Johnson was giving President Calvin "Silent Cal" Coolidge a run for his money. That was when he finally spoke more than two words while making a public statement, but not about baseball. He spoke for Silent Cal. "Some people criticize the President because he doesn't come out of the White House and go up and down the country making speeches. This to my mind is one of the reasons he should be continued as head of the government. He is keeping his feet on the ground and attending to the job."[27]

Chapter 9

Giant Killers

If, as Walter Johnson suggested, Calvin Coolidge was to be "continued as President of the United States," Coolidge knew what he had to do: get to the opening game of the 1924 World Series. He was scheduled to speak that afternoon at the dedication and unveiling of a monument to the First Division soldiers lost in France in World War I. Priorities being what they were that particular day, the World War I event was moved to the morning so the president could get to the game. Coolidge was the second president to attend a World Series game. President Woodrow Wilson attended a 1915 game in New York.

The weather cooperated. Saturday, October 4, was a sunny Indian summer day with the high expected to be in the mid 60s. The president finished his speech at the dedication around 1 P.M. After a quick lunch, the president and his party were hustled into his limousine and escorted by motorcycle police to the ballpark. People lining the route cheered as the motorcade passed. The police and secret service had to clear a gauntlet through the crowd of thousands who congested the streets outside the park. The president and the First Lady didn't get to their box until shortly before 2 P.M. They were among the last of the 40,000 fans to arrive. In the president's party were Speaker of the House Frederick Gillett and his wife and the president's secretary, C. Bascom Slemp, and his wife. The president wore a pearl gray fedora with his suit. His wife was in white from hat to shoes with a white satin scarf. The president sat down and lit his customary after-lunch cigar.

Among the celebrities in the crowd were humorist-writer Will Rogers, who was besieged by photographers; heavyweight boxing legend James "Gentleman Jim" Corbett; and America's first show business superstar, George M. Cohan, known coast to coast as an actor, singer, dancer, playwright and composer who wrote "Give My Regards to Broadway," "You're a Grand Old Flag" and "Yankee Doodle Dandy." He sat with a delegation from Broadway "filled with silk shirts and green spats."

The marine band played for two hours. The army band, 100 strong in light blue and white striped uniforms, marched around the field pulling up at home plate. The crowd was described by scribe Francis P. Daly: "Millionaire bankers and brokers, august Senators, eminent judges and learned doctors, members of divinity, distinguished scientists and brilliant lawyers literally rubbed elbows with human mortals of far lesser degree — former convicts, bootleggers, housebreakers, gamblers and all the remaining flotsam and jetsam in the melting pot of democracy whose human lava boiled over the immense theater of sport."

Walter Johnson and Peckinpaugh were presented with cars. Johnson received the green Lincoln that had been on display all week. The American Automobile Association gave him a lifetime membership and Mutual Insurance Company gave him full insurance for the life of the car. Peckinpaugh got a Peerless from his fans in Cleveland. Johnson finally lost his famous cool. "The only one who did not enjoy the brief ceremony was Johnson, for he suffered from stage fright of the most violent type."

Looking mortified, Johnson sat inside the floral horseshoe on the front bumper and posed for 100 photographers. The crowd rose and cheered for five minutes. The car was filled with flowers for his wife and his mother, who was seeing him pitch for the first time in the big leagues.[1] Back at her home in Coffeyville, Kansas, American flags were flying all over town as they were in Hughestown and Pittston, Pennsylvania.

The Giants lineup was Lindstrom, 3b; Frisch, 2b; Youngs, rf; Kelly, cf; Terry, 1b; Wilson, lf; Jackson, ss; Gowdy, c; and Nehf, p. Despite McGraw's contention that the Giants had the edge in experience, three of the starters were rookies — Hack Wilson in left, Bill Terry at first and Freddie Lindstrom at third. Lindstrom was 19 and starting in place of Heinie Groh, who tore up his knee on September 19 while trying to stretch a single into a double. Groh was 34 but was having a good year as the Giants' lead-off batter. The day after Groh went down, Frankie Frisch, the second baseman and second-place hitter, sprained his hand on a head-first dive into home. He was safe and scored the last of his league-leading 121 runs. His start in the World Series was his first appearance since the injury. Cleanup hitter High Pockets Kelly led the N.L. in RBIs and hit 21 home runs, one fewer than the entire Senators team. Of the Senators' 22 home runs, only one was hit at home, where opponents hit only seven.

The anemic home run numbers and the Senators' league-leading 104 triples were functions of Griffith Stadium's immenseness. It was said to be the largest playing field ever in a World Series, even with the 15 rows of temporary seats between left-center and center. Under normal conditions it was 407 feet down the left-field line, 421 to center, and 423 to deepest right-center. No

Bucky's family at the 1924 World Series. From left, brother Merle, Merle's wife Hattie, Bucky's mother and his stepfather, Mr. Rosencrance (Library of Congress Digital Collection).

wonder the Giants hit more than four times as many home runs as the Senators. But the Giants were also the only major league team to bat .300, and they led both leagues in hits and runs. Even so, the Senators had batting stars. Rice led the A.L. in hits, Goslin led in RBIs, and Bucky led in sacrifices with 46. The Senators led the A.L. in ERA at 3.34. The Giants were third in the N.L. at 3.62.

The Senators were free of injury, and their lineup was the same as it had been in nearly every game since McNeely joined in early August: McNeely, cf; Harris, 2b; Rice, rf; Goslin, lf; Judge, 1b; Bluege, 3b; Peckinpaugh, ss; Ruel, c; Johnson, p.

Bucky handed the president the first ball to throw in and introduced him to Babe Ruth, who was the only exception to the secret service rule that the president should not receive any visitors to his box. After the band played "The Star Spangled Banner," all attention was given to the president's box.

The president tossed the ball to umpire Tom Connolly, who had to jump to catch it. Umpire William Dinneen yelled, "Play ball," and Connolly tossed the ball to Walter Johnson.[2]

The Giants went in order in the first. In the Senators' first, McNeely flied to left. Bucky stepped into the box. He had been calm all day as he bantered with the president, took infield and made out his lineup card. He'd slept well. He felt fine. But as he dug in for his first World Series at-bat, the magnitude of it all overwhelmed him. "Then it hit me. My knees turned to water. I didn't know what I'd do when he pitched the ball. I was petrified. I stepped out and talked to myself. You've got to pull yourself together. All of a sudden I was all right, but I'll never forget that moment of panic."[3]

He grounded out to short.

Kelly led off the Giants' second with a home run into the fifth row of the temporary bleachers for a 1–0 Giants lead. Goslin fell into the first row of seats while chasing the ball. In the Giants' fourth, after Johnson struck out Youngs and Kelly, Terry hit a home run almost to the same spot as Kelly's. They seemed to fall only inches apart.

The Nationals made it 2–1 in the sixth. McNeely doubled, went to third on a ground out by Bucky, and scored on a ground out by Rice. It stayed that way until the ninth. With one out, Bluege singled. Peckinpaugh doubled to left, and Bluege scored to tie it. Pandemonium broke loose in the stands. Even the president, who had stoically sat without cheering through the first eight innings in a bow to impartiality, leaped to his feet. A newspaper flew from the crowd and hit him in the back. Hats and seat cushions were tossed onto the field. The game was stopped for 10 minutes while the objects were picked up. When the game resumed, Peckinpaugh got to third on a ground out but was left there when Johnson flied out.

In the 12th the Giants scored twice. Gowdy walked to start it. Nehf batted for himself and singled to center. McNeely stumbled, recovered, then threw wildly for an error, and Gowdy and Nehf advanced to second and third. McGraw sent up Jack Bentley, a left-handed-hitting pitcher who had batted .265 during the season, to hit for Lindstrom. He walked, loading the bases with no outs. Frisch grounded to Bucky, who made the out at home. Youngs singled in a run and Kelly drove one in with a fly ball.

The game went to the bottom of the 12th with the Giants leading, 4–2. Mule Shirley led off while batting for Johnson. Giants shortstop Travis Jackson, who had led the N.L. with 58 errors, dropped Shirley's easy pop-up for a two-base error. McNeely flew out for the first out, and then Bucky lined a single to center to score Shirley to make it 4–3. Rice singled Bucky to third, where he was the tying run, but Rice, inexplicably, was thrown out at second trying to make a double. Billy Southworth, who had entered the game as a pinch-runner for Bentley in the top of the inning, made the peg. Goslin hit a slow ground ball toward second. Kelly, who had been moved from center to second after Lindstrom left for the pinch-hitter, charged in, barehanded the ball and in one motion threw to first where Terry made a barehanded catch just as Goslin's foot came down on the bag. Umpire Bill Klem called Goslin out. Bucky, who had crossed home plate with what he thought was the tying run, raced down the line and joined Goslin in shouting a few profane words into Klem's face.

Nehf and Johnson both pitched complete 12-inning games. Johnson struck out 12, but uncharacteristically gave up six walks and 14 hits, throwing 165 pitches. Nehf gave up 10 hits and struck out three. Having defeated Johnson in Washington, the Giants were sudden favorites. The Senators had been 11 to 10 favorites before the game, but afterwards it was 8 to 5 Giants, and they were drawing money. McGraw saw it that way, too. "Nehf, in my mind, out pitched Walter Johnson today and our chances of winning the series were considerably bettered. We got a break in the 12th inning by Rice trying to stretch his single into two bases. But that was the only break we got while the Senators had many."

He cited Rice throwing out a runner in the 9th inning Gowdy lining into a double play in the second, and Jackson failing to catch Shirley's fly in the 12th as breaks for the Senators.[4]

Bucky, in his *Post* story, brought up the breaks that McGraw didn't mention, such as the Giants' two home runs into the temporary stands that would have been outs. Bucky admitted the fence was short for the Senators, too. Later in the Series the short fence would pay off for Bucky. He didn't criticize Rice for attempting to stretch his single. "The ball was fumbled in the outfield and Rice, a fast runner, thought he could make it. That's good baseball."

Bucky half-apologized for yelling at Umpire Klem after the last play. "Really the play could have been called either way. I was on third with what looked like the winning run, Goslin sent a slow roller to second, Kelly gathered it in and shot it to first. Klem called Goslin out, but it looked to me like he was safe and I told Klem so. I went a little too far with Klem, but whatever I said was in the fever of the moment. And for that reason Landis should give due consideration for what happens in the heat of the battle."[5]

The plea worked, for nothing was made of Bucky's encounter with Klem. The surprising reaction to the first game was the suggestion that Walter Johnson looked and acted nervous. "Walter Johnson could have borrowed a little of the cool of the President."[6]

Having waited 13 years for the opportunity, Johnson was despondent after the game. He hung his head in the locker room and didn't talk to reporters.[7] Having gone down at home with their Old Master, the Senators were under extreme pressure to win Game 2. The president didn't add to it. He stayed away and listened to the game on the radio from his yacht, the *Mayflower*, off Virginia. The only lineup change was by McGraw. He moved Kelly to first, started Meusel in left field and benched Terry. Though the rookie was 3-for-5 against Johnson in Game 1, McGraw didn't trust him against left-handed pitching. Bucky's starter was lefty starter Tom Zachary. The 6'1", 28-year-old left-hander was 15–9 in the regular season with a 2.75 ERA. The Giants loaded the bases in the top of the first on two singles and a throwing error by Bucky. He made up for the error in a flash as the next batter, Meusel, grounded to Peckinpaugh, and he and Bucky turned one of their patented double plays, the first of three Bucky would turn in Game 2. In the bottom of the first, after two easy outs, Rice singled to center and stole second. Goslin hit a home run into the permanent bleachers in left, unleashing a deafening roar of cheers unlike anything ever heard in Washington.

In the Giants' fourth, Youngs led off with a single, setting up the Senators' second double play, this one started by Bucky to Peckinpaugh. In the Senators' fifth, after Zachary struck out and McNeeley grounded out, Bucky hit a fly ball to left-center. As the ball was in the air, fans in the temporary seats were on their feet shouting, "Come on ball, come on here."[8] It did, landing close to where the Giants' home runs had come down the day before. The score was 3–0 Senators. It stayed that way until the Giants picked up a run in the seventh, with Kelly scoring as the Senators turned their third double play, this time started by Bluege to Bucky.

Zachary was rolling along until the ninth when the Giants rallied and tied the game, 3–3. Frisch walked and Young flew out. With Frisch running, Kelly lined one into the right-center gap. Rice made a great play to stop it from going to the wall and threw to Bucky. Jennings waved Frisch home as Bucky turned and threw. The ball beat Frisch home but was a little high. Ruel pulled it down and tagged Frisch in the chest as he slid. The crowd thought he was out, but Klem, behind the plate for Game 2, called him safe. Kelly stayed at first. Meusel hit a hot grounder between first and second. It looked like a hit, but Bucky got to it and made the out at first, with Kelly getting to second. Wilson singled to right. Rice made another good play and throw, but Kelly dove over Ruel to avoid the tag and landed on the base with his hands first, tying the game. Wilson went to second on the throw. Bucky went to the mound and called for Marberry, who promptly struck Jackson out with three fastballs to send the game to the bottom of the ninth.

In the bottom of the ninth Judge hit a foul for home run distance and then walked. Bluege bunted him to second. Peckinpaugh doubled past Lindstrom down the left-field line, Judge scored easily, and the game was over. As Peck reached second, the crowd surged onto the field and fought to carry him on their shoulders. They packed around the dugout hoping to get a glimpse of their heroes but none emerged. It took 40 minutes to clear the field. Nobody knew it then, but Peckinpaugh had injured his knee running out his game-winning hit.

With two great games won in the winning team's last at-bat, the Giants-Phillies scandal was forgotten. McGraw took heat for not walking Peck in the ninth. Frisch wanted to walk him, according to Judge, who was on second base and heard Frisch call for a walk. McGraw wouldn't. It did seem like good strategy with Ruel and Marberry due up. Lindstrom was a sensation at third. In the fourth he dove for a ball Bluege hit, rolled over, got up, and made the throw in time.

"We are just as good as they are and what's sauce for the goose is sauce for the gander," Bucky said after the game. "We found our true form today and there won't be any more nervousness on the team after this.

"It took a lot of nerve for young Marberry to go in there and stop the Giants the way he did with three pitches. I expect to shoot him right back at them tomorrow and he will be just as cool then. I never saw him nervous or worried."[9]

Ted Sullivan, who wrote a report for the *Post*, said the Senators' double plays "surpassed anything for swiftness and neatness I ever saw." That was quite a statement considering Sullivan had seen a lot of ball. He was 73 and had been a manager and umpire in the 1880s.

After Game 2, with no travel day scheduled, the teams hurried to the station for the trip to New York for Game 3 in the Polo Grounds. Flowers were delivered to McGraw's office but he refused them, saying, "That's the biggest jinx in baseball."

The Polo Grounds took on a festive atmosphere of its own, though not up to Washington standards. After all, the World Series was not a novelty in New York as it was in Washington. The 1924 Series was the Giants' fourth consecutive, the previous three having been against the Yankees. Four fans in sombreros said they were rooting for any player who came from north of the Rio Grande and west of the Mississippi. Among the celebrities at the Polo Grounds for Game 3 was Al Jolson, the singer, comedian, and actor who was a friend to sports figures, including Johnson and McGraw. Baseball royalty included Cobb, Ruth and Christy Mathewson, who would die exactly one year later on October 7, 1925.[10]

The announced paid crowd was 47,608, the largest ever at the Polo Grounds. A surprisingly large and loud minority were rooting for the Senators. Bucky made his first lineup change, going with Leibold leading off in center field in place of McNeely, who was 1-for-9 in the first two games. Bucky's selection of Marberry to start the game was something of a surprise. He had

Mogridge, Curly Ogden and Paul Zahniser available. Mogridge hadn't pitched since September 24. Ogden hadn't been used for a full two weeks, and Zahniser had not pitched since he threw one inning on September 27.

Marberry threw smoke but was wild. In the second he walked one, hit a batter and threw a wild pitch. Bucky contributed an error and the Giants scored twice. They scored one more in the third. Peckinpaugh lasted two innings, limping around on the field in obvious pain. Bucky pulled him in the third inning, moving Bluege to short and replacing Peck in the lineup with unknown Ralph Miller, who had joined the team in late July and had played in only nine games. Miller hit a sacrifice fly in the fourth, scoring Rice, who had walked and reached third on a double by Judge, who later scored on a bases-loaded walk to Tate, batting for Marberry. McGraw's starter, Hugh McQuillan, also left in the fourth, replaced by Patrick "Rosy" Ryan, who got the last out.

In the Giants' fourth, Ryan shocked the baseball world by hitting a two-strike home run off Russell, who relieved Marberry, into the upper deck in right. It was the first home run by a National League pitcher in a World Series and it was Ryan's first of only two he would hit in a 10-year career. He also drove in a run in the eighth with a ground out. The Giants won, 6–4. Frisch was the fielding star, twice ranging into the outfield to steal hits from Goslin. In the fourth he caught one racing away with his back to the infield. In the fifth he ran one down along the right-field line.

The attendance record was broken again the next day with 52,000 in the Polo Grounds for Game 4. Among them was Giant-rooter Jack Dempsey in a field box behind first base. Nearby, Griffith lit his first cigar. He would go through one an inning.[11]

Peckinpaugh couldn't go. Bucky started Miller at third, hitting eighth, and Bluege at short. He went back to McNeely in center and leading off and sent Mogridge to the mound. Right-hander Virgil "Zeke" Barnes, who was 16–10 with a 3.06 ERA in 35 games in the regular season, started for the Giants.

Bucky finally got some production out of the leadoff spot, which had been 1-for-13 in the first three games. McNeely went 3-for-5 in Game 4 and scored twice as the Senators evened the Series at 2–2 with a 7–4 win. With the score 1–0 Giants in the top of the third, Mogridge struck out for the first out. McNeely singled to left. Bucky singled to right. Rice grounded out to second, with McNeely and Bucky advancing to third and second. Goslin hit a line shot deep into the lower deck in right for a three-run homer. "The blow was the mighty punch of all those that have been launched in the current post-season games. It shot like a bullet."[12]

In his *Post* article Bucky wrote, "I should imagine another Babe Ruth has been discovered. The ball that Goslin hit was absolutely the hardest hit of the series."

One scribe described the homer as a cannon shot. "That line drive whizzed into the startled customers in the lower tier of the right field stands with the speed of a French '75." That was a reference to an artillery piece.[13]

The Goslin shot gave the Senators a lead they never lost. McNeely and Bucky started another rally in the fifth with back-to-back singles. Bucky's hit sent McNeeley to third, from where he scored on a wild pitch while Bucky went to second. Goslin came through again, singling Bucky home to make it 5–1. It was 7–2 in the bottom of the eighth when Mogridge walked two batters. Bucky went to the mound. He and Mogridge went down on their haunches and talked it over. Despite a five-run lead, Bucky brought in Marberry, who made his third consecutive appearance. He gave up a double to Wilson, the first batter he faced. One run scored, but Bucky, relaying a throw from Rice, threw Meusel out at home. Marberry got a ground out to end the inning. Marberry stayed on in the ninth. He gave up two hits and a run, but struck out two, including Kelly, who batted as the potential tying run, to end the game. Marberry, Bucky wrote in his *Post* story, "is as dependable as an Atlantic City lifeguard."

With the fourth game completed, the money for the players' pool was made. The total was $331,092 — $148,991 for the winners and $99,327 for the losers, with the remainder going to each league's second and third place teams. Goslin, who was 4-for-4 with four RBIs, thanked Babe Ruth for hitting advice.

"Babe came to me before the game and said I was swinging wrong." Goslin corrected his swing and said, "You could see the result. I owe a lot to the Babe."[14]

Bucky supplanted Frisch as the fielding star of the game. *Post* scribe Baxter was effusive in his praise. "In the seventh Harris made two of the greatest fielding plays on ground balls the game has ever seen or will soon see again."

On one he ranged behind the second-base bag. The second he went behind first into right field. "How he managed to reach the spots where the plays were made was well nigh miraculous, how he recovered in time to make the throws defies description or explanation."[15]

The *Times* was a little less complimentary, calling the plays "a great stop" and "a fine stop."

On the play in the eighth when Bucky threw Meusel out at the plate, McGraw blamed Hughie Jennings, who was coaching third. "I disagree with Jennings' judgment. Meusel should have been held at third."[16] The friends had a falling out over McGraw's reaction and they didn't patch it up until the winter.

The momentum swung back to the Senators with the Game 4 win, as they could come back with Johnson with three days' rest for Game 5. Surely he wouldn't lose two in a row with so much at stake. But he did. The old smoke didn't blow. The Giants made 13 hits off Johnson and won easily, 6–2. He struck out only three batters. It was just a lost baseball game, but it felt more like a funeral. The assumption was Johnson had pitched his last game and was going to retire after the Series.

Baxter in the *Post*: "Had fortune chosen to follow the wishes of countless thousands, Johnson's last appearance in the major leagues would not have been written with ink wrung from his own soul as it was."[17]

The *New York Times*: "When Johnson's own World Series came along he couldn't win a game. Giant bats penned one of the saddest stories ever known to baseball yesterday. After the name of Walter Johnson they wrote 'finis.'"[18]

Headline in the *Post* game story: "Defeat of Johnson becomes tragedy of 1924 World Series."

In the story was this: "And it was a pity that 'Finis' could not have been written at the end of Johnson's major league baseball career in a more fitting manner, for today was his last appearance on the diamond."[19]

Such was Johnson's stature throughout baseball that the Polo Grounds crowd's reaction to the Giants' win was vastly understated. They felt for the Old Master. Bucky didn't have time for the Johnson epitaphs. He was taking the Senators home, where they played .610 ball. And they left New York with a win. Griffith won the coin flip for home field for the seventh game, the last time a coin flip would be used to determine home field for a World Series seventh game.

Back in Washington the next morning, Bucky said in his *Post* story he was impressed with the Giants' fans and organization. "It was marvelous the way the New York fans treated us. In all my baseball career I have never seen such sportsmanship on a foreign field. Even now I'm not sure whether the New Yorkers are rooting for the Giants or the Griffmen."

When Bucky wondered who the New York fans were rooting for, he may have been making a little joke, but it wasn't entirely funny. There were thousands of fans in the Polo Grounds rooting for the Senators. Among them were the Senators' fans who had managed to get tickets, and Yankee fans who landed tickets, hated the Giants and McGraw, and rooted for the American League. Thousands, if not millions, of New Yorkers were migrants from all over the country. Their loyalties were not with the Giants or Yankees, and many of them embraced the Senators as underdogs or out of patriotism. The case could be made that the Senators of 1924 were the first "America's team."

Bucky was impressed, too, by the quick getaway his team got after Game 5. "When we left the Polo Grounds a dozen motorcycle policemen accompanied us to the station and we never had to stop. Traffic all along the way was blocked for us, one of the finest tributes to baseball I have ever seen. No other city could have arranged a demonstration like that, not even Washington."[20]

Maybe not, but there was a pretty good demonstration in Washington when the Senators arrived at Union Station, where 5,000 cheering fans greeted the Senators with "a rousing reception, much like that accorded victorious football teams by college students."[21] For the do-or-die sixth game Bucky put Peckinpaugh back in the lineup. His knee was not much better and heavily bandaged, but even a gimpy Peck was a better option than the inexperienced Miller, who had failed to cover third in the fifth game, blowing an easy force out. McGraw's starter was Game 1 winner Nehf, who had four days' rest. Bucky went with Game 2 winner Zachary on three days' rest. Intermittent rain in the morning gave way to sunshine, and by game time the temperature was in the high 50s. President Coolidge and his party were back in his box for Game 6. Also in the crowd, estimated at 35,000 to 37,000, in a box on the other side of the Washington dugout was Pennsylvania Governor Gifford Pinchot, who was thrilled to meet the boy coal-picker from his home state who ran the Senators baseball team.[22] The crowd was a little subdued compared to the crowds of Games 1 and 2, probably due to the quick, efficient pitching, lack of scoring and desperate nature of the game. The crowd was close to evenly divided between men and women. Asked by a *New York Times* reporter why she wasn't cheering in the ninth inning, one female said, "It's not time for applauding, it's time for praying."

The fans provided a welcome bit of levity by booing Ruth when he didn't stand for the seventh-inning stretch, while Cobb, two seats away, laughed.[23] Lindstrom started the game by trying to bunt for a hit, but Bluege threw him out with a barehanded play, setting a precedent for the game for pitchers and fielders. The Giants did get a run in the first. Frisch doubled. Youngs hit back to Zachary, who caught Frisch between second and third. He was put out in a rundown but managed to get Youngs to second, who then scored on a Kelly single. The Giants would get only five more hits—four singles and a second double by Frisch in the third, the last Giant to get beyond first base.

It was still 1–0 when the Senators batted in the fifth. Peckinpaugh, who was 2-for-2 with a walk, singled to left and Ruel sacrificed him to second. Zachary grounded out to first, with Peckinpaugh advancing to third with two outs. McNeely walked and stole second. Into the box stepped Manager Harris. He took the first pitch for a strike and swung and missed at the second. He fouled off the third pitch, and then took two wide ones to run the count to 2–2. Nehf threw an inside curve. It was close but went for a ball. Then Nehf went against the book on Bucky. He threw one on the outside part of the plate and Bucky singled into right between Frisch and Kelly, scoring Peckinpaugh and McNeely and giving the Senators a 2–1 lead. Bucky's single was one of only four hits by the Senators.

Bucky's two RBIs held up into the ninth. Leading off the Giants' ninth, Youngs popped easily to Bluege at third for one out. Kelly singled to right on a 1–2 count. McGraw sent Southworth in to pinch-run. Meusel hit two foul balls, then hit a ground ball past the mound toward second base. Peckinpaugh, noticeably limping, fielded the ball behind second base. He twisted his body back toward the bag and backhanded a throw to Bucky, who caught the ball barehanded for the force out on Southworth. Bucky threw to first but too late to double up Meusel. Peckinpaugh's effort was too much for his knee. He tried to take a few steps but couldn't. Teammates rushed from the dugout to help him. "A couple of teammates put their shoulders under his arms and half carried him, Peck hopping on one foot. Another teammate bent over and started to hoist the shortstop on his back, but Peck would have none of that. When he left the field he intended to walk off, even on one leg."[24]

Bucky called Peckinpaugh's play "the gamest exhibition I ever saw on a baseball field."

Bucky pulled third baseman Miller, moved Bluege to third and brought in Tommy Taylor to play second, even though Taylor had a broken bone in his throwing hand. Taylor hadn't played regularly since he filled in for Bluege for 14 games in July. The Senators had one more out to get with a third baseman at shortstop and a third baseman with a broken throwing hand. But Zachary didn't let Wilson, the final batter, put the ball in play. He struck him out swinging on four pitches. The Senators had forced the World Series to the final game for the first time since 1912.

Sam Rice was the fielding star. He made three running catches. In the first he caught a ball hit by Meusel that looked like it was headed for the first row of the temporary bleachers for a two-run homer. Instead, Rice leaped right at the fence and caught it. In the third Rice charged hard on a ball hit by Lindstrom, catching it knee high. In the fifth he went to the foul line and caught a ball hit by Nehf that was about to drop inside the chalk. Also in the fifth, Bucky made a fielding gem, going into right field to flag down a bid for a Texas Leaguer by Meusel. That was just the type of play Griffith and Bucky had worked on so diligently in the spring of Bucky's rookie season in 1920.

Bucky went to Griffith's house the evening after the sixth game with an idea for the seventh contest the next afternoon. Normally Bucky wouldn't need to have strategy approved by his boss, but with what he had in mind he figured he better run it by the Old Fox. Bucky wanted to start a right-handed pitcher and then bring in a lefty after one batter, hoping to get McGraw to take Terry out of the game, or at least force Terry to bat against lefties. Terry was 6-for-12 to that point in the Series with a triple, home run and two walks, all against right-handed pitchers.

Griffith went along with the plan. It wasn't so radical that it was never attempted. Managers had done it before, enough so that the gambit had nicknames such as the "cover" or "beard" pitcher. But to do it in the final game of a World Series was pretty daring.[25] As Bucky left Griffith's house to go home and get some sleep, fans were already lining up outside the box office preparing to spend the night. Most had blankets and pillows, a few had cots. But by morning there were fewer in line than had been for the previous three home games because scalpers worked over the line overnight, getting up to $50 for tickets. The fans who were scalped should have held out, as every fan still in line when the box office opened got a ticket. Some 200 boys who stormed the gate and tried to crash it were let in in the eighth inning.[26]

Before the seventh game a moment of silence was called for Jake Daubert, who died a day earlier of natural causes at age 40 while still an active player. A two-time National League batting champion, he also hailed from Pennsylvania hard coal country and escaped life in the mines through baseball. Daubert was born in Shamokin, Pennsylvania, which also produced the Coveleski brothers.

Bucky announced his lineup. Peck, who could not put weight on his leg, was out. It wasn't just his fielding the Senators would miss. He was 5-for-12 with two doubles and two walks in five games. One New York writer said flatly that the Senators could not win without him. "When Peckinpaugh went out the Senators' chances probably went with him."

There was a perplexed murmur when Curly Ogden was announced as the Senators' starting pitcher. Mogridge had been the expected starter. Ogden struck out Lindstrom to start the game. He then walked Frisch, and Bucky pulled the beard off and brought in Mogridge. He struck out Youngs and then Bucky held his breath as Kelly grounded to Taylor at third, who got the throw across to Judge with his bandaged broken hand. Terry was slated to lead off the second and McGraw let him bat against the lefty; he grounded weakly to Bucky. With two out, Taylor muffed his second chance, allowing Jackson to reach on the error, but Mogridge struck out Barnes, the opposing pitcher, to end the second. In the top of the fourth Terry came around again. McGraw let him bat and Mogridge struck him out. In the bottom of the fourth Bucky hit his second home run of the Series, again dropping one in the temporary bleachers in center. Two were twice as many home runs as he had hit in the regular season and one-third as many as he had hit in his career. The score was 1–0 Senators after four.

In the top of the sixth the Giants scored three. Youngs walked and Kelly singled, sending Youngs to third. Terry was up and McGraw let him bat until

Bucky touches home after his home run in the seventh game of the 1924 World Series. It was his second of the Series. He hit one during the season. The catcher is Hank Gowdy; bat boy is unidentified (Library of Congress Digital Collection).

he went down 0–2 to Mogridge. Then McGraw blinked and sent Meusel up to pinch-hit. He hit a sacrifice fly, scoring Youngs to tie the game. Wilson singled, sending Kelly to third. Marberry could have gotten out of it, but suddenly the Senators' fielding, which had been sparkling, fell apart. Judge booted a grounder by Jackson for a two-base error while Kelly scored. Then Bluege made an error on a Gowdy grounder and, with two unearned runs, it was 3–1 Giants. Marberry got Barnes to fly out and stuck out Lindstrom to end the inning. If there was any consolation, Terry was out of the game.

In the eighth with one out, Barnes was working on a four-hitter and still owned that 3–1 lead. Leibold pinch-hit for Taylor and doubled. Ruel, who was 0-for-19, singled to left. Leibold went to third. Bucky sent Henry Tate up to bat for Marberry. Tate, who had hit .302 in only 43 at-bats during the season, mostly as a pinch-hitter, drew a walk to load the bases. McNeely popped to left, too short for Leibold to tag, and the moment belonged to Bucky. Bucky grounded a single to left, scoring Leibold and Ruel to tie the game. But this was no ordinary single to left. It was within Lindstrom's reach at third, but the ball hit something and bounced into left field, an eerie pretext of what was to come. As Baxter put in the *Post*, "For the benefit of those who did not see the stunt this time, she repeated it." To Baxter, "she" was Lady Luck.

The eruption of sound after Bucky's hit had barely died down when the crowd's cheers were renewed to a crescendo as the Senators took the field in the top of the ninth with Walter Johnson walking to the mound. Strangers were hugging each other in the stands. Some were said to cry.[27] Bucky handed Johnson the ball and gave him a pat on the back. The Giants had the top of the order up. Johnson got Lindstrom to pop to Miller, who had replaced Taylor at third. Frisch lashed a triple to center. The Old Master was on the hook for his third World Series loss. He looked at Bucky, who put up four fingers. Johnson walked Youngs intentionally. Johnson found a reserve of power and struck out Kelly on three flamers. Then Meusel grounded to third and Miller made the play. In the bottom of the ninth the Senators had runners at first and third with one out, but Miller hit into a double play.

Johnson walked Wilson to start the tenth, but struck out Jackson and got Gowdy to tap back to the mound for a double play to end the inning. In the 11th, with two Giant runners on, Johnson struck out Frisch and Kelly to end the inning. In the 12th, more drama, as Meusel singled while leading off but he got no further. Johnson struck out Wilson, Jackson grounded out, and Gowdy flied to left.

What happened in the bottom of the 12th is the stuff of World Series legend. The 1-for-20 batter who should have been out got a second chance and hit a double and the ground ball to third that should have been an easy out instead ignited a near riot. Miller grounded out to second while leading off. Ruel popped a foul fly near home plate. Giants catcher Hank Gowdy threw down his mask, stepped on it and fell as the ball dropped in the dirt next to him. Given new life, Ruel doubled to left on the next pitch, his second consecutive hit after the 0-for-19 start. Bucky let Johnson bat and he reached on an error by Travis Jackson, his third of the Series. Ruel stayed at second. McNeely was next, and Bucky was on deck. McGraw motioned to Lindstrom to come in even with the bag at third to take away the bunt. McNeeley fouled off the first pitch then swung at the next and hit a hard hopper toward Lindstrom, a double-play ball. This game was going to the 13th. But Ruel, the Senators' slowest runner, ran hard to third, hoping to get in Lindstrom's way. Then it happened. The ball hit something, a pebble — or the hand of God as some Senators fans believed — and took a wild hop over Lindstrom's head. In left Meusel didn't break on the ball when it was hit. Even so, when he reached it, everyone expected him to make a throw home, where Ruel was headed in what looked like slow motion. But Meusel picked up the ball and casually put it, some say, in his pocket or his glove and ran off the field as Ruel crossed home.

At 5:04 in the afternoon of October 10, 1924, the Washington Senators were champions of the baseball world.

As the game ended the fans poured onto the field so quickly McNeely was surrounded before he reached first base. He was lifted on the shoulders of the fans and thumped, pummeled and hugged. His buttons were pulled from his shirt and the upper part of his uniform was torn to shreds. Men and women grabbed and kissed him. Two policemen rescued him, using nightsticks to beat back the crowd in front of the dugout so McNeely could get to the locker room. Meanwhile, cushions, torn-up programs, newspapers, hats, and even overcoats were thrown from the upper tier onto the dugout and field. Fans danced on the top of the clubhouse. The sound of horns, bells, whistles and 40,000 screaming voices could be heard for miles. The Secret Service men encircled the president and his wife in their box near the dugout, but the fans had no interest in presidents. They were after Senators.

In the immediate aftermath, the players milled around the clubhouse in a state of shock. They laughed, they cried, they lit cigars. Bucky was so caught up he forgot to put his clothes on after his shower and ran around naked, though with his hair neatly combed, congratulating his teammates.[28] At 6:30 P.M. there were still 10,000 fans around the outside entrance to the clubhouse. While most of the players were able to get away safely, Johnson, Bucky and few others stayed in the clubhouse while waiting for police to regain control and clear a way out. Johnson passed the time talking over plans for a hunting trip with Paul Zahniser. Finally, the cops ran him through a gauntlet to his car. As he drove away from the park, he was "followed by an endless stream of humanity in an endless snake dance."

Bucky got a snake dance, too. "Stanley Harris made his triumphal progress from the ballpark to the hotel in a manner more like that of a monarch. Cheering thousands prevented his car from moving at more than a snail's pace."[29]

At the Shoreham Hotel where Bucky lived, several hundred baseball fans from all over the country, including attractive young women from states as far south as Florida and as far west as California, mobbed the lobby. Ranking army and navy officers and officials of the district and national government tried to pull rank for an audience with the great Boy Wonder. Elevators went out of commission, stairways were jammed, and guests headed to dinner could not get to the dining room. It took a "squadron of devoted friends who formed themselves into a football flying wedge" to get Bucky safely into his room, where his brother, Merle Harris, and Pittston Pitt owner Max Marcus were waiting.

Outside the crowd sang a parody of "Sidewalks of New York."

East Side, West Side, all around the town
When Barney Johnson is twirling its three up and three down
Have no fear of losing we will win in a walk
And John McGraw will go sneaking back to the sidewalks of New York.

All over the city tens of thousands of fans took over the streets while blowing horns, shaking rattlers, firing pistols, and lighting fireworks in the wildest celebration ever seen in baseball. Automobile horns blared incessantly and trolley bells rang away among the immovable mass of people and machines that clogged Pennsylvania Avenue.

In Hughestown a miniature version of the D.C. celebration broke out. Led by a band, an impromptu parade of nearly every man, woman and child in the little town marched from "Hamtown" through Pittston to the cacophony of church bells, fire engine sirens and locomotive whistles.[30]

N.W. Baxter was effusive in his praise of Bucky. "The heart of a lion, the soul of a leader, the tact of a diplomat, the brain of a master tactician and the courage of a great fighter carried the youthful manager to the great finale of the world's series." Baxter engaged in a bit of hyperbole, suggesting Bucky had won the game single-handedly.

> Harris was the rock that would not yield. He stood in the breach while his infield crumbled about him and white of face he brought back within his halting colleagues the courage and skill that seemed about to desert them for the first time since June.
>
> With virtually no aid from his teammates and supported mainly by his will to win he drove three runs across the plate — one with a homer — when these runs meant the game, $50,000 and the title of world champions. He met "The Master Mind" of baseball, John McGraw, on his favorite chess board and out-guessed and out-generaled him.
>
> He fought with all the desperation of a man about to die and all the calmness of the man who will not lose.[31]

Plenty of second-guessing went on in the aftermath. McGraw was panned for not switching Youngs and Meusel between left and right field — as he had earlier in the game — when McNeely batted in the 12th inning. Youngs had a much better arm and McNeely was a dead pull hitter. Bucky took some heat for ordering Johnson to intentionally walk Ross Youngs twice late in the game. Both free passes to Youngs, who was slumping, put two men on base for the Giants' best hitter, High Pockets Kelly, who hit a home run off Johnson in the first game. But Bucky knew what he was doing. Youngs was a left-handed batter and Kelly was right-handed. Youngs may have been only 5-for-25 in the first six games, but three of those hits were off Johnson. After both free passes Johnson struck Kelly out. Johnson pitched to 17 batters, struck out five, and gave up two hits and three walks. Bucky was as happy for Johnson as for himself or the city. "It's hard to analyze my feelings but the biggest thrill I've gotten out of the moment of my life was the glorious comeback of Walter Johnson," he wrote in his report for the *Post*.

Bucky, Goslin, Peckinpaugh and Judge were the Series batting heroes. Bucky and Goslin led in hits with 11 each. Three of Goslin's hits were home runs, tying a record held by Babe Ruth. Goslin led in RBIs with seven. Bucky hit two home runs into the temporary bleachers and led in runs scored with five. Peckinpaugh was 5-for-12 in four games for a .417 average. Among the players who played all seven games, Joe Judge quietly led in batting average at .385. He had 10 hits and walked six times for a team-leading .484 on-base percentage. McNeely was only 6-for-27, but three of his hits were doubles, and he scored four times. Ruel had been hitless in his first 19 at-bats but it didn't matter because he recorded hits in his last two and scored the ultimate deciding run. Zachary was 2–0 with a 2.04 ERA in 17⅔ innings; Marberry gave up one earned run in eight innings. Johnson was 1–2 with an even 3.00 ERA in 24 innings and 20 strikeouts. Mogridge was 1–0.

The day after the game the players who were still in town regrouped at the stadium. Bucky handed out their checks. Several of the players had to leave right after the game to join charity contests and barnstorming commitments. Their checks were mailed. "This is my last job as manager for this year and I will certainly be glad to get the rest," Bucky said.

Already back in New York by then, McGraw broke his silence. "We had some tough luck, but the Griffmen played a lot of good baseball and I want to compliment Stanley Harris and his men. Harris has put Washington on the baseball map and I never saw a city so wild with joy as Washington when we pulled out. Landis said that though Washington deserved to win, it must be acknowledged we had some hard luck. I told the Judge [Commissioner Landis] just to add $2,000 to each player's check and we'll call it square."[32]

The Senators' individual payouts were $5,959.64. Each Giant received $3,820.29. They were the second-highest player shares ever, surpassed only by the 1923 Giants-Yankees Series.

Chapter 10

Down with His Best

"In Washington there were popular demonstrations just about this time four years ago unlike anything ever tolerated in the United States with the single exception of armistice night, but today's news tells of the dismissal of Bucky Harris, the hero of that night's insane rioting and nobody, including Mr. Harris himself, seems to care."[1]

By the time the above was published on October 3, 1928, Clark Griffith readily agreed with it. He was convinced he had two men named Harris in his employ: ballplayer Bucky Harris and manager Stanley Harris. Bucky the player was the tough little coal miner with dirt under his nails who was a role model for his teammates and took no quarter between the lines from any man, regardless of how big in stature or legend. Stanley the manager was the manicured, mild-mannered gentleman who moved in Washington high society, never raised his voice, and didn't discipline his players.

Bucky had a good time with his celebrity in the aftermath of the 1924 World Series. He made public appearances, received exotic gifts and came in high in a straw poll for president. Two days after the Series ended, Bucky, the players and their families were honored guests at a dinner dance at the Congressional Country Club. The club president, Representative Joseph Himes of Ohio, presented Bucky with an honorary membership. He was only the third person so honored.[2]

The day after the seventh game Bucky went to a college football game at American League Park and saw Georgetown University beat King College of Tennessee, 21–7. He sat with the Georgetown fans and signed hundreds of programs. During halftime he went on the field and posed for photographs with Georgetown captain Fred Sheehan.[3] It was reported that Mrs. Glen Stewart, the wife of the wealthiest man on the Eastern Shore of Maryland and the top dog breeder in the country, was going to give Bucky a $5,000 Irish wolfhound, Billy Shamrock. Billy was registered with the London and American Kennel clubs.[4]

Bucky agreed to play in an exhibition game in western New York. On the way he stopped in the Polo Grounds where he was one of 60,000 fans to watch Notre Dame beat Army, 13–7, in football. On October 29 he went home, arriving by train in Wilkes-Barre. An automobile parade escorted him back to Pittston about five miles away. Thousands of miners, who were off for a union holiday, lined the route while cheering, waving American flags and setting off Roman candles. In Pittston he was met by his mother, brother Merle, old basketball buddy Gary Schmeelk, an entire troop of state police, the Pittston police force, and fire engines from all of the surrounding towns. The parade stopped at Gilmartin Park in Pittston where 2,000 kids who were let out of school waited for him.[5] That night there was a banquet in his honor at the state armory where he had played basketball with the Pittston Pitts. He didn't play any basketball that fall or winter though he did have offers, which, he said, could have netted him $10,000.

In his column on November 2, which he called the "Illiterate Digest," Will Rogers listed the country's straw poll preferences for president. "At last the American people are aroused. They have found a medium through which to express their individual preferences for President of the United States. Will Rogers Illiterate Digest is the only fair and honest test of the merits of the candidates' popularity.

"The vote so far proves that if the people had anything to do with the nominations personally instead of it being done by a half-dozen men in the back rooms of some hotel, why America would be a Democracy."

The leaders in the Rogers poll were: Walter Johnson, Red Grange, Knute Rockne, the Prince of Wales (all in feminine handwriting), Rudolph Valentino, Henry Ford, Kermit Roosevelt, and Bucky Harris.

On November 6 Bucky spoke to the D.C. Fire Department at Assembly Hall on behalf of the Red Cross. The next day he addressed the police department. He offered a silver baseball bat autographed by the Senators as a prize for the first fire or police station that enrolled 100 percent in the upcoming roll call for donations to the Red Cross. Two days later he was in Charlottesville, Virginia, where he saw Georgia beat Virginia in football, 7–0. He was introduced over the public address system and he stood and waved to a rousing reception.

When the *Christian Science Monitor* reported the city of Washington spent $523,346 to see the Senators win the World Series, the Visiting Nurse Society, chronically in need of funds, issued a press release. It showed tables of percentages with Washington at the top in "baseball standings" and at the bottom behind Boston, Cleveland, New York, Detroit, Cincinnati, Pittsburgh, Philadelphia, St. Louis, and Chicago in "Nursing Standing."

Bucky agreed to let the nurses use his name to boost their cause, saying, "I'm going to do my best to put them in the championship class."[6]

On November 9, the day after Bucky's 28th birthday, Bucky and Griffith dispelled rumors they were feuding. The two-year contract Bucky had signed in February was torn up and he agreed to a new one-year contract for 1925. Details were not made public, but Bucky said, "You can rest assured that I did not sign for less." A fair guess would be in the area of $15,000 to $17,000. It was speculated that George Sisler signed as player-manager of the Browns for $20,000 in 1925, but Sisler was 32, had five more years of service, and he was one of the game's all-time great hitters.

Bucky angrily denied claims by New York and Boston writers that he was at odds with Griffith. "There's absolutely no truth to them at all. Somebody's been having a pipe dream or something and you can go as strong as you like in denying even the slightest intimation that there has ever been any friction between Griff and me."[7]

One of the stories was attributed to Bob Quinn, president of the Red Sox, who said Bucky was demanding $18,000 and threatened to quit if he didn't get it. On November 14 Bucky received a telegram from Peckinpaugh. His leg was healed and it didn't bother him on a hunting trip to Canada. On December 1 the Senators and Giants announced an agreement to barnstorm together in the spring of 1925. Six of the games were already arranged: two in New York, two in Washington, one at the Giants' camp in Sarasota and one at the Washington camp in Tampa.

Griffith and scout Joe Engel were in Hartford at the time for the minor league meetings, where Engel said he was confident Walter Johnson would pitch again but admitted he hadn't yet signed a contract. While Johnson had said back in February that 1924 would be his last season, a week after the World Series when he returned to Washington after a short barnstorming trip, he hinted he might come back to the Senators. "While I had but one proposition in mind when I announced last February that I hoped to make 1924 my last season with Washington, I am now considering several."

His main pursuit was an effort to buy the Oakland club of the PCL. This deal was on again and off again from October through the end of the year. Johnson's kids were reaching school age and he wanted to settle somewhere. Griffith and Bucky were accepting of anything Johnson wanted to do. "I wouldn't want to do anything to stand in the way of Barney's becoming a magnate," Bucky said. "And for Walter's sake I would like to see him put through the deal, as it is an ambition he has had for years. At the same time for my own sake and the club's sake I would like to see the old boy back here pitching us to another pennant and world's series."[8]

Cal Ewing, the Oakland owner, met Johnson in Washington after the minor league meetings. Ewing praised Griffith and Bucky for letting Johnson pursue a deal. Few other owners would have treated Johnson so considerately, he said. Johnson offered $385,000 cash for the club. Even so, the deal fell through. The first week of January in 1925 Ewing declared the deal officially dead and took the Oakland club off the market. In December Griffith and Bucky were at the league winter meetings in New York. They let it be known they brought the checkbook with the World Series bankroll to purchase "ivory, either finished or crude."[9]

There was plenty of talk but no deals were made. On December 10 Bucky finally made a deal, but nothing significant. He sold infielder Ralph Miller and pitchers Benson Brillhart and Dan Hankins to Wichita. Miller was the only one who actually played with the Senators in 1924. The others had been cut the previous spring, but the Senators still had first rights to them.

Then on December 12 Bucky made a deal for a big-name player when he traded By Speece and Carr Smith for Stan Coveleski, who was a hard-coal country native. Coveleski, whose real name was Stanislaus Anthony Kowalewski, was born on July 13, 1889, in Shamokin, Pennsylvania, a coal mining town 80 miles southwest of Hughestown where he worked full-time

In 1925 Bucky acquired Stanley Coveleski (left), a fellow hard coal miner. Thought to be past his prime, he led the A.L. in ERA for the 1925 Senators. The catcher is Muddy Ruel (Library of Congress Digital Collection).

in the mines starting at age 12 for $3.75 per week. He was the youngest of five boys, four of whom would play professional baseball. Following the lead of his older brother Harry, who won 81 games for the Phillies, Reds, and Tigers, he changed his name to Coveleski (sometimes spelled Coveleskie). Though the scribes sometimes called him "The Big Pole," his friends and teammates called him "Covey."

Coveleski threw a variety of pitches from a variety of motions, but was mostly known as a spitball pitcher. He was one of the 17 spitballers grandfathered in when the pitch was outlawed in 1920. Like Big Ed Walsh, another spitballing hard-coal miner, Coveleski developed excellent control of his spitball. He doctored the pitch with alum, a natural crystal used in making baking powder. He kept the alum in his mouth, where it became gummy. He averaged 20 wins and 41 starts between 1916 and 1922 with the Indians. In 1920 he was 3–0 with three complete games and a shutout in the Indians' World Series victory over the Brooklyn Robins. His ERA for the Series was 0.67 ERA, and he walked only two batters in 27 innings. On August 17 that season he was the opposing pitcher in the game where Ray Chapman died after a beaning by Carl Mays. After a subpar year in 1924, when Coveleski was 13–14 with a 4.04 ERA, the Indians made the deal with Bucky and the Senators. This was one of the best trades Bucky ever made. Smith never played another major league game, and Speece was 3–5 with a 4.28 ERA in mop-up action for the Indians in 1925. Coveleski won 20 as well as the ERA title for the Senators.[10]

Two days after getting Covey, Bucky bought Walter Dutch Ruether from Brooklyn, where he had been 8–13 with a 3.91 ERA in 1924. He was 31 and reputed to be hard to handle. He had clashed repeatedly with manager Wilbert Robinson in Brooklyn. The scribes and the fans were worried about the Senators' aging pitching staff. Coveleski and Ruether didn't allay those fears. Covey would be 36 that July. Vean Gregg, a pitcher the Senators had bought after the World Series from Seattle for $10,000, was 40. Johnson was 37. Bucky liked veteran pitchers. "There are lot of good tunes in an old violin and this also applies to good games in old pitchers."[11] Fred Marberry, Curly Ogden, Allen Russell, and World Series hero Tom Zachary were referred to as the "junior division" of the Senators staff. All were in their late 20s, except Russell, who was 31.[12]

Clark Griffith and Bucky agreed to take part in a New Year's Day modified marathon in Washington, Griffith as the official starter and Bucky as the prize presenter. Collegiate runners from Princeton, Dartmouth and the Naval Academy were entered in the seven-mile race. There were also entrants from the Washington Canoe Club, the Hilton Club, and 30 from the Baltimore Hikers.[13]

Bucky and Griffith went to Hot Springs early in February to get in some golf. As they did not allow players to play golf during the season, they advised players to arrive early, too, if they wanted to hit the links. Bucky met and played with Walter Hagen, who gave him some tips on getting distance on his drives. Hagen, who had once considered a baseball career, was the reigning champion of the British Open and the PGA Championship.

Though Walter Johnson's deal to buy the Oakland franchise fell through, that didn't mean he was back with the Senators. When the team reported for spring training in Hot Springs on February 16, he was home in Reno, Nevada, a holdout for the first time in his career. Though there were reports that Johnson had signed, that was news to Bucky. "When I left Tampa last Friday he had not signed a contract. Whether he has done so since, I do not know. I don't know what the hitch is."[14]

The hitch was Johnson wanted $25,000. Two days after Bucky's statement, Johnson suddenly showed up in Hot Springs. He had agreed to a contract over the wire, but didn't sign until March 3 in Tampa. Terms were not disclosed, but he received two years in the neighborhood of $30,000 for each.[15] From Hot Springs the Senators left for Tampa on March 2 in a special car provided by the Missouri Pacific Railroad, which used the Senators as an attraction. A full-page picture of the team appeared on the dining car menus. Having failed to buy a minor league team, Johnson said he was investing in Florida real estate. Griffith cautioned against buying land off maps, predicting that Walter was making a mistake trying to play "the other fellow's game."[16]

Griffith didn't get to be "the Old Fox" for no reason. It's not clear how Johnson made out investing in real estate in the Sunshine State, but Bucky tried it years later and wound up taking a bath in the proverbial Florida swampland.

A local teenager by the name of Al Lopez from Ybor City, the Spanish section of Tampa, Florida, showed up at camp. He said he was a catcher and asked Bucky for a job. Bucky let him catch batting practice and warm up pitchers, including Walter Johnson, at the Senators' training camp. It was an experience Al Lopez never forgot. Within five years Lopez would be a starting catcher for the Dodgers, the beginning of a 40-year career as a player and manger.[17]

March 4 was Inauguration Day in Washington, and Bucky sent a telegram congratulating his friend Calvin Coolidge, who had won the election in November. With a booming economy, no crisis abroad, and a split Democratic party, Coolidge had won by one of the biggest landslides ever, defeating Democrat John W. Davis and Progressive Party candidate Robert LaFollette, 53 percent to 28 to 16.

Bucky's old mentor, Hughie Jennings, was managing the Giants when the spring series between the 1924 World Series opponents began on March 9. McGraw was in Cuba. The Giants won the first two games, 8–7 and 2–1 in 12 innings. On March 15, the first appearance of the now-famous infield of Judge, Harris, Peckinpaugh, and Bluege drew cheers from the surprisingly large crowd. On March 14 Commissioner Landis appeared at the Senators' home, Plant Field, and presented the players with World Series championship medals before a game against the Boston Braves. The Senators led the game, 9–3, but lost, 12–10, prompting Frank Young, who was covering the spring games, to write, "After having been reminded before the hostilities started by Commissioner Landis that they are the champions of baseball and given medals to prove it, the Harrismen proceeded to show just how the national game should not be played."

Over in St. Petersburg, Miller Huggins was not counting on the Senators playing like that. He blamed the pitching for the Yankee failure in 1924 and promised a stronger team in 1925. The Yankees added Urban Shocker to their staff, and Huggins predicted Sam Jones would have a much better year. Ed Barrow, business manager of Yankees, was reluctant to give the Senators credit for winning the A.L. pennant in 1924. "They took things easy on the theory the Senators were sure to blow it," he said of the 1924 Yankees. "They didn't bear down early in the race."[18]

In an interview with a scribe who called Bucky "the managerial Horatio Alger," Bucky said he wasn't counting only on Ruether, Coveleski and Vean Gregg. "They don't represent all the paper strength we have gained. We almost lost the pennant and the world's series because we did not have an adequate reserve infielder. We have him now in Mike McNally who can jump in and play second, third or short." McNally, from Minooka where the O'Neill brothers were from, was another of Bucky's coal-mining buddies. A journeyman infield utilityman, he had filled that role for the Red Sox and Yankees since 1915, averaging 50 games a season. He would be of little help to the Senators in 1925, getting in only 12 games, the last of his career.

"Bluege and McNeely will be better for the experience they gained last year," Bucky said further in the interview. "Bluege looks like one of the great infielders in the league right now. Peckinpaugh has completely recovered. Ruel, Judge, Rice, Goslin, and Zachary are as good as ever and Johnson and Mogridge have plenty of baseball in them."

He expected no problem with Ruether. "He may have gained a reputation as a hard man to handle but he has given no intimation to me. If I know my own name he will pitch his arm off for the Senators.

"Coveleskie is hardly the pitcher he was in 1920 but few believe he is altogether over."

Harris predicted they would win 25 between them. Covey didn't talk to the press much, but the stories that he was done got under his skin. "Now, what I want to know is how can you come back when you never went? Less than two full calendar years ago I led the American League in earned runs, I won 13 and lost 14 games. Last year I had an off season. I was not in shape. I figure I'm due to have a good year this season. I'm feeling better now that I did at anytime last season. Just because Cleveland let me go everybody figured I was done."[19]

As interest grew among fans in Florida, teams committed to training there permanently and development was spurred. St. Petersburg spent $35,000 renovating a ballpark and gave it to the Yankees. New roads and a bridge reduced the automobile ride from St. Petersburg to Tampa from 56 miles and three hours to 19 miles and less than an hour between 1924 and '25.

On March 27 Bucky talked to Billy Evans. "I know the other seven clubs regard us lucky, that we got all the breaks. It has been my experience that winning teams get the breaks. Incidentally they make the breaks with aggressive play.

"I am banking on my pitching staff to carry the burden. That's why I have gambled with veterans rather than rookie phenoms. Vean Gregg is close to 40, but he should be a whale of a relief pitcher able to go at top speed four or five innings."[20]

Walter Johnson was a big ticket in Dixie that spring. Wherever the Senators played, the fans clamored to see him pitch. This worried Bucky, but Griffith insisted he make appearances. On April 3 he pitched five innings in New Orleans. On the 5th he pitched two in Mobile and then four the next day against the Giants in Birmingham.

The Senators and Giants gave the fans a good show with a series of tight games. The Giants led the series 5–1, but by the time the teams reached Washington where they were supposed to play two games, the Senators had won the last four to even the series at 5–5. The Giants won the first game in D.C. 11–2, the only game that hadn't been close. The second game was rained out. Forty-five minutes after the game was called the teams were on a train to New York, where they would play the last two games of their series before the regular season began. With the Giants leading 6 games to 4, Bucky was so serious about winning and evening the series, even with the season opener only two days away across town at Yankee Stadium, he brought Johnson to close the first of the two games and got ejected from the second one after one pitch. Bucky and umpire Will Walker, who had been traveling with the teams, had a running feud going back to a game on March 11 in West Palm Beach. When McNeeley claimed he was hit with the first pitch in the second game in New York, Walker said no and Bucky came out of the dugout to argue. Walker wouldn't argue with him, saying, "Get out and stay out. I'm tired of arguing with you."

The Senators won the game without Bucky, 11–5, before 15,000 fans to even the series at 6–6.[21] The next day the Senators went across town to open the season at Yankee Stadium before 55,000 shivering fans. By the end of the game the temperature was in the 40s. Ruth was in the hospital with indigestion. His understudy, a rookie named Ben Paschal, hit a home run as the Yankees won, 5–1. Urban Shocker, one of the 17 legal spitball pitchers in the majors, pitched a seven-hitter in beating Mogridge. It was noted that Yankee shortstop Everett Scott played in his 1,800th consecutive game. Bucky's lineup was identical to the one he used most often in the latter part of 1924 and in the World Series when Peckinpaugh wasn't injured: McNeely, cf; Harris, 2b; Rice, cf; Goslin, lf; Judge, 1b; Bluege, 3b; Peckinpaugh, ss; and Ruel, c. The Yankees' win in the first game was not the start of a trend. It was just the opposite. Opening Day would turn out to be the only day the Yankees spent over .500 all season. The Senators won the next three games and three of four from the Yankees in Washington a week later. In the fourth game of the opening series, Ruether pitched a complete game and Judge hit a grand slam. Ruth was operated on for what was described as abscesses in his intestinal tract and was expected to be hospitalized for two weeks. By the time Ruth played his first game on June 1, the Yankees were in seventh place, 13 games behind the first-place A's. That's where they would finish, seventh, and 28 games out. Ruth, coming off consecutive seasons where he hit .393 and .378 with 45 and 39 home runs, played in 98 games and hit .290 with 20 home runs. Sam Jones lost 21 games. Shocker was 12–12. Pennock was 16–17, and Waite Hoyt went 11–14. The Yankees were seventh in the league in batting and runs scored. They were 7–15 against the Senators and 9–13 against the A's. The most notable thing that happened to the Yankees in 1925, though it was little noted at the time, was their discovery of a new first baseman. On June 2, the day after Ruth returned, Wally Pipp sat and a kid named Lou Gehrig, 17 days shy of his 22nd birthday, took his place.

On April 29 Bucky and Griffith gave up on pitcher Paul Zahniser. He had appeared in 24 games in 1924 but refused to sign a contract for 1925. He was traded on April 29 to the Red Sox with rookie outfielder Roy Carlyle and $5,000 for utilityman Joe Harris, who was 33. Asked how he would use Harris, Bucky said, "I can't answer that question. The only thing I'm sure about the deal is it brings us added hitting strength and I plan to use it anywhere I see a chance."[22]

Bucky was right about the added hitting. Harris played 100 games at first, in the outfield and as a pinch-hitter. He batted .323, slugged .573, and was second on the team in home runs with 12 in 300 at-bats. Goslin hit 18.

President Calvin Coolidge presents Bucky with a watch at the White House in May of 1925. Coolidge was a guest at Bucky's wedding after the 1926 season. Third from the left is the president's secretary, Edward T. Clark (Library of Congress Digital Collection).

In one two-week stretch in August and September, after Judge was hit in the head with a pitch by the Tigers' Whitehill, Harris played first every day and batted .405. Meanwhile, in Boston, Zahniser went 5–12 in 1925. In 1926 he led the league in losses with 18 and then was out of baseball except for a one-game comeback in 1929.

On May 1 in Washington before a Ladies Day game versus the A's, the 1924 American League pennant was raised on the center-field pole. Griffith and Bucky took first tugs on the rope and then the players in order of seniority took turns. The festivities, and the ladies, pulled a crowd of about 22,000 despite a chilly drizzle.[23]

The Senators spent most of the summer chasing the Athletics. After splitting a double-header with Boston on Memorial Day in Washington, they were 25–15 and four games behind the 28–10 Athletics. On June 26 the Senators played the first of five consecutive games against the A's, two in Philadelphia and three in Washington. The Senators, 42–22, were 1½ games behind the A's, 43–20. The Senators won four of the five games to take over first place by a half-game. Johnson won the first of the five, beating Lefty Grove, 5–3, in Philadelphia for his 11th win against five losses. The A's won the second game, 3–1, but the Senators won the next three in Washington by a combined score of 17–2. Coveleski threw a shutout to raise his record to 9–1, Ruether won a game to raise his record to 8–2, and Johnson won again to raise his record to 12–4. The Senators hit the rails after the sweep and won three more in Boston. Marberry won the first one, 6–4, in 10 innings and the Senators blasted away the next two days, winning 11–4 and 11–0. Coveleski threw the shutout and the Senators increased their lead over the A's to two full games.

The Senators hit a slump in mid–July, losing three of four in St. Louis and two of three in Detroit, to fall into second place, percentage points behind the A's. From Detroit the Senators went to Cleveland (where they swept three) and New York (where they won two of three). But they lost ground to the A's, who won 12 of 14 in Detroit, Chicago and St. Louis and at home versus Boston. When the Senators got home on July 28, they were 59–34, 1½ back. The A's were 60–32.

The A's continued to win, taking two of three at home from Detroit and Chicago between July 28 and August 4, when they beat the White Sox, 9–3, to lead the Senators by two games and three in the loss column. The A's stayed hot through the middle of August, winning eight of 11 from August 6 to the first game of a double-header on the 15th. The Senators kept pace and even picked up a half-game by winning nine of 12.

When the A's lost the second game of the double-header in Boston, there was no cause for alarm among the A's. How could they have known at the time that the loss would be the start of one of the most precipitous collapses in baseball? The A's went to St. Louis from Boston, where they were swept in three one-run games. The Browns' Elam Vangilder was the winning pitcher in relief in all three games. The Browns scored two in the seventh inning of the first game to win, 7–6. Vangilder pitched the last 3⅔ innings. The second game was 6–2, Browns heading into the ninth. The A's scored six in the top to go ahead, 8–6, before Vangilder came in and got the last two outs. In the bottom half the Browns scored three runs against two of Mack's best pitchers, Slim Harriss and Eddie Rommel, and won, 9–8. In the third game Vangilder pitched the last 1⅔ innings and the Browns again won in the bottom of the ninth with two runs off rookie Lefty Grove. With one out and no runners on Harry Rice tied the game with a home run. Bobby LaMotte singled, bringing up manager Dick Sisler, who won the game with a triple. The A's fell into second place, one game behind the Senators, who swept the White Sox while the A's were swept by Vangilder and the Browns.

The next day in Chicago, the Browns lost their fifth consecutive game while the Senators lost in Detroit. The next two days both teams won and the lead remained one game. Then, beginning with a loss in the last of the four-game series in Chicago, the bottom fell out of the 1925 season for the A's. They lost 12 consecutive contests, getting swept in Cleveland, Detroit, Washington and New York and losing the last two of the 12 to the Senators in a Labor Day double-header in Philadelphia on September 7. Attendance was 30,000, a top-five crowd for the season in Philadelphia. Johnson won the first game, 2–1, for his 19th win. The Senators won the second game, 7–6. Bucky was on base seven times in the double-header. He was 4-for-6 with two walks and was hit by a pitch, stole a base and was part of three double plays in the second game. In the eighth the A's had the bases loaded with one out, down by a run. Bishop hit a ground ball to Bucky. He touched Welsh, the runner, coming from first, but Welsh tangled with Bucky and the umpire called interference. It went for a double play to end the inning. The game ended on a vintage Peck-to-Harris-to-Judge double play.

The A's finally ended the losing by winning the last two games of the Washington series over the next two days, but it was too late. The Senators had won nine of 14 during the A's losing streak, and even after the two A's wins, the Senators' lead was seven on September 9. The Senators were 85–48. The A's were 76–53. The Senators and A's had one more game to play against each other, a make-up contest played on September 13 in Washington that ended in a 6–6 tie called by darkness after 11 innings. During that game, Goose Goslin and Bucky got into a heated argument in the dugout. Goslin misplayed two balls into triples in the fourth and sixth innings. Bucky said something to Goslin after the second misplay and the argument ensued. It's not known what Goslin said, but it must have been ugly, as Bucky fined him $100 and suspended him. Bucky backed off the suspension (Goslin was in the lineup the next day), but the fine stood.[24]

On September 19 Bucky heard some boos from the hometown fans in the ninth inning of a double-header against the White Sox. The Sox were winning, 17–0, and Lyons had a no-hitter going. With two outs in the ninth Bucky sent up Veach to bat for mop-up pitcher Ballou. The fans, who by this time wanted to see Lyons finish the no-hitter, let Bucky know. Veach singled to right field.[25]

Over in the National League, by mid–September the Pirates were in the same position as the Senators in the A.L. They had an eight-game lead over the Giants with two weeks to play. The Pirates and Senators clinched a day apart. The Pirates went first, beating the Phillies on September 23. It was a win fitting a championship team. The Phillies had the bases loaded with one out in the ninth. Huber hit a fly ball to left. Left fielder Wright caught the ball running away, then turned and threw out the Phillies' Durning at the plate to end the game.

The Senators clinched the next day at home, winning a double-header against Cleveland, 4–3 and 6–2. Goslin was the hero of the first game with a home run in the first inning and a ground-rule double in the 10th into the

Bucky signs autographs for unidentified women on Ladies Day on September 8, 1925. Bucky attracted a lot of women to Griffith Stadium and married one of them, Betty Sutherland, daughter of a U.S. Senator (Library of Congress Digital Collection).

area in center where the World Series bleachers were under construction. The double scored Rice with the winning run. Ruether won his 18th game against seven losses. He didn't walk a batter in the 10 innings and struck out four.

Spencer Adams, who was filling in for Bucky at second base, caught a pop-up to end the second game, a 6–4 win. The fans swarmed the field, but the celebration was muted compared to the chaos of a year earlier. After the clinching game the Browns came to the Capital for a three-game series. With the pennant clinched, Bucky fielded a lineup of mostly subs and rookies.

Bucky was on the bench with a badly injured finger as the Senators clinched. Two days earlier Bucky had tried to score on a double-steal play in the first inning of a game against the Indians. While tagging Bucky out Indians catcher Myatt stepped on the middle finger of Bucky's right hand, splitting it open. The cut was stitched. The injury was severe and made worse by the fact that the misshapen finger had been injured twice earlier in the season and multiple times in Bucky's career. Trainer Martin said Bucky would be out 10 days.[26] The Senators won the game, 3–2, behind Coveleski, who picked up his 20th win. He complained of a stiff back the next day. Neither Bucky nor Coveleski played again until the World Series.

Statistically the Pirates' batting rated over the Senators. The Pirates led the majors in batting average, slugging, runs, doubles, triples and stolen bases. They scored 912 runs. From July 24, 1924, to June 25, 1925, they went 150 games without being shut out, a record until 1993. Pirates second baseman Eddie Moore batted .298, the only Pirate regular to hit below .300. He scored 106 runs, hit 29 doubles, and had 77 RBIs. Third baseman Pie Traynor hit .320, with 39 doubles and 14 triples, scored 114 runs, and had 106 RBIs. The first-base platoon of George Grantham and Stuffy McInnis hit .326 and .368, respectively. Shortstop Glen Wright played all but one game, batted .308, slugged .480, tied for the team lead in home runs with 18, and had 121 RBIs. He led the N.L. in assists and double plays, surprisingly making two more than Bucky, though in 91 more innings.

The Senators scored 828 runs, fourth in the A.L. Among the Senators' infielders, none of the regulars scored 100 runs; Bucky was the only one with more than 90, with 91. And none of the Senators infielders had as many as 80 RBIs. Bluege had 79.

Around the Pirates' outfield, from left to right, Clyde Barnhart batted .325 with 85 runs and 114 RBIs; leadoff hitter Max Carey batted .343 and scored 109 runs and led the N.L. in steals with 46; and Kiki Cuyler batted .357 with league-leading totals in runs (144), triples (26), and total bases (366), still a team record. He slugged .598 and was second to Carey in steals with 41.

In the Senators' outfield only Goose Goslin had numbers to compare.

He batted .334, scored 116, batted in 113, hit 18 home runs, and led the league with 20 triples. Sam Rice in right hit .350 and was the only Senator besides Goslin to score more than 100 runs, but he hit only one home run and slugged .388.

The Senators' pitching led the major leagues in ERA at 3.70. The Pirates were third in the N.L. at 3.87. Coveleski and Johnson won 20 each for the Senators. Coveleski led the A.L. in ERA at 2.84, Johnson was fourth at 3.07. Dutch Ruether was 18–7. Marberry was used strictly in relief and led the major leagues in games (55), games finished (39), and saves (15).

The Pirates did not have a pitcher like Marberry, but neither did any of the other major league teams. The Pirates did have five pitchers who won 15 or more games with winning records. Lee Meadows won 19; Ray Kremer, Johnny Morrison and Emil Yde 17 each; and Vic Aldridge, 15. The Pirates' best-known pitcher was Babe Adams, who by 1925 was no babe. He was 43 and in his 18th season. He was the only pitcher in the Series who predated Johnson, having started in 1906. He won three games in the 1909 Series for Pirates. In 1925 he was 6–5 in 23 games, 10 of them starts. Adams and Johnson never met until the night before the first game, when Adams visited the Senators' hotel to meet Johnson.[27]

The Senators were generally considered to be a better fielding team at most positions except third base, where Pie Traynor led the majors in putouts and double plays and the N.L. in assists. The Senators' Muddy Ruel led all catchers in putouts and double plays and the A.L. in assists. Goslin and Rice were first and second in outfield assists, and Joe Judge led all first basemen in fielding percentage. Bucky was second in putouts and assists and first in double plays in the American. But Walter Johnson said the numbers weren't the whole story. "Harris is not being praised half enough for his fielding. Others no better get big headlines. Well, he goes out and makes wonderful stops and some runner is called out and that's all there is to it. Those who don't see the plays never hear anything about this and it isn't like Bucky to whine about that either."[28]

McGraw said Ruel could be a difference maker. "No doubt in my mind that Muddy Ruel is a far smarter backstop than any on either team. The Senators have a distinct advantage with Ruel whether he hits well or not. His keen mind and smoothness as a catcher will be a stabilizer for the whole club."[29]

The Pirates sent back $500,000 to applicants for tickets after selling out of the reserved and box seats for all their home games. Numerous celebrities, politicians and prominent people were expected to come to the city for the Series, but they were out of luck without tickets unless they were willing to deal with scalpers or stand in line for one of 10,000 $2 bleacher seats to be sold the day of the game. The city solicitor said he was unable to find a state law against scalping, and the city ordinance only said tickets couldn't be resold on the streets. Storefront offices were opened, where tickets with face values of $5.50 reserved and $6.60 for box seats were going for $10 to $30. Of course, there were scoreboards and game reenactments all over Pittsburgh and Washington, and 10 million were expected to hear the radio broadcast.[30]

The Washington party of 60 arrived in Pittsburgh on the evening of October 5, two days before the first game. They were met by cameramen, but not a lot of supportive fans. The Senators were no longer beloved underdogs. The glow of 1924, when fans all over the country rooted for them, was gone. They were big boys now, having won a second consecutive pennant and having improved by 11 games, winning 96. The Pirates, who had won 98, were — if not underdogs — sympathetic favorites, being from a small major league town and not having been in a World Series since 1909. The scribes were split on who would win, but most baseball men liked the Pirates. Writing in the *New York Times,* Bucky's old mentor, Hughie Jennings, wasn't caught up in any sentiment. He saw the Pirates as vastly superior and predicted they would win in five games. The Pirates were healthy except for Moore, who had a bad finger, but not one to rival Bucky's digit. Bucky's finger was still swollen. It would affect his play, though he wouldn't admit it until later. The skinny on Covey's back changed from day to day. One day, reports said he was responding well to treatments; the next he was out for the Series. On the eve of the first game he was said to be cured. Peckinpaugh's wheels were iffy. His knee never really came all the way back and he had a sprained ankle, too.[31]

Pirate manager Bill McKechnie was 11 years older than Bucky and was in his fourth year with the Pirates. As manager he liked his routines. He stayed with his everyday lineup and with his pitching rotation and used his starters in relief frequently. Though as a player he was known as a good bunter and once led the Federal League in sacrifices, he didn't bunt a lot with the 1925 Pirates. None of the Pirate regulars had as many as 20 sacrifices. Three Senators had more than 20, including Bucky, who led the major leagues with 41. Bill McKechnie remains the only manager to win World Series titles with three different teams. He won more than 1,800 games and was elected to the Baseball Hall of Fame in 1962. As a manager Bucky was more likely to break routine, and he would do so as the Series progressed. The Pirates' batters were known to hit lefties hard. Bucky was determined to limit their opportunity against his southpaws. It was foggy and chilly during the teams' workouts the day before the first game, a harbinger of weather to come later in the Series. The fans who came out saw Goslin hit 12 home runs in batting practice.[32]

The weather was fine — for the opener at least. There was lots of sunshine and the fall foliage sparkled in the mountains around the city. The game was

Pirates manager Bill McKechnie, left, and Bucky got a kick out of watching President Calvin Coolidge throw out the ceremonial first ball at the third game of the 1925 World Series in Pittsburgh (Library of Congress Digital Collection).

a sellout, 41,723. Babe Ruth was there before the game in the Senators' dugout wishing them well. Honus Wagner and Ty Cobb, who played against each other in the 1909 Series, were introduced and the fans went wild. For the game, Wagner and Cobb sat in the press box with John McGraw and Jennings. Pennsylvania Governor Pinchot threw out the first ball.[33]

Walter Johnson was masterful in the opener. It was said his fastball was as hot as ever and his curve was breaking more sharply than usual. He gave up five hits, a walk and struck out 10, including Cuyler twice. He received a standing ovation when he batted in the eighth and visibly blushed.[34] Joe Harris, who got the start in the outfield over McNeely, hit a solo home run in the second. Rice had the big hit — a two-run, two-out double in the fifth.

Babe Ruth was impressed by Johnson. "I have watched Walter Johnson pitch a lot of ball games, but I don't believe I ever saw him when he was better than yesterday. His fast one was breaking a good six inches, he had a sweeping curve that he mixed in to get the batters off balance, and he was just wild enough to be effective."

Pennsylvania Governor Gifford Pinchot greets Bucky in Pittsburgh before the 1925 World Series (Library of Congress Digital Collection).

Wilbert Robinson, the Brooklyn president, said Johnson had a good plan. "Johnson beat the Pirates because he drove them back on their heels. Men such as Traynor and Wright are free swingers who like plenty of room around the plate. By keeping the ball in on them Johnson cramped their style. That was brainy stuff by Johnson."

Stuffy McInnis, who struck out on three pitches while pinch-hitting for Meadows in the eighth, said the good pitching wasn't all about the pitchers. "Johnson got me, and got me good, but fans should remember that the field has been greatly reduced in size by the extra seats. Those seats have not been painted. That yellow and white glare from the raw timber into which the batter looks is horrible on the eyes."[35]

That night Christy Mathewson died in New York. John McGraw left to be a pall bearer. The next day both teams wore black armbands and marched to the flag pole where the band played "Nearer My God to Thee" and the "Star Spangled Banner."

In the second game Aldridge and the Pirates beat Coveleski, 3–2. Bluege was beaned in the sixth inning and taken to hospital for observation, where he stayed two days. He was replaced by Charles "Buddy" Myer, who had four games of major league experience. Bucky was 0-for-3 again with a sacrifice.

The third game, which was the first game in Washington and was postponed for a day by cold and rain, featured one of the greatest and most controversial catches in World Series history. With the Senators leading, 4–3, in the eighth, Marberry relieved and struck out the first two batters. Pirates catcher Earl Smith hit a ball to right field that was headed for the temporary bleachers, which would have made it a home run to tie the game. Rice made a headlong dive into the fans and climbed out a few seconds later holding the ball. Umpire Cy Rigler called it a catch. McKechnie ran out to confront Rigler, demanding to know how he knew Rice had actually made the catch. McKechnie appealed to Landis, who refused to get involved. The call stood. Asked if he caught the ball, Rice would only say the umpire called it an out. The controversy wouldn't die. In 1965 Rice wrote a letter, sealed it and gave it to the Baseball Hall of Fame to be opened when he died. He died in 1974. The letter read, "At no time did I lose possession of the ball."[36]

The third game should have been controversial for another reason, though not much was made of Bucky's choice for a starting pitcher because the Senators won, 4–3. Afraid to go with a lefty, Bucky passed over Ruether, an 18-game winner who hadn't pitched since September 24, and started Alex Ferguson, who had started only four games for the Senators since they bought him from the Yankees in mid–August.

In Game 4 before 38,701, Johnson was again on top of his game in a 4–0 win. He gave up six hits, all singles, and no Pirate runner reached third. He struck out only two, but had the Pirates hitting weakly on the ground. Bucky handled a record 13 chances with six assists and seven putouts. Batting in the third inning, Johnson singled to left and was thrown out trying to stretch it into a double. He limped off the field. Martin said he had a charley horse, but he finished the game. Goslin and Joe Harris hit back-to-back home runs in the Senators' second inning when they scored all their runs. The Senators led the Series, 3–1. Only once had a team come back from a 3–1 deficit to win a World Series. It happened in the first World Series, in 1903, when the Boston Americans came back from a 3–1 down to win a nine-game series. It had never happened in a seven-game series.

Aldridge and the Pirates won Game 5, 6–3. Bucky again refused to start his left-handers, instead going with Coveleski on two days' rest. The Pirates had 13 hits and stole three bases. Joe Harris hit his third home run for the Senators. Bucky brought in the lefty Zachary in the eighth and he realized Bucky's fears, giving up a double and single to the first two batters he faced —

Clark Griffith and Bucky board a train on October 5, 1925, heading to Pittsburgh for the World Series (Library of Congress Digital Collection).

righties Wright and McInnis. Marberry pitched to two batters in the ninth, but he didn't appear in the last two games. Back in Pittsburgh the next day, the Pirates forced a seventh game with a 3–2 win. After writing in his game story in the *Post* after Game 5 that he was going to pitch Ruether in Game 6, Bucky did not. He instead went back to Ferguson. Ruether, an 18-game winner, did not pitch to a single batter in the Series. The Senators scored runs in the first and second to lead, 2–0, but Kremer shut them down the rest of the way. Moore's home run in the fifth was the game-winner. In the ninth, Joe Harris hit a tremendous shot to center. The 40,000-plus fans went silent as the ball fell toward the temporary bleachers where it would have tied the game. But the ball hit six inches from the top of the screen in front of the bleachers and Harris had to settle for a double. He was there with one out, but Judge popped to first and Bluege grounded to third to end the game. In the eighth Bucky, who was 2-for-17 to that point, sent Veach up to pinch-hit for him with the tying run on third. Later he would admit his finger limited him and he shouldn't have played in the Series at all.

Game 7 was postponed a day by rain. It was thought to be an advantage to Johnson, giving him an extra day of rest. But the day off did not improve the weather; it got worse. It was foggy with a cold rain the morning of October 15 in Pittsburgh and it stayed that way all day. It had rained off and on for 24 hours, including periods that were very hard. The field was soaked by morning. There were puddles in the outfield as well as on the baselines, pitcher's mound and batter box. By the time the game started, the rain had slowed to a drizzle, but that was no help.

James Harrison of the *New York Times* described the game with flowing prose.

> It was the wettest, weirdest and wildest game that 50 years of baseball has ever seen. Water, mud, fog, mist, sawdust, fumbles, muffs, wild throws, wild pitches, one near fist fight, impossible rallies — these were mixed up to make the best and worst game ever played this century.
> Players wallowing ankle deep in mud, pitchers slipping as they delivered the ball to the plate, athletes skidding and sloshing, falling full length, dropping soaked baseballs — there you have part of the picture that was unveiled on Forbes Field this dripping afternoon. It was a great day for water polo. Johnny Weismuller would have been in his element. The web-footed amphibians would have had a field day. But it was the last possible afternoon that you would pick for a game of baseball on which hung the championship of the country. And still the game was packed with more thrills to the square inch than any other game could possibly be. This is a broad statement, but it was a broad game — a game painted on a broad canvas.[37]

So much sawdust was mixed into the mud that after the game it was said Walter Johnson looked like he was covered with oatmeal.[38] Why was it played? Commissioner Landis huddled with Bucky and McKechnie before the game and said, "A lot of people have gone to a lot of trouble to come to this game. I am not going to disappoint them. We are going to finish this game if it is humanly possible. I want you to give them a good game."[39]

McKechnie started Vic Aldridge on two days' rest, probably because he had two complete-game victories. He didn't make it out of the first inning. Rice singled and went to second on a wild pitch. Bucky flew out. Goslin walked and he and Rice advanced to second and third on another wild pitch. Aldridge walked Joe Harris and then Judge to force in a run. Bluege singled and everybody slid up a base in the mud. The score was 2–0. Morrison replaced Aldridge to face Peckinpaugh, who was awarded first on catcher's interference, forcing in a third run. Ruel reached on an error by Moore while Judge scored the fourth run. The bases were still loaded with only one out when Johnson struck out and Rice flied out to left. On any normal day a 4–0 lead by Johnson would have been a win in the book, but this was not a normal day. The drizzle turned to a steady rain by the third inning; by the fifth it was pouring. It was so dark cigarettes glowed. Fans in the infield grandstand could barely make out the outfielders' forms.

In the second the Pirates got two runners on, but Bucky made an unassisted double play, somehow getting to the bag without slipping and throwing to Judge to end the inning. The Pirates made it 4–3 in the third. Morrison singled to center to start it and Moore doubled him home. Carey singled, knocking in Moore. Carey reached second on a ground out, stole third and scored on a single by Barnhart. The Senators went up, 6–3, in the fourth. After Rice singled to right with one out, Bucky was called out on strikes. Goslin singled, and Joe Harris doubled Rice and Goslin home.

In the fifth McKechnie made a pitching change, bringing in Kremer, who retired the side in order. In their half of the fifth, the Pirates made it 6–4 on doubles by Carey and Cuyler. The Senators went down in order again in the sixth as Bucky struck out again. The Pirates tied it in the seventh. Moore reached on an error by Peckinpaugh, who slogged after a pop-up in short left and got there but dropped the ball. Carey doubled to left, scoring Moore. Cuyler sacrificed Carey to third. Barnhart grounded to second with the infield in and Bucky held Carey at third and made the out to first. Then Traynor tripled to right, scoring Carey. Traynor tried to round the bases as the ball plopped and stopped in a puddle, but Bucky threw him out after taking a relay throw from Rice. The score was 6–6 going to the eighth. Peckinpaugh hit a home run to put the Senators up, 7–6, in the top of the eighth. Marberry was available but Bucky let Johnson bat, and he popped to the catcher to end the inning.

When Johnson got the first two outs in the eighth, Bucky's call to leave him in looked safe, but then disaster struck. Between the mud, which covered his shoes, and his leg, which was still sore from the charley horse, Johnson couldn't get much on his fastball. Smith doubled with two outs and Yde ran for him. Johnson complained that he couldn't get any footing and the game was stopped while the grounds crew spread sawdust around the pitching slab.

It didn't help Johnson. Carson Bigbee, who had been 0-for-2 as a pinch-hitter, batted for Kremer and doubled Yde home to tie the game. Johnson walked Moore and Carey grounded to Peckinpaugh, who pulled Bucky off the bag with his throw to second for his record-setting eighth error of the Series. Some of the players looked at Bucky but Johnson did not. Even with Marberry fully rested (having pitched only 2 and ⅔ innings in the Series), Bucky made no move. Cuyler doubled home Bigbee and Moore, the 15th hit and eighth double off Johnson. Barnhart popped to second to end the inning on Johnson's 130th pitch, but the Pirates led, 9–7, and needed just three outs.

McKechnie brought in Red Oldham to pitch the ninth. Oldham, a little-known 32-year-old lefty, had pitched in only 11 games during the season and none in the Series. The Senators had the top of the order up. Rice was called out on strikes on a 2-and-2 count. He argued with Umpire McCormick, but Bucky, who was the next batter, got between them. Bucky took the first two pitches for strikes and then lined to second. Goslin was next and was called out on strikes on three pitches without taking a swing, looking as though he could not see the ball in the gloom. Johnson, dripping wet, sat on the top step as the Senators batted in the ninth. None of the players went near him or said anything to him, sensing he wanted to be alone.

In the clubhouse after the game Bucky offered no excuses but did complain mildly about the seventh game being in Pittsburgh. In previous World Series when an ultimate game was forced, a coin flip decided the site. But in 1925 for the first time the schedule was made in advance, with the Pirates getting the seventh game at home. "It's a tough one to take, but what's the difference?" he said. "It's over now and Pittsburgh can celebrate as we did last year. I don't see the justice of the rule which compelled us to play the final game here. The old way of tossing a coin to decide where the final game is to be played is best, since it gives both teams a chance."[40]

The second guessers criticized Bucky less for his decision to leave Johnson in the seventh game than for his decision to pitch Coveleski in the fifth game on

Bucky let Walter Johnson, pictured, finish the seventh game of the 1925 World Series and drew the wrath of A.L. President Ban Johnson (Library of Congress Digital Collection).

two days' rest and to let him bat with two outs in the fourth and runners on second and third. Many fans thought he should have gone with a lefty that day, Ruether or Zachary, and if the game was lost he would have had Coveleski for the sixth game on three days' rest.[41]

American League president Ban Johnson didn't agree with those fans. When the Senators got to Union Station in Washington that night after the seventh game, there was a telegram waiting for Bucky from Chicago. After a token congratulation for a "game fight," Johnson accused Bucky of blowing the Series by leaving Walter Johnson in the seventh game "for sentimental reasons" and called the decision "the crudest blunder in the history of baseball."[42]

Bucky answered the charge the next day. "Sentiment played no part in my decision to pitch Johnson. He pitched wonderful ball. I regard it as a reflection on Walter to have such a thing said of him. President Johnson's remarks, if his telegram has been quoted correctly, are gratuitous and would have been better left unsaid."[43]

As far as Bucky was concerned, he went down with his best.

Chapter 11
Boy Wonder No More

Among the one-quarter million new customers Bucky and the darlings of the capital drew to Griffith Stadium during the summer of 1924 was Miss Elizabeth Sutherland. The youngest of five sisters, she was the 18-year-old debutante daughter of Howard Sutherland, a former West Virginia senator. Sutherland was the government's Foreign Property Custodian, a high-profile job created in the wake of World War I in which he oversaw the confiscation of enemy or hostile alien property in the United States. Betty or Liz, as she was called by her friends, sat in a box near the Senators' dugout at home games and followed the road games at home on her radio. "I'd rather see a good ball game than eat," she once said. Betty played piano, was an amateur actress, played tennis and golf, and rode horses.

Though she didn't say so, she especially liked ball games where one of the teams was managed by a handsome young manager from Pennsylvania. Betty told a friend she wanted to meet Bucky Harris. Robert V. Fleming, who was the president of the largest bank in the capital, was a mutual friend of both and he made it happen in the summer of 1925. He hosted a dinner party and made sure place cards for "Miss Sutherland" and "Mr. Harris" were next to each other. A match was made.

Prior to meeting Betty Sutherland, Bucky had not made a lot of friends outside baseball circles since his arrival in the capital in 1920. The first couple of winters he went back home to Hughestown, where he felt comfortable playing basketball with coal miners. He felt out of place anywhere else, especially in cosmopolitan Washington. He was quiet and shy and, as a high school dropout, unsure of his own intelligence. He didn't talk much except about baseball.

A relationship such as the one Bucky and Betty had wasn't out of bounds. Walter Johnson, a one-time hayseed farmer, had married the daughter of Congressman Ernest Roberts. Even so, it was speculated that Sutherland might have preferred his daughter had chosen a diplomat or titled foreigner. Her parents were said to be properly impressed to have Bucky as a nice friend but hoped she was not considering marrying him.

Night after night as they courted, the couple listened to the radio at the Sutherlands' home. After weeks of this, for an hour or two every evening he finally told her his life story. Betty's parents came to like Bucky. He wasn't the ruffian they might have expected a coal-miner-turned-professional baseball player to be. He was a gentleman. In time they withdrew their objection to the match. Their engagement was announced May 14, 1926.[1]

One evening after a ball game in which Bucky purposely got hit by a pitch with the bases loaded and two outs in the ninth to force in the winning run, the couple went to the Sutherlands' house. Over dinner Liz told her father what happened at the game, saying Bucky didn't get out of the way.[2]

"Why Liz," said Sutherland, "Bucky wouldn't do anything as unsportsmanlike as that."[3]

Bucky's son Stanley was familiar with the story and said it fit Sutherland's personality.

"Our maternal grandfather was as straight-laced a guy you could ever run into," Stanley said. "He was a senator. If a constituent sent him a box of matches, he'd send it back saying, 'I can't accept that.'"[4]

Betty Sutherland had a lot of company at the Senators' games in 1925. In 1923, the season before Bucky became manager, the Senators had drawn 357,406, sixth in the American League. For 1924 the attendance jumped more than 230,000, to 584,310, third best in the A.L. In 1925 the team drew a record 817,199, by far the largest in franchise history and third in baseball after the Yankees and Tigers. Griffith knew that Bucky Harris was good for his team's bottom line and Bucky knew it, too. He may have been born on top of a coal mine, but baseball — to his way of thinking — was more like a gold mine. Bucky was always one of the first to sign and had never quibbled. But in November of 1925, he became a holdout. That's when he declined to sign a one-year deal Griffith proposed. He passed his time courting Betty, working on a few player deals, and watching a horse named Bucky Harris run at Pimlico. On November 26 he signed a deal to manage the Coral Gables team in the Florida Winter League, a six-team circuit that also signed Frankie Frisch and George Sisler as managers. Players came from the International, Texas, Southern, Pacific Coast and Eastern leagues and the American Association. Griffith didn't object to Bucky managing but insisted he not play.[5] On December 12 Bucky and Griffith met but did not reach an agreement. The next day Bucky left for Miami with Walter Johnson and Al Schacht in Johnson's automobile.

In mid–January Bucky wrote a letter to Frank Young of the *Washington Post* explaining his position. "I like baseball so well that it naturally is on my mind. However, I am not satisfied with the terms Mr. Griffith has offered me. Anyway, the team we have, it won't take much to get an attack going, so that isn't worrying me.

"I might say that I am just as anxious to sign as Griff is to have me, due to the results we have enjoyed and in consideration of the money the club has received the past two years, I believe I am entitled to insure myself in the future by getting a three-year contract at a figure I have given Mr. Griffith."[6]

Based on experience, Griffith didn't like multi-year deals. He believed players performed better under the pressure of year-to-year contracts. Bucky was a different case. Griffith couldn't deny the attendance figures and he loved Bucky like a son. He relented, and on January 27 signed a three-year deal in Tampa. Terms weren't released, but it was speculated to be worth $100,000. In 1928 when the deal expired, *Post* columnist Shirley Povich said it had been worth $100,000.[7]

No sooner had Griffith signed Bucky than he usurped his authority. He was so angered by holdouts Peckinpaugh and Ruel he declared they would be bench warmers in 1926. In February Bucky came up from Miami to Tampa for the start of summer camp and declared he was through with golf, saying it was ruining his baseball swing. Oddly, he didn't order his players not to play as he had in the past. Though Griffith and Bucky made a lot of runs at deals for players in the offseason, they didn't get any players who had an impact. Bucky talked up the deal for Bullet Joe Bush as a winner. On February 1 the Senators sent Zachary and Win Ballou to the Browns for Bush and Jack Tobin. Bucky was ecstatic about the deal, saying it "assured his team of a third American League pennant."[8]

Bush had plenty of experience. He was 33, had been pitching in the majors since 1912, and had 11 seasons of 200-plus innings on his arm. He had a 2.67 ERA in 60 innings in five World Series with the A's, Red Sox and Yankees. He was 14–14 in 33 starts for the Browns in 1925, one of them a one-hitter against the Senators on August 27. Walter Johnson got the only hit, a double in the sixth inning.

Bucky's hopes for Bush ended with one line drive. On April 18, in just his second start, Joe was working on a one-hitter against the Yankees in New York with one out in the ninth when he was hit on the knee by a sizzling line drive by Earle Combs. His next start came a week later, losing a complete game to the A's, but he never really recovered. He was 1–8 with an ERA over 6.00 when Griffith released him on June 24, 1926. Bucky Harris would later say, "If I had to name the most disappointing event in the race, I'd probably say it was the failure of Joe Bush to win for us. I banked heavily for him to come through for us, but lost."[9]

Without Bush, Bucky relied on his same old big four from 1925: Walter

Johnson, Stan Coveleski, Dutch Ruether and Firpo Marberry. His only concessions to youth were a pair of 26-year-olds from North Carolina, General Crowder and George Murray. Each started 12 games. Crowder went 7–4 and Murray, 6–3. The other prominent new player was rookie infielder Buddy Myer. He had been bought from New Orleans at the end of 1925 and got in four games with the Senators. He started the season as Peckinpaugh's backup, but wound up being the regular once Peck's legs gave out for good. Peckinpaugh played in only 57 games. Playing shortstop, Buddy hit .304 with 132 hits, 18 doubles and one home run for the Senators in 1926 in 132 games. He was the only player different in the regular lineup in 1926. Clark Griffith traded Myer to the Boston Red Sox after he got off to a slow start in 1927. Griffith regretted the trade and gave up five players to get Myer back in 1929.[10]

An infielder named Stuffy Stewart came from Birmingham at the end of 1925. He was extremely fast and was the greatest base stealer in Southern Association history. In 1926 he was used 34 times as a pinch-runner, scoring 13 runs and stealing six bases. In 1926 and 1927 he was also used as a late-inning substitute at second base for Bucky, signaling the beginning of the end of Bucky's career as a player.

The Senators won 15 fewer games in 1926 than they had in 1925, dropping to fourth place at 81–69. But the story of the 1926 A.L. season was more about the Yankees' resurgence than the Senators' collapse. The Yankees started the season 13–3. In May they won 16 consecutive games, scoring an average of almost seven runs per game. On May 26 the Yankees were 30–9 and the Senators were nine games out at 22–19. Through June, July and August, the Senators struggled to stay around .500. On August 23 they were 59–59 and in fifth place, 16 games behind the Yankees. Between August 24 and September 6, the Senators won 13 of 14 to raise their record to 72–60. They passed the Tigers and Athletics to move into third place, but it was too late to catch the Yankees, whom they trailed by 10 games.

The Yankees cooled off in September and finished 91–63, three games ahead of the Indians and eight ahead of the fourth-place Senators. The Yankees got full years out of Ruth and, of course, Gehrig. The Babe ran away with the major league titles in RBI (146), runs (139), and home runs (47), and batted .372. Gehrig hit .313, was second in runs with 135, and led in triples with 20. Herb Pennock, Urban Shocker and Waite Hoyt combined to win 58 games for the Yankees. As a team the Yankees slugged .437 and had an ERA of 3.86. The Senators slugged .364 and had a team ERA of 4.34.

Only Walter Johnson won as many as 15 games for the Senators, and he lost 16. Marberry was the only Senators pitcher to perform up to form. He led the league in appearances (64), games finished (47), and saves (22). The

Senators lost the Yankees' number in '26, losing 12 of 22 to them after going 15–7 and 13–9 the two previous seasons. As troubling as the drop to third place was the 300,000 drop in attendance, to 551,580.

On September 12, 1926, Bucky and Betty set a wedding date. He surprised her with a set of keys to a house he bought at 2202 Wyoming Avenue known as Senators' Row. The next-door neighbors were Chief Justice and Mrs. William Howard Taft. Taft was the 27th president of the United States, having been elected in 1908. He served only one term and lost his reelection bid. The wedding was October 1, 1926, five days after the Senators' last game of the season. They were married in the Sutherlands' home at 1841 R Street Northwest. Bucky was five weeks short of his 30th birthday. Betty was 21.

Though at one time the wedding was expected to be one of the main events of the Washington social scene in the fall of 1926, it was instead small and quiet, owing to the death of Betty's older sister, Mrs. George Lyon. Her husband, Dr. George Lyon, was Bucky's best man and the flower girl was the Lyons' daughter, Betty's niece, Berkley Lyon. Betty's sister Margaret was her only attendant. The wedding was performed in front of "immediate family and a few intimate friends," which included President Coolidge and his wife. The wedding cake was decorated with a figure in a Washington Senators uniform. They went to New York after the reception and from there sailed to Europe for their honeymoon.[11]

There was a changing of the guard among baseball managers in 1927. Superstar player-managers were out. Sisler, Speaker, Cobb and Collins all retired as managers after the 1926 season. Jack Hendricks, the manager of the Cincinnati Reds, predicted their retirements meant the beginning of the end for player-managers. In seven seasons as player-manager, Cobb had never finished higher than third and was sixth in 1926. Eddie Collins tried it for three years and finished sixth, fifth and fifth. Sisler also lasted three years. He had one season over .500, in 1925, but dropped all the way to seventh in 1926. Speaker won a pennant and World Series in his first full year as player-manger in 1920, but nothing since.

Rogers Hornsby was the player-manager with the N.L. and World Series champion Cardinals in 1926 but was traded to the Giants for Frankie Frisch and Jimmy Ring after the season. Though Hendricks was right in his prediction, it would take some years for playing managers to fade away. In 1927 there were seven, including Bucky. Dave Bancroft was a player-manager with the Boston Braves but was released in 1927 following a second consecutive seventh-place finish. Ray Schalk was player-manager for the White Sox in 1927 but was fired in July of 1928 when he appeared in only two games as a player. Bob O'Farrell took over for Hornsby with the Cardinals in 1927, his only full year as a manager, and was also the backup catcher. Hornsby managed the Giants for the last 33 games, filling in for the ailing McGraw. Stuffy McInnis was officially a player-manger in 1927, his one and only season as a major league manager, but he appeared in just one game with the Phillies, who lost 103 games. In 1928 Bucky and Hornsby, who had moved on to the Boston Braves, were the only active player-managers.

At the winter meetings in Chicago in December of 1926, Griffith declared Walter Johnson was the only player he would not trade. Bucky had gone alone to the minor league meetings a week earlier but did not make a deal. In Chicago, talk of trades, such as Joe Judge for Sisler and Muddy Ruel for Wally Schang, turned out to be nothing but rumors. Bucky shot down Ruel-for-Schang the minute it came up. He did not consider Schang anywhere near Ruel's class as a fielding catcher.[12] Nothing happened at the meeting, but a deal was struck on January 16 that broke up the famous double-play combo of Peckinpaugh and Harris. Peck was traded to the White Sox for pitchers Hollis "Sloppy" Thurston and Leo Mangum. Peck and Bucky had both led the A.L. in double plays every season from 1922 to 1925. Time was chipping away at the Senators' 1924 championship team.[13]

With Buddy Myer gone, Bobby Reeves became the everyday shortstop in 1927. A football and baseball star at Georgia Tech, Reeves was signed right off the campus by Joe Engel and reported directly to the Senators in June of 1926. Leibold, who had alternated in center with McNeeley, was gone, and 39-year-old Tris Speaker was the everyday center fielder in 1927. McNeely backed up at all three outfield positions. The Indians released Speaker on January 31, 1926, and the Senators signed him before the day was out. He had a decent season, batting .327, his last as a full-time player.

The Senators' starting pitching was completely revamped for 1927, with three new pitchers who set a record for the oddest collection of names — Hod, Sloppy and Bump — if nothing else. Sloppy Thurston won 13 games. Hod Lisenbee, a rookie, won 18, and Bump Hadley, also a rookie, won 14. The Senators improved by four games from 1926 to 1927 and bumped up from fourth to third place, but finished 25 games behind the soon-to-be-legendary 1927 Yankees, who won 110 games. Griffith Stadium attendance dropped another 25,000, to 528,976.

On Thursday, September 22, at Griffith Stadium, the Senators beat the Browns, 10–7. The story line of the game the next day was the win moved the Senators into third place. The historical significance of the game was not known at the time: Walter Johnson had pitched the last innings of his career. He started but lasted only 3⅓ innings, giving up nine hits and six runs. In his only at-bat he hit a home run. He would make one more appearance in 1927, pinch hitting for Tom Zachary in the ninth inning of a 4–2 loss in Yankee Stadium. His last major league appearance was a mere footnote in a game in which Babe Ruth hit his record 60th home run of the season. Johnson finished the season 5–6, appearing in only 22 games.

On October 16, saying "he didn't want to be in the way next year," Johnson asked for and was given his unconditional release. "I hate like everything to think of not being with the Washington team next season and hate to think of the possibility that I may, for business reasons, have to leave Washington where I have been treated royally by the fans. I have no definite plans. I have saved up a little money and am looking around for a good investment."[14]

Griffith could have sold or traded Johnson for value, but he promptly granted his request for an unconditional release and said he would ask all teams to let Johnson clear waivers, which was necessary for his unconditional release. On October 26 Johnson signed a two-year deal to manage Newark of the International League. Salary was not disclosed, but it was said to be "the highest ever paid to a player-manager outside the major leagues."[15]

Since the day he arrived in the nation's capital in 1919, Bucky Harris had been as solid a Senator as any other than Walter Johnson, but by the winter of 1927-28 small cracks appeared in his relationship with Griffith. Billy Evans was the general manager of a new deep-pockets regime that had taken over Cleveland, and Evans was in Washington in December talking to Griffith about buying Bucky to manage the Indians. Griffith didn't sell, but on the other hand he didn't say anything, which left some people to wonder why he was quiet. In the past Griffith had always publicly supported Bucky when trade rumors surfaced. For example, a few years earlier, he said he wouldn't send Bucky to the Yankees for any three players.

It seemed strange when a few days later Griffith dismissed Bucky's pitching coach, Jack Onslow, who had been credited with helping rookies Bump Hadley and Hod Lisenbee post winning seasons. Griffith told *Post* scribe Frank Young the change was Bucky's idea, while Bucky said it was Griffith's.

On December 14 the deal that had been rumored a year earlier happened. The Senators bought George Sisler from the Browns for $25,000. Sisler would have been worth several times that amount a few years earlier when he was considered the greatest first baseman in the game. After his famous .420 season in 1922, he missed all of 1923 with severe sinus infections that caused headaches and double vision. He came back in 1924 and agreed to be the Browns' player-manager. His average dropped to .305.

In 1927 he was relieved as manager and had a decent season, hitting .327 with 201 hits. But the Browns were under new ownership in 1928 and they were determined to reconstruct the team. As Sisler was turning 35 in March of 1928 and had been with the Browns 13 years, he was expendable. The Sisler experiment was a failure in Washington. Little used except as a pinch-hitter with an occasional spot start, he was sold to the Boston Braves for $7,500 on

May 27 after batting .245 in 49 at-bats. Not much else went right for the Senators in 1928.

In March, amid whispers that Bucky was too soft as a manager, Griffith ordered him to impose stricter discipline in spring training. Bucky laid down the law at camp. Bucky said he would no longer be "a good fellow" but intended to tighten the reins, saying, "I feel my job is at stake. I don't believe I ever before took baseball as seriously as I am taking it this year. Looking back I can see where on several occasions, conditions confronted me which I now feel were partly my fault. I had my own heart wrapped up in the game and the team and took a little too much for granted in assuming that my players looked at things in the same manner."

Golf was an example of what he was talking about. A year earlier he had stopped playing, saying it was ruining his swing. He didn't ban it for the players, perhaps hoping they would get the hint and follow his lead. They didn't, so for 1928 he ordered the players not to play after March 15. "I really mean this. If I catch any player cheating here on this, I intend to order him from camp and to suspend him until he gets into condition after the regular season opens. After the season opens it is going to cost any player golfing $500 in fines. The game seems to get such a hold on players that all they think and talk about is golf," Bucky said.

He also clamped down on "clowning," as he described it. "I want the boys to take their baseball seriously beginning from now. Even in these exhibition games they must give me all they have and I expect them to be on their toes at all times and to give me 100 percent effort. The slightest letup no matter by whom, means the bench." He put in a system of fines based on salary, making it clear stars would be fined more. He warned catcher Hugh McMullen he would be fined $10 for the next infraction after he failed to slide in an exhibition game.[16]

A few days later Griffith said the Senators would contend with the Yankees for the A.L. pennant. The team's strength, he said, were the nine men on the roster who were part of the 1924 and 1925 championship teams. Of the nine — Ruel, Marberry, Zachary, Bluege, Judge, Rice, Goslin, Tate, and Harris — only Goslin would have a season reminiscent of 1924 and 1925 in 1928. He led the A.L. in batting at .379 and the team in home runs with 17 and RBIs with 102. Ruel hit .257. Bucky had a horrendous season. Beset by nagging injuries, he batted .204 in only 99 games. On April 16 an x-ray showed a chipped bone in his right instep. He came back in a week, but after going 2-for-15 he had to admit he had rushed his return. "I realize that I made a mistake in not remaining out a little longer when I first hurt my foot and do not intend to repeat that stunt."[17]

The collapse of the Senators was completed in 1928. They fell below

.500, at 75–79, and finished 26 games behind the Yankees, who won another 101 games. In July of 1928 Joe Engel found another diamond in the rough, a player who would turn out to have a profound impact on Bucky's life in baseball for years to come. Engel bought 21-year-old infielder Joe Cronin from Kansas City of the American Association for $7,500. Engel bought Cronin at a beer festival from George Muelhbach, brewery owner and owner of the Kansas City team. Later Muelhbach said, "It was the beer bidding, not me."[18]

Bucky quickly saw something in Cronin. "Cronin was the most nervous and fidgety youngster you ever saw. All arms and elbows when he broke in, but I put him in the lineup immediately. Griff was sweet on Bobby Reeves and wired me on the road that Reeves would never be a ball player unless he plays everyday. I wired Griff back: 'Neither will Cronin.'"[19]

Cronin started at short the rest of the season. He hit .242, but two seasons later he batted .346 for manager Walter Johnson, as the Senators won 94 games and finished second. Despite Bucky's attempt to impose discipline in 1928, he was blamed for not having a tight enough managerial rein. He was accused of not following up on his spring edicts. It was said the players weren't in shape coming out of Tampa, and then when the season started he tried to get them in shape by conditioning under the grandstand. They didn't play well until August. In games he proved to be too easy a taskmaster. Poor baserunning, failure to back up plays and a lack of hustle were allowed to go unpunished. Rumors flew that he was on the way out. He said he wanted to stay in Washington, even offering to take a salary cut.

The day of the final game, after a meeting in Griffith's office, he walked down the clubhouse steps with a grim smile and said, "Well boys, I'm through."[20]

On October 2, he was relieved of his managerial duties. He was not released. Griffith still held his rights as a player. To the extent that the criticisms of Bucky were true, he was the victim of his own success. He was one of the youngest players on the team when he took over as manager in 1924. He didn't feel it was his place to discipline them and there was little need for discipline. The veterans played hard for him in 1924 and 1925. Subsequent teams were not like that.

Post columnist Shirley Povich opined on the Harris-Griffith relationship.

Bucky Harris was one of Griffith's greatest disappointments. Griffith will not admit it in so many words but when he talks about Bucky you get a drift of blighted hopes and sad reminisce. For Griffith had plans for Bucky. When the contract for $100,000 was handed to Bucky, Clark Griffith was ready to step down and let younger hands relieve him of the responsibility of president of the club. On Bucky Harris he had built his hopes of a successor. Bucky was no mere manager. He was to be an officer of the club. A new clubhouse was being built and Bucky's office was already receiving its appointments. But the Bucky Harris of

1926 was not the Harris of '24. Baseball was no longer an obsession with Bucky. He had made new friends and moved in new circles. He was no longer the first man on the field and the last to leave. Bucky was growing older, less ambitious.

He spent less time in his office. During 1926 and '27 Bucky managed the ball team and that was all, Griffith was back in the clubhouse running the business affairs as he had run them since 1912 when he bought the team.[21]

If Griffith and Bucky had such a relationship, where Bucky was expected to take over as club president, it was news to a lot of people. Griffith had always been something of a control freak, and it's doubtful he was going to make Bucky his successor. Griffith remained club president into his 80s. And it was not fair to say Bucky did nothing but manage the team on the field. He engineered a lot of the deals that made the 1924 and 1925 teams winners and had some of the failed deals forced on him by Griffith, notably for fading stars Sisler and Speaker. But it was true that Bucky changed. He was no longer the "mine boy" or the "boy wonder," and he did "move in new circles," as Povich put it. At the end of his first tenure in Washington, though, it was his personality that did him in and that did not change as he aged. When not on the field playing, Bucky was soft-spoken and easy going. He didn't like imposing strict rules off the field. He trusted men to act like men, not boys. Curfews were for children. As long as the players showed up on time and played hard, he didn't think it was any of his business what they did with their free time. Bucky never called out a player in front of other players for bonehead plays or errors. He spoke to them privately, man-to-man. When he played he had blow-ups with umpires, but as a dugout manager he rarely did. In 1924, when he played every day, he was ejected three times. In 1928, when he played 99 games, he was tossed once.

On October 12 Griffith announced his choice for manager: Walter Johnson. Though a wildly popular choice with the fans, it was an odd choice in that Johnson was as mellow and good-natured as Bucky, and it was hard to visualize him being a disciplinarian any more than Bucky was. A few days after Johnson signed, a letter writer to the *Post* gave Bucky a nice sendoff.

> And now that Johnson is coming back home, in our new found joy let's not be guilty of failure to remember and failure to express our gratitude to the grandest, most beautiful gesture ever made on a ball field, the moment when Bucky Harris took his future in his hands and ordered Johnson to the hill in that never to be forgotten afternoon. Johnson with his stout heart and strong arm delivered the ball game.
>
> Bucky Harris with his stout heart and his love for Johnson delivered the opportunity. Who knows but that fine turn of faith, exhibited when fate seemed to turn her smile, gave Walter the dazzling speed and perfect control of old. For his superb act of faith and friendship, Bucky Harris deserves the undying gratitude of every baseball fan.[22]

Chapter 12

From Detroit to Boston

In Detroit owner Frank Navin was looking for a manager to replace George Moriarity, the former player and umpire who resigned after two seasons as manager, following fourth- and sixth-place finishes. Because Bucky was still a player, he was valuable trade material. Griffith wanted to accommodate Bucky, saying if Bucky could negotiate another managerial job, Griffith would help him even if he had to give him away.[1] It almost came to that. Detroit wanted Bucky and he wanted Detroit. Losing Bucky meant the Senators needed a second baseman and the Tigers had a fine one in Charlie Gehringer, but Tiger president Frank Navin wouldn't part with Gehringer. True to his word, Griffith made the deal, accepting Jackie Warner, a third baseman. Warner never played a game for the Senators, who released him before the 1928 season began. He later caught on with the Dodgers where he played 48 games in three seasons.

Bucky signed with Detroit on October 28. Second base was in good hands with Gehringer, who batted .320 with 74 RBIs in 1928, and Bucky immediately said he didn't expect to be a playing manager except in emergencies. His first duty was announcing the purchase of outfielder Roy Johnson for $75,000 from the San Francisco Seals, where he hit .359 in '28.[2] Not yet on the job a week, Bucky had an assessment of the Tigers' chances in 1929. "From what I have seen and the way matters are taking shape there is much to enthuse about. I don't want to make ridiculous predictions but I will be disappointed if we don't finish higher than last season."[3] The Tigers were sixth in 1928 at 68–86.

On November 11 Bucky obtained George McBride's release from Newark to be his number one coach. McBride had been Bucky's teammate and manager in 1921 with the Senators. Given free rein by Navin to make deals, Bucky was busy at the winter meetings. He traded starting shortstop Jack Tavener and pitcher Kenneth Holloway to Cleveland for pitcher George Uhle. He also sold back-up infielder Johnny Neun to Toledo and traded platoon first baseman Bill Sweeney to Toronto for Dale Alexander, whom the Tigers had signed in 1924. Called "the Ox" or "the Moose," the 6'3", 210-pound right-handed hitter had won the International League Triple Crown in 1928.

At the meetings John A. Heyder made a radical proposal for 10-man lineups, with the 10th man being a batter for the pitcher. Ironically, Heyder was the National League president; the A.L. owners called it a joke and refused to bring it to a vote. Billy Evans, the Indians' business manager, said if the rule was passed, "We would have to bring Larry Lajoie back into the fold." White Sox manager Russell Blackburne said his pitchers would assassinate him if they couldn't bat. Bucky said it would ruin baseball.[4] Heyder was way ahead of his time. The designated hitter for the pitcher rule was adopted by the American League in 1974.

Bucky arrived in Phoenix, Arizona, for spring training on February 24. Early in camp Bucky worked out at third base but continued to insist he wasn't going to play. "No, I'm to manage the club. But I could play third or second if the occasion arose."

Bucky brought Emil Yde to camp from Indianapolis. Yde had good seasons pitching with the Pirates in 1924 and 1925 and had pitched a game against the Senators in the 1925 World Series. But his pitching fell off the next couple years and the Pirates sold him to Indianapolis, where he was 19–12 and batted .371, frequently pinch-hitting. It was expected the Tigers would experiment with him as an outfielder because of his hitting ability, but Bucky said he intended to use him as a pitcher because he needed lefties. In the second week of March, Bucky said the Tigers were as good or better than the 1924 Senators. Catching, where Eddie Phillips and Pinky Hargrave platooned, was the only weak spot. He liked 23-year-old Jonathan Stone, hailed as the best-looking young Detroit outfielder since Ty Cobb. He also liked outfielders Harry Rice and Roy Johnson from PCL.

The Tigers had a rough time with the Chicago Cubs in spring games. They played a five-game series in Wrigley Field in Los Angeles and the Cubs won all five games. A record crowd of 26,000 came out for the first game on a Sunday. The Cubs won, 13–3. They won the next four games —13–3, 8–4, 13–8 and 10–2. In the 10–2 game on April 2, Hack Wilson hit a home run over the right-field bleachers and out of the park. The teams played 10 games overall, including five more in Texas and Arizona. The Cubs won eight of the 10.[5]

Bucky was impressed, calling the Cubs "the greatest ballclub I have ever seen placed on a field and that includes the Yankees."[6] After the first thrashing by the Cubs, Bucky was a little more circumspect about hits team's chances. "It's a hard task this taking over a new club and trying to put out a winner the first year. I'm not entirely sure of the qualities of my club yet. I believe the Tigers will be a troublesome outfit."[7] He planned to move Harry Heilmann to first base to accommodate an outfield of Johnson, Rice and Stone. Heilmann was benched during the Cubs games, and on March 29 it was reported Bucky would ask waivers on Heilmann for his failure to observe training rules. The next day Bucky gave him a second chance if he showed a sincere desire to obey the rules. As the season approached, Bucky had second thoughts about not playing. He was so down on Heinie Schuble, the projected starting shortstop, that Bucky tried playing second and putting Gehringer at short. He tried it for three days then ditched the idea. Gehringer was a second baseman. Bucky asked Navin to look for a shortstop.[8]

Alexander was the hitting star of the exhibition season. Bucky was considering starting him over Harry Heilmann, with whom Bucky continued to clash. Their relationship was hard to figure as Heilmann was 34 and had never been known as a troublemaker. Bucky, meanwhile, had his reputation as the manager without strict rules, especially for veterans. Before the Tigers left Los Angeles for Cleveland, where they were to open the season on April 16, Bucky and some of the players visited Paramount Studios. They met stars and directors and watched filming of scenes from *Thunderbolt* with George Bancroft and *The Insidious Dr. Fu Manchu.*[9]

Bucky's pitching staff consisted mainly of front-line starters Uhle, Earl Whitehill, Vic Sorrell and Ownie Carroll and spot starters and relievers Augie Prudhomme and Yde. The everyday lineup was Alexander, 1b; Gehringer, 2b; Marty McManus, 3b; Schuble or Yats Wuestling, ss; Johnson, Rice and Heilmann, of; and Eddie Phillips or Pinky Hargrave, c.

The Tigers played decent ball for the first three months. At the end of June they were 38–33 and in fourth place, 13 games behind the A's and eight games ahead of the sixth-place Senators. But they tanked in the second half, going 33–51 to finish 70–84 and in sixth place, two games behind the fifth-place Senators. Bucky's prediction of improvement was modestly correct, by four games. The pennant-winning A's punished the Tigers, winning 18 of 22. The second-place Yankees won 13 of 22 and Washington 12 of 22 versus the Tigers.

The Tigers' hitting kept them out of the cellar. They led the A.L. in team batting at .299; slugging, .453; runs, 927; and doubles, 337. Gehringer made it easy for Bucky, who played in seven games, to stay on the bench, leading the league in runs, doubles, triples and steals while batting .337. Alexander led the A.L. in hits with 215 and was third behind Al Simmons and Ruth in RBIs with 137. Heilmann and Bucky made peace and Harry batted .344 and slugged .565 with 15 home runs and 120 RBIs. The pitching was a disaster. The Tigers were dead last in team ERA at 4.96. They gave up the most hits and runs, 312 more than the pennant-winning A's.

Bucky was only a little overboard on his pre-season assessment of the Cubs. They did win 98 games and won the N.L. pennant by 10½ games over the Pirates, but lost the World Series to the A's, 4 games to 1.

On June 5 the Tigers visited Washington for the first time in 1929. "It's certainly good to be here again," he said, "but I don't feel at home in the visitors locker room."

The fans gave him a loud, long reception of cheers when he went to the plate to give the umpire his lineup card. Firpo Marberry, Bucky's favorite game saver, started for the Senators and pitched a complete-game five-hitter as the Senators won, 8–2. In what was an unlikely coincidence, Bucky was ejected from his first game back in Washington for the only time that season — twice in the same game. In the seventh inning he was ejected by Umpire McGowan for "remarks held as not being in good taste." Coach George McBride was tossed with him. In the ninth Bucky was caught directing coach Bennie Myer, who was presumably managing the game, from the top step of the tunnel. Umpire Campbell chased Bucky back into the clubhouse.[10]

Attendance surged by almost 400,000 in Detroit in Bucky's first season to 839,176, third-best in the A.L. after the A's and Yankees. Bucky's reward was a contract for 1930, signed in early September of 1929. Terms were not disclosed. With some of that increased revenue Bucky tried to improve the Tigers for 1930. He bought Elias "Liz" Funk, who hit .385 with 39 doubles and 13 home runs with Hollywood in the PCL in 1929 and .625 in the playoffs. The amount paid for Funk was not disclosed, but given his numbers it was likely in the neighborhood of $50,000 and two players to be named. Bucky bought pitcher Elon "Chief" Hogsett from Montreal in the International League. Though Hogsett was given his nickname for reputedly being part Cherokee, he said he was only ¹⁄₃₂ Cherokee on his mother's side. Even so, the Indian tag stuck, and in 1929 when he led the International League with 22 wins for the Montreal Royals, he was made an honorary member of the Iroquois Nation in a ceremony at home plate. The local Indians gave him the name "Ranantasse," meaning "strong arm."

The Tigers acquired him, reportedly for $40,000 and unknown players, in August of 1929 and he joined the team at the end of the IL season. There were "hints of something funny in the deal," reported the *Toronto Star*. Kenesaw Mountain Landis, commissioner of baseball, went to Montreal in early September to investigate but found nothing amiss. Hogsett played in two games at the end of 1929.[11]

In May of 1930, with Funk in the outfield, Bucky traded Harry Rice, Ownie Carroll and Yats Wuestling to the Yankees for Waite Hoyt and Mark Koenig. Koenig was only 25 and had been the starting shortstop for the Yankees in 1926, 1927 and 1928 while hitting .290. In 1929 he hit only .230, splitting time as a backup at third and short, while the Yankees played fiery youngster Leo Durocher at short. He was hitting .240 when the Yankees traded him to the Tigers. Hoyt, 30, had won 22 and 23 games in 1927 and 1928, respectively, but slumped to 10–9 with an ERA of 4.24 in 1929 and was 2–2 with a 4.58 in 1930 when the trade occurred. Neither player helped the Tigers much. Hoyt took a regular turn and was 11–10 with a 4.71 ERA. Koenig took over as the regular shortstop and hit .238 in 96 games. Hogsett was a good find. At 17–13 he led the team in wins. Funk, a regular in the outfield, was only fair compared to his PCL numbers, batting .275 with 64 RBIs.

For all the tinkering, the Tigers only improved by five games, going 75–79 in 1930 and finishing sixth. The Senators were the surprise of the league. They improved from 71 wins to 94 and finished second, eight games behind the A's in Walter Johnson's second season as manager. It was the Senators' biggest season-to-season improvement since Bucky led them from 75 wins to 92 from 1923 to 1924.

Bucky just couldn't make a winner out of the Tigers. In 1931 they slumped to 61–93 and seventh place, 47 games behind the A's, who won their third consecutive A.L. pennant. That August Bucky, having faith in rookie Merv Owen to hold down third base, traded Marty McManus to Boston for a back-up catcher and his old Senators' glory days buddy, Muddy Ruel. On June 12 against the Red Sox at Fenway Park, Bucky started at second base. He batted three times and was 0-for-2 with a walk. It was his 1,263rd game as a major league player and his last. He was a career .274 hitter.

On December 12, 1931, Bucky's mother had appendicitis surgery in the Pittston Hospital. Ten days later her condition took a serious turn for the worse. The first week of January, Bucky and Liz went to Pittston. They were there for 10 days and were at his mother's side when she died on January 16. She was buried in the family plot in St. Peter's Cemetery.

In 1932 the Tigers improved by 18 games and posted a winning record for the first time under Bucky. It was one of his better managing jobs as he coaxed a 79–75 record out of a team with such no-name starters as shortstop Billy Rogell, center fielder Gee Walker, first baseman Harry Davis and, by now, journeyman pitchers Whitehill and Sorrell. Rookie Tommy Bridges won 14 games.

The Tigers' spring camp was in San Antonio, Texas, in 1933 and Bucky didn't know what to make of an enormous Jewish kid from New York City. Hank Greenberg, 22, was 6' 4" and 210 pounds and attracted a lot of attention for his size, good looks (some said the best in baseball) and ability to hit the ball a country mile. Bucky did know what he wanted to do with 23-year-old rookie pitcher Lynwood "Schoolboy" Rowe, who was a half-inch taller than Greenberg. On March 7 Bucky said he was going to throw Rowe into the fire: "I'm going to start him in the first series we play in Detroit. If he is beaten, I'll send him back on the mound again. And if he is beaten again, I'll send him back again."[12]

Was Greenberg a case where Bucky, inexplicably, didn't get it? It seemed that way, but years later Greenberg believed Bucky did right by him by keeping him in the minors from 1930 to 1932. Bucky, based on what happened in 1933, believed Greenberg could have used even one more season down on the farm. Bucky had talked Navin into buying Harry Davis from Toronto for $50,000 after the 1931 season and made him his regular first baseman in 1932, when he hit .269 with four homers and 64 RBIs. Davis was considered a good fielder and Bucky loved fielding. He was determined to have Davis play first base. He tried Greenberg at third, where he was much worse than at first, where he was no Joe Judge.

After the third base experiment Bucky didn't speak to Greenberg for 10 days. At one point when the team went to Norfolk for a spring game, Bucky took a break and went home to Washington. Del Baker managed and put Greenberg at first and he had a single, double and triple. Bucky still didn't want to play him regularly. Finally, under pressure from Navin, and with Davis slumping, Bucky's hand was forced. Reluctantly, he played Greenberg in 117 games. He batted .301 with 33 doubles and 12 home runs.[13] Maybe if Bucky had played Greenberg another 40 games, Bucky wouldn't have wound up resigning after the 1933 season. Back in the spring he predicted the Tigers would finish third or higher and said he would resign if they didn't. "It is the finest team I have managed," he said of the 1933 Tigers in camp. "It is young, willing and possessed with great natural ability. We will crowd teams like Cleveland and Philadelphia."[14]

One reason for the optimism was his old game-saver, Fred Marberry, acquired by the Tigers from the Senators the previous December with pitcher Carl Fischer for Earl Whitehill. During the spring Bucky said Marberry would be his game finisher. In 1932 with the Senators, Marberry led the league in games, 54, and saves, 13. His record was 8–4, and he was on the mound to close 26 games.

But in 1933, Bucky, who along with Griffith had developed Marberry as a relief pitcher, curiously turned him in to a number-one starter. He led the Tigers in starts, 32, and was second in complete games with 15. Bucky used him in relief only five times. To a degree the strategy worked, for he led the team in wins with 16. But it must be asked if the Tigers would have been better off with Marberry in his usual role?

To the extent that one game can make or break a season, the Tigers' contest in Washington on July 23 was that game. Oddly, it was a game the Tigers won with a late rally and one from which Bucky was ejected. The Tigers were behind, 6–2, after seven but scored nine times in the eighth and won, 12–8. Bucky didn't see the rally. He had been tossed by umpire Bill McGowan in the sixth inning after shouting something profane at Washington pitcher Monte Weaver, which was what Griffith and the fans had wanted to see when Bucky was on their side. In his five seasons with Detroit, Bucky was ejected four times, twice in Washington. It doesn't seem likely that was a coincidence.

The Tigers knocked the Senators out of first place that day and lifted themselves to fourth by a game. That was the good; the bad was the July 23 game was the last of the season for Schoolboy Rowe. He was 7–4 with a 3.58 ERA, eight complete games, one shutout and 75 strikeouts in 123 innings to that point. He made his 15th start that day, but didn't get out of the third inning, leaving with a sore arm.

On September 23, 1933, Bucky kept his word and resigned with two games left in the season. Navin was willing to accept that Bucky's spring prediction was hyperbole and tried to talk him out of quitting, but Bucky stuck to his promise. "Perhaps somebody else can do better. I am not going to sit around and blame the breaks. I dislike to sever my connection with the Tigers, but under the circumstances feel that it is the only fair thing to do. I honestly believed we had a club that would finish in third and no lower than fourth."[15]

Someone did do better, much better. That December Navin made two deals that paid off in 1934. He visited Mack's house sale in Philadelphia and bought Mickey Cochrane for $100,000 and appointed him manager. Then he traded John Stone to the Senators for Goose Goslin. In 1934 Cochrane provided a huge upgrade at catcher over Johnny Hayworth, who hit .245 with 45 RBIs in 1933. In 1934 Cochrane batted .322 with 76 RBIs in 129 games. Goslin, 33, batted .305 with 13 home runs and 100 RBIs. Greenberg played all but one game at first base, batted .339 with a league-leading 63 doubles, 26 home runs and 139 RBIs, and while he was second in the league in errors, he was nowhere near the butcher Bucky had considered him to be. Gehringer led the league in hits and runs. Even Rogell, a player Bucky always liked, came through by increasing his RBI total from 57 to 100. Rowe recovered from his sore arm and led the team with 24 wins. Bridges won 22. It would all add up to a pennant for the 1934 Tigers, who won 101 games.

But that spring nobody was predicting a pennant for the Tigers, least of all Bucky, who had moved on to the Red Sox. Bucky signed with the Red Sox on October 30. He succeeded McManus, who took over in the middle of 1932 when John Shano Collins resigned. McManus had been Bucky's third baseman with the Tigers in 1929 and 1930 before being traded to Boston during the 1931 season for Ruel. Boston released him after a seventh-place finish in 1933.

Red Sox owner Tom Yawkey and his general manager, Eddie Collins,

Bucky's one-time idol, considered Peckinpaugh and Babe Ruth before hiring Bucky. Yawkey was born Thomas Austin into a wealthy family of lumber and iron ore magnates. When Tom's father died, his uncle, Bill Yawkey, who owned the Tigers, adopted him and he became Thomas Austin Yawkey.

Over the winter of 1932-33, Yawkey, then 30, was hunting on his 50,000-acre South Carolina estate with Eddie Collins, whom he had met through another hunting buddy, Ty Cobb. Collins mentioned the Red Sox were for sale and urged Yawkey to buy the team. Yawkey said he would if Collins would agree to be the GM. On February 21, 1933, Yawkey collected on his trust, which was estimated at $40 million. On February 25, 1933, he paid Bob Quinn $1.5 million for the Red Sox. He spent another $1.5 million to refurbish Fenway Park. He was willing to spend on players, too.[16] Terms of Bucky's contract were not disclosed, and it's difficult to hazard a guess. Yawkey was rich and generous, but the Depression was in full force and a lot of teams were reducing salaries. True, Ruth made $80,000 in 1930, but the days when managers were almost always paid more than the players were ending. It's not unreasonable to guess Bucky signed for $40,000 to $50,000. After he signed, he made the same vow he had made a year earlier in Detroit: "I've only signed for one year. If I can't get results in that time someone else deserves a chance."

At the press conference when he was introduced, Bucky's personality came through. "Harris, modest and soft-spoken, had little to say as he made his bow at the Boston baseball writers luncheon at Fenway Park. Most of his remarks were about yesterday's college football games."[17]

In November Yawkey bought three players from the A's for $125,000. Most of that amount, $100,000, was for Lefty Grove, while the rest went for Rube Walberg and Max Bishop. Bishop was a second baseman and an on-base machine, having drawn 100-plus walks for five consecutive seasons. In 1933 he batted .294 and walked 106 times in 117 games. His on-base percentage was .446. Walberg had a mediocre season, going 9–13 in 1933, but Grove was one of the top pitchers in the game. In 1933 he led the A.L. in wins with 24 and complete games with 21.

Bishop was happy to play for the Red Sox. "I'm tickled because I believe the Red Sox are going places in the league; second, because it's going to be great to work under Bucky Harris for an owner who isn't afraid to spend money; and third, because I've always liked Boston and the sportsmanlike appreciative fans there. If I had my choice of a team to be sold to I would have picked Boston."[18] Bucky had definite plans for Bishop: "Max Bishop, one of the former A's, is sure of second base. There isn't anyone who can push him off. He is also certain of the lead-off position in the batting order."[19] On December 15 the Associated Press had reported 30 A.L. players changed teams since the end of the 1933 season. In addition to the trio from Philadelphia, the Red Sox also got infielder Bill Cissell from Cleveland and outfielder Carl Reynolds from the Browns.

Bucky turned down an offer from the Senators of left-handed pitcher Bob Weiland for Goslin. He had to regret that one. Weiland went 2–10 in 1934 while Goslin went to Detroit, drove in 100 runs, and won a pennant with the Tigers. Bucky had the sad duty of releasing Dale Alexander, the big first baseman who had led the league in hits as a rookie with the Tigers in 1929. The Tigers traded him to Boston during the 1932 season when they signed Harry Davis. Alexander had a huge year in Boston in 1932, batting .372 in 101 games, but on Memorial Day in 1933 he injured his leg while sliding into home plate. Red Sox trainer Doc Woods used a new deep-heat treatment on him that aggravated the injury. He finished the season but never played again.

A happy coincidence for Bucky in going to the Red Sox was Joe Judge was there. The Red Sox had picked him up on a waiver claim the previous July as a reserve. The unhappy part was Bucky had to release him, too. He departed in May, 10 days before his 40th birthday. In January Judge, seeing the writing on the wall, recommended the signing of first baseman Eddie Morgan, formerly of Cleveland. Morgan was in New Orleans and subject to the draft. "I told Collins to grab Morgan and he told me I was to blame if a lost my job."[20] Morgan turned out to be the everyday first baseman in 1934 and batted .267 with 75 RBIs.

It was around this time the Tigers acquired Cochrane. Shirley Povich, in his *Washington Post* column "This Morning," wasn't impressed. "There is no reason to view the Tigers with alarm despite their acquisition of Mickey Cochrane. Cochrane has yet to prove himself the managerial equal of Bucky Harris. The Tigers, however, figured to be a front-division occupant along with the Yankees, Nats and Red Sox."

In his office at Fenway on January 10, 1934, Bucky talked about the American League. "Washington is still the club to beat. Too many ifs dot the Yankees prospects and now that Mickey Cochrane has left Philadelphia to take over my old job in Detroit, you can bank on the A's pitching not being anything to boast about. I think the league has more balance than it has enjoyed for years. Don't be surprised to find the American League race the same neck and neck affair that thrilled the National League last season." He said he was banking heavily on Grove and promised not to use him in relief, as had been done in Philadelphia.[21]

On February 4 Povich interviewed Bucky and asked about the Tigers. "I recommended Mickey Cochrane for the job and he's the kind of man they need, but the Tigers have their weaknesses. I see where they are going to leave up the left field screen I erected because we didn't have any long left field hitters. But the auditing department kept count of the hits out there and discovered the screen robbed the Tigers of more home runs that it did the opposition."[22]

In early March Bucky was quoted in a Detroit paper as saying the Tigers didn't have much of a chance and he expected the Red Sox to finish ahead of the Tigers. Cochrane was happy to hear that. "I'm going to put that clipping on the bulletin board and have everyone read and remember it. Harris and his Red Sox will be very much surprised when they meet us, for Harris is managing one team that we're going to beat."[23] Cochrane offered to bet Bucky that the Tigers would finish ahead of the Red Sox and said, "Bucky had gone crazy from the elevation mixing with millionaires and everything."[24]

As fate would happen, the Tigers opened the exhibition season against Boston in mid–March. The Red Sox won, but Bucky didn't refer to Cochrane's comments and he didn't gloat. "What can anybody say at this time of year? If certain players come through, we have a chance up there. If not we'll have to do some more building."[25]

The Red Sox had nine left-handed pitchers in camp. "You can't have too many good ones," Bucky said. "Bob Grove is a fair country pitcher, and Walberg, a lot of hitters would be pleased if he broke an arm or something."[26]

Bucky was happy with outfielder Roy Johnson, who had been with him in Detroit. He was high on catcher Rick Ferrell and he liked his infield of Eddie Morgan, Max Bishop, Bill Cissell and Billy Werber. He always liked veteran pitchers and didn't mind having Herb Pennock, the 40-year-old former Yankee star. He also liked Fred Ostermueller, a rookie who won 16 games at Rochester in 1933. Bucky was satisfied if not thrilled with his players. Everything was fine as long as he had Lefty Grove.

But he didn't. Grove hadn't thrown a pitch all spring. On April 9 it was revealed why. He had arm pain. In what seemed like an odd remedy, he had three infected teeth removed. Hoping against hope, Bucky said, "I believe that will clear up the trouble."

Grove believed it, too. "I'm out to get this trouble corrected. If I ever started a season in which I wanted to do my best, it's this one. I honestly believe I'm working for the best outfit I ever saw. Bucky Harris, Eddie Collins and Tom Yawkey. I'll pitch my head off for them and to do that I have to have my arm in shape so I don't pitch it off too. I'm going to be ready, let the teeth fall where they may." He said he could pitch steadily at a certain speed but "when I put speed on it I feel it."[27]

On April 13 Bucky announced Gordon "Dusty" Rhodes would be the pitcher in the opening game of the unofficial three-game city championship with the N.L. Boston Braves. The Red Sox won two of the three games, with Walberg pitching a complete game in one of them, but the Braves claimed the city title for having won two previous games in Florida.

As the season opened Grove was in disbelief. In an interview with Grant-
land Rice in the *Los Angeles Times* on April 13 in his "Sportlight" column,
Grove said, "Here I go 15 years without knowing what a sore arm is and then
I get sore before I've thrown a ball, just at the time I'm set for my best year.
I can't believe it will last long but I won't sleep much until I know for sure."

Bucky was depressed. "You can understand how any manager would feel
when he sees 25 ball games on the point of blowing up in front of his nose
just as the season is ready to start. We were all set to shoot for third place and
I believe we could have made it until this terrible thing happened. I still can't
believe it will work that way."

As it happened the Red Sox were supposed to host Washington on Opening Day. The game was switched to Washington to accommodate President
Roosevelt's schedule, but it was rained out. The teams took the train together
to Boston to open with single games on Tuesday and Wednesday, April 17
and 18, and a Patriots' Day double-header on Thursday. Grove was not
expected to pitch for another week. Gordon Rhodes was the Opening Day
starter for the Red Sox, who lost that one but split four games.

On April 23 Grove tested his arm against the Holy Cross College team.
He gave up four hits in five innings, including a tremendous home run by Ed
Moriarity. He struck out four, walked one and hit one. But the arm still hurt.
He gave it a go against major league batters on May 5 versus the Browns and
wished he hadn't. He faced five batters, walked two and gave up three hits.
All five scored but the Sox managed to win, 13–12. On May 19 he started for
the first time in St. Louis, pitched a complete game and won 4–1, and hit a
three-run home run. It was noted that his fastball lacked zip and he struck
out only four, but it was encouraging enough to give him a second start four
days later in Cleveland on May 23. He pitched another complete game and
won, but gave up 10 hits, five runs and again struck only four. On May 28
he started again but was hammered in Detroit, giving up 12 hits in 5⅔ innings.

From Detroit the Red Sox went to Philadelphia, where Grove sat in the
A's hot room, known as "the sweatbox." "There's 45 electric bulbs there and
you could cook a barbecue. They've got the best clubhouse and that sweatbox.
There's nothing like it anywhere," he said.[28]

He pitched 20 minutes of batting practice that day and reported no pain,
but the discomfort returned the next time he pitched. On June 9 he gave up
a record six doubles in one inning against the Senators and 15 total hits in
seven innings. On July 9 Grove had his tonsils removed. Dr. Harry P. Cahill,
a throat specialist at St. Elizabeth's Hospital in Boston, operated. The team
left Sunday night for a long western trip without him. The scribes had fun,
saying he gave up three teeth for his arm and now he was going to give up
his tonsils. It sounded crazy, but Collins and Bucky hoped the operation

would help him.[29] In the end nothing helped Grove. He appeared in only 22 games, 12 of them starts. He finished with an 8–8 record and an ERA of 6.50.

In his July 12 "Sportlight" column, Grantland Rice praised Bucky's work. "Bucky has turned in one of the season's best jobs. He has kept the ball club, picked to finish sixth or seventh, up around third place. Most of his ballplayers are castoffs. Harris as a manager is entirely different than Cochrane, who is emotional, full of fire and spirit. Bucky belongs to the colder logical school."

Rice had a point about the job Bucky did in 1934. The Sox peaked at nine games over on July 18 with a 47–39 record. At that point they were in third place, 6½ back of Tigers. They slumped after that and by September 16 were 70–71. The finished .500, 76–76, an improvement of 13 games over 1933 when they were 63–86. They were 8–14 against the pennant-winning Tigers. It was the Sox's first .500 season and first-division finish since 1918.

On August 3 Bucky conceded the race to the Yankees and Washington. "Figure it out for yourself. We had every reason to expect Grove to win 20 games. He has won only four and it's a question whether his arm will be in shape to start another game in August. Yet we are only nine games or there-abouts back of the leaders. With Grove in shape and taking his regular turn there is no doubt we would be right on top of the heap."[30]

Bucky had hard luck with pitchers. Walberg also was injured and started only 10 games and was 6–7. In early May, Yawkey bought George Pipgras from the Yankees with infielder Billy Werber for $100,000. Pipgras, who won 16 in 1933 for the Yankees, developed arm trouble and appeared in only two games with the Red Sox in 1934. Just how bad Bucky's luck with Grove was became evident the next season. Grove won 20 and led the league in ERA at 2.70.

There were a couple of highlights in 1934. On April 22 a Fenway record-breaking crowd of 45,500 paid to come out for a Yankees game and 8,000 were turned away. The crowd spilled onto the field and ground rules were made for the first time. Mounted police kept the crowd in check behind the roped-off sections in right and center field. The Yankees won, 8–1.

When the Senators returned to Boston for a three-game series on August 4 and a double-header on August 5, the Senators were in fifth, 5½ games behind the fourth-place Red Sox. Senators manager Joe Cronin predicted a Washington sweep and that his team would catch and pass the Red Sox and finish in the first division. The Red Sox won two of three. The Senators fell to seventh at end of season; Red Sox finished fourth.

On September 24 the Red Sox eliminated the Yankees from the A.L. race, 5–0, in Yankee Stadium on a four-hit shutout by rookie lefty John Merena in his second major league start. Ruth, limping in obvious pain, started in right. He walked in the first inning and called for a pinch-runner. He received a rousing ovation from the crowd of only 2,000 as he walked to the dugout in what would be his last home game in the famous house he built.

On October 26, Bucky, to his great surprise, was released.

"I had no inkling I was going to be released. I knew I was working on a one-year contract, but I thought I had done well at Boston under the circumstances. However, that's baseball and apparently I'm on the open market for a job."[31]

Chapter 13

Back to the Capital

"There's no use denying it. I'd turn 18 handsprings if I was offered the Washington job again," Bucky said that after he was dismissed by the Red Sox in October of 1934. "There isn't another spot I'd prefer. I'd like to start over with a clean slate and stand or fall on what I might do. But no job has been offered me. That's up to Mr. Griffith to decide."[1]

Griffith had a decision to make about a manager for 1935. On October 26, 1934, he sold his player-manager, Joe Cronin, to the Red Sox for shortstop Lyn Lary and cash. The Red Sox released Bucky the same day. Yawkey had chosen Cronin over Bucky at considerable expense. The cash involved in the trade was reported to be between $150,000 and $250,000. It was said Cronin increased Yawkey's investment in the Red Sox to $3 million. Cronin was given a five-year contract and unlimited financial support to acquire players. The deal had been in the works since the World Series. Eddie Collins, Yawkey's vice president and GM, said, "When we were in Detroit Tom asked me who I wanted to manage in 1935. I said Mickey Cochrane. When Tom laughed, I warned him that my second choice, Joe Cronin, was just as hard to get."

Collins was shocked Griffith let Cronin go. After all, Cronin was practically family. He was married to Mildred June Robertson, Griffith's adopted daughter, and he had some success with the Senators, leading them to a pennant in 1933. But Yawkey pulled off the deal, as he told Collins, by making Griffith an offer that will "jar him for the rest of his life."[2]

Cronin had come to the Senators in Bucky's last season as manager in 1928. It was Bucky, over Griffith's objection, who made Cronin the Senators' regular shortstop in July of 1928. Cronin succeeded Walter Johnson as manager in 1933 and immediately took the Senators to an A.L. pennant as manager and the everyday shortstop while leading the league in doubles. Griffith had to like that because it came with an attendance increase. Even though the Depression kept the figures from approaching the heady days of 1924 and 1925, the Senators were fourth in the major leagues in 1933. Griffith valued loyalty but valued money more, so when Yawkey made him the offer for Cronin, he couldn't refuse.

But would Griffith bring Bucky back to Washington? In fact, Bucky never really left Washington. It was home. While he was in Detroit and Boston he spent the winters at home in Washington with his family, which by 1934 had grown by three. Proof of Bucky's commitment to home was his house. In April of 1932 he bought a home at 4932 Hillbrook Lane Northwest. The home was designed and built in their Spring Valley development by famous architects W.C. & A.N. Miller. It was there that Shirley Povich visited in February of 1934 and described Bucky's home life. "Stanley Raymond Harris Jr., 6, was risking permanent deafness with one ear jammed against a speaker whose strident tones were already informing the immediate community that the radio was on in the Harris household; Sally Harris, 3, was succeeding in eliminating the crease from Daddy's trousers with a sustained and relentless tugging; Dickie Harris, 10 months, was propped against the back of the divan contemplating the reactions of the 59-cent dollar on the world's money markets and how it would affect the price of teething rings."[3]

Though Bucky had been gone from the Senators for five years by the end of the 1934 season, he had never left Griffith's mind. He visited privately with his old boss whenever the Tigers or Red Sox were in Washington and he drank, played cards and smoked cigars with Griffith in the winters. No one knows what they talked about, but it's not hard to imagine, given their father-and-son-like relationship, that they discussed scenarios for Bucky's return to Washington one day.

On October 28 Bucky visited Griffith at his office. Griffith said it didn't mean anything. They were friends and always visited. Griffith said there was no hurry to hire a manager and with a laugh said he would handle the job himself if it came to that. Ruth, Hornsby, Sam Rice and Joe Judge were being considered. One rumor suggested Ruth was offered $15,000 and a cut of the gate but was holding out for $30,000. Either amount seemed like a pittance considering the Babe earned $80,000 as a player and Bucky had been paid $100,000 for his last three seasons in Washington.[4] Griffith said Ruth was not being considered. "I greatly respect Babe as a man and for his great work in the game. He is of managerial timber I believe, but he is definitely out of the picture for management of my ball club."[5]

Griffith said he did not want a player-manager and wanted a manager respected by the fans. Bucky fit both counts, and he emerged as the frontrunner in November. On November 14 he finally signed a one-year deal. The compliments flew.

"I believe I have in Harris the best man obtainable," Griffith said. "I think he can get the best there is in a player. It takes bad years for a manager to really learn baseball. Harris has been through the mill and there are few that know more baseball than he does."

Bucky, by now 38, said, "I think Griff has a wonderful bunch of boys here. I thought they would win the pennant last year. They were going great until they were blasted by injuries. Washington will miss Cronin. Lyn is a fine young shortstop and he's improving, but he isn't Cronin yet."[6]

The irony was doubly delicious. Boy Wonder II replacing Boy Wonder I and vice versa. Coach Al Schacht was released in order to go with Cronin. Bucky signed Joe Judge to replace Schacht. When the Cronin deal first went down, it was said to be for $150,000. By the time Bucky signed, the price for Cronin was being reported as $200,000. Even the lower price was a bloody fortune during the Depression. As usual, Bucky's salary wasn't reported, but it was suspected to be from $10,000 to $15,000, roughly a third of what he made yearly in his last Washington contract. But Bucky wasn't complaining about the money. "This is the best break I've had since 1924. It's really a thrill to come back to Washington. There's something about coming back to your hometown that makes a fellow want to dig in."[7]

When the Senators won the A.L. pennant in Cronin's first season as manager in 1933, his top two pitchers, General Crowder and Earl Whitehill, ranked first and second in pitching victories in the A.L. with 24 and 22. Lefty Stewart won 15. Left fielder Heinie Manush led the league in hits and triples and first baseman Joe Kuhel drove in 107 runs. Cronin led the league with 45 doubles and the team in RBIs with 118. But in 1934 the Senators crashed from 94 wins and first place to 66 and seventh place. General Crowder, it turned out, was burned out. He had pitched in 102 games and 626 innings in 1932 and 1933 combined. In 1934 he pitched only 100 innings and was 4–10. Whitehill and Stewart, both age 35, flopped in 1934, too, going 21–22 combined.

Given those statistics, Bucky wanted Griffith to use some of the Cronin money to sign pitchers for 1935. To that end nothing happened at the winter meetings in New York City before the season. The Yankees were willing to part with pitching but wanted Buddy Myer and Heinie Manush rather than money. The only nibble was talk of a deal with the Cubs, where Griffith would swap his second baseman, Luke Sewell, for rookie pitcher Lester Tietje, but the Cubs wanted a pile of cash on top and that killed the deal.[8]

Bucky got back on the speaking circuit in Washington after signing in October. On December 12 he was a guest speaker at the Optimist Club luncheon but was not in a positive frame of mind. He said he and Griffith were not to that point able to strengthen the seventh-place ballclub despite the Cronin money. Griffith let Bucky off the hook as early as December. "I'm not passing the buck to Bucky. I know what he's up against unless the winter

brings some deals for pitching. I'm taking the rap for what happens next year."
He insisted Bucky was the best manager available. "I believe I have made the
wisest choice possible. I except no man in baseball when I call Bucky the
greatest manager on the field."[9]

With Christmas coming, Griffith had still not spent any of the Cronin
money and Povich didn't like it. "Griffith is in a position to go into the market
for talent but so far he has done Bucky wrong. He has ordered Monte Weaver
to change his diet, telegraphed Bob Burke to have his tonsils extracted, placed
Linke under the care of a specialist and wired Earl Whitehill to return from
his Far Eastern trip. At best Bucky will have only a reconditioned staff.

"Couldn't cry poverty to the holdouts like Whitehill. Bucky is taking
the rap. Anything the Nats, as currently constituted, achieve during the 1935
season will be achieved despite Griffith."

Griffith responded, "We had 27 different cases of injuries or sickness last
season. There wasn't a week when Cronin could put a regular lineup on the
field. You've got to throw the whole season out of reckoning. I admit we need
pitchers, but look over the rest of the ball club, there's a lot to see. Thirty-
four beat anything. Even my wife broke her ankle and the concessionaire
strained his back."[10]

On January 3, 1935, at the annual stockholders meeting the Washington
baseball club failed to declare a dividend despite the $250,00 received from
Boston in the Joe Cronin deal in October. There hadn't been a dividend since
1931. Even so, Griffith said the team nearly broke even and said he was "perfectly well satisfied" with the team's 1934 financial statement. The Senators
were the second-best road draw to the Yankees, according to American League
data. But a decade later, 1924 and 1925 remained the team's most profitable
years.[11]

On January 21 Bucky tossed the center tap to start a basketball game
between the Heurich Brewers of Washington and the Newark Mules of the
Eastern League as part of the official dedication of the new basketball arena
built by Chris Heurich. The arena, located at 26th and D Streets Northwest,
was jammed to capacity. Bucky received a rousing ovation when he was
announced along with Joe Judge and Nick Altrock. Newark won, 43–34.
Honey Russell scored 17 for the winners.[12]

That same day Yawkey was in D.C. to make the Cronin deal official.
Yawkey met with Bucky, a meeting described as one between a man fired from
a $15,000 job and the man who fired him but remained friends.

"Just because a man loses his job that's no reason he should lose a friend,"
Bucky said. "Those are my sentiments, too," Yawkey said. "Bucky knows how
I feel about it. He knows Joe Cronin is the only man on earth I'd hire in his
place. Bucky would be manager of the Red Sox today, if I didn't have the

chance to get Cronin. Don't forget we get both a shortstop and a great manager and that's no reflection on Bucky."

Yawkey praised Bucky for his handling of rookie Billy Werber in Boston in 1933. "Things were not all milk and honey with Werber at the start of last season. He was a bust at shortstop and the fans were riding him hard. The kid made 14 errors in 22 games until Bucky moved him to third base and you know what he did at third."[13]

Bucky met with the Arch McDonald Hot Stove League at 77 P Street Northeast. Chocolate and cookies were served and club members had photos taken with Bucky.[14] A couple days later he was the honored quest at the Washington Baseball Writers Association Dinner. Bucky got the biggest applause of the evening when he was introduced as the baseball manager "who would not lie to reporters."[15] Bucky was the guest on a few radio shows in February. On the Bill Coyle show on WMAL, he was billed as "The Man Who Came Back."

In mid–February Griffith went to Miami to golf, fish and heat up the telegraph while looking for a pitcher. He bristled when a reporter asked him if his new minor league ball clubs — Selma of the Southeastern League or Panama City of the Georgia-Alabama-Florida League — were semi-pro teams or honest-to-goodness minor league teams.

"They may not produce any major leaguers but you've got to take that chance," Griffith said. Bucky agreed: "The trading at the recent major leagues meeting, virtually none at all, discloses the scarcity of good ballplayers. We've got to dig our own garden."[16]

The team was due on February 24 in training camp in Biloxi, Mississippi, where the Senators had been training since 1929. On February 27 four pitchers and two position players were holding out. One day Griffith said, "They were ungrateful renegades who are blind to their own welfare." The next day they were simply young fellows who were at odds with him on the salary question. The holdout pitchers were Earl Whitehill, Bobby Burke, Jack Russell and Lefty Stewart. The players were shortstop Lyn Lary and first baseman Joe Kuhel.[17]

Bucky arrived in Biloxi on March 1. He stepped off the train with Altrock and was greeted by the mayor, his official family, and representatives of the chamber of commerce. Altrock, an honorary chief with the West End Fire Department, was escorted to the fire house for a shrimp dinner atop a speeding hose cart with sirens blaring.

Bucky went to see Griffith, who was sick in bed at his hotel. They didn't discuss the holdouts. "We never discuss players' salaries, Griffith and I. That's his job. I don't interfere because I know he wants no interference.

"I'm starting from scratch, you know. I don't know any of these lads and perhaps it's lucky for them. I didn't sign to manage the team until the season was over and none of these rookies are my choice. Perhaps it's better for them that it's that way. I'll have an open mind and it will be strictly up to them."[18]

On March 26 the Edgewater Golf Course in Biloxi conducted a tournament for the Senators. Bucky won a playoff for the title. Nobody won much of anything the rest of the year. The Senators did move up from seventh to sixth place, 27 games behind the pennant-winning Tigers, but they won only one more game, 67, than they had in 1934.

What games they did win were won with hitting. The Senators were second in the A.L. to the Tigers in team batting average and runs scored. Second baseman Buddy Myer led the league in batting at .349. Bucky played rookie Jake Powell, who hit .361 with 20 homers for Albany in the International League in 1933, in center field every day and he hit .312 with 98 RBIs. Cecil Travis hit .318. Griffith and Bucky gave up on Lyn Larry, who was batting .197 when they traded him to the Browns in June for back-up infielder Alan Strange. Ossie Bluege, who at 35 was the only player left from the 1924–25 teams, took over at short and hit .263. The batting could not overcome the atrocious pitching. The Senators were seventh in team ERA at 5.25, edging the Browns at 5.26.

Griffith never did buy a top-flight pitcher with the Cronin cash. The best he could do was acquire Bobo Newsom from the Browns for $40,000 in May when he was 0–6. He went 11–12 for the Senators with a 4.45 ERA. Whitehill remained the number-one starter and went 14–13 with a 4.29 ERA. Bump Hadley was number two and was 10–15. Ed Linke, a rookie who had pitched 11 innings at the end of 1934, was the fourth starter. He was 11–7 despite a 5.01 ERA, getting 6.55 runs of support per nine innings.

The Senators hung around until late May. They were 17–15 on May 27 when Whitehill beat the Indians, 6–5. They then lost eight straight, including a Memorial Day double-header in Yankee Stadium, and never saw .500 again. In June, during a string of seven losses in nine games, Bucky publicly gave up on most of his players, as reported by Povich.

> Disgusted with his ballclub as presently constituted, Manager Bucky Harris will seek the permission of owner Clark Griffith to trade any or every man on the team with the exception of his regular infield, outfielder Jack Powell and pitcher Henry Coppola, the *Washington Post* has learned. Before another season dawns, Harris hopes the Washington club will be hardly recognizable to Washington fans. The deadline on trades having expired a couple weeks ago, the Nats are unable to act this season, but Harris is looking to the future.

Powell, who was leading the league in RBIs at the time the story broke, and Coppola were kept off the block due to their youth. Coppola didn't have much of a record but was 21 and had a hot fastball.[19]

Bucky started on his remake of the team as soon as the 1935 season ended. On October 1, 1935, he selected pitcher Pete Appleton from Montreal in the Rule 5 draft. Appleton had last played in the major leagues as Peter William Jablonowski in 1933. In December he acquired outfielders Carl Reynolds and Roy Johnson from the Red Sox for Heinie Manush. He then sent Johnson and Hadley to the Yankees for pitcher Jim DeShong. Both pitchers came through in 1936. DeShong led the team in wins with 18. Appleton went 14–7 and led the team in ERA at 3.53. Newsom led the league in starts and went 17–15. Whitehill was 14–11. The team ERA dropped by nearly a run, and the Senators improved by 15 games, going 82–71 and landing in fourth place, 20 games behind the Yankees, who won 101.

Bucky's second term in Washington would last six more seasons, through 1942. But the hope inspired by the winning season in 1936 waned quickly. The Senators dropped back below .500 in 1937 and stayed there. They finished fifth in 1938 and then sixth, seventh, sixth and seventh from 1939 through

Bucky, back for a second term in D.C., greets A's Connie Mack before the 1938 Opening Day game in Griffith Stadium (Library of Congress Digital Collection).

1942. Each year Bucky was retained with a one-year deal. Each spring there was renewed hope of obtaining better players, but no major deals were made. Some interesting players came along, including two future Hall of Famers: pitcher Early Wynn and outfielder Al Simmons. Wynn, who would go on to win 300 games, was 19 when Bucky gave him his first three starts in September 1939. In the last of the three games in Washington before a crowd of only 600, he pitched against the A's. Before the game Ben Chapman of the A's asked Bucky who was starting. Bucky pointed to Wynn. Chapman laughed and predicted he'd get four or five hits off him. "If you do the last three will be from the prone position," Wynn said. Asked if he would knock down his mother, he said, "It depends how good she was hitting."[20] Chapman got one hit off Wynn.

Bucky brought Simmons from Detroit in April of 1937. He was beyond his prime but he hit .279 and .302 in his two seasons under Bucky. Mickey Vernon was a rookie in 1939. Vernon, a slick-fielding first baseman, would play 20 seasons. He was Bucky's starting first baseman in the last two seasons of his second term, in 1941 and 1942, and for all of Bucky's third term, from 1950 to 1954. He was a two-time A.L. batting champion.

George Case was the starting center fielder and lead-off batter for Bucky from 1939 to 1942. Considered one of the fastest men in baseball, he led the A.L. in steals all three seasons and scored more than 100 runs in three of the four.

In 1940 Bucky and Griffith promoted Sid Hudson from Class D, where he was 24–4 with a 1.80 ERA in 1939. He won 17 as a rookie. Bucky Harris called him "the cleverest young fellow I've seen come along since Schoolboy Rowe broke in under me with the Tigers in 1931. Fellows like him don't learn how to pitch in a couple of years. He's in an advanced stage because he's just naturally a pitcher."[21]

In 1938 Bucky selected Dutch Leonard in the Rule 5 draft from Atlanta. Brooklyn had released him after the 1936 season. Leonard led the Senators in wins with 18 in 1939. He was Bucky's kind of ballplayer. In April of 1942 he broke his leg sliding into first base while trying to beat out an infield hit. "That's a tough blow to take, but Leonard would not have been injured if he was not such a fine ballplayer. He is one of the few pitchers who is bearing down even when he is not pitching. Another man might have been content to be tagged out."[22]

On September 27, 1942, after a long talk with Griffith, Bucky resigned from the Senators. He telephoned the Washington papers with the news and said he didn't want to comment further. Later he did issue a statement. "It is with regret that I have decided to resign as manager of the Washington baseball club due to the pleasant relationship I have had with Mr. Griffith and my many friends in the organization and with the newspaper men and Washington fans. However the time has come when a change may prove beneficial to all concerned. I'm acting at an early date with the hope if there is an opening in baseball for me I will be free to consider it."[23]

Bucky did have a "pleasant relationship" with the writers, but by the end of 1942 Griffith was getting weary of his laid-back style and the fans had turned on him. Attendance in 1942 was 14th of the 16 major league teams and the fans who did come out took to booing Bucky when they saw him, which wasn't very often. He stayed in the dugout.

A close friend said that wasn't Bucky Harris the coal miner hiding out in the dugout; it was Stanley Harris scion of the nation's capital. "Stanley began thinking too much of self-respect. When he was a younger man, not too long out of the coal mines, he didn't have any inhibitions. When he came up in the world socially and had a few of the rough edges knocked off, his whole demeanor changed. Stanley wanted to be a smooth fellow. The rowdy business of stomping out on the field and making scenes lost its appeal for him."[24]

Chapter 14

Fired in Philly

Bucky Harris lost favor with the fans and even Clark Griffith by the end of 1942. The fans wanted him to confront umpires more often. Officially, Bucky resigned, but that was likely by mutual agreement with Griffith after their long talk. Griffith wasn't likely to re-sign him in any case. Griffith argued with him over his lack of fire and his refusal to leave the dugout. But around the leagues, baseball people defended Bucky. Shirley Povich talked to some of them during the World Series. One A.L. manager said, "Only one man could have done better than Harris with Washington last season, Houdini. Harris kept Washington eight games out of the cellar and ahead of the A's with a team that was worse than the A's."

Yankee manager Joe McCarthy said, "What did they expect from Harris at Washington anyway? Do they want him to tear out of the dugout and make a scene over a decision at first base when his team is behind 10–1 in the ninth? That grandstand stuff don't go."

Povich said Bucky was handicapped by a lack of talent, writing, "The Washington farm system was the cross Harris bare."[1]

There was truth to it all. Bucky was a mellow fellow and getting more so as he aged. The Washington talent pool was weak. And baseball owners and GMs still thought Bucky was a capable manager. Teams liked managers with experience, and rumors surfaced quickly as to where Bucky was headed. For the first time, N.L. teams were in the mix. The Dodgers and Cubs were considering having talks with Bucky.

On October 11 Griffith signed Ossie Bluege to succeed Bucky. Bluege, 42, had last played in 1939. In 1940 he was on the roster as a player but acted as a coach and did not play. In 1941 Griffith offered him a contract as a coach at a reduced salary and he refused. In 1942 he changed his mind and was Bucky's top coach. By hiring Bluege to manage, Griffith stayed true to his pattern of hiring loyal players as managers, but he didn't keep his promise to hire a fire-breather. Bluege was not a flaming personality. He was more like

Bucky and Walter Johnson. He was soft spoken and rarely argued with umpires.

That November, Bucky entertained himself by watching his new favorite team in his new sport, the National Football League's Washington Redskins. He visited the Redskins' locker room after they beat Philadelphia, 30–27, on November 1 to congratulate his friend, Redskins assistant coach Turk Edwards, who called Bucky the team's number-one fan. The following week the Redskins beat the Chicago Bears, 28–0, at Griffith Stadium. Two weeks later Bucky traveled with the team to New York to watch the Redskins beat the Giants. Led by quarterback Sammy Baugh, the Redskins went 10–1 and beat the New York Giants, 13–7, in the NFL championship game in Griffith Stadium in front of 36,006 paid. After the game, thousands of the fans rushed the field, tore down the goal posts, ripped up the sod and even forced their way into the locker room to celebrate with the Redskins.

Redskins owner George Marshall had moved the team to Washington from Boston in 1937 and shared Griffith Stadium with the Senators. Bucky and Marshall, who met in Bucky's early days as a Senator player when Marshall ran a chain of laundries in D.C., were the same age and remained friends for 50 years. They were even roommates for a time. In 1937 Bucky missed out on the investment opportunity of a lifetime. Bucky's son, Judge Stanley Harris, recalls what happened:

> Marshall was a sports nut. He and Dad developed a good relationship, but Marshall was so damned intrusive. I don't know what Dad's salary was. This must have been after he came back from Detroit. Marshall was having trouble. There was no TV, no lights, pro football was not that big. Marshall came to Dad and asked for his help. He said he'd sell Dad a substantial stock in the Redskins for $10,000. Dad liked football but didn't have much faith in Washington as a sports town. He turned it down. He could have been one of the principal stockholders of the Redskins. That was when he invested in some swamp land in Florida.[2]

Bucky told the same story in an interview late in his life, though he put the dollar figure lower. "When George Marshall moved the Redskins from Boston in 1937, he ran short of money. He wanted to borrow $5,000 from me in exchange for stock in the team. I couldn't see it. I didn't think Washington was a good football town. You see how wrong I was."[3]

World War II was on when Bucky resigned from the Senators and that may have been a factor in why he agreed to resign. He was 46 but wanted to serve. He applied for a commission in the Army Specialist Corps. He made the announcement at the District Umpire Association banquet, where he was the honored guest on October 23. He was expected to pass the physical and serve in the Specialist Corps in the Welfare and Recreation Division, most likely in organizing sports activities for the troops. But the corps was disbanded.[4]

The first time Bucky was mentioned as a candidate to manage the floundering Philadelphia Phillies came on February 23, 1943. The 1942 season was the 10th disastrous season for the Phillies under owner George Nugent. In the last five seasons under Nugent, from 1938 to 1942, the Phillies finished last every season and had an overall record of 225–534, a .296 winning percentage. The National League bought Nugent out in a forced sale and then flipped the team to William Cox, a 33-year-old lumber millionaire, for $325,000.

Cox, who played baseball at Yale and was the owner of a race horse and one-time owner of a football team in a failed professional league, signed Bucky on February 25. Cox chose Bucky over Bill Dickey, Pepper Martin and Lefty O'Doul.[5] When he signed with the Phillies, Bucky said he chose them over the Brooklyn Dodgers. The Dodgers, who had won 102 games in 1942 (but not the pennant, as the Cardinals won 106), had a new general manager, Branch Rickey, who was worried about manager Leo Durocher's army draft status and was considering other managers. Durocher was 36 and married but had no dependents and was classified 3-A, eligible, though a long shot, to be drafted. In November, reports surfaced that Durocher applied for a commission with the navy, which Durocher denied. After several negotiations Durocher signed a one-year contract with the Dodgers in November. But in January, Durocher was ordered to take a draft physical in St. Louis. He passed, was reclassified 1-A, and was ordered to report for a final physical. Then on March 1 he was rejected due to "an old ear injury."[6]

Though Rickey never publicly said he was going to sign Bucky, he must have talked to Bucky about coming to the Dodgers between the time Durocher was reclassified 1-A and the time Bucky signed with Cox on February 25. This seems likely because Povich reported the Dodgers had offered Bucky $20,000 and Bucky explained why he chose the Phillies over the Dodgers. Povich called reports that Bucky had signed for $10,000 "way out of line," pointing out that would make him the lowest-paid manager in baseball. Povich claimed Brooklyn's offer was close to $20,000 and speculated Bucky received as much from Cox as he had made at Washington in 1942, $14,750.[7]

"I saw Harris play in 1924," Cox said. "About five years ago I saw him again in an exhibition game in Atlanta. I like the way he handled the players. When I got the Phillies I asked 10 men who should know what they thought of Harris and every one of them rated him A-1. He is a man who can get the most out of any player."

Cox said he received a telegram from Yawkey advising him to sign Bucky. Terms weren't disclosed but Bucky said he hoped it would be for a long time and that he wouldn't have taken it if it wasn't attractive.[8] Why would Bucky chose the moribund Phillies over the Dodgers and for less money? For the same reason the National League sold the team to Cox: the league and Bucky were taken in by Cox's "dynamic personality," to use Bucky's own words.

"It may seem funny taking a job with the Phillies when I had a chance to go to the Dodgers. But there are many circumstances to consider. I found Cox to be a charming fellow whose ideas about building up a ball club are much like my own. I want to make a fresh start with him and the Phils are not in such a bad place to start. The war has sort of equalized things. A tail-end club of last year can be up there next season."[9]

Bucky's first act was to retain Chuck Klein as player-coach. Coach Hans Lobert left to go to the Reds, where he had played in 1906. Bucky went back home to Washington after signing and back to Philadelphia a few days later. Cox met with Mack, billed as a meeting of the oldest, 80, and youngest owners in the league. "My meeting with the grand old gentleman was one of the big moments in my life," Cox said.[10]

Unfortunately, the situation was not as positive for Bucky Harris. The Phillies, unlike nearly every other team, didn't lose any regulars to World War II from 1942 to 1943. Between 1917, when the Phils finished second, and 1943, a span of 27 seasons, they finished higher than .500 once and above seventh place only four times. The previous 10 of those pathetic seasons were under Nugent, who made sloppy deals to get rid of every decent player the Phillies had. In August of 1932, during what would be Chuck Klein's Triple Crown and MVP season, Nugent called the Cubs' offer of $100,000 and Babe Herman for Klein ridiculous. But it was Nugent who wound up being ridiculous. He sold Klein to the Cubs in November for $65,000 and three players who would play a total of 65 games for the Phillies. Nugent got Klein back after his peak for pitcher Curt Davis, who posted double-figure wins for the Cubs for the next four seasons, including a 20-win campaign.

The day he signed Bucky, Cox wagered a carton of cigarettes with a Philadelphia sportswriter that the Phillies would be sixth at the end of the first month of play and would finish the season in sixth place or better.[11] The bet seemed harmless but in retrospect it should have been seen as a red flag. Cox won the first part of the bet. At the end of May the Phillies were in sixth place and only three games under .500. The Phils were so bad that Warren Giles, general manager of the Cincinnati Reds, suggested a special National League rule that no waiver list would be withdrawn until the Phils selected a player.

On March 26 Bucky invited all free agents of organized baseball to report to training camp in Hershey, Pennsylvania, and show what they could do. "We have to keep the players now on the roster if only because of quantity.

I'm pretty confident on their record a lot of them aren't major league players, but under the present conditions I can't be too fussy."

In early March he went to New York on a "talent hunt." He traded Alan Glossop and Lloyd Waner to the Dodgers for Babe Dahlgren, who didn't show up to camp. He was due to report March 10. Cox telephoned San Gabriel, California, but was unable to contact Dahlgren. He finally came in on March 23, almost two weeks late. Bucky signed a rookie pitcher saying he might be the "Dizzy Dean" of the Phils' training camp. He was 24-year-old Bill Webb of Atlanta, Georgia, who pitched for Mobile of the Southeastern League. He pitched one inning in 1943, which constituted his entire major league career.

Somehow Cox got the idea the Phillies needed "commando training" to make them winners. He hired a guy named Harold Anson Bruce, an internationally known track and field coach, as trainer. Commando training consisted of exercises for runners and jumpers, including such routines as the "pinwheel thrust" and the "gorilla hedgehop."[12]

"I know nothing about baseball," Bruce said, "but I do know that most of the players are not in top physical condition. You can see they're slow and sloggy and overweight. I will guarantee that the Phillies will be the best-conditioned club in baseball. Whether they have the playing talent to match the others, I don't know. But if the issue may be decided on physical condition, then the Phillies will win." He might have added, "or at least they won't be breathing hard after they lose." The conditioning was said to be a combination of the American, Swedish, German and other systems of calisthenics, some of which dated to Egyptian days. An important part of the physical program was running. "Some of these men never have run a sustained mile in their lives. I'm working them up gradually, but before we are through I will have them ready to run three miles."[13]

Cox and Harris were on the telephone morning, noon and night trying to make trades, but they were hamstrung by a deal Nugent had made before he was bought out. He had traded first baseman Nick Etten, probably the Phillies' best player, to the Yankees for Allen Gettel and Ed Levy, who refused to report to the Phils. The Phillies wanted Etten back. Commissioner Landis ruled he had to stay with the Yankees and the Yankees would have to send other players to the Phillies, who turned out to be Al Gerheauser, who went 10–19 in 1943, and a catcher named Tom Padden, who got in 17 games. Meanwhile in 1944, Etten led the A.L. in home runs. In 1945 he led in RBIs.[14] Gettel stayed in the minor leagues until 1944. Levy sat out 1943, and both played for the Yankees in 1944.

When two outfielders hit .071 and .196 in the spring, a scribe writing about retiring players wrote, "Some others must have been retired and didn't know it." A typical lineup for 1943 turned out to be: Mickey Livingston, c; Jim Wasdell, 1b; Danny Murtaugh, 2b; Pinky May, 3b; Glen Stewart, ss; and Coaker Triplett, Buster Adams and Ron Northey in the outfield. Babe Dahlgren played more games than any of those players, splitting time at first base, third base and shortstop.

On July 27 the Phillies were in St. Louis, where they lost a doubleheader, the Cardinals' 10th and 11th consecutive wins. Bucky opened the newspaper the next day and learned, the same way sports fans all over the country did, that he had been fired and replaced by Fat Freddie Fitzsimmons.

"This is the most shocking thing that has happened to me in my entire life," he said. Three things made it all the more shocking. One, the Phillies, at 38–52, had already won only three fewer games than they had in all of 1942. And two, the board of directors made the announcement. Bucky was on the board, and at the board's previous meeting, Bucky had asked Cox to leave the room and then talked the other members into giving Cox a raise. Cox said it was a mistake that Bucky learned of the firing in the papers, but didn't know how it leaked out. It was shocking also because Bucky, as with everywhere he managed, was loved by the fans, scribes and ballplayers in Philadelphia. Shortly after Bob Montgomery of Philadelphia won the lightweight boxing championship, he was asked who he thought was then the most popular man in his hometown. His answer was Bucky Harris.

"Clubhouse friction" was reported in all the stories as the main reason behind the firing. To the extent it was true, it was caused by Cox, not Bucky. Cox was always in the clubhouse after games wanting to talk to players. Bucky reportedly suggested diplomatically that it would be better if Cox sent for the players he wanted to talk to rather than visiting the clubhouse.[15] This didn't sit well with Cox. Cox also insisted on taking infield with the team, so Bucky hit the fungoes as hard as he could at him. This may have been as much the reason for the firing as anything.[16] The players rebelled at the firing and voted to go on strike if Bucky were not rehired, if only to be given the dignity of being able to resign. Bucky went into the dugout the next day and talked the players out of striking, saying they were professionals and to go out and play. So Bucky was out, the only time he was ever fired during a season.

Afterward Bucky said he had worked for "the lowest terms I have ever had" and that he had been promised a share in the profits. There may have been a profit, too, as the Phillies set an attendance record that year, and 51 of their 77 home games had already been played by July 28. The Phillies played .424 ball under Bucky and .404 under Fat Freddy, finishing seventh and preserving Bucky's record of never having managed a last-place team.

Cox made an apology of sorts. "We regret the manner in which Mr. Harris was informed of his dismissal. It was certainly not intended to happen that way. We wish to emphasize that he was to be given the opportunity of resigning if he wished to do so."

Then Cox took his shots. In an eight-page statement read to reporters at his hotel room, Cox said he fired Bucky because he couldn't get the team out of the second division and allegedly for saying nothing could be done because "the Phillies are a seventh-place club" and that "he had no intention of running a school for ballplayers." He said Bucky called the players "those jerks" at a board meeting on July 12. Cox said, "Harris stated that if the owners of the club did not have confidence in him they should get a new manager and that was quite all right with him. It had happened to him before and he could get along in baseball."[17]

Bucky reacted to the eight-page statement.

> It has taken Cox three days to get together a complete set of lies for his own defense. It is amazing how one person could figure out so many lies. If I said any of those things I would be the first to admit them. The only accusation by Cox that has a semblance of truth is the one about the Phillies being a seventh-place club. If there is a jerk connected with the club it is Cox, and he is an all-American jerk.
>
> I hope that the controversy will be brought to a close. I have no control over any statements Cox may make but I do not wish to prolong the incident of my release. For the good of the Philadelphia team and in the interests of baseball, I desire to make no further comment."[18]

In New York Cox got in the last shot. "Harris was looking in the mirror when he said 'he is an all–American jerk.'"

In November, Landis ordered Cox to a meeting to defend himself against allegations he bet on Phillies games in 1943. Cox called the allegations ridiculous and denied them, but when he failed to appear for the hearing Landis banned him from baseball for life. A few days later Cox admitted he had bet $25–$100 on about 20 Phillies games in April and May and then stopped when he learned it was against the rules. In a radio interview he said, "I made some small and sentimental bets before I learned of the rule against it. I leave it to the public and my friends to decide whether I was wrong."[19]

Chapter 15
Shuffle Off to Buffalo

Bucky went home for a few days after he was fired. On August 12 he was back in Philadelphia and one of 11,129 who saw the Phillies win a double-header, beating Pittsburgh, 2–1 and 2–0, to move into fifth place. He openly rooted for the Phillies and Fitzsimmons. He dismissed a rumor that he would manage the Atlanta Crackers for the rest of 1943.

In October Bucky accepted an offer to manage Buffalo in the International League. If anyone thought going to the minor leagues represented loss of prestige for a 47-year-old man with 20 seasons of major league managerial experience, Bucky wasn't one of them.

He said he didn't mind one bit going to the minors and cited other former major league managers in the minors, such as Gabby Hartnett at Jersey City, Fred Haney at Toledo and Rogers Hornsby in the Texas League.[1]

There was some speculation that taking the Buffalo job was a precursor to a position as an executive with Detroit. The Bisons had a working relationship with the Tigers. Bucky had not burned his bridges in Detroit and the field manager there was Steve O'Neill, the brother of Bucky's old double-play partner, Jimmy O'Neill. The pay was major league in Buffalo, too, estimated to be $15,000 with an attendance bonus of up to $3,000.[2]

The AP said even without the bonus Bucky was the highest-paid manager in the minor leagues. Arch Ward in a *Chicago Daily News* column said Bucky's pay was as much as Bluege got for managing the Senators in 1943. And his contract had one more perk. The club's general manager, John Stiglmeier, said under his contract Bucky could leave immediately if offered a major league job. That loomed as a possibility before Bucky even stepped on the field at Buffalo.[3] A story in the *Washington Post* on December 1 said new Phillies owner and GM Bob Carpenter was talking with Herb Pennock and if he turned down the job, Bucky was next. Carpenter never called.

End-of-the-year columns ranked the Bucky-Phillies story as one of the top sports stories of the year, ranked with Great Lakes beating Notre Dame in football. Povich tabbed the Bucky story number five and the biggest surprise in sports in the year.

In January Branch Rickey said he didn't think the minor leagues would be able to operate in 1944 because of the war.

"In normal years we would have 39 or 40 players under contract and there would be a half-dozen more who would be in our training camp not under contract. We would have 20 players to turn back to the minors.

"But this year the big leagues are desperate. The Giants will have only 27 players under contract and Brooklyn about the same. There will be no surplus for the high minors so I doubt their ability to operate."

Bucky didn't agree. "All leagues, majors as well as minors, face hardships next season and we need men at the top with fight and determination, not the likes of Rickey, who would give up easily."

Bucky said the minors would meet the problem by signing free agents, taking what they can get from the majors, and perhaps bringing back older veterans. "We'll make it somehow and it should be very interesting. Perhaps my Buffalo club is lucky, but we have 32 players on our reserve list. We can operate with as few as 18, Mr. Rickey notwithstanding. He has not suggested the big leagues quit."[4]

Bucky had been in Buffalo during the previous world war as a player in 1918 and 1919. Back as manager in 1944, he did something he hadn't done since 1936: he managed a team to a winning record. The Bisons had a typical wartime roster of older and teenaged players (two were 18 and 13 were 28 and older), including 45-year-old Earl Whitehill, who had pitched for Bucky in Washington. The Bisons went 78–76 and finished in fourth place.

There was speculation the International League ball was juiced in 1944 as the Bisons had a tremendous hitting season. Mayo Smith, a reputed good-field, no-hit center fielder, had the greatest batting year of his 18-season minor league career. He hit .340 and led the league. Smith would play in only 73 major league games, all in 1945 with the A's, but he was later a manager for nine seasons, winning the World Series with the 1968 Tigers.

Edward "Shovels" Kobesky, a coal cracker of Bucky's ilk from Scranton and a 14-season career minor leaguer, hit 26 home runs, had 129 RBIs, and batted .328, all career highs. Versatile Otto Denning, who had played in 129 major league games with the Indians in 1942 and 1943 combined, played first base, catcher and the outfield and hit 21 home runs with 99 RBIs.

The Bisons' top pitchers were Mike Roscoe, who was 16–10, Walter Wilson, 18–14, and Henry "Prince" Oana, a 38-year-old from the island of Oahu in Hawaii. Henry's father was of native Hawaiian descent. His mother was Portuguese. The 6'2", 190-pound right-hander was a high school football, basketball and baseball star and one-time slugging outfielder who led the PCL in extra-base hits in 1933. He converted to a pitcher late in his career. Though dark-skinned, he was not too dark for pre–1947 big league baseball, playing in 30 games over three seasons in the majors, but dark enough to face some bigotry when he played in Atlanta in 1934.[5]

The Bisons lost four games to three to Baltimore in the first round of the IL playoffs, Bucky's first postseason since 1924. Attendance was 198,907, only 10,000 less than the National League's Boston Braves, and was considered a success.[6]

During the playoffs in Baltimore on September 18, Bucky was asked about rumors that once more had him going back to the Phillies. "I haven't signed with the Phillies and nobody has approached me in that connection. Neither have I signed a Buffalo contract for 1945. If and when I do, it will be with the understanding that I be free to accept any major league offer that comes along. I would be very happy to come back to Philadelphia as a manager. I'm receptive."[7] The next day Fitzsimmons was rehired by the Phillies for 1945. On October 5 Bucky re-signed with Buffalo for $15,000, which was about the same as 1944.

When Casey Stengel quit as manager of the Boston Braves, Bucky was considered a candidate for the job. It went to Bob Coleman. Povich said Bucky would have turned it down anyway because he was due to graduate from Buffalo to Detroit.

On February 28 Bucky was named Buffalo's general manager on top of being field manager. Again it was speculated that the move was all part of his grooming for the GM job with the Tigers, where Jack Zeller was sick and wanted to retire. Bucky was missing some action at home. His son, Stanley Jr., was the starting first baseman for Wilson High School in Washington. One of his teammates was Dud DeGroot Jr., son of the Redskins coach. On June 5 young Stanley reached the quarterfinals of the Washington Post Cup School Boy golf championships, where he lost, 5 and 4.[8]

The Bisons dropped to sixth place in the IL with a 64–89 record in 1945. Attendance dropped to 129,436. Of the 35 players in the Bisons camp at Hershey in 1945, 15 were 4Fs and six were discharged veterans. Among the players was Lloyd Brown, 41, who had pitched for Bucky at Washington in the 1920s. He won 12 games in 1945 for the Bisons.

Bucky eventually used 40 players, ranging from teenagers like Art Houtteman, Billy Pierce and Emery Hresko, to veterans like Brown and Ollie Carnegie, who hit .301 and four home runs at age 46, giving him 296 career home runs and 258 as a Bison.

Houtteman and Pierce had long major league careers. Pierce pitched in 18 major league seasons and was a three-time complete-game leader, two-time 20-game winner, and a one-time ERA leader in the A.L. for the White

Sox. He won 211 games. Houtteman had an 87–91 career record in 12 seasons but did win 19 with the Tigers in 1950.

First baseman John McHale batted .313 and hit 22 home runs. He had a brief stay in the majors as a player, but a long stay as an executive in Detroit, Milwaukee/Atlanta and Montreal. He was the expansion Expos first president. In 1946 Bucky remained the Bisons GM but stepped down as field manager in favor of Gabby Hartnett. The Bisons went 78–75 and finished fifth. Attendance more than doubled to 293,813, the highest it had been in 43 years. The end of the war had a lot to do with the attendance spike, but so did the Montreal team, which sold out nearly every game thanks to an infielder named Jackie Robinson, who led the league in batting at .349, stole 40 bases, and scored 155 runs in just 122 games. He led the Royals to a 100-win season and the pennant in a runaway, by 18½ games.[9]

A notable for the Bisons was right fielder Vic Wertz, who hit .301 with 19 home runs and 91 RBIs. He would spend 17 seasons in the American League with five different teams, batting .277 with 266 home runs. The IL season ended on September 8. Two days later the speculation about Bucky going to a major league team front office proved true. On September 10 Bucky was hired, not by the Tigers, but by the New York Yankees.

Chapter 16

Yankee Doodle Bucky

Bucky wasted no time joining the Yankees. Yankees president Larry MacPhail announced Bucky was being hired on September 10, 1946, and on September 12 Bucky reported to the team in Detroit. Del Webb, Dan Topping and MacPhail had purchased the Yankees from the Ruppert family in 1945 for $2.8 million. Webb and Topping loaned MacPhail $900,000 to buy about 10 percent and named him president because he was a baseball man. He had been president of the Cincinnati Reds and Brooklyn Dodgers.[1]

MacPhail stressed unequivocally Bucky would not be the team's manager. "Bucky is joining us strictly in an administrative capacity," MacPhail said. "He is not considered for any kind of job on the field."[2]

On September 13 Bucky said he was surprised to be hired and was in full agreement with what MacPhail said. "I have worn that uniform long enough and I don't intend to put it on again. I accepted only an executive job and I don't intend to go back on the field. Exactly what my duties will be, I am not sure yet."

MacPhail wasn't exactly sure either. He didn't even have a title for the job. One facet of it was to scout players, a job MacPhail said he and VP George Weiss were too busy to do. MacPhail also said Bucky would be "a contact man between the front office and our players."

Given Bucky's reputation as a players' manager, the description of Bucky as a go-between from the players to the front office made some sense. But no other major league team had a position quite like it. As Povich put it:

It sounds as if Larry MacPhail invented a job for Bucky Harris. Thus the Yankees add another echelon in what is already the most involved set up in the big leagues.

At the top is MacPhail who is president of the club, and standing at his back are two men who produced the money to buy the Yankees, Del Webb and Dan Topping. Hovering up front, too, is George Weiss, with the official title of vice-president in charge of the Yankees' farm system, and until Harris came along, Manager Bill Dickey was next in command.

Harris fits in apparently as a buffer between Dickey's playing hands and

MacPhail. The latter's sanctum seemingly is now off limits to players who have a grievance. No other club president ever needed a contact man, but then there is no other club president named Larry MacPhail.

Before MacPhail hired Harris he called Clark Griffith for a personal recommendation and heard this: "Harris can work for me anytime. You're getting one of the finest men in baseball."

The Bucky-to-Detroit theory did not die. "With the Yankees, Harris may merely be sitting out for a couple of years until he moves on to Detroit as GM. Walter Spike Briggs, who will come into control when his father retires, is smitten with Harris' talent for running a ball club. More likely, Spike was smitten with Bucky the man. Spike remembered Bucky from his days as Detroit manager and held him in high esteem."[3]

Dickey took over as manager of the Yankees in May of 1946, after Joe McCarthy stunned the baseball world by abruptly resigning. McCarthy had managed the team since 1931 and for a record 1,460 games. His seven World Series titles were a record at the time. The official version of the resignation was that McCarthy had resigned on his own out of the blue. He made the announcement by wire from his farm near Buffalo. From the telegram: "My doctor advises that my health would be jeopardized if I continue. This is the sole reason for my decision which, as you know, is entirely voluntary on my part."

MacPhail wired back, "As you know I have been extremely reluctant to accept your resignation, even though I understood the reason why you feel you should not continue."[4]

The truth was McCarthy didn't get along with MacPhail. As Arthur Daley put it in his column in the *New York Times*, "Marse Joe is an ultraconservative man who hates change, emotionalism, gloss or glitter. Larry is a radical who relishes change, flash, color, excitement and argument. Temperamentally they were as far apart as the poles."

Daley said the exchange of telegrams was a charade. "Denials will be formally made that the split was anything but amicable."

Writing in *The Sporting News*, Dan Daniel pulled no punches. "There is no doubt in my mind he was asked to quit."[5]

It was right after a confrontation with pitcher Joe Page that McCarthy resigned. McCarthy didn't like Page, a noted partier. He berated him on a plane from Cleveland to Detroit in front of the team and reporters for breaking curfew and threatened to send him back to Newark. A public outbreak was out of character for McCarthy, and it was rumored McCarthy was drinking heavily. If that was the case, he was no different than anyone else among the Yankee brass. Two years later McCarthy was back managing in Boston.

Dickey, 39, the back-up catcher who played in 50 games in 1946, replaced

McCarthy. On September 10, the day Bucky was hired, the Yankees were 16 games behind the Red Sox. Dickey, saying he found MacPhail "a bit difficult to get along with on three or four occasions," said he would not return in 1947 citing "personal reasons."

Less than 24 hours later Bucky had his first assignment with the Yankees. He announced that Dickey was out immediately and would be replaced by coach Johnny Neun for the last 14 games of the season.[6]

MacPhail stuck to the story that Bucky would not replace Neun for the 1947 season and Bucky stuck to his line that he wanted to stay in the job he had, whatever that was. Bucky did allow he might change his mind for a "sufficiently handsome offer." Leo Durocher was under consideration, but as he was getting $70,000 from the Dodgers, it was believed he would stay there. Durocher said he had not been approached by the Yankees. Money was not the reason the Yankees didn't want Durocher. "The Lip" came with a lot of baggage, such as past associations with gamblers and mafia types, and he wasn't regarded as being up to Yankee standards.[7]

On October 27 it looked for all the world like Chuck Dressen would get the job. He had a two-year contract with the Dodgers but signed a contract with the Yankees. Only a day earlier Dodger president Branch Rickey said he would not release Dressen from his two-year deal as Dodger coach unless he was hired to manage another major league team. MacPhail insisted Dressen had signed "nothing more than a contract making him an employee of the Yankees."[8]

Finally on November 6 the news came down. Bucky Harris, two days shy of his 50th birthday, was the man for the Yankees. "It cannot be said Impresario Larry MacPhail failed to extract all the dramatics the situation had to offer," wrote one scribe. Bucky signed a two-year contract for $35,000 per year. Dressen was named his top assistant at $15,000.[9]

In his column Daley cheered the selection of Bucky. "The baseball writers will applaud his selection because Bucky is a blunt, outspoken fellow who never equivocates or hides behind the moth-eaten excuse, I was misquoted. Nor will he take any nonsense from MacPhail."

To illustrate this Daley told a story from when Bucky was with the Phillies in 1943. Scribe John Kieran reported that he called the A's "a bunch of swell headed stiffs." Asked if he was quoted correctly, Bucky said, "You don't think John Kieran is the sort of fellow who makes up stories, do you? Of course I said it."

Two weeks after he signed Bucky, MacPhail said Durocher had indeed approached Dan Topping about the Yankee job and that Bucky had recommended Durocher for the position after scouting the Dodgers in September. MacPhail admitted Bucky had agreed to take the Yankees job on October 23, but the announcement was held up for 12 days as a personal favor to Durocher, who was about to open negotiations with Rickey.

Under pressure to make money so he could pay Webb and Topping, MacPhail installed the best and most expensive lighting system in major league baseball, strengthened the team by loading the minor league system, and chartered airplanes for the team to travel. In 1946 the Yankees became the first team to top two million in attendance.

But the players did not like MacPhail. He was obsessive about the image of the Yankees. He fined Joe DiMaggio $100 for refusing to pose for a special promotional newsreel, the first and only time DiMaggio was ever fined by the team. He fined Johnny Lindell $50 for telling young players they didn't have to attend every banquet arranged by the Yankee publicity department. When players refused to fly, MacPhail told them they'd have to pay for their own train transportation.

MacPhail flew into a rage at Phil Rizzuto and George Stirnweiss. He called them "bastards" for meeting with Jorge Pasquel, who was working outside the frame of organized baseball by scouting talent for his Mexican League and offering generous contracts.

MacPhail took advantage of eased travel restrictions after the war and took the Yankees on spring trips through the Caribbean and Latin America, hoping to make a killing. He saved money by bunking players at army bases. Some of the older players later complained, saying the trip in 1946 had been the reason for their mid-season slumps. DiMaggio was one of the biggest complainers, but MacPhail wouldn't relent, as the 1946 trip made the team a lot of money.

The 1947 trip was even longer.[10] MacPhail took the Yankees to San Juan, Puerto Rico, Caracas, Venezuela, and Havana, Cuba. The San Juan leg was underwritten by Serralles Brothers, distillers of Don Q Rum. The Yankees stayed in the Hotel Normandie. It was built like a model of the French Liner. Don Q sent a case of rum to every players' room. That was a bit much, even by Bucky's lax training standards. He had the rum confiscated.

The Yankees played a series of games, some of them against American blacks at Sixto Escobar Parque in San Juan. When the Yankees lost one to a local team, Ponce, people embraced and jumped up and down, crowds paraded in the streets, bands sprang up out of nowhere. Don Q arranged a trip to St. Thomas in the Virgin Islands. Bucky refused to let the Yankees go, wanting them to get in shape for upcoming games against Puerto Rican teams. Charlie Dressen and the writers made the trip as tourists.[11]

The Dodgers flew to Havana for three games against the Yankees. Memphis Engelberg, a horse player of repute and a friend to MacPhail, was in the same box as Dressen and Durocher, adjacent to the box MacPhail was in.

When Commissioner Happy Chandler found out, he suspended Durocher indefinitely and Dressen for 30 days and fined MacPhail $2,000. Chandler had warned Durocher before about his associations. Back in the States at a dinner in Newark, MacPhail was quoted as saying Chandler didn't have enough evidence to suspend Durocher for two minutes, let alone for the season. That was the beginning of an ever-widening rift between MacPhail and Chandler and between MacPhail and Durocher, who wasn't buying MacPhail's defense of him. He believed MacPhail set him up.

April 27 was Babe Ruth Day, not just in Yankee Stadium, where 58,000 came out to see the Babe in the flesh, but all over the major leagues. The ceremony and speeches were piped into all the other baseball parks around the country that day. The Babe, who had throat cancer, appeared shrunken and weak, wearing a camel's hair polo coat and matching cap and talking in a low rasp. The players hung from the dugout like apes, mouths agape in the great one's presence. The Yankees could have used a bit of the Babe in uniform that day. They were shut out by the Senators to drop to 7–5 on the season.

Though the 1947 Yankees had a lot of proven players, they had problems, too. Tommy Henrich was 37 and coming off a .251 season. DiMaggio had two surgeries on his left heel. Red Ruffing was gone. Spud Chandler (20–8 in 1946) was 37.

Bucky was worried about shortstop Phil Rizzutto, whose best seasons were behind him. In 1946 second baseman Joe Gordon, third baseman Stuffy Stirnweiss, Joe DiMaggio and Phil Rizzutto all had the least productive batting seasons of their careers to that point. DiMaggio missed 22 games, the fewest of the four.

In 1947 the four had better batting seasons, but Bucky, in conjunction with MacPhail, made some moves that paid off. They gave up on Nick Etten. Etten had served the Yankees well in the war years at first base, leading the A.L. in home runs in 1944 and RBIs in 1945. In 1946, at age 34, he was overmatched. They sold him to the Phillies in April where he got in only 14 games, the last of his career. MacPhail said he would spend up to $150,000 for a first baseman, but Bucky went with one they had acquired in January for free. Bucky decided to give George McQuinn, who turned 38 in May of 1947 and had been released by Mack after the 1946 season, a shot at first. McQuinn had averaged around .290, double-figure home runs and 80 RBIs in eight seasons with the Browns before spending a season with the A's. Bucky always liked his fielding and saw him as a clutch hitter.[12] There were two other major changes in the starting lineup in 1947. Left fielder Charlie Keller, who had led the team with 30 home runs in 1946, injured his back on June 5. He was only 31 but his career was effectively over. He played in only one more game in 1947 and hung around as a backup for three more seasons. Bucky moved

Stirnweiss to second base to replace Joe Gordon, who was traded to the Indians for pitcher Allie Reynolds, and put Billy Johnson at third. All the moves worked. McQuinn hit .304 with 80 RBIs, Johnson hit .285 with 90 RBIs and Lindell hit .275 with 67 RBIs. DiMaggio boosted his average 25 points and had 97 RBIs, Rizzutto put 20 points on his average, Allie Reynolds won 19 games, the Yankees won the pennant, and Bucky was a genius.

But if he was a genius, it wasn't because of what he did with the lineup or Allie Reynolds; it was because of what he did with Joe Page. In April, Page was regarded, at best, as the Yankees' fourth or fifth starter. On April 19 he started the Yankees' fourth game of the season and didn't get out of the fifth inning. He faced 20 batters, eight of them reached base and four scored. He was responsible for all four runs in a 4–2 loss in, of all places, Washington. Bucky didn't use Page again for 11 days. On April 30 Bucky called his number in the fifth inning in St. Louis. He faced four batters and walked them all. They all scored and the Yankees lost, 15–5. Page's ERA was 14.40.

After that debacle, Bucky didn't know what to do with Page. He used him three times to mop up losses in the first three weeks of May, but by the end of the month he was considering sending him back to Newark.

Then came the inning that changed the Yankees' season, Joe Page's career, Bucky's legacy and, according to author Bill James, the history of baseball. Appropriately, it happened before a single-game record crowd.

On Memorial Day, 74,747 paid the see the Red Sox–Yankees game in the Stadium. In the third inning Yankee starter Specs Shea, already trailing the Red Sox, 3–1, got in trouble with runners on second and third with no outs. Bucky brought in Page for a last chance. Page didn't know it, but Bucky decided that if Page got bombed, he was going to ship him back to Newark. Page got Ted Williams to bounce to first, but McQuinn made an error to load the bases. Page got behind York, 3–0. In the dugout Bucky said to no one in particular, "If he throws ball four he goes to Newark now."

York swung and missed the next three fastballs. Page fell behind Bobby Doerr, 3–1. Then he struck out Doerr on two tailing fastballs. He got the third out on a fly out.

Page pitched the rest of the game, held the Sox to two singles and struck out eight in seven innings, and the Yankees won, 9–3. DiMaggio had three hits, including a three-run home run.[13]

Beginning that day in May 1947, Bucky, as he had with Marberry 23 years earlier, converted Page into a dedicated relief pitcher who became a dominating closer. From 1944 to 1946 combined, Page appeared in 70 games, 42 as a starter, and did not record a save. Under Bucky in 1947, he won 14, led in saves with 17, was second in games with 55, struck out 117 in 141 innings, and had a 2.48 ERA. In 1948 he led in games, 56, and was second in saves.

He appeared in 111 games combined in the two seasons, the most in baseball. He led in games finished in both seasons and started only three games. Casey Stengel inherited Page when Bucky was fired after the 1948 season and in 1949 Page led the A.L. in games, 60, and saves, 27. Page's success led to widespread use of the closer concept.

In 1949 Page led the A.L. in games, 60, and saves, 27. From 1949 to 1952 the closer concept exploded. In 1946 no pitcher pitched 50 games in relief. Ten years later 20 did and five of those topped 60. James, in his book *Bill James Guide to Baseball Managers*, argues the modern-day use of closers began with Bucky's use of Joe Page in 1947.[14]

Page had something going for him in Bucky's mind other than his fastball. Page was a Pennsylvania coal miner. He grew up in the soft coal region in the southwestern part of the state where his father was a locally well-known spitball pitcher. Joe worked on and off in the mines in a variety of jobs, including electrician, loader and coupler until 1943.

At 22 he was hit by a car and had to have an operation to graft bone to his left shin to avert amputation. The injury didn't seem to hurt his pitching, but it kept him out of the army.

He made a fast rise through the minors, starting from Class D Butler in the Pennsylvania State Association, where he was 11–3 in 1940; to Augusta in the Sally, where he was 12–12; to Newark, where he was 7–6 in 1943 and 14–5 in 1944 as a starter. He spent only six years in the majors, from 1944 to 1949. He finished his career with Escogido of the Dominican League, retiring in 1956 at age 35.

From 1947 to 1949 he was the highest-paid relief pitcher in baseball. Though it's not known what his salary was, one story suggests that Bucky earned Page an extra $20,000 in 1947.

Page initially turned down the Yankees' contract offer for 1947 when MacPhail did not offer a raise. MacPhail said, "If you sign this contract, on the first and fifteenth of each month, I'll ask Bucky and if he says 'Page is my boy,' I'll hand you $2,500 in $100 bills."

Eight times out of 11 paydays Bucky said, "He's my boy." MacPhail paid out $20,000 to Page.[15]

John Lardner, a sports columnist and brother of Ring Lardner, once said of Page: "Joe had a lot of stuff. He drank a lot of stuff. He was a switch drinker. He could lift a glass with either hand."

Bucky was known to lift a glass or two himself. In 1947 and 1948 he would greet writers after games by lifting a glass of whiskey over his head and saying, "Gentlemen, Joe Page."

For a time Page was a roommate and buddy to Joe DiMaggio, but when he came back to the room too late and too drunk time after time, DiMaggio insisted on a different roommate. Bucky believed Page didn't really grasp just how hot his fastball was and that he lacked confidence. Bucky went to DiMaggio and asked him to boost Page's self-esteem, saying, "Tell him he scares hitters to death."[16]

That 9–3 win over the Red Sox when Page emerged as a relief pitcher was the fourth game of a four-game series. The Yankees won the first three games, the third one, 17–2, and outscored the Sox 40–5 in the four games.

The Yankees went into the series in sixth place and emerged in second, three games behind Detroit. On June 20 in the midst of a four-game sweep of the Tigers in New York, the Yankees moved into first place to stay.

On September 15 the Yankees were playing the Browns in New York. The game lasted four batters before it was washed out by a sudden rainstorm. Once the game was postponed, the Yankees hung around the clubhouse waiting. Bucky sat in his office with the door open. MacPhail burst in with the news. The Red Sox had lost the first game of their double-header. The Yankees had a 13-game lead with 11 to play. They were champions of the American League. Writers, broadcasters, team personnel, anyone else with access poured in after MacPhail to "extend their felicitations to the popular 50-year-old manager who only a year ago hadn't the faintest idea he would ever manage a major league team again." MacPhail was put in front of a radio microphone. "This is a big moment for me, but all I can say is it couldn't have happened to a nicer guy, meaning Bucky Harris, and here he is."

Bucky quickly passed on the credit. "All the credit belongs to this wonderful bunch of kids who won the pennant for me."

Asked how the pennant compared to the two he had won as "the Boy Wonder," he said, "That was so long ago I can't remember. But after 22 years it's a great feeling to lead another winner."

Yankee secretary Arthur Patterson brought out a huge silver cup the Yankees had won in a spring exhibition series in Venezuela. It was filled with champagne. "Beat the Dodgers in the series and I'll buy a bigger cup," MacPhail shouted over the din.[17] The Dodgers had an 8½-game lead in the National League. They clinched on September 22 when the Cubs beat the Cardinals.

Bucky pulled a mild surprise in the first World Series game on September 30 in Yankee Stadium, starting rookie Specs Shea over Allie Reynolds. Both were right-handers. Shea had a fine season, going 14–5 in 23 starts, but Reynolds was 19–8 with 17 complete games in 32 starts and was considered the staff ace. Bucky didn't think Reynolds had the toughness to take the pressure. The Yankees won, 5–3, scoring all five runs in the fifth on three hits, three walks and a hit batsman. Lindell had a two-run double. Shea gave up a run in the first, then faced only one over the minimum in the second through the

Bucky, as manager of the Yankees, meets Brooklyn manager Burt Shotton before the 1947 World series.

fifth. But Bucky pulled him for Page to start the sixth. Page gave up single runs in the sixth and seventh, then shut down the Dodgers in the eighth and ninth.

Reynolds started the second game, and if there was anything to Bucky's concern that Reynolds didn't pitch well under pressure, the Yankee batters eviscerated that factor, scoring 10 runs in an easy 10–3 win.

Before Game 3, the Dodger band played "For He's a Jolly Good Fellow" for Leo Durocher and his actress bride, Laraine Day, who were in a box near the Dodger dugout. He shook the band leader's hand and she blushed.[18]

In Ebbets Field for Game 3 — before a crowd of 33,000, less than half what the first two games averaged — the Dodgers made it 2 games to 1 with a 9–8 win. Brooklyn scored six in the third. The Dodgers' version of Joe Page, Hugh Casey, pitched one-hit ball over the last 2⅔ innings.

In the bottom of the ninth in Game 4, Bucky made a decision that is infamous in World Series annals to this day. With a 2–1 lead he put the potential winning run on base with an intentional walk; the potential was realized. The run scored and the Dodgers won, 3–2.

The circumstances were strange indeed in that ninth inning. Yankee starter Floyd Bevens, who was 7–13 during the season with an ERA of 3.89, entered the ninth with an unlikely no-hitter, leading, 2–1. The Dodgers scored their run in the fifth on two of Bevens' eventual 10 walks, a sacrifice bunt and fielder's choice. With one out in the ninth, Bevens walked Carl Furillo. Jorgensen fouled out for the second out. Brooklyn manager Burt Shotton sent Pete Reiser out to pinch hit for Casey. Reiser would have been starting in the outfield had he not sprained his ankle sliding in Game 3. After the game the Dodgers' team doctor said, "He will play only by some miracle tomorrow."[19]

The ankle injury must have been bad, as Reiser would make only one other appearance in the Series, also as a pinch-hitter. While Bucky took a lot of heat for walking Reiser, only the fourth ball was intentional. The count was 2-and-1 when Gionfriddo, pinch-running for Furillo, stole second on ball three. Then Bucky ordered the fourth ball to Reiser, a left-handed batter, with righty Eddie Stanky coming up. Eddie Miksis ran for Reiser. Lavagetto, also a righty, batted for Stanky and on the second pitch, Bevens' 137th of the game, Lavagetto doubled off the right-field wall and the Dodgers evened the Series. It was Lavagetto's only hit in seven at-bats in the Series. Bevens pitched 2⅔ innings in the seventh game, the last of his major league career.

Hundreds of fans, a half-dozen ushers and three cops ran after Lavagetto as he sprinted for the dugout after the winning runs scored. Soda vendors threw their white hats in the air. Fans lingered in the right-field corner, worshiping the spot on the wall where Lavagetto's line drive hit.[20]

Bucky defended himself. He reasoned that with a three-ball count, if Bevans tried to come in with a pitch to Reiser, he might have done what Lavagetto would do. And Bucky wasn't sure of the full extent of Reiser's injury. "I ordered him put on, yes, and I'd do the same thing tomorrow."[21] He did do the same thing "tomorrow." In Game 5 he walked Reiser in the ninth to load the bases and Shea struck out Reese to end the game.

Back at the Stadium the Yankees won the fifth game, 2–1. Shea pitched a four-hitter with seven strikeouts and drove in one of the runs with a single. DiMaggio hit a home run for the winning run. The next day the Dodgers forced a seventh game by winning, 8–6, in the contest legendary for Gionfriddo's catch of DiMaggio's home run bid. The Dodgers led, 8–5, going into the bottom of the sixth inning when Gionfriddo was brought in as a fielding replacement. Snuffy Stirnweiss and Yogi Berra were on base when DiMaggio drove the ball to the 415-foot marker on the visitors' bullpen. Gionfriddo ran at least 90 feet, only once turning back to find the ball. No more than two feet from the bullpen he did a half turn, leaped and grabbed the ball in his web as he fell into the bullpen gate. The Dodgers in the bullpen said the ball would have carried over the gate and tied the game. In one of the most famous images in baseball history, the usually emotionless DiMaggio shook his head and kicked at the dirt in frustration as he rounded second.

Bucky came back with Shea on one day of rest to start Game 7, but pulled him with one out in the second after he gave up three consecutive hits — a triple and two singles. Bucky brought in Bevens, who gave up a double before getting out of the inning, but the Dodgers led, 2–0.

In the bottom of the fourth, while the Yankees scored twice to take a 3–2 lead, Bucky ordered Reynolds and Page to warm up. After the third out, as the Yankees took the field for the top of the fifth, Bucky told his coach, Frankie Crosetti, to call the bullpen. John Schulte, the bullpen catcher, said Reynolds was throwing fast and with control. Back-up catcher Ralph Houk, the same Ralph Houk who would manage the Yankees for 11 seasons in the 1960s and 1970s, said he could catch Page bare-handed. Ignoring the assessments, Bucky called for Page. Page stopped the Dodgers cold, retiring 13 consecutive batters and facing the minimum 15 through five. The Dodgers' Eddie Miksis got a single with one out in the ninth, but then Bruce Evans bounded into a double play to end the game. The Yankees won, 5–2, and were world champions. The official scorer gave Page the win, though he came in with a one-run lead.

The net receipts were $2,021,348, making the 1947 Series the first $2,000,000 World Series. Attendance was a record 389,763. For all that, the winners' shares were only $5,830. Bucky had received more in 1924. The Dodgers' shares were $4,081.

There were some firsts. Bucky became the first manager to win a World Series with two teams. The Series was the first with a black player and the first one televised, though only in New York, Philadelphia and Washington, D.C.

In the clubhouse, Bucky's hand shook as he raised a glass for a toast. "Gentlemen, Joe Page. What a way to win. That man Page. What a pitcher when the chips are down. He was great. If that wasn't the greatest World Series, it will do until a better one comes along. Whew! I'm glad it's over and proud of my club."[22]

Chapter 17

Fired Before Hired

A footnote to the 1947 season and World Series was the relationship Bucky developed with a 21-year-old rookie and D-Day veteran named Lawrence Berra. After the war, but before he was discharged, Yogi played for a navy team and stroked several hits in a game against the Giants. He was property of the Yankees at the time, and Mel Ott, the Giant manager, tried to buy him from MacPhail for $50,000. On leave, Yogi showed up at the Yankee office in his navy uniform. MacPhail wasn't impressed. "Here was a funny looking guy in a sailor suit. He had a homely face, no neck and the build of a sawed-off weight lifter. My first thought was, do I turn down $50,000 for this?"[1]

Because of his body type, the Yankees made him a catcher. They were going to need one. Dickey was about to retire. They sent Yogi to Newark, where he batted .314 and hit 15 homers in 77 games. He was a September callup at end of 1946 and played in seven games.

Spring training in St. Petersburg in 1947 was not the first time Bucky encountered Yogi and he was happy to have him on his side. "Harris knew I could swing the bat," Yogi said. "He remembered me from the International league in '46 when he managed Buffalo."

Bucky agreed. "If I had a gun I'd have shot the little pest a hundred times. Every game we played against Newark he murdered us."[2]

Berra was the Yankees' hottest hitter in the spring of 1947 with a 14-game hitting streak. Yogi was a scribe's dream and they had a ball writing and talking about him. They focused on his comical demeanor and malapropisms more than his long home runs. Yogi quickly became a caricature regarded as an unintelligent, but lovable, oaf. He forced himself to laugh along, taking jokes such as he was the only catcher in league who became better looking with his mask on. Even umpires joined in the fun.

Bucky was happy with the distractions caused by Yogi in spring training. His presence overshadowed the Yankees' problems with age, injuries and pitching. Yogi's batting style was odd but effective. He swung at anything he could reach. His low center of gravity was an anchor. With long arms and good hand-eye coordination he put balls in play. He never struck out more than 38 times in a season and only 414 times in his 20-year career. Bucky built Yogi up as a hitter, making a prediction that would prove to be accurate, but he also played along with the gibes.

> Don't think he's a dope. Try to remember he hasn't had much schooling and is at a disadvantage in conversation. Just don't sell him short when he's up there at the plate. He's going to kill a few people with his bat and they won't think he's funny at all. I'll make a prediction about Yogi. I'll say within a few years he'll be the most popular player on the Yankees since Babe Ruth. People are going to feel sorry for him when he makes a mistake and go wild when he does the right thing and wins a ball game. Henrich, Rizzuto and DiMaggio have a lot of fans who admire them, they are great ballplayers. But I mean more than that. People are going to love this little guy because he's such a character. He's funny to look at and sometimes he makes ridiculous plays. But he's got personality and color. That's crowd appeal and it makes people pay their way into the ballpark.[3]

Yogi appreciated the support. "He was always trying to build up my confidence and morale because it had gone down the year before. He built me up to writers probably because he didn't want their gibes to affect my confidence, but even Bucky called me 'The Ape.' After batting practice he'd say, 'Did you see that Ape hit the ball today?'"[4]

With DiMaggio and Lindell hurt, Berra started the season in right field. Though Bucky invited Joe "Ducky" Medwick to camp to coach Yogi on outfielding, Bucky didn't think he had the grace to play in the garden, saying, "We'll make a catcher out of him if it kills us."[5]

As the season progressed, Yogi was receiving a lot of criticism for his fielding and catching and poor hitting against lefties. DiMaggio supposedly dressed him down for asking not to catch the second game of a double-header. Bucky asked players and reporters privately to take it easy on him. "He can be a great ballplayer. He won't be if his spirit is broken by criticism. He's very young and has a lot to learn. In a few years he'll be the biggest player in the game, the closest thing to Babe Ruth. But only if you fellows help the public to understand and love him instead of making him look like a simp."[6]

Though Bucky constantly worried about Yogi behind the plate, he didn't want his pitchers to feel uneasy with Yogi. Once Page shook off Yogi with Ted Williams batting. Page threw a fastball and Williams hit a home run. Bucky let everyone in the dugout know Yogi had called for a curveball in. At the end of the inning Bucky winked at Page and told him in the future he should have more faith in his little catcher.[7]

In the first two games of the 1947 Series, Bucky, wanting Yogi and Lindell in the lineup, started Yogi at catcher, where he had started 48 games during the season. When reporters asked Bucky how he would contain the Dodger speedsters, especially Robinson, Bucky said Yogi had held his own against Robinson in the minors. Yogi was 0-for-7 batting in the first two games and threw out one of five runners in stolen-base attempts. Though the Yankees won both games, Bucky gave in to the critics in Game 3 and started another rookie, Sherm Lollar, who had started only eight games all season. Bucky sent Yogi up to pinch-hit for Lollar in the seventh and he hit a home run, the first pinch-hit home run in series history.

In the fourth game during Bevens' lost no-hitter, Yogi took a lot of the heat. The Dodgers' first run came when Yogi threw the ball into center field on a stolen-base attempt by Reese, who came all the way around and scored. In the ninth Al Gionfriddo stole second. On the Lavagetto game-winning hit, Yogi called for fastball up and away and Lavagetto hit the two-run double to the right-field corner and the Dodgers won, 3–2.

Bevens said he threw the pitch Berra called even though he didn't want to. Berra said he called for the pitch the scouting reports recommended. Both cried after the game. Bucky defended Yogi, "Cookie was 35 and on his last legs. The scouting report said you could get him with fastballs."[8]

The writers blasted Yogi in the Series. He fielded poorly, batted 3-for-19, and the Dodgers ran wild, stealing five bases in the first two games. As Arthur Daley of the *New York Times* put it, "The Dodgers stole everything from him but his chest protector."

Bucky defended him. "Berra got a number of bad breaks in the series. For one I don't think he fully recovered from the illness that knocked him out in early September, although he assured me he felt all right. For another, the strain on a first-year catcher working in the World Series is terrific and to make matters worse the laxity of our pitchers holding runners just about sank him."[9]

During the celebration after the seventh game Yogi put his arm around Bucky and thanked him for having faith in him. Bucky said Yogi would be his regular catcher the next year.[10] There were high expectations for the Yankees in 1948. Writing in *Baseball Digest*, John P. Carmichael said the Yankees would win by a dozen games, as they had in 1947. Most scribes around the country agreed. The Yankees did have a good season in 1948, winning 94 games, only three fewer than they had in 1947. But these three games would be enough to separate the Yankees from first place — and separate Bucky from the Yankees, as things turned out.

On June 2 the Red Sox were 15–24 and in seventh place. They won 14 of their next 16 and by June 22 had risen to fourth place at 26–24, seven behind the league-leading Indians. In the second half of July the Red Sox went on another hot streak, going 17–2 and moving into first place by a half-game over the Athletics and by two over the Indians and Yankees on July 30. But the Red Sox lost their next three in Cleveland, and on August 1 the A's were in first with the Indians, Red Sox and Yankees all one game out. The A's faded in August, but the Indians, Red Sox and Yankees engaged in one of the greatest day-to-day pennant races in the history of the game.

The Yankees started the A's slide by sweeping a three-game series from them on August 19–21. After a win on the 21st, when DiMaggio hit his 27th homer, the Yankees were in third, 1½ games behind the second-place Red Sox and three behind the leading Indians. The Yankees weren't as streaky as the Red Sox. Their best second-half hot streak started after they split a double-header with Detroit on August 29, when they were in second, a half-game behind Red Sox. The Yankees won their next eight, but when the winning streak ended with a loss in the second game of a double-header to the A's in the Stadium on Labor Day, they had gained nothing during an 8–1 run. They were still a half-game behind the Red Sox, who were 8–1 in the same span.

When the Yankees when to Boston for three games on September 8–10, tickets were going for $40 on the street. When the Yankees lost the first two, they were in danger of dropping 4½ back if they were swept. But Joe DiMaggio hit a game-winning grand slam in the 10th inning straight over his brother Dom's head and halfway up the bleachers to keep the Yankees in the race. It was one of the few balls Dom didn't get to in 1948. He set a record for center-field putouts, 502, that lasted more than 30 years.

The Indians got hot at the right time. After losing to the Yankees, 6–5, on September 14, with Eddie Lopat beating Bob Lemon and Page saving, the Indians were two behind the Yankees and four back of the Red Sox. The Indians won their next seven and 11 of 12. On September 29, when Feller beat the White Sox for his 19th win, the Indians had a two-game lead over both the Sox and Yankees with one series left in the season. The Indians were home versus Detroit for three. They were 12–7 against the Tigers, who were 77–75.

The Yankees and Boston had a day off, then closed against each other with two games in Fenway. After the Tigers beat the Indians in the first game of their series on October 1, with two games left for each team the standings were:

Indians	95–57	
Yankees	94–58	1.0
Red Sox	94–58	1.0

The possibilities were dizzying. Any of the three teams could win the pennant outright, either Boston or the Yankees could tie the Indians for first place, or all three teams could end up tied for first. But the end came quickly for the Yankees. They were eliminated on the next-to-last day, losing to Boston, 5–1. Ted Williams went 2-for-2 with a home run, a double and three walks. Meanwhile, the Indians beat Detroit. That night Tiger manager Steve O'Neill called Bucky and Joe McCarthy to apologize for not pitching his right-handed ace, Fred Hutchinson, against the Indians, explaining that Hutchinson had a 102-degree fever.

"That was nice of Steve. He's in a spot," Bucky said.[11]

The next day the Red Sox's only hope was to tie for the pennant by beating the Yankees again while having the Tigers beat the Indians. The night after the Yankees lost and were eliminated, Joe DiMaggio rode with his brother to Dom's house in a Boston suburb for a family dinner. The Yankees and DiMaggio didn't have much to play for the next day and some may have even speculated DiMaggio and the Yankees would lie down and give the pennant to Joe's brother and McCarthy, who was the Red Sox's manager. But on the car ride Joe told his brother he would personally see to it that the Yankees would knock the Sox out the next day. Dom said he might have something to say about that.[12]

Bucky was in the same mind as DiMaggio. He pulled out all the stops to win that last game, using his four best pitchers, four pinch-hitters and a pinch-runner, but the Red Sox won, 10–5. Dom DiMaggio hit his ninth home run of the season. Joe DiMaggio went 4-for-5. After he singled in the ninth, Bucky took him out for a pinch-runner. Joe had played hurt all season. Head down, he limped back to the dugout while 35,000 Red Sox fans rose to their feet with an ovation. He tipped his cap. In center field Dom got misty-eyed. "My glasses clouded up. As Joe reached the top step I did something that was to me as involuntary as breathing. I reached up and took off my cap."[13]

"Bucky said, 'You've had enough,'" DiMaggio said, "I had Charley horses in both legs and my right leg hurt like fury." The ovation lasted a few minutes after he disappeared into the dugout. DiMaggio called it one of his greatest thrills.[14]

DiMaggio led in the A.L. in home runs with 39 and RBIs with 155, and Tommy Henrich led in runs with 138. The Yankees were second in the league behind Boston in runs. It was the Yankee pitching that couldn't keep up with the Indians, whose team ERA was more than a half-run lower. For Cleveland, Bob Lemon and Gene Bearden won 20 and Bob Feller won 19. Bearden led in ERA at 2.48 and Lemon was tied for second. Feller led in strikeouts, 164, and Lemon was second. Feller's ERA was a little high by his standards at 3.58, but it was lower than any of the Yankees' big three of Allie Reynolds, Eddie Lopat and Vic Raschi. Specs Shea was a disappointment, going 9–10. Even Page, who appeared in 55 games and finished 38 to lead the league, had an ERA of 4.26 and a losing record.

August 13 lived up to its reputation as a Friday the 13th, at least for 18 fans in Chicago. That night the Indians' Negro League and barnstorming circuit legend Satchel Paige made his second major league start and shut out the White Sox, 5–0. He was announced as the starter earlier in the week and the game sold out in advance. Official attendance was 51,000, but another 10,000 to 15,000 tore down a turnstile and filled every possible standing space. Eighteen people were injured. Officially a rookie, Paige finished 6–1 with a 2.48 ERA in 27 games.

On August 14 Bucky changed his lineup. McQuinn at first, now 39, was slumping, hitting .203 over the previous month. Stirnweiss at second was hitting .216. Despite having told Berra he would be his everyday catcher in 1948, Bucky moved Yogi to right field, shifted Henrich from right to first, and put Bobby Brown at third. Gus Niarhos became the regular catcher. Bucky had seen something the statistics would verify. The Yankee pitchers walked fewer batters and struck out more with Niarhos catching instead of Berra.[15]

Yogi's relationships with the umpires was one explanation for the statistical difference. Umpire Bill McKinley said of Yogi, "not a bad guy, but a pest. He was always turning around saying something."

Umpire Joe Paparella joked Yogi was "not only a great catcher but a great umpire." But Bucky wanted Yogi's bat in the lineup, so he hid him in right field. On the season Yogi hit .305, with 14 home runs, 24 doubles and 98 RBIs in 125 games. The Yankees were 60–44 before Bucky made the lineup change — that's .576 ball. They were 34–16 after, .630. As always Bucky was insightful and had the courage of his convictions to make the changes. If only he had done so a week earlier, things might have been different.[16]

The biggest baseball news of 1948 was the death of Babe Ruth on August 16. While the Babe lay in state in Yankee Stadium, the Yankees were in Washington for a midweek three-game set. After they won the first game, DiMaggio took a 2:00 A.M. train from Union Station to New York to be a pall bearer for Ruth. He returned in time for the third inning of the second game.[17]

The pennant race and the continuing post-war economic boom were good for baseball's bottom line. The minors expanded to 58 leagues with 438 teams. The majors and minors drew 68,802,447, breaking the record of the season before. Cleveland set records for home, 2,620,627; road, 1,762,399; single game, 86,288 and double-header, 82,781, attendance. The Yankees drew 2,373,901, a franchise record not broken until 1979.[18]

While the Red Sox were beating the Yankees that last day, the Tigers pulled a surprise by beating the Indians. This set up a one-game playoff for the A.L. pennant the next day in Fenway Park. Cleveland won, 8–3, as Bearden won his 20th game. The Indians beat the Boston Braves, 4 games to 2, in the World Series.

On the day of the one-game playoff, the *New York Times* reported Bucky's contract would not be renewed for 1949. The announcement came after a meeting among president Dan Topping, general manager George Weiss and Bucky. No one was surprised. "Harris, undeniably popular with the players, press and public, was sort of living on borrowed time, so far as his connection with the Bombers was concerned,"[19] wrote Povich. Bucky had told Shirley Povich a week earlier he expected to be fired, saying, "They haven't said they want me to stay on and it's clear they don't."[20] Bucky suspected all season he was not wanted and became convinced when Weiss flew into Detroit while the Yankees were there in mid–September. Weiss and Bucky were talking in a hotel lobby when one of the writers asked Weiss, "Can we take your visit here as a vote of confidence for Bucky as manager?"

Weiss, who never knew what to say to writers, stammered and didn't get an answer out. Bucky interrupted, saying, "The heck with that. What's to be gained by bringing that up now."

Bucky beat himself up later for bailing Weiss out. "At the time it seemed to make sense. Later I have often asked myself how would Weiss have explained firing me if we won in '48? He would have, you know, because I was done back in French Lick. What a dilly of an explanation that would have been."[21] French Lick was a reference to the meeting the Yankee brass had there back in 1946.

During that final Cleveland-Detroit series, Weiss flew into Cleveland to watch a game, then tried to duck out. He refused to answer questions about Bucky when reporters caught up with him.[22] "Bucky's failure to get a vote of confidence from his Yankee bosses indicates he's out unless they win the pennant and perhaps even if they do."

To understand why Bucky was doomed, go back to the aftermath of the Yankees' World Series triumph in 1947. Larry MacPhail's reaction to the Yankees' championship was a strange one. He resigned. One newspaper account of the post-game happenings said MacPhail announced he was quitting right after the game in the clubhouse. Other accounts indicate he didn't resign but was fired at the post-game celebration at the Biltmore Hotel later that evening, which became a drunken brawl.

"MacPhail became a raging drunk, punching and harassing members of the press and the Yankee organization. Topping dragged him into the kitchen and literally beat some sense into him. MacPhail was chastened briefly, then MacPhail canned Weiss only to be cut loose himself the next day when co-owners Dan Topping and Del Webb made Weiss the GM and bought MacPhail out for $2 million. He doubled his money, but was lost in alcohol, drugs or mental illness."[23]

A couple years later Bucky told the full story of why he thought he was fired by Weiss. As he explained it, he was fired before he was hired. Before Bucky was hired as Yankee manager, he was at an organizational meeting in French Lick, Indiana, after the 1946 World Series. "Every scout, manager and farm system man was there. MacPhail outlined each man's duties. I wasn't the manager then, but something like Larry MacPhail's ambassador. Later that fall I agreed to manage the team after MacPhail couldn't get anybody else he wanted."

At the meeting MacPhail put Bucky in charge of the top minor league teams, Newark and Kansas City, farms which were born and nurtured under Weiss. This began what would be an ever-widening rift between Bucky and Weiss and Topping, who grew to hate MacPhail and saw Bucky as MacPhail's hire. "I didn't realize it then but that was the moment I was done. Only one more moment had to be added, (and) that when MacPhail left the club."[24]

Other excuses for the firing were proffered. Pitchers under Bucky couldn't hold runners on. And the old bugaboos surfaced. He had to rely on MacPhail for constant guidance, as he had with Griffith. And as he had under Griffith, he was accused of being too nice of a guy. Red Barber said it worked, "Bucky ran a happy ball club in New York. He managed quietly and didn't raise his voice. He had a group of grown men and treated them as such."

Roger Kahn wrote, "That was one way of looking at matters. Another way was less kind. Harris was no disciplinarian."[25]

Weiss said players, Lindell and Page to name two, were drinking too much and he blamed Bucky. "Harris is too damn easy going. He's lost control of the game."[26]

And Weiss didn't like Bucky's meddling in minor league affairs. In 1948 Bucky rode Weiss about bringing up pitcher Bob Porterfield from Newark and outfielder Hank Bauer from Kansas City. Bucky insisted in pointed statements to the press that he needed Porterfield. "I didn't care what they thought when I insisted they bring Bob Porterfield up from Newark," Bucky said.[27]

Weiss relented on Porterfield in mid–August but didn't bring up Bauer until the Kansas City season ended. Bucky was far from a yes-man and that's what Weiss wanted. As Daley wrote in the *Post*, "Bucky always had been an outspoken fellow who said precisely what he thought with a frankness that could border on being downright embarrassing. This quality endeared him to the press, but it could hardly have done the same with the front office."[28] Most of the players didn't want Bucky fired.

To Yogi it was obvious that Weiss had no use for Bucky in 1948, saying Weiss called Bucky "a four-hour manager" because he didn't eat, drink and breathe baseball. "I was sad to see Bucky go. He was a good guy and good to me. When I was struggling behind the plate Bucky told me not to worry. He wanted my bat in the lineup."

After the 1948 season the New York baseball writers awarded Bucky, right, the William J. Slocum Award as the top New York baseball figure of the year. Johnny Mize, left, received the Sid Mercer Award as outstanding player.

Tommy Henrich: "I never played for a smarter manager or more guttier guy than Bucky Harris."

DiMaggio: "This club would be crazy to let Harris get away. He's done a great job and they're lucky he wants to stay. If you can't play for Bucky, you don't belong in the major leagues."[29]

The New York baseball writers let it be known whose side they were on. They awarded Bucky the William J. Slocum Award as the top New York baseball figure of the year.

Chapter 18

Padre Bucky

Rumors persisted that Bucky would replace manager Burt Shotton or even president Branch Rickey at Brooklyn. Bucky doubted the rumors but welcomed them. "I have no knowledge of it," Bucky said, "but if they want me I would love to have the job."[1]

Another report had it he would replace Steve O'Neill at Detroit as soon as Spike Briggs returned from Europe. Spike coveted Bucky, but he exaggerated his own power in Detroit. His father was still calling the shots.[2] The obvious question was: How about a third term in Washington? Bucky visited Griffith when he got back to Washington after the World Series, but so what? He always visited the Old Fox during offseasons.

In early December San Diego entered the Bucky sweepstakes. Would Bucky Harris accept a demotion from the New York Yankees to a minor league team 3,000 miles away? It sounded crazy, but he said he would consider it. In mid–December there was a concrete offer from San Diego, which was entering the first season of an agreement as Cleveland's top farm club. Cleveland Indians owner Bill Veeck was being lobbied hard by vice president Hank Greenberg to hire Bucky for San Diego. Bucky may have seen San Diego as a stepping stone to a job with the Indians, telling Povich, "If I do go back to the minors it won't be with the idea of making a career of it. Baseball's only charm for me is the big leagues."

In pitching himself, he admitted he'd made mistakes. "I think I'm a better manager today than ever before because I've profited by my past mistakes," likely a reference to his laxity on discipline.[3]

In San Diego fans were getting excited, but the local paper reported Bucky was still considering a Washington offer. Bucky met with Veeck and San Diego president Bill Starr on December 16 in Cleveland and agreed to one-year deal, although he didn't sign. Money was an issue. The terms were said to be "very attractive." Reports had the salary ranging from $15,000 to $20,000. In his column in the *Washington Post* Povich said it was $22,500, which was higher than the salaries of at least five major league managers.

The prospect of Bucky Harris managing in San Diego was front-page news in the *San Diego Daily Union* under a headline describing Bucky as the "Little Man." Starr said, "I am elated that Bucky Harris has accepted the Padre managership. He is one of the great men in baseball today and we are privileged to have him."

Around town the fans were elated and stunned to be getting a two-time World Series champion as manager.

Art Billings, a Ryan Aeronautical executive and Pittsburgh Pirate scout, said, "This adds atmosphere to the baseball picture here and I believe his appointment assures the Padres considerable help from the Cleveland Indians. After all, he's a big man in baseball and he wouldn't take a job if he didn't have a guarantee of player talent."

Joe Brewer, a local restaurant owner, was quoted as saying, "Next to the new ballpark I'd say this is the best thing that ever happened to San Diego baseballically thinking."

The local high school baseball coach said, "I don't see how the Padres could have picked a better man."

Lt. Col. Walter Yaecker, a retired Marine officer and Padres box holder, said, "Harris has done some wonderful work with men who were considered mediocre. He's great for young players. He commands respect."

Eugene Harris, a local luggage dealer, had experience with Bucky as a fan. "I have followed his career since 1920 and saw him play back in '25. As a baseball manager and gentleman he has no peer or par."[4]

That same day in Chicago at the winter meetings, the major leagues turned down a request of PCL president Clarence Rowland of the Hollywood team to increase the players' draft price from $10,000 to $25,000 and extend from four to six years the period PCL teams could retain a player before he became eligible to be drafted by the major leagues.

Right after the new year Bucky signed with the Padres. Veeck called him one of the top three managers in the big leagues. Povich made a prediction. "Harris will be back in the majors before long and make the Yankees eat their words."[5]

By hiring Bucky, Veeck showed he didn't carry a grudge. Back in July Bucky had managed the American League in the All-Star Game. Veeck pulled Feller out of the game, leaving Bucky with three pitchers. Bucky was livid and went on a tirade against Veeck prior to the game.[6]

On February 1, Bucky arrived in San Diego after a 10-day drive across the country during which he battled rain, sleet, snow and wind. He was happy for the warm weather. "Southern California looks and feels mighty good. I hope it looks and feels as good at the end of the season. They tell me I've got the toughest job in a tough league, but I'm ready."

Asked about the Yankees, he said, "I think it would be better just to skip the subject. That's something I'm trying hard to forget."[7]

The last time Bucky had been in California was with the Tigers 17 years earlier for an exhibition game with the Hollywood Stars. Bucky brought Red Corriden with him from the Yankees as a coach and inherited Jimmie Reese. This was the first time the Padres had two coaches. It also let Bucky manage from the dugout while the coaches manned the coaching boxes. Bucky also stepped into a new field featuring a new perk for the PCL — a dugout-to-bullpen phone.[8]

San Diego, Los Angeles, Hollywood, Oakland, Portland, Sacramento, San Francisco and Seattle comprised the PCL in 1949. The league played a 188-game schedule, with teams going into visiting cities for a week at a time. Fred Haney, who managed in the majors before and after, was the Hollywood Stars manager. Charlie Dressen was at Oakland and Lefty O'Doul was with the Los Angeles Angels. In February Bucky spoke at the California Football Writers Association banquet. Jesse Hill, USC's track coach who played under Bucky at Washington in 1936, said, "He's the best manager in baseball and always has been."

Padres president Bill Starr said, "We feel San Diego has the best setup in minor league baseball, with a working arrangement with the world champion Cleveland Indians and a world championship manager."

Again asked about the Yankees, Bucky said, "I guess I was lucky to win the pennant and World Series in 1947 and a poor manager not to repeat in 1948."[9]

On March 5 Bucky's starting lineup in the Padres' first exhibition game included three former major leaguers in Dain Clay, 30, and Steve Mesner, 31, Reds starting outfielders during the war, and Max West, 33, who hit 43 home runs and drove in 124 in 1947 for the Padres and was taken by the Pirates in the Rule 5 draft. After hitting .178 in 87 games with the Pirates in 1948 he was released and then re-signed by the Padres.[10] A future major leaguer was 19-year-old pitcher Gordon Jones, who would pitch in 11 seasons in the majors with six different teams, from 1954 to 1965. The exhibition schedule concluded with a game against the Indians on March 28. At that point Veeck was supposed to leave some talent behind for Bucky.

Bucky was in his 26th season as a manager, having worked in both the majors and two years in the minors at Buffalo, but 1948 presented the new experience of managing black players. San Diego had integrated the PCL in 1947. He had managed against blacks, including the pioneers Larry Doby in 1947 and Jackie Robinson in the 1947 World Series. Little is known about Bucky's racial proclivities, but he certainly wasn't an outright racist. During the 1947 Series he said nothing about Robinson. It wasn't until years later that he offered any comment at all about Robinson's impact in the 1947 World Series. "I didn't regard him too fondly at that time. He didn't hurt us much, but he almost killed my shortstop Phil Rizzuto with those rolling football blocks trying to break up double plays. I admired Jackie as a player. He had a lot of obstacles to overcome."[11]

Later in his career Bucky would play a part in the racial integration of two American League teams. By the spring of 1948, Veeck, who in 1947 signed Larry Doby as the first black American League player, had 14 blacks in his system and was referred to as "the Abraham Lincoln of baseball."[12] Among the blacks on the Padres roster in March of 1948 was the PCL pioneer from the previous season, catcher John Ritchey, along with Art Wilson, Parnell Woods, and the flamboyant 6'5", 240-pound Luke Easter.

Easter was turned over outright to the Padres via a new working agreement and couldn't be recalled unless, as one writer put it, "he could be reacquired let's say in case of emergency."[13] The 26-year-old outfielder/first baseman was born in Mississippi and grew up in St. Louis. A left-handed batter and right-handed thrower, he was cat quick around first base and a good fielder. A broken ankle on the St. Louis sandlots and the war set Easter back a couple of years. In 1946 he batted .415 with 152 RBIs with the Cincinnati Crescents in the Negro League and hit a 500-foot home run to the center-field bleachers at the Polo Grounds. In 1947 and 1948 he batted .336 and .376 for the Homestead Grays with more than 100 RBIs each year. Veeck signed him after he led the 1948-49 Puerto Rican winter league in batting with a .402 average for the Mayaguez Indians and assigned him to San Diego.[14] Easter reported to Bucky in Ontario, California, on March 5. The next day he bought a new car, a 1949 Buick with four portholes on each side amidship, prompting Bucky to joke, "I'm the manager and I only have a three-holer."[15]

On the first pitch Easter saw in batting practice on March 7, he hit a 475-foot home run. That afternoon in a game against Sacramento he hit a 390-foot home run. On March 20 he blasted one 415 feet. Against Seattle he hit two triples, and manager Jo Jo White said he never saw two balls hit harder in his life. By March 27 he was 18-for-38 with four home runs. In an exhibition game that day against the major league White Sox, Easter hit a two-run home run in a 9–7 win.

Bucky thanked Veeck and coined a nickname for the ever-smiling Easter. "Veeck is the man who turned Luke Easter loose in the Padre pasture and if he can come up with a couple more like 'Happy,' the Padres will have little worry."[16]

Easter was a sensation around the PCL and a gate attraction. When he took batting practice everybody stopped to watch. Almost everyone had a comment. One coach said of him, "His shoulders are so broad that when he wears one of his pinstriped suits it looks like he forgot to remove the coat hanger." Seattle manager Dick Barrett said, "He's made a Christian out of every Rainier pitcher."[17]

L.H. Gregory, a veteran Portland sportswriter described an Easter homer this way: "It was a high drive straight out from the plate over the pitcher's head. It cleared the fence in deepest right center by the margin of a three-story building; and, carrying on, was perceived to bounce on the roof of the gray foundry building there and carom out of sight." Gregory estimated the home run at 450 feet.[18]

Easter had a subtle sense of humor. One day Dolph Camilli was coaching first for the Sacramento Solons and was riding Easter, who was playing first.

After few innings Easter asked Camilli what his name was.

Camilli said, "Joe Blow."

Easter answered, "I ain't never heard of you, Mr. Blow."

Frank Finch, a writer for the *Los Angeles Times*, wrote, "He sports a diamond ring that looks like a headlight on the Santa Fe Chief. I asked him where he got it and he said he stole it."[19]

Rain canceled a March 19 exhibition game with the Hollywood Stars. Bucky used the day off to go to Los Angeles to meet with some Cleveland brass.[20] Bucky wouldn't say what they talked about, but speculation suggested it was about personnel. Veeck promised to stock the Padres with talent, but Bucky and the fans were worried the Indians weren't following through.

On March 28, two days before the start of the PCL season, the Indians came to San Diego and beat the Padres, 10–5. Max West hit two home runs. Easter had a rare off day, going 0-for-5, but in 14 spring games he hit .429 with 15 runs scored, 12 RBIs, six doubles, three triples, four home runs and a .918 slugging percentage.[21]

The Indians left behind four players for Bucky and the Padres — pitchers Will Hafey and Lyman Linde, outfielder Bobby Wilson and infielder Artie Wilson, who was called "Li'l Arthur" and was described in the *San Diego Union* as "a spidery little Negro clever afield and dangerous from the left side of the plate."[22] Wilson would prove very dangerous, in fact. He led the PCL in hitting in 1949 at .349.

On March 30 the Padres opened against the Hollywood Stars at home, Lane Field, in San Diego. The *Union* had high hopes for the team. "There has been pennant talk based chiefly on the fact that Harris, one of baseball's best, is at the helm."

Bucky was cautious. He shunned the miracle worker label and said he was contacting other major league teams for pitching help. Reserved seats were sold out for the opener and a crowd of 8,500 was expected, but steady rain held the crowd down to 4,580 and stopped the game in the eighth with the score tied, 3–3. The Stars, who had knocked the Padres from sixth to seventh place in the final week of the 1948 season, won the next two games. On April 3 the Padres evened the series, winning a double-header, 10–8 and 7–3. Easter was 5-for-9, with a home run in each game. On April 5 they opened a seven-game series with Oakland, the defending league champions managed by Dressen.[23]

The Padres won five of the seven, including a double-header to end the series. Max West went crazy against Oaks pitching with nine consecutive hits, including a 5-for-5 performance in the first game of the double-header that he won for the Padres, 14–13, with a two-out, two-run homer in the bottom of the ninth, his third of the game. In the second game Easter was 3-for-3 with a home run in an 8–0 win.

They began their first road trip in Oakland on April 12, drawing 13,071, the Oaks' best Opening Day crowd ever. The Padres won 10 straight on the road before losing the second half of a double-header on April 17 in Portland.

On May 12 Easter hit two home runs in Los Angeles in a win over the Angels. On May 16 the Padres split a double-header at Los Angeles before 23,083, the largest crowd ever at Wrigley Field for a PCL game. After a long argument, Bucky played the game under protest over a pick-off play in the third. In the *Los Angeles Times* the next day he was pictured out of character, with his finger in the umpire's chest protector.[24]

Early in May Veeck sent Bucky a gift, a black Cuban third baseman by the name of Minnie Minoso. Minnie Minoso broke camp with the Indians in 1949, making his major league debut on April 19. But he played in only nine games and batted under .200. Cleveland stuck with veteran Ken Keltner at the hot corner. Two years later the White Sox turned Minoso into an outfielder, where he earned Rookie of the Year honors and won two Gold Gloves.[25] The Padres hit a couple of slumps, inevitable in the 188-game season, but did manage to win 95 games. It sounds funny, but with 95 wins they were only three games over .500. They finished tied for fourth place.

Artie Wilson led the league in batting at .349. West led in homers with 48 and RBIs with 165. Minoso hit .297 with 22 homers. The pitching was questionable, but the real reason the Padres didn't finish higher was they lost Easter. On June 21, after hitting .357 with 23 homers and 87 RBIs in 73 games, Easter was called to Cleveland for an operation on his chipped kneecap. He recovered and on August 11 he was called up to Cleveland.[26] His major league career was brief due to injuries, but productive. He hit 28, 27, and 31 home runs in his three full seasons, 1950–52. In 1952 he was *The Sporting News* A.L. Player of the Year. He was shot to death by armed robbers coming out of a bank in Euclid, Ohio, in 1979.[27]

The final standings of the first five places were Hollywood at 109–78;

Oakland, 104–83; Sacramento, 102–85; and San Diego and Seattle both 95–92. Irv Noren, who batted .330 with 29 homers and 129 RBIs for Hollywood, was the league MVP.

On September 26 the Padres and Seattle played one game to decide fourth place and a spot in the playoffs. The game was played in San Diego, but Seattle was the home team after winning a coin toss. Attendance was 10,930. Seattle led, 6–4, in the top of the ninth when San Diego scored five to pull out a 9–6 win. Minoso was the batting hero, going 4-for-5 with a double, two singles and his 22nd home run of the season. He hit a solo home run in the eighth and a three-run double in the ninth. For the first time in six seasons the Padres finished out of the second division. And for the first time since 1942 they reached the playoffs.[28] They were tops in the league in combined home and road attendance. They drew 533,000 at home and 1,031,038 combined.

And they weren't done yet. After a day off the playoffs started on September 28, with first-place Hollywood versus third-place Sacramento and San Diego versus the second-place Oakland Oaks, also known as the Acorns. It was Bucky Harris versus Chuck Dressen, manager and coach, respectively, of the 1947 world champion New York Yankees.

The teams had split 26 regular-season games. The first three games of the playoffs were in Oakland. The series went seven games, with the Padres winning the seventh contest, 18–2, with 17 hits. Minoso was 5-for-5 and scored six runs. West was 3-for-5.

In the finals against Hollywood, the Padres won the first two games. West hit his 50th home run in the first contest and Minoso hit one in the second game, but Hollywood won the next four to take the series in six. Attendance was woeful. The highest single-game mark was 8,753 in San Diego for game three. It was windy and cold in Hollywood for game six and only 1,951 paid to see the Stars win the championship. The payout was only $550 for the winners and $356 for the losers.[29]

All told, the Padres played 201 games and were 101–99, not counting the 14-game exhibition season in March. Padres president Starr and the Padres' fans, who were not used to winning seasons and playoff games, wanted Bucky back.[30]

Chapter 19

A Third Term

During the PCL playoffs in early October, Bucky was offered a contract to return to San Diego for 1950. In mid–October it was speculated Bucky was negotiating with Griffith for a return to Washington. Griffith did not deny he talked to Bucky, but insisted nothing had been settled. Griffith said he contacted Bucky to ask about Irv Noren, whom he eventually purchased on Bucky's advice, and asked Bucky if he had signed for 1950.

"He said no," Griffith said, "but that he wanted to speak to me in Washington before committing himself. I think pretty well of Bucky, but he's just one of the men I'm considering."[1]

Bucky was heading east and was expected home around October 20. Starr said Bucky had promised to let him know if he would be back for 1950 by the end of the week. Factors pointed to Bucky returning to Washington. Griffith always appointed an old-time star, he always liked Bucky, and he had offered Bucky a front-office job the previous year. On October 18 Griffith admitted he was negotiating with no one other than Bucky and hoped he would accept the job. Griffith was a little hurt that Bucky didn't jump at the offer a couple weeks sooner, but Bucky was in a sweet bargaining position as the highest-paid minor league manager in San Diego, where he was wanted back with a raise.

Cleveland vice president Hank Greenberg said San Diego president Bill Starr was pretty upset. "He called me this morning to persuade Harris to return to San Diego, but I explained that we owed Bucky the chance to return to the majors. It's with reluctance that we let him get out of our organization but with nothing better than San Diego to offer him, we can't obstruct him."[2]

Bucky's wife was contacted at her home in Chevy Chase, Maryland, and said she hadn't heard Bucky was coming back to Washington but wouldn't be surprised. "But when is he going to get out of the monkey suit and get a front office job? He and Mack are the two oldest managers in baseball, aren't they?"[3]

The first time Griffith had fired Bucky back in 1929, it was said Bucky was "getting too high-horse and big-shot." The second time he absolved Bucky of any blame for the team's poor records but felt the team needed new faces, including the manager. Povich, who always followed Bucky closely, said Bucky had changed. "Harris isn't the same raw meat, up-and-at-'em guy who took the Nats to pennants in the 20s when he was barking at umpires, cracking down on his ball players and kicking up a fuss generally. He matured and developed a new calm as a bench manager."[4]

Through it all Bucky and Griffith remained friends and in the offseason Bucky always sat in the continuous pinochle games in Griffith's office. Griffith always maintained a soft spot in his heart for Bucky, and thought of him as a son. On October 22 Bucky signed for three years for a reported $27,000 a year with attendance incentives that could earn him more than the $90,000 he was paid for managing the club from 1926 to 1928. Griffith didn't quibble over his request for a three-year deal, despite the fact that none of his managers since 1928, when Bucky's first three-year deal ran out, had been given more than a one-year agreement. "We agree that we face a long-range program."

Griffith said Bucky would have a greater role than just field manager. "Stanley's judgment on players always did have my respect and no manager in the league will have as much freedom in the front office as he."

Bucky said Griffith agreed to spend some money. "Mr. Griffith won't turn me down on the players I want and I already have ideas."

Griffith agreed to offer Oakland $100,000 for Jackie Jensen. "That's the kind of thinking I mean. Griff used to swoon when the price tag was higher that $15,000. Of course, prices were relative in those days. Griff is catching on. He didn't squawk when I told him to offer $70,000 for Noren."[5]

Bucky might have stayed in San Diego and moved up to Cleveland if the Indians made a move with Lou Boudreau. But that didn't seem likely, and he wanted to get back to the majors. As it turned out, Boudreau was released after the 1950 season.

Bucky addressed the idea that PCL was major-league quality. "San Diego is a nice town. The pay is fine. So are the folks, But it's still bush. It's just what it's rated, triple A and no more, it's certainly not the majors. There wasn't a team out there that wouldn't have been murdered by big-league company."

Writing in the *New York Times,* Al Gold blasted Bucky.

You can have Bob Hope, Groucho Marx and Jack Benny. When we want a belly laugh from now on we're going to tune in on Bucky Harris. That from a gent who's taking over at Washington of all places. Washington used to be major all right, but that was a long time ago. Washington ain't major now. There's considerable doubt whether the current Senators are baseball players at all.

How does Brother Harris think Washington would have fared in the PCL last season? We'll answer for him. Washington couldn't have made the first division. Washington might even have finished eighth.

He was paid $25k. If he really thinks the Padres were punks, he should give most of it back. On switching from San Diego to Washington he's going up in classification, but down in class.[6]

It can't be known how the 1949 Senators would have fared in the PCL, but they didn't fare well in the A.L., going 50–101 and finishing last, 47 games out and with the third-lowest attendance in the major leagues. And they didn't have any players like Luke Easter, Minnie Minoso or Irv Noren. Their best player was first baseman Eddie Robinson, and he hit .294 with 18 home runs and 78 RBIs. Their number-one starter was Sid Hudson, and he lost 17 with a 4.22 ERA.

Bucky knew what he was getting into. "I'm walking into an eighth-place club and apparently there is a lot of work to do."[7]

Chapter 20

The Cuban Connection

"A Republican will do anything to get to Washington" and "One more and he'll tie FDR" were the jokes heard when Bucky came back to manage the Senators in 1950. Even before the 1950 season dawned, Griffith and Bucky made it known they were willing to deal in an attempt to remake the club. They agreed Robinson was the only untouchable. They would consider trading anyone else, including starting third baseman Eddie Yost. As it would turn out, they kept Yost and traded Robinson in May with infielder Al Kozar and pitcher Ray Scarborough to the Chicago White Sox in exchange for pitcher Bob Kuzava, second baseman Cass Michaels and outfielder Johnny Ostrowski.

In November the Senators claimed San Francisco pitcher Steve Nagy, Hollywood shortstop George Genovese, and wildman Seattle catcher Newton Grasso from the PCL for $10,000 each. In Seattle Grasso had been fined $1,200 and tossed from 23 games in three years. He was known to throw his shin guards and mask all over the field. He was popular with fans, though, who would phone the hotel or park to learn if he was in the lineup that day. He calmed down quite a bit with the Senators in 1950, but still managed to get ejected from three of the 75 games he played.[1]

On November 21 Griffith cut a cake in his stadium office with scores of friends and family — including nine grandchildren — to celebrate his 80th birthday. He said he intended to carry on actively with the club for a long time. Bucky and Joe Cronin, the Red Sox's general manager, were introduced as "my two boy managers." D.C. Mayor Robert Barrett gave Griffith a television set on behalf of the city's 1800 policemen.[2]

Bucky hadn't burned any bridges in Detroit or Boston and he was highly regarded throughout baseball, but he always carried a grudge against the Yankees. During the winter meetings he talked to Casey Stengel in New York in the Commodore Hotel lobby and couldn't help giving Stengel a little shot over his lack of power to make trades, a power Bucky had under Griffith. "Stengel won't move on our deal. He wants to give us a lot of trash for Eddie

Robinson. And he had the nerve to suggest we could also make a deal for Ray Scarborugh. When he said that, I thought I'd jolt him. I told him we'd make a deal for Scarborugh and that Griffith was talking to Joe McCarthy and they were getting pretty close. Stengel raced upstairs to report to the Yankee bosses. Maybe it will revive our deal."[3]

To Bucky the biggest acquisition in 1950 was Irv Noren. Bucky got an eyeful of Noren when he was the MVP of the PCL in 1949 with the champion Hollywood Stars, a Dodger farm club. A 6'0", 190-pound Swede from upstate New York, Noren was a tremendous all-around athlete. After an army hitch, he was signed by the Dodgers for $5,000 out of Pasadena Junior College, where he was the Southern California Junior College basketball player of the year. He played basketball briefly with Jackie Robinson on an AAU team and with the Chicago Gears in the NBA with George Mikan. In 1949 he hit .330 with 29 homers and 130 RBIs with Hollywood despite missing three weeks with appendicitis. Bucky watched him work out a few times in the spring of 1950 and said, "Kid, the center field job is yours."[4]

He had a nice rookie season, hitting .295, with 98 RBIs and a league-leading 20 assists. He had flashes of absolute brilliance, and Bucky often said he was potentially one of the best center fielders in baseball. Noren was happy in Washington. "It's great to be a Senator; Bucky is a regular guy to work for," Noren said.[5]

Bucky as he appeared during his last term as Senators manager, from 1950 to 1954. He was in his mid-to-late 50s during this time.

The dealing for players continued into the season, and by the end of 1950 the Senators were a much different team. In June after dealing Robinson, Bucky tried Noren at first, but wanted him in the outfield, so he got Mickey Vernon back from Cleveland for pitcher Dick Weik. Though Vernon wasn't the hitter he was when he hit .353 to lead the league in 1946 with the Senators, he did hit .306 with 65 RBIs in 90 games for Bucky in 1950.

Bucky inherited pitcher Sid Hudson, who had been a regular starter since he won 17 as a rookie in 1940. In 1950 he lost 17, a league-leading number. He last pitched in 1950 on September 27, lost, and went home to Texas. What was known was his elderly mother had a bad fall. What wasn't known until the next spring was his arm was shot. Always an over-the-top thrower, he couldn't throw without debilitating pain in his shoulder. In camp Bucky and Griffith didn't give up on him. They turned him into a sidearm pitcher and he led the team in wins with a 14–14 record in 1951.[6] All the roster tinkering produced 17 more wins for the Senators in 1950 and a jump from eighth place to fifth. To at least one writer, such improvement made a case for Bucky as manager of the year.

> His many friends felt sorry for him when he took over the Senators last spring. He had few talented players and most were so used to losing they went through the motions on the field. You might say anything Harris did would be an improvement, but it wasn't the extent of the improvement that makes the case for Bucky.
>
> He jumped the Senators to fifth with 17 more wins by tactful but firm handling of the players; through smart trades and common sense handling of the games. Harris turned the Senators from a joke into a scrappy team that gave everyone a fight. Bucky, a battler all his life, wouldn't stand for quitting. He developed a winning habit in men who never had it before. Bucky has two years left on his contract and he thinks he can make the Senators a contender.[7]

The Senators weren't just the most improved team in the American League; they were also the most interesting, thanks to their Cuban connection. Though Cubans had played in the majors as early as 1911, no major league team ever had more Cubans at one time than the Senators in the late 1940s and early 1950s, when Griffith developed an affiliation with the Havana Cubans of the Florida International League from 1946 through 1953.

In 1950, five Cubans pitched for the Senators. Three made only brief appearances, including Carlos Pasqual, the older brother of Camillo Pasqual, who later would be a star for the Senators and the Twins after the franchise moved to Minnesota. The two Cuban pitchers who stuck were Sandy Consuegra and Connie Marrero. Not everybody was happy with the Cuban invasion. Four Cubans in camp were too many to suit outfielder Roberto Ortiz, who was a fifth Cuban. He was the only bilingual among them and had to speak for the other four. Ortiz complained about being Bucky's interpreter, but only a little as he probably realized his English was the only reason he was carried in 1950. He played in only 39 games and hit .227. Ortiz wasn't much help to Bucky when the Cuban pitchers were on the mound. In September he sold Ortiz to the Phillies and went looking for a bilingual catcher for 1951.

Fermin "Mike" Guerra, a 38-year-old journeyman back-up receiver, fit the bill. In December the Athletics sold Guerra to the Red Sox with the expectation he would be sent on to the Senators for catcher Al Evans. "I've just got to have him," Bucky said. "He's the only guy who can tell those Cubans what I want them to do."

But when the Red Sox balked, Bucky was angry, telling anyone who would listen the Red Sox had no reason to keep Guerra except to hurt the Senators. The Red Sox didn't agree to a deal until May of 1951. Until then Bucky tried to get by using pidgin English and hand signals. When he finally obtained Guerra, he was relieved. Bucky, who refused to learn a word of Spanish, and the Cubans, who refused to learn all but the most rudimentary English, were at loggerheads before Guerra arrived. "I was getting weary of all that sign language and grunting," Bucky said. "At least Guerra got me out from under that load. We can make Guerra happy. We're the only team with our own built-in Spanish quarter and it's working out all right. I don't understand their jabbering, but they all seem to be happy."[8]

Of the three Cubans who pitched for the Senators in 1951 Conrad "Connie" Marrero was the one who had the biggest impact competitively, comically and culturally. A squat, cigar-chomping right-hander of indeterminate age, Marrero became a favorite of the fans and Bucky. When asked his age, Marrero would point at his uniform number, 22. That was such an obvious lie they listed him at 32. Reggie Otero, the manager of the Havana Sugar Kings, told Bucky Connie was 42. When Bucky confronted Connie, he said, "Otero, he lie. This many more." He held up three fingers, laughed and walked away.

During the first three months of the 1950 season Marrero existed on eggs and steak, they being the only things he knew how to order. After the first road trip in 1950 he was asked his impressions of the major league cities and said, "St. Louis, too hot. Chicago, too cold. New York, too rush."

He was described this way by one writer: "His legs are so short he appears to batters to be buried up to his waist. He creaks like a windmill and throws just hard enough to reach the catcher. His only English is the profanities his teammates taught him. He has a delivery and motion like no other pitcher. The right-hander puts his left foot in the bucket toward first base. When he is ready to throw he resembles an orangutan heaving a 16-pound shot. Hitters call his pitches junk."

Once when the writers asked him what he threw, he said, "Everything but my cigar." The writers said Marrero was a dead ringer for Sitting Bull and nearly as old. He ran a farm and pitched as an amateur in Cuba for 16 years and became known as "El Premier" or "Grade A." His first professional jobs were in the Mexican League and with the Almendares in the Cuban winter league. He played three seasons for Washington's Havana team in the Florida International League and was 70–25. When Marrero first came to the Senators in the spring of 1950, Bucky was incredulous. "If anybody were to tell me he's a pitcher I'd say he was crazy."

Bucky thought the Cuban players were temperamental, quick to squabble among themselves and generally hard to handle. But after being around Marrero for a while, he grew to like him. They became fast friends. Whenever Bucky's name was mentioned around him, Marrero would pull on his cigar and say, "Buck-ee Harris, my friend." The feeling was mutual. Bucky kidded him about his size, 5'5", 160 pounds, and the senoritas.[9]

As a rookie in 1950 Marrero was 6–10 with a 4.50 ERA and batters couldn't wait to hit against him. In 1951, having pitched all winter in Cuba, he was in mid-season shape, and with a knowledge of the hitters, he did better. He was the Opening Day starter in Philadelphia and beat the A's, 6–1, in the first game in A's history not managed by Connie Mack. After winning two games in Philadelphia, the Senators went back to D.C. for their home openers, a day-night double-header against the Yankees on April 20. This was only nine days after President Truman removed World War II hero General MacArthur from command in Korea. When Truman threw out the first pitch before the game, a smattering of cheers was overpowered by boos from the 27,000 fans. An announcement after the eighth inning asking the fans to remain seated until the presidential party left the park was roundly booed. The unpopularity of the president didn't bother the Senators baseball team, which won both games.[10]

Marrero faced the A's again on April 26 and pitched a one-hitter. "He threw Eddie Joost knucklers and other slow pitches that sent Joost wild, at first jumping up and down and cursing Marrero. Then he laughed and called him El Payaso the clown."[11] Marrero struck out Joost three times that day. On the last of the strikeouts Marrero hitched his pants, adjusted his hat, played with the rosin bag, and went into a double windup. Joost stood there and took strike three.

While Marrero won his first five starts, fellow Cuban Sandalio "Sandy" Consuegra won three and the Senators got off to their fastest 13-game start in 20 years. When Marrero beat the White Sox, 7–1, on May 3 in Chicago, the Senators were 10–3. On May 12 Marrero beat Boston, 5–4, and struck out Ted Williams on a knuckler. "It didn't turn around once as it floated up to the plate. I swung at it and ducked," Williams said. Bucky usually gave Marrero six days' rest. When asked to pitch on four against Detroit, he did.

He gave up 16 hits and walked six but won, 11–6. Bucky just shook his head in amazement.[12]

The Senators' promising start in 1951 fizzled. Beginning May 20, the Senators lost nine consecutive and 18 of 20 through June 10. They also had losing streaks of 11 in August and nine in September. They finished 62–92 and in seventh place, ahead of only the St. Louis Browns. They were seventh in A.L. team batting, ahead of only the Browns. They were dead last in home runs with 54, 32 fewer than the Browns and only 12 more than major league leader Ralph Kiner. Third baseman Eddie Yost and right fielder Sam Mele tied for the league lead in doubles with 36. Those numbers were functions of Griffith Stadium's mammoth dimensions instead of the power by Yost or Mele. Yost led the team in home runs with 12. Mele had five and led the league in grounding into double plays. Hudson, the arm pain back, dropped from sidearm to underhand pitching and slumped to 5–12 with a 5.09 ERA. Marrero was the best pitcher. Pitching every sixth day, with a few exceptions, he was 11–9 with a 3.90 ERA in 25 starts.

Bucky had been around too long to be discouraged by one set-back season. He continued to wheel and deal for players. One of his finds was Texas cowboy Pete Runnels, who had played in 78 games in 1951 and hit .278. Bucky installed him as the full-time shortstop in 1952. When Runnels checked into a hotel in Washington before the start of the season, there was a rodeo in town and 40 cowboys were staying at the same hotel. Runnels was seen there in a ten-gallon hat, fancy cowboys boots and a beaded shirt, modeling clothes for a men's store he worked for in Lufkin, Texas. In the spring of 1951, when Runnels was up from Texarkana in the Big State League, Bucky took one look at him and said, "That kid has a base hit stroke."

Bucky was impressed with him as a shortstop who could hit to all fields, comparing him to Cecil Travis. "He seemed a couple years away from the majors, but when he hit .356 at Chattanooga they brought him up in July and nobody ever got him out of there," Bucky said.[13]

Bucky bet coach Clyde Milan that Runnels would have the highest average on the club in 1952. It didn't happen. Jackie Jensen, another of Bucky's acquisitions, beat him out by one point, .286 to .285, but Bucky's evaluation of Runnels would bear out in time. He hit .310 for the Senators in 1956. After a tremendous slump in an injury-plagued 1957, when he hit .230, the Senators traded him to the Red Sox for Albie Pearson and Norm Zauchin. In Boston Runnels turned into a star. From 1958 to 1962 he batted .322, .314, .320, .316, and .326, twice leading the league and making three all-star teams.

Bucky and Griffith clashed over Gil Coan. A one-time wonder boy of the Southern Association, he was *The Sporting News* minor league player of the year in 1945. Griffith was in love with the kid, and even after he hit .238 and .218 in his first two seasons with the Senators in 1948 and 1949, Griffith wouldn't let him go. He nixed a deal with Detroit for pitcher Dizzy Trout for Coan. Griffith didn't want to give up on Coan, saying, "Coan has everything it takes to be a great player except confidence at the plate. Maybe Bucky can help him. He knows how to deal with young players."

Coan did develop into a pretty decent average hitter under Bucky for a couple of years, hitting .303 in both 1950 and 1951. But he was done after that, never living up to Griffith's belief in him.

He dropped almost 100 points, to .205, in 1952. His slump started in the second half of the 1951 season. He was hitting .350 in early July. Coan had no theory. "I was a bum from March to October and never snapped out of it," he said, referring to 1952. "I'm not blaming Harris. He went a long way with me. I didn't get a hit in my first 20 at-bats. Bucky went farther with me than I'd have gone with myself if I was managing."[14]

Griffith rebuffed Bucky's request to shop Coan for a trade over the winter of 1952. But Coan turned 31 that May and time was running out. After the 1953 season Bucky traded Coan to the Orioles for Roy Sievers.[15]

In 1952 a lot of the scribes expected the Senators to finish last, behind even the Browns, who were rebuilding. Bucky made a spring vow to keep the Senators out of the cellar, saying, "I'm too old now to run a last place club for the first time."[16]

To keep the vow to stay out of the cellar, Bucky and the Senators made more player changes than any other team in the league. As if to concede the pitching was hopeless, Bucky signed Bobo Newsom, who was 44 and hadn't pitched since 1948, to a fifth term in Washington. Bucky unloaded 17 players from the spring roster. Some were rookies up for trials but he also got rid of veterans. He traded Sam Mele to the White Sox for Jim Busby. It was a wash statistically in 1952, but Busby was five years younger. In 1953 Busby hit .312 with 82 RBIs, forcing White Sox general manager Frank Lane to admit Bucky had got the better end of the deal.[17]

The deal that helped the most was made in May when Bucky traded his former golden boy for a failed golden boy. He traded Irv Noren and Tom Upton to the Yankees in exchange for Jackie Jensen, Specs Shea, Jerry Snyder and Archie Wilson. While managing San Diego Bucky had seen Jensen with Oakland, where he batted .261 with nine home runs and 77 RBIs in 1949, the same year Jensen married bathing beauty and golden blonde Olympic diving champ Zoe Ann Olsen. Enticed by an offer of $75,000 guaranteed with an annual $25,000 salary for three years by Oakland owner Brick Laws, Jensen left the University of Southern California after his junior year to join Oakland. At USC he had led the Trojans baseball team to the title in the first

College World Series and the football team to a 10–1 season as the first Trojan to rush for 1,000 yards.

Laws didn't expect to keep Jensen for three seasons, figuring, correctly, he could sell him at a profit before that. Bucky recommended Jensen to Griffith, but the price was a little steep for the Old Fox, and Jensen went to the Yankees for $100,000. The Yankees brought Jensen up in 1950 as a backup to Joe DiMaggio. He hit only .171 in 70 at-bats. He had a decent spring in 1951, tied with DiMaggio in home runs, but Stengel benched him on the way north and went back to a veteran outfield. In June he was hitting. 298, but they sent him down to Kansas City. He was angry about the demotion and money. The Yankees were supposed to pay him the $25,000 he signed for with Oakland, but they made it a $10,000 salary with $15,000 as an incentive bonus that he could not reach in Kansas City. He complained about Stengel to a writer, in confidence, he thought, but his complaints were published with the headline "Jensen fed up with Yankees." When he reported, Stengel chewed him out, saying, "I'm running this club and nobody tells me who to play." In 1952, with the emergence of a kid named Mickey Mantle, Jensen became expendable.

When he got to Washington, his first conversation with Bucky was positive.

"No pep talk, no nothing,' Jensen said, "but he made it sound like I was the right fielder and third place hitter for a long time to come. It made me feel good."

He declined to be part of a story to be named. "It's great to be an ex–Yankee," but he added, "It's nicer with Washington. Bucky Harris doesn't panic if you go hitless or lose a ball game. He doesn't single out individuals. With Stengel it was always 'watch that curve ball' or 'watch for that changeup.' Bucky leaves you on your own up there."[18]

Bucky knew Frank "Specs" Shea well. He had a winning season for Bucky as a rookie with the Yankees in 1947, going 14–5. He was the winning pitcher in an all-star game and won two World Series games. After he injured his neck when he was knocked down as a batter by Earl Caldwell, he pitched only 56 innings in 1949. By 1952 the Yankees had given up on him and he hadn't pitched an inning when he was traded in the Noren-Jensen deal. Bucky had inside information that Shea was ready to go and insisted he be in the trade. In his first three games he gave up only two runs and struck out 21 with an ERA of 0.70.[19]

Most of the roster changes worked for the Senators and they were the surprise of the American League in 1952. The team reached a peak on July 1 when the Senators climbed to second place after a 10–4 road trip. But they lost three of four in double-headers in New York on July 3 and 4 and never threatened again. Still, in the end they improved by 16 games to finish 78–75, the first over–.500 finish since 1945, and only three games out of third place. Bucky was given credit for getting production out of players considered retreads, such as Shea, Jensen and Bob Porterfield, whom Bucky got from the Yankees during the 1951 season. In 1952 Shea was 11–8 with a 2.93 ERA. Jensen batted .286 with 10 home runs, good for second on the team, 80 RBIs and led the league in steals. He had a 20-game hitting streak in June and early July, and Stengel picked him for the all-star team over five outfielders who had received more votes.[20]

Porterfield had a team-low ERA at 2.72, but had a losing record at 13–14 due to dismal run support of 2.76 per start. Shea received 4.24 runs per game. Marrero was 11–7 with a 2.93 ERA. Eddie Yost led the team with 12 home runs and runs scored with 92 and paced the league in walks with 129 and made the all-star team. Runnels hit .285 with 64 RBIs. Bucky didn't use a relief specialist as he had so effectively in the past. The closest pitcher to fill that role was Sandy Consuegra. He led the team in games finished with 14 and was 6–0 with a 3.05 ERA. He appeared in 30 games, only two as a starter.

Two weeks after the 1952 season ended, Bucky was rewarded with a two-year deal estimated at $35,000 per, a raise of $10,000 over the previous three seasons.

"Stanley Harris will be my manager as long as I am president of the club," Griffith, 82, told the *Post*. He was happy with his team finishing fifth after being pegged by most for seventh or eighth.

On reports that Stengal was getting $100,000, Griffith said, "I was tempted to give Stanley a contract for $101,000 contingent of drawing 3,000,000. That's as absurd as Stengel's salary reports."

Griffith set the stage to take the blame for future failures. "I have always claimed Stanley is the best manger in the league and that still goes. When we don't finish in the first division, it's my fault for not providing him with the material."[21]

The 1953 season started with a tragedy. Coach Clyde Milan, 65, collapsed after hitting fungoes in 80-degree heat in Orlando and died two hours later at the hospital. Dr. Frank Gray said he died of a heart attack and that before he died, Milan told Gray he had been having chest pains but never told anyone.[22] He had been with the Senators since 1909, when he came up with Walter Johnson. He had been a coach under Bucky, Bluege and Kuhel for 15 seasons.

Bucky revived another retread in 1953 in second baseman Wayne Terwilliger. Bucky was hard on second basemen and had gone through several during the previous three seasons. The Cubs and Dodgers had given up on

Terwilliger, who had only 125 at-bats at St. Paul in 1952. But Bucky, based on the advice of an unnamed friend, bought him from Brooklyn.

Terwilliger made the everyday lineup and batted .253. Vernon had a big rebound season at age 35, leading the league in batting at .346 and doubles with 46 and topped the team with 115 RBIs. Jensen batted .266 with 10 homers and 84 RBIs. Porterfield led the league with 22 wins. Chuck Stobbs was 11–8 with a 3.29 ERA but couldn't live down the 565-foot home run he gave up to Mantle on April 17. Batting righty, Mantle hit the ball to left-center, over the bleachers, where it hit near the top of a National Bohemian beer sign that was 15 feet above the stands. The beer company painted a giant baseball on the sign where the ball hit. "That thing haunted me most of the summer until Bucky had it painted out," Stobbs said.[23]

The Senators stayed on an even keel in 1953. They finished 76–76, which was enough to inspire some hope for 1954. But the hope was dashed. Porterfield slumped to 13–15. Shea and Marrero were 5–15 between them after combining for 17 wins in 1953. The Senators fell to sixth place at 66–88 in 1954, a season in which the Indians won 111, the Yankees 103 and the White Sox 94.

Despite the poor finish in 1954, as late as September 24, when the Senators beat the Red Sox in a double-header, they were only one game out of fourth place and a share of the World Series money. The first game of the double-header was Johnny Pesky's last as a player, two days before his 35th birthday. Bucky had acquired him in June as a backup. Before the double-header Griffith announced Bucky was resigning. The press release read, "After a long conference with Bucky Harris this past week concerning the future of the Washington Senators ball club a decision was made to let Bucky resign."

Bucky agreed to go along with that statement, but the next day when he was asked what happened, he intimated in two different *Post* stories he was tired of going along with what he saw as a charade: managers who were really being fired agreeing to resign.

"It was apparent my contract wasn't to be renewed. I was tired of telling little white lies about it. I asked Mr. Griffith to announce I was resigning to get it over with."

In another *Post* story he said, "You can believe what you want. Maybe it's better that way. I've been through it before. I was shoved. I didn't plan to make any announcement. I hate to leave Washington. It's been my home for thirty years, but that's one of the hazards of baseball. I don't know what I'm going to do. I have no offers."[24]

Chuck Dressen was hired to replace Bucky at $45,250 for 1955, at least $10,000 more than Bucky earned in 1954. In 1955 the Senators plummeted to 53–107.

Chapter 21

Killebrew and Kaline

Bucky's 18th and last season as Senators manager in 1954 may have ended in a sixth-place finish and only 66 wins, but it was not without its interesting subplots. One involved a 17-year-old from Idaho by the name of Harmon Killebrew. He was recommended to Griffith by his friend, Republican Senator Herman Welker, who it was said had also discovered pitcher Vernon Law. Killebrew's story was beyond belief. Said to be 6 feet tall and 195 to 210 pounds, he looked much bigger with a Paul Bunyan-esque upper body. He was selected as Idaho's high school player of the year in baseball and football and he was rated as the top quarterback in the nation. He batted .500 in high school and was hitting higher than .800 in the semi-pro Idaho-Oregon Border League when Ossie Bluege, who had been kicked upstairs after being fired as manager after the 1947 season, was sent to Idaho to scout Killebrew. Seeing was as beyond belief as hearing. In the three semi-pro games Bluege saw, Killebrew batted 12-for-12 with four home runs, including one stepped off by Bluege at 435 feet. He also had three triples and five singles and a line drive that hit the shin of an outfielder and bounced back to the infield. Bluege said Killebrew had the best swing he'd ever seen.

The Senators outbid 12 other teams and paid $50,000 for Killebrew, roughly $450,000 in 2010 dollars, making him the first bonus player in Senators history. For that he gave up a football scholarship offer from Oregon. On June 19, 1954, 10 days before his 18th birthday, he signed with the Senators. He flew on a prop to Chicago where the Senators were playing the White Sox, was met at the airport by Bluege's brother, and was taken to the Senators' hotel where, knees shaking, he was introduced to Bucky. The next day he made his debut as, of all things, a pinch-runner.

Bucky didn't know what to do with the kid, who by bonus rule he had to carry. He was slow, threw with a stiff wrist (some observers said he threw like a girl) and was a butcher at third base, where Yost was entrenched. He was confused, nervous, and bewildered. Bucky saw the potential but didn't play him. Bucky believed Killebrew was four or five years away from contributing in the major leagues. He got in only nine games in 1954. Calvin Griffith, Walter's adopted son who was taking a greater role with the team, and Senator Welker wanted him to play. Bucky's refusal to play Killebrew may have been a factor in his leaving the Senators after 1954. Calvin wanted a different manager. But Dressen also didn't play Killebrew in 1955 and, with the bonus rule expired, he wound up in the minors at Charlotte, Chattanooga, and Indianapolis. He proved Bucky right when in 1959, his first year as a regular, he led the A.L. with 42 homers.[1]

Bucky's son, Dick, was signed by Sherry Robinson out of Wake Forest in 1954 and assigned to Hagerstown, Maryland, in the Piedmont League, after cutting his teeth playing for Truro in the Nova Scotia League, a summer league for top college players. Dick had another year of eligibility when he left Wake, where he hit .314. Listed at 6 feet and 158 pounds, one scout said of him: "Good fielder, quick hands, good instincts, runs well, but weak bat, probably won't go higher than AA."[2]

Dick said at the time his father had not particularly encouraged him to pursue baseball, nor did he discourage him. "I considered that a good sign. I have an older brother who is a lawyer in Washington. He played baseball at the University of Virginia, but dad advised him to lay off the pros."[3]

Dick spent 1955 and 1956 in the military. When he got out he was assigned to Charlotte and decided to give it three years, telling himself if he didn't make the majors by then he'd pack it in. True to his word, he retired from minor league ball after the 1959 season. By his own admission Dick was a classic no-hit, good-field middle infielder who had trouble with the curveball. His best year was 1958 at Class A Charlotte, where he hit .249 with nine home runs as the everyday second baseman. He was promoted to AA Chattanooga late in 1958 and 1959 where he played with Harmon Killebrew, Bob Allison, and Jim Kaat.

Dick, whose signing bonus was $35, said being Bucky's son was more of a disadvantage than an advantage. For example, there was the abuse from fans. "After ball games we'd go get a beer," Dick said. "Some of the people in the bar were saying some negative stuff about me being Bucky's son. My teammates went over to them and said we don't want to hear that anymore, let's go outside. So they were sticking up for me.

"Only once did it get to me. During a game somebody was yelling 'Bucky's little Bo Bo. Too bad you can't play like your dad.' That's when I charged the fence down in Charlotte and the first baseman stopped me.

"Dad, he only saw me play ball, I think, three times. And one time in Charlotte he paid to get in. Didn't want anybody to know he was there. Didn't even go to Mr. Howser to get in free. He carried on a conversation with people next to him. They were yapping about how Dick can't play as good as his dad. Dad never said a word until the game was over, then he said, 'You know, by the way, I never introduced myself. I'm Dick's father, Bucky Harris.' They about dropped over."

Bucky's son, Stan Jr., a retired federal judge, had a similar experience. He was tagged as Bucky's son as early as 1943, when he made the starting lineup at first for Woodrow Wilson High School. The Associated Press picked up a picture of him that ran in papers throughout the country with the caption "A chip off the old block." When he played in the army, people would take shots at him. "Little snotty things. Once I hit a routine fly ball and the PA announcer said, 'You'll have to hit a lot better than that to make the big leagues.'" Stan said his father never saw him play competitively in high school, college or with the army.[4]

Another 1954 subplot was the debut of Carlos Paula. On September 6 in Griffith Stadium, Bucky penciled in Paula to start in left field and bat fifth. Thus the Senators became the 12th of the then 16 major league franchises to break the color barrier. Why had it taken so long? There is no clear answer. Griffith never made any effort to scout and sign American black players, but he did let the Homestead Grays of the Negro Leagues play half their home games in Griffith Stadium. In 1943 Griffith asked Josh Gibson and Buck Leonard if they wanted to play major league ball. They said yes, but he never got back to them. Writer Leonard Koppett argues Griffith was too old and undercapitalized to do what Rickey did.[5]

In any case, that it took seven years after Jackie Robinson's debut for the major league team representing the capital of the United States — in a city with a 54 percent black population — to finally field a black player sounds like fodder for a sensational story. But no one seemed to care, not even the city's black baseball fans. The newspaper accounts of the game mention Paula in the last sen-

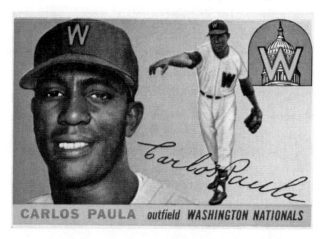

CARLOS PAULA outfield WASHINGTON NATIONALS

Bucky was the manager when Carlos Paula, pictured in a Topps baseball card, became the first African American player to play for the Senators in September of 1954.

tence. "Paula, the first Negro to break into action with the Senators in a regular season game, played in the first game and did contribute two hits including a two-run double."[6]

Paula's appearance was decidedly a nonevent. Happening as it did in a holiday double-header on Labor Day, attendance was only 4,865, almost 2,000 below average for the season and 12,000 below what the Yankees had drawn the day before for a Sunday afternoon game. The next day Paula played again and attendance was less than one-tenth of Monday's at just 460. Played in 95-degree heat between sixth- and seventh-place teams, the game drew the smallest crowd since Griffith Stadium opened in 1911.[7] Three days after Paula integrated the Senators, the city's schools opened under an integration policy for the first time.[8] Why the lack of interest in Paula? For one thing there was a general lack of interest in baseball in Washington. The team's season attendance was 505,000, 15th among the 16 major league teams. Another factor may have been Paula was Cuban. Washington baseball fans were used to Cubans. An African American might have generated more excitement among D.C. blacks.

Back in the spring a different player had been expected to be the first black to play for the Senators in the regular season. Angel Scull, also a Cuban, was pushing Paula for right field. Scull was Bucky's early favorite. Scull was 5'8" and 160 pounds, ran well and reminded Bucky of himself. "Never saw such a cute one," Bucky said. "It would be a shame if he got homesick or fouled up with all the ability he's got. He's a little demon out there."[9]

Scull was a singles hitter with tremendous range in the outfield and a great arm. Paula, on the other hand, was big, 6'3" and 195 pounds, and powerful. Bucky soured on Paula early in the spring as he was fishing for bad balls but warmed to him later. "I have to like what I see. He can whack the ball. He has that size and gets some extra leverage into his swing. And he isn't fast for a big man, he's fast for a man of any size."[10]

Bucky expected one or maybe both of the players to make the team in the spring. He liked the idea of carrying them both as support for one other. Worried they might be turned into heroes, which would hurt them on the field, Bucky asked Senators vice president Calvin Griffith to enlist the cooperation of leaders of the black community in Washington to ease the way for Scull and Paula. Griffith asked a bilingual Howard University student to help.[11] But when April came, Paula and Scull, without explanation, did not make the cut. Paula was sent to Charlotte in the Sally League and Scull was sold to Havana. Topps issued a baseball card for Scull for 1954, but he never appeared in a major league game.

Meanwhile, in Detroit, Spike Briggs had inherited the presidency of the Tigers from his father, Walter Briggs, in 1953. Spike had worked for the Tigers since 1934 after graduating from Georgetown, where he played second base. He was christened Walter Briggs Jr., but his father didn't want him to be called "junior" so he called him Spike, which suited the son. It was said Spike hated "junior" so much that employees could be fired for using it. Spike was a powerful and persuasive figure in Detroit. As chairman of the sports committee for Detroit's 250th birthday in 1951, he brought in the National Rackets championship, a Charles-Wolcott title fight, AAU National Gymnastic meet, National Table Shuffleboard Championship, National Open golf tournament, fencing, diving, the American Legion Junior Baseball World's Series and the MLB All-Star Game.

During Bucky's first year of his first tenure at Detroit in 1929, Spike was in high school, and he had the run of the clubhouse and the field. But when Mickey Cochrane took over in 1930, he and the owner clashed over Spike. Cochrane thought he was a distraction and didn't want him around. Bucky had liked having him around and they got along well. Spike never lost his boyhood admiration for Bucky and he lobbied his father for years to bring Bucky back. When Jack Zeller retired as GM in 1945, Spike tried to get Bucky the job, but his father gave it to George Troutman. After the 1954 season Tiger manager Fred Hutchinson, who had been the Tiger skipper for three seasons, asked for a multi-year contract. When Hutchinson refused to accept a $40,000 one-year contract as manager for 1955, Spike finally got Bucky. He was 58 by then and had been in baseball since 1916.[12]

Twenty-one years earlier Bucky left a young Detroit club that went on to win two pennants for another manager. The 1955 team was similar to his 1929–1932 teams in that it had a lot of young talent. Among the young players were Frank House, Bill Tuttle, Harvey Kuenn and 20-year-old Al Kaline. When Bucky met him, Kaline was not yet three years out of high school in Baltimore, where he hit .333, .418, .469 and .488, and was the first to make the *Baltimore Sun* high school all-star team four years in a row. His father and grandfather had been amateur players. His father, Nicholas, was a bare-handed catcher from the Eastern Shore of Maryland that produced Home Run Baker and Jimmy Foxx. In the summers during high school, Al played three games on Sundays in different leagues with men old enough to be his father. While Al changed in the car, his father drove from field to field. When he graduated, all 16 teams made offers or expressed interest. The Tigers were looking at Tom Qualters and wanted Kaline only if he didn't insist on a signing bonus. Scout Ed Katalinas convinced them otherwise. Nicholas insisted the family get $15,000 for him to sign in June 1953, but settled for the minimum $6,000 a year for three years. Al reported directly to the Tigers on June 24, 1953. He was used only as a pinch-hitter until his first start on September 16 in Boston, where he went 3-for-5. Kaline played in 30 games and hit .250 in

1953. In 1954, after incumbent starter Steve Souchock broke his wrist in winter ball, Hutchinson put Kaline in right field to open the season.

After Kaline hit a low wall abutting the foul line and developed water on the knee, Briggs ordered a group of boxes torn out to make more room. The area became known as "Kaline's Corner." After he hit .276 in 138 games in 1954, he received a raise to $12,000 in 1955. He signed for $20,000 in 1956. In 1955, Bucky's first year back, Kaline came in to camp a married man and 20 pounds heavier. Bucky made him the full-time right fielder. He hit safely in the first 14 games. On April 16, after going 4-for-5 with three home runs, two in one inning, he was batting .560. It was the first time a batter had hit two in one inning since DiMaggio in 1936. The writers told him he would be in the record books with DiMaggio.

Kaline seemed unfazed, but the next day he confessed to Bucky that he didn't sleep that night.

"How could he?" Bucky said. "Just think what's ahead of him."[13]

What was ahead of him, at least in 1955, was a break-out season in which he led the A.L. in average, .340, and hits, 200. He hit 27 home runs with 102 RBIs. Thanks to Kaline and Ray Boone, who led the league in RBIs, and Kuenn, who led in doubles and hit .306, the Tigers won 11 more games than they did for Fred Hutchinson the year before. They finished 79–75, their first .500-plus season since 1950. When the Tigers played a series in Washington in 1955, *Washington Post* writer Bob Addie asked some of the players why the Tigers were playing well. "The consensus was they were playing under a relaxed manager."[14]

Ten days in June of 1956 were all it took to seal the Tigers' fate (and Bucky's, as it would turn out). On June 15, the Tigers were 27–26, tied for fourth with the Red Sox, but only two out of second place. Beginning the next day the Tigers lost 10 of 11 games, with the 11th one being a tied game stopped by rain. By the time they won again, beating the Athletics in Kansas City on June 28, the Tigers were 28–36. They never recovered enough to contend, but they did go on a torrid streak from August 21 through the end of the season when they played .729 ball, going 27–10 to finish 82–72. That was good for fifth place, and fifth was only three games out of second.

During the hot streak down the stretch, second-year pitchers Frank Lary and Paul Foytack were 7–0 and 5–3, respectively. Paul Foytack's lack of control and consistency almost drove Bucky to distraction in the spring, but Bucky kept sending him out there and he turned into a first-rate starter. Foytack was from Scranton, just a few miles from where Bucky grew up. As a senior at Scranton Tech High School, he was 6–1 with 81 strikeouts. He graduated in June of 1948, signed with Tigers for a $4,000 bonus and went to Toledo. He made it to the Tigers in 1955 but pitched only 49 innings and received only one start. In 1956, after he shut out the Senators on five hits with seven strikeouts on May 9, Bucky put him in the regular rotation for the rest of the season.

Foytack, now 79 and living in Tennessee, remembers Bucky and the 1956 season when he was 25. "He was a great guy. He really was. We were from the same area and I used to tease him all the time. I'd keep him laughing and he'd say, 'Foytack, you're crazy.'

"He didn't act like a smart aleck. He treated you the way he wanted to be treated. I thanked him for pitching me every fourth day and I'm sure everybody else did. I completed 16 games and was ashamed of it."[15]

The 16 complete games Foytack pitched came in 33 starts, second on the team to Lary. He pitched 256 innings, also second to Lary, who led the league with 294. Foytack led the team in strikeouts and was third in the league with 184. He led the league in walks with 142.

Lary, whom Bucky liked to call "Bulldog," led the league in starts with 38 and wins with 21 and was second in complete games with 20. Lary, now 80 and living in Alabama, also remembers that 1956 season and Bucky. "He was a pretty old fella. He'd been in baseball a long time. He knew baseball well. I played for a lot of good managers and he was one of them. He let you play the ball game. He gave me a good chance to pitch. I wasn't put on the bench, I can tell you that. He was kind of quiet. He wasn't jumping on nobody. That was a nice thing about him."[16]

Lary started against Cleveland in September and gave up 10 hits and six walks but only one run. He stranded 15, only three under the record. He left the bases loaded twice and a man on third two other times. Someone in the press box said, "You have to say one thing about Harris, he's not going to be hasty about this."

Bucky usually let Lary be Lary on the mound. "You have to stick with Frank a lot more than most pitchers. He has a remarkable ability to get himself out of trouble. Just when you think he's on the ropes he suddenly pulls himself out of a hole and seems to be as strong as ever. He has tremendous determination to make good. Has more of that than almost any player I've known."[17]

Despite the strong finish in 1956, Bucky was in trouble. During the June losing streak Briggs said he had no immediate plans to fire Bucky. It was likely Briggs stuck with Bucky because of his respect for him and because he had the franchise up for sale and thought it was better to keep Bucky so the new owners could pick their own manager. Instead, he blamed the players' lack of hustle and poor coaching for the failed season. He regularly blasted the coaches in the papers. He said third-base coach Billy Hitchcock was blowing calls. Joe Gordon quit over the criticism. Briggs complained about GM Muddy

Ruel, saying, "He gets more money than the president and he hasn't done one thing since he's been GM."[18]

That was an odd thing to say about a GM who brought Kuenn, Kaline, Lary, Foytack and other young players to Detroit and who, it was believed in some quarters, was under orders not to sign black players. From 1945 to 1952, the Tigers had plunged from world champions to cellar dwellers, yet Walter Briggs did not sign a black player or develop any African Americans in Detroit's minor league system. The Tigers were the second-to-last team to put a black player on their major league roster. Though they beat the Red Sox by a year at the major league level when they played Ozzie Virgil in 1958, the Tigers were the last team to sign an African American to a contract. That wasn't until August 1953. Some claimed it was no coincidence it didn't happen until 18 months after the death of Walter Briggs. While no definitive quote on the subject of race by Walter Briggs ever saw the light of print, many black Detroiters believed Briggs had vowed never to have black players as long as he was in charge of the club. George Lerchen, a Detroit native who played with the Tigers' farm system in the late 1940s and 1950s and for the Tigers in 1952 and 1953, was quoted in the book *The Detroit Tigers: Club and Community*, saying, "It was well known that any scout who signed a colored player would be fired."[19]

Bucky's own racial attitudes aren't known. Bucky's son, Stanley Harris, said he never heard him discuss race. There is no quote attributed to him about race other than an expression of sympathy for Jackie Robinson for what he went through in 1947. He knew Robinson when Robinson played for Montreal and Bucky managed Buffalo. He managed against Robinson in the 1947 World Series. He had a good relationship with Luke Easter and the other blacks in San Diego. While it's true he never publicly urged any of the teams he worked for to break the barrier, he was the manager of the Senators when they played their first black player, Carlos Paula, and the general manager in Boston when the Red Sox became the last team to break the color barrier in 1959. In the Boston case, Bucky wanted Pumpsie Green to make the team out of spring training but was overruled.

As early as September 20, 1954, there were reports that Red Sox GM Joe Cronin and field manager Pinky Higgins were going to San Francisco and that Bucky would take over the GM job. Sports editor Jerry Nason of the *Boston Globe* said Cronin was going to San Francisco to "do spade work for the American League which ultimately will put them into a major league operation on the coast." The Sox owned the San Francisco team in the PCL.

Sportswriter Larry Claflin of the *Boston Evening American* predicted the same thing. He believed Bucky would be brought in as an assistant to Cronin and "will be general manager with full authority after Cronin departs."

But Sam Cohen of the *Boston Daily Record* quoted Yawkey as saying in a telephone interview from his South Carolina plantation, "Cronin and Higgins going to San Francisco. That's a hair-brained thing if I ever heard one."

Having said that, he refused to comment on Harris. In early September a deal was closed to sell the Tigers for $5,500,000 to Fred Knorr, a Michigan radio executive and the head of an 11-man syndicate. Knorr leveled the usual criticism at Bucky. He was too nice of a guy, too mild-mannered.

Knorr said, "The next manager will be a fiery, active guy who will inspire his players and get out there on the field and fight for them."[20]

When Bucky read that description, he submitted his resignation. "That eliminates me," he wrote in a letter to Spike, who was kept on as GM. The letter was dated September 5. It was released by Briggs on September 27.

"As you know," read the letter, "I prefer to try and get winning results by exercising my best judgment percentage wise."[21]

Harris said he left behind a sound nucleus for a pennant contender. Briggs defended Bucky. "We've had our ups and downs. The way Bucky brought the team back during the final two months of the season is tremendous. I wish him the best for the future."

Bucky and his wife, his second and much younger, moved out of their suburban Grosse Point home the day before the letter was released and put their furniture in storage. Bucky took his shots at the new owners. "I know just the man for the Tiger job," Bucky said. "I mean Emmett Kelly of the circus. He has everything they want in a manager.

"If they want a television actor they should have known better than to hire me. I've never been what they call a fiery type. I've always backed up my ballplayers on a question of rules, but I've never seen an umpire reverse himself on a judgment play. I never liked the idea of abusing an umpire to show him up, anymore than I'd like the idea of somebody abusing me. Maybe things have changed since the advent of TV and you have to give people a show. Well, I'm not that way."[22]

On September 30, 1956, Bucky managed his 4,410th — and last — major league game. His Tigers won. In the context of his career he went out a winner. The 82 wins by the 1956 Tigers were the most for a Bucky team since the 1948 Yankees and tied for the sixth-most wins in a season in his career.

Once and for all, Bucky was out of the "monkey suit."

Chapter 22

Trouble in Beantown

On July 21, 2009, 75-year-old Elijah "Pumpsie" Green threw out the ceremonial first pitch at Fenway Park, 50 years to the day that Green broke the color barrier for the Red Sox, the last major league club to integrate. Green's debut with the Red Sox came on July 21, 1959, against the White Sox at old Comiskey Park in Chicago, when he entered the game in the top of the eighth inning as a pinch-runner. Among those who witnessed the historic moment was Red Sox general manager Bucky Harris. By then Jackie Robinson had played 12 years and retired; Willie Mays, Hank Aaron, Ernie Banks, Frank Robinson, Vada Pinson, and Bill White were established National League stars. In 1959 Johnny Roseboro, Charlie Neal, Jim Gilliam and Maury Wills would help the Dodgers win the World Series. The American League was slower to develop black stars, though A.L. pioneer Larry Doby was still playing in 1959 and men such as Vic Power, Minnie Minoso, Bobby Boyd, Willie Tasby and Elston Howard were impact players. Across town the National League Braves, who by 1959 were in Milwaukee, had integrated nine years earlier with Sam Jethroe, who was the 1950 N.L. Rookie of the Year.

So what took the Red Sox so long to integrate? Why were they last? Critics say the answer is simple — out and out racism, especially on the part of Mike "Pinky" Higgins, the manager since 1955, and owner Tom Yawkey. There is plenty of evidence to support the accusation. In April of 1945 Jethroe, Marvin Williams and 26-year-old Jackie Robinson were given a tryout in Fenway before then-Boston manager Joe Cronin. The tryout was a token gesture to the black press in Boston and City Councilor Isadore Muchnick, who was threatening to ban Sunday baseball in Boston if the Sox didn't give evidence they were thawing on integration. In interviews with the *Boston Globe*, Jethroe, who died in 2001, said, "I remember Cronin telling us that we all had the ability to play in the big leagues but that blacks simply weren't being allowed at that time."[1]

Robinson, Williams, Jethroe and others in attendance also remembered hearing someone yell, "Get those niggers off the field."

No one knows who yelled it, but it did happen.

In a radio report on National Public Radio on October 11, 2002, Juan Williams talked about the shouting of the slur, saying, "But with only management in the stands, someone yelled 'Get those niggers off the field,' according to a reporter who was there that day."

In 1972 Robinson told the *Boston Globe*, "We knew we were wasting our time. It was April 1945. Nobody was serious then about black players in the majors, except maybe a few politicians."[2]

Howard Bryant, a Boston native, recounts the same story in *Shut Out: A Story of Race and Baseball in Boston*, where he writes flatly, "The Red Sox were one of the most racist teams in baseball."

Clark Booth, writing in the *Dorchester Reporter* around the 50th anniversary of Pumpsie's debut, wrote, "Destiny got sidetracked by the person who, as Robinson was finishing his infamous tryout at Fenway Park on the morning of April 16, 1945, yelled from the shadows deep in the grandstands behind home plate, "Get those blankety-blank N-word off the field!"

While some believe it was Yawkey who yelled the slur, Booth doubts it.

> But I find that much hard to believe. While I don't doubt the depths of his antebellum hang-ups on the subject of race, I don't think Yawkey was that dumb. He was, after all, a Yale man and therefore plenty wise to all the ways he could express his displeasure and exercise his will or just plain get even without descending to such common vulgarity and risk making a fool of himself.
>
> It's more likely that the profane utterance that still so scars Red Sox history probably came from one of the clubhouse employees, a rowdy bunch. But their antics, I firmly believe, would have been heartily approved by their employers.[3]

In 1959 Cronin, by then A.L. president, offered to *Jet* magazine a lame defense of the 1945 decision not to offer Robinson and Jethroe contracts that amounted to saying let someone else go first. "The color line hadn't been broken yet and we didn't own any team where we could play them. I certainly regretted not taking Robinson, but there is no truth to the charge that the Sox practice discrimination. We just were never able to sign a Negro player we wanted and Tom Yawkey is a fine man. He has colored help on his plantation in South Carolina, takes excellent care of them, pays good salaries and they are all happy."[4]

In 1949, the Red Sox gave up the chance to sign Willie Mays. As Juan Williams reports, "one of the team's scouts decided that it wasn't worth waiting through a stretch of rainy weather to scout any black player."[5]

Booth cited the Red Sox signing of bonus babies as proof of their racism. In the 1950s the Red Sox signed 17 bonus babies. "Every single blessed one of them was a white boy. Did anyone pause to wonder why? If so, there's no record of it. It's as if they were blind."[6]

A *Boston Globe* story from 2000 claimed the Red Sox signed a black player before Green. "The spin over the years is that the Sox didn't sign a black player until Pumpsie Green in the late '50s. Not true. They signed Piper Davis, a Hall of Famer in the Negro Leagues, and took him to spring training in 1950. They also gave him a $5,000 bonus, which was huge in those days. Davis was a second baseman, but he couldn't beat out Bobby Doerr so the Sox sent him to Scranton, Pennsylvania, which was their No. 3 minor league club, where he would be allowed to play. Piper played a few weeks, hit better than .300, but decided he would be better off back in the Negro Leagues."[7]

Davis did not receive a $5,000 bonus. If he had, the Red Sox would have been forced by the bonus baby rule to carry him on the major league roster. The Red Sox bought him for Scranton for $15,000 in August of 1949 from the Birmingham Black Barons, where he was the manager and the Negro Leagues leading hitter. Though it was intimated he would make the Red Sox in 1950, there's no evidence the Sox took Davis to spring training in 1950 and he certainly did not play in any spring games for the Red Sox. It is true Davis left Scranton on his own and went back to the Negro Leagues where he was making better money.[8]

Green's Fenway Park debut against the Kansas City Athletics on August 4, 1959, was a major event. He started in the lead-off spot and played second base. Fenway didn't get many black fans then, but for that game, several hundred turned out. The game sold out, so Sox management roped off a large section of center field for hundreds of standing-room fans, all of them black.

Green lives in the San Francisco area and Scott Ostler of the *San Francisco Chronicle* interviewed him at the time of the 50th anniversary of his debut. "It seemed like I was lightheaded," Green says, "because they were screaming and hollering. Boy, I just don't know. So I went and got my bat and on my way up to home plate, the whole stands, blacks and whites, they stand up and give me a standing ovation. A standing ovation, my first time up! And the umpire said, 'Good luck, Pumpsie,' something like that."[9]

Green cleared the path for black pitcher Earl Wilson, who came up a week later. In 2005 Paul Harber of the *Boston Globe* uncovered more evidence of the entrenched racism in the Red Sox organization when he found this in a Wilson scouting report: "Well-mannered colored boy, not too black, pleasant to talk to, well-educated, very good appearance."

Wilson told the *Globe* in 1980, "It never bothered me what people said in the stands in Boston. What I heard in the South was so much worse. I just wondered why it took me so long [six years] to get there. I was ready long before that."[10]

What was the role of Bucky Harris in Green's breaking of the Red Sox's color barrier in 1959? For a man who knew five United States presidents, married a senator's daughter and once had William Howard Taft for a neighbor, Bucky was outwardly apolitical. If he had an opinion on the sociopolitical aspect of integrated baseball, he never told anyone about it. His sons say they never heard him discuss race. But he did have a little bit of a history with black players.

He was the general manager of the Buffalo Bisons in the International League when Jackie Robinson played for Montreal. He managed against Robinson in the 1947 World Series, and the only time he was quoted on Robinson he was sympathetic. Black players were the stars of his San Diego team in 1949 and he was friendly with them, especially Luke Easter. And it was Bucky who made the first Senators lineup with a black player in it.

For all that, Bucky was never proactive about bringing black players into the game, but in that regard he was no different than most veteran baseball men, such as Ted Williams. Much has been made of the fact that Williams went out of his way to greet Green warmly and treat him like any other teammate, helping ease his way. But it's also true that by 1959, Williams had been with the Red Sox for 14 years, during which time he never made a public complaint about the team's racism.

Bucky was hired by the Red Sox on the day of the first game of the 1956 World Series. The announcement said Bucky would be a "special assistant" to general manager Joe Cronin, making Bucky fourth in the hierarchy of President Tom Yawkey, Cronin and field manager Mike "Pinky" Higgins. Higgins was a hard-drinking Texan and alleged "man's man" from the old school and an open and unrepentant racist. Higgins was Yawkey's drinking buddy, and Bucky sometimes joined them in Yawkey's office for happy hours.

In one biography, Ted Williams claims the drinking got out of hand. Sometimes Bucky "was so far gone that the office help had to guide his hand through his signature of the official papers." And "Higgins with a lot of personal problems which he drowned, he liked to say, with cherry bombs."[11] A cherry bomb is a drink made with vodka, creme de cacao and grenadine syrup.

There is some circumstantial evidence one of the "special" aspects of Bucky's position was to be a front man on race relations and pave a way for the integration of the Red Sox. Two years went by before such evidence emerged. For his first two seasons in Boston, Bucky seemed content as the GM's assistant. He and his young wife, Marie, enjoyed the nightlife in Boston and their beautifully appointed vintage home. Bucky liked making deals while staying out of the limelight. Several of the trades made in 1957 and 1958 bore Bucky's imprint, notably the trades of Milt Bolling, Russ Kemmerer and Faye Throneberry to the Senators for Bob Chakales and Dean Stone; Billy Goodman to the Orioles for Mike Fornieles; Albie Pearson and Norm Zauchin to the Senators for Pete Runnels; and Ken Aspromonte to the Senators for Lou Berberet.

In January of 1959 Cronin was elected president of the American League and Bucky was elevated to general manager and vice president, replacing as GM the man who had replaced Bucky as manager 23 years earlier. Bucky, 61, was described as stunned and happy. "I learned only an hour ago from Joe who called from Chicago," Bucky said at a hastily called press conference at Fenway. "It's so sudden that it kind of stumps you. Replacing Joe is not the easiest thing to do, but I'll just have to dig in and do it."

In the Ted Williams book *Hitter* by Ed Linn, Williams said Bucky was a reluctant GM. "Yawkey always felt guilty about letting Bucky go. He was, alas, doing Bucky no favor. Bucky had a gorgeous young wife, and until Yawkey felt the need to go rummaging around his conscience he had been living a perfectly happy life. Bucky was an administrator. Bucky wasn't an executive."[12]

One of the first questions Bucky was asked was how he would handle Ted Williams. Bucky smiled and said, "Let him handle himself."

Williams would handle himself between the lines, but Bucky had to sign him first. Williams was 40 and had missed 25 games in 1958 with injuries, yet was coming off his seventh season of leading the A.L. in batting. He was renewed for something said to be "upwards" of $125,000 for the 1959 season after a 25-minute meeting with Bucky.

That winter, be it trades or dealing with 1958 A.L. MVP Jackie Jensen, who was livid over the Williams contract, whatever Bucky did, that was mere backdrop to the one big looming story of 1959, Pumpsie Green. Green had been bought by the Red Sox in 1956 from Stockton and worked his way up the chain, from Albany to Oklahoma City to Minneapolis, the Sox's AAA club.

With pressure on the Red Sox, who did not employ a black person even as a janitor or vendor, to integrate in 1959, Green was sent to the Red Sox spring training camp in Scottsdale, Arizona, where he wasn't allowed to stay in the team hotel. He had to be shuttled back and forth every day from the Hotel Adams in Phoenix, 17 miles away. Green had a tremendous spring and batted .400 for a while despite finishing 2-for-19. In spring games he batted .327, led the team with four home runs, and was selected "best prospect in camp" by the Boston baseball writers. He went north with the team and played in exhibition games on the way to Boston. It seemed certain he was going to make the team, and Bucky told reporters that when the Red Sox broke camp.

Then on April 8, two days before the Red Sox were scheduled to open the season in Yankee Stadium, Higgins demoted Green to Minneapolis, which caused an uproar throughout Boston and baseball.

"Pumpsie Green is just not ready," Higgins told the press. When Larry Claflin asked Higgins if he would recall Green later in the season, Higgins called Claflin a "nigger lover" and spat tobacco juice on him.[13]

Booth described Higgins as a "Svengali who held Yawkey totally under his sway" and writes that Higgins told one writer, "There'll be no niggers on this ball club as long as I have anything to say about it."[14]

The Boston NAACP chapter was outraged by Green's demotion, organized protest pickets at Fenway Park, and asked for a hearing on bias charges against the Red Sox before the Massachusetts Commission. Yawkey said nothing. Bucky was sent out to face the commission and the press. In an article in *Jet* magazine Bucky said, "The fact that we have 12 Negro players in our farm system speaks for itself. As to the '45 tryouts, I think anyone would have wanted Robinson and Jethroe if they had known they would develop as they did."[15]

It fell to Bucky to release a letter to the Massachusetts Commission describing the Red Sox defense against the bias claim. The letter weakly claimed the Red Sox signed players, "regardless of race, color or creed." And the letter said, "The charge that the decision to option Pumpsie Green to Minneapolis was prompted by bias has no foundation. The truth is he was optioned to give him an opportunity to play regularly and develop his profession."

Lacking hard evidence, the commission cleared the team of the bias charge. In *Jet* Robinson spoke out. "There is no question in my mind about the Red Sox being prejudiced. But in the case of Pumpsie Green, who can say they are not right and he needs seasoning? The Red Sox have spent so much money all these years trying to buy a pennant by buying broken down

PUMPSIE GREEN
Second Base-Shortstop

Boston
Red Sox

Bucky was a key figure in the integration of the Red Sox in 1959. Bucky fired racist manager Pinky Higgins to clear the way for Pumpsie Green, pictured in a Topps baseball card.

ballplayers. Milwaukee, the Dodgers, Giants, Cincinnati, Pittsburgh, anybody who wants a Negro player has found them and good ones. There is no question that if the Red Sox wanted one they could find one. Maybe it's not Green, but in all this time there could have been others."

While the Red Sox were in Washington for a three-game series from June 30-July 2, Bucky was in Philadelphia working on a trade. Yawkey called him there and sent him to Washington to settle, according to Yawkey, rumors that Higgins would be fired. The Boston papers were saying Higgins had agreed to resign at the end of the road trip in Baltimore on July 5 or that he would never resign and would have to be fired.[16]

In any case, Bucky did not go to the team's hotel in Washington, as expected, where some reporters were waiting. In *Hitter* Williams says, "He went roaming his old haunts and disappeared for two days, although Bucky sightings were periodically posted in the press box."[17]

From Washington, where the Red Sox lost all three games to fall into last place at 31–42, the team traveled to Baltimore by bus. When they arrived at the Lord Baltimore Hotel the night of July 2, they found their missing general manager waiting in the hotel lobby. Bucky took Higgins to a late dinner and a long talk. At the end of their dinner, Higgins said he would not resign until he talked to Yawkey. He called him the next day and agreed to step down.

Yawkey had a press conference in Boston, the first he had called in 26 years, where he said "Releasing Higgins was one of the toughest things I ever had to do in baseball. We're close friends."

Yawkey said he didn't blame Higgins for the team's poor play.

"It's always unfortunate when a ball club goes poorly that the manager has to take the rap. It might not be his fault and it might be."

Yawkey said when Harris went to Washington, there was no intention of replacing Higgins. "However, his visit immediately started press speculation that a change was impending. It was said these reports brought the situation to a head with fan opinion playing a part."[18]

Yawkey's press conference did not answer this question: Did Yawkey send Bucky to Washington with orders to fire Higgins or to give Higgins a public vote of confidence that he would be retained, which Bucky defied? A little over a year later, in September of 1960, when Yawkey fired Bucky, Povich wrote the latter was true. "Bucky was fired for firing Higgins and hiring Bill Jugus to replace him without consulting Yawkey."[19]

This is a credible claim. Consider the Red Sox went 44–36 in the second half of 1959 under Bill Jurges, after having been 31–42 under Higgins, yet Yawkey brought Higgins back to replace Jurges in 1960. On June 1, 1960, Yawkey gave Jurges the manager's death sentence: a vote of confidence and assurance he would not be fired. Just nine days later, Jurges was given what was called a leave of absence. Officially, he was released for health reasons and succeeded by coach Del Baker as an interim. The *Christian Science Monitor* saw through it. "According to the official announcement Jurges felt the mounting pressure of 25 setbacks in 30 starts since the middle of May had left him physically and mentally unable to continue as manager, but recent developments made many critics suspect the move had actually come via front office pressure."[20]

In any case, a week after Higgins was fired, Green was called up, an unlikely coincidence.

After Green's debut, Roy Campanella said something about Bucky. "I haven't seen Green play any baseball this season, but if I know Sox general manager Bucky Harris, I figure the club thinks a lot of Green. They dealt Bobby Avila, an 10-year veteran to Milwaukee to make room for Green and that certainly shows some decision."[21]

It was a good point. Whatever Bucky's complicity in the stalling by the Red Sox on integration, by firing Higgins and letting Avila go he finally made it happen. And whatever Bucky's racial attitudes may have been, it seems clear when he looked at ballplayers, he saw only ballplayers.

The Sox tumbled from fifth place and 75–79 in 1959 to seventh place and 65–89 in 1960. Ted Williams played in only 113 games as a 41-year-old, Jensen and Sammy White retired, and every starter but Runnels had sub-par years. But the poor record gave Yawkey had a convenient excuse to get rid of Bucky and replace him with Higgins, who won his promotion to the front office by managing the Red Sox's 1960 collapse on the field. Yawkey and Higgins continued to defy integration. The Red Sox did not develop an African American rookie with star potential until Reggie Smith in 1967.

During his four years in a Red Sox uniform, Green batted .244 in 327 games, with 12 home runs, 69 RBIs and an on-base percentage of .353. He was traded to the Mets at the end of the 1962 season and played 29 games for New York in 1963 before retiring. It took decades for the Red Sox to live down the racist label, if in fact they have. When the team was sold in 2002 John Henry, the new principal owner, said, "I think we have to make a statement not just in baseball but in our community that diversity is an issue that hasn't been fully addressed in the past and certainly has to be fully addressed."

And Larry Lucchino, president and CEO of the Red Sox and part of the new ownership, said the club's history has included "an undeniable legacy of racial intolerance."[22]

Chapter 23

Senior Citizen

On the morning of August 19, 1975, a 78-year-old man in his bathrobe sat in a hard maple chair in his room in the Westwood Retirement Home in Bethesda, Maryland, and listened to people 400 miles away in Cooperstown, New York, talk of him and for him. Baseball Commissioner Bowie Kuhn, who grew up in Washington, D.C., and was a scorecard boy in Griffith Stadium, said, "Your commissioner was just a little kid when he met Bucky Harris and I have a special emotion and love for Bucky."

When Bucky heard Kuhn through the special direct line phone hooked up by the C & P Telephone Company between the Cooperstown platform and his room, he could say only, while trying to control himself, "I'm a little touched, so I think I better not try to talk."[1]

His son, Stanley, then a United States attorney and now a retired federal judge, spoke for and accepted Bucky's induction into the Baseball Hall of Fame as his father and some friends, including Charlotte Winters and her son, listened in Bethesda. Povich described the son's talk as "personal and filled with the particular muscle of life that is Bucky Harris."

When Stanley finished his talk, Kuhn said, "Bucky, are you there and how you doing?" And Bucky said of his son, "He's a little wound up, isn't he?" and the laughter of the hundreds who heard him in Cooperstown Park could be heard in Bucky's room.[2]

Among those who were in Cooperstown for Bucky's induction was a large family group, among them the judge's wife, Becky, and their three sons, Bucky's younger son, Dick, Bucky's daughter, Sally Gooch, and Stanley's mother- and father-in-law, Mr. and Mrs. William Colson. From the old Pennsylvania coal country came Drew Smith, Bucky's brother Merle's grandson, and Smith's wife, Mary, and mother Jean, Merle's daughter. Among the players there for Bucky were Ossie Bluege, Firpo Marberry and Stan Coveleski from the 1924-25 team; Sam West, George Case, Ken Chase (who played under Bucky in his later times in Washington) and Yogi Berra.[3]

Bucky's second wife was not in the picture at this point. It is known Bucky and his first wife divorced in June of 1950. Not much could be learned about Bucky's second wife. Stanley knew little about her. He didn't know her maiden name, how they met or when they married. Stanley said bluntly he believes "she bailed with the Parkinson's."

Drew Smith, Bucky's great nephew whose mother was Merle's daughter, said Bucky and his second wife visited his mother's home once. He said her name was Marie. He estimates she was 20 years younger than Bucky and they seemed to be well matched. "She liked to party, have a good time," he said, "and so did Bucky."[4]

Whatever happened to her, she wasn't around when Bucky was inducted, and Bucky's son, Stanley, explained why Bucky wasn't in Cooperstown that day, either. Bucky had Parkinson's disease, but was otherwise healthy. The tremors associated with the disease were eased somewhat by the new drug L-Dopa. Stanley and his brother Dick thought their father, by now living alone, would be able to make the trip when voted into the hall, and he had said he would go when he was elected in February. But his doctors advised him not to go, as Parkinson's can be aggravated by emotional stress.

Initially Stanley urged him to go. "I said, 'Dad it would be great to go up to Cooperstown and see your old friends,' thinking it would be a great thing for him. Finally it became apparent we were depressing him by pushing him. I said, 'Dad, I'll accept.' He broke into a grin. 'That would be great. I want them to remember me the way I was.'"[5]

A reporter in Bucky's room during the induction wrote this description: "Hundreds of miles away with a wide soundless grin splitting his lips, Mrs. Winters kissed him gently on the cheek. In 15 minutes it was over. Once or twice he plucked self consciously at his bathrobe. He dropped his right hand below the folds of his robe to hide the tremor. In Cooperstown they adjourned for lunch and a ball game. In Bethesda Bucky retired for a nap and some TV."[6]

—◦◦◦—

After he was fired by Yawkey, Bucky got a job with the White Sox, which he could do from Washington. The Sox hired him as a scout, not for young players, but to evaluate other teams and their players as football teams did. It was a relatively new concept in baseball. Bucky was meticulous about the work. He filled out sheets on the players' physical, mental and even social characteristics. He prepared an exhaustive rundown of every Washington player, including those sent to the minors, for Sox manager Al Lopez and less-detailed assessments of other A.L. teams. For the two seasons Bucky worked for the Sox, 1962 and 1963, they were 23–13 against the Senators.[7]

After the 1962 season Bucky quit the White Sox when the club insisted key personnel live in Chicago all year.[8] Bucky lived in Kensington, Maryland, was 66, and didn't want to move.

The Griffith era in Washington D.C. ended in 1960 when the Senators were sold by his heirs to a group who moved the team to Minnesota. Clark Griffith had died at age 86 in 1955. Bucky had been among the honorary pall-bearers, which included U.S. presidents. In 1961 a new era of Washington baseball began when the city was awarded a new franchise under the A.L. expansion to 10 teams, the Los Angeles Angels being the second expansion team. In 1963 the old joke about Bucky needing one more term in Washington to tie FDR came true when he was hired by the expansion Senators' general manager, George Selkirk, as a an aide for player evaluations and special assignments. The job was to include scouting major league teams in Florida during spring training and working out of Washington during the season evaluating major leaguers. A little welcome-home party for Bucky in Selkirk's office turned into a reunion for Bucky with three men who had been rookies under him — Senators field manager Mickey Vernon and coaches George Case and Sid Hudson.[9]

Appropriately Bucky was with the Senators until the end. On September 30, 1971, he was one of only 14,000 who attended the Senators' final games, a double-header with the Yankees, before they moved to Texas to become the Rangers. In a final irony, the last game was not completed. In the top of the ninth hundreds of fans swarmed the RFK Stadium field, tearing up the bases, tearing out tufts of infield grass, and carrying away the ball boys' chairs. Three policemen guarded home plate. Three men were arrested. The game was stopped and forfeited to the Yankees.

Bucky was 73 then and had cataract surgery. He had poor lateral vision and didn't drive but still worked for the Senators as a consultant. Asked if he would go to Texas, he said, "Heavens no. I'm still shocked. I keep thinking how it's going to be around here next season without baseball. I've lived in the Washington area for over 50 years and I guess I'll feel the loss of the Senators as much as anybody."[10]

To his surprise Bucky remained well known in the Washington area as he aged. He marveled at the mail he got asking for autographs. He reluctantly went along with a lavish banquet thrown for him to celebrate his 50 years in baseball. In September of 1965 he donned the Washington uniform one last time to manage the Senators' front-office team against a press–TV team before a Senators-Yankees game. Later that year he was deeply honored when the Washington Baseball Writers named their manager of the year award the Bucky Harris Award. Bucky was there at Shoreham Hotel when the first Harris Award was presented to Dick Williams by Joe Cronin in 1965. The 1970 banquet was star-studded. Ted Williams received the Harris Award from Bowie Kuhn. Williams had to be coaxed to go and relented after being told he didn't have to wear a tux or tie. Gil Hodges received N.L. award, presented by Earl Weaver. President Eisenhower's grandson, David, gave the Most Improved Senator award to Ed Brinkman. Astronaut Frank Borman, the Apollo 8 commander, presented the Sam Rice Awards for best hitters to Killebrew and Aaron.[11]

For the 100th anniversary of baseball in 1969, when Bucky was 72, Bucky was named to the Senators' all-time team in a vote by fans along with four of his teammates from the 1924 team: Rice, right field; Goose Goslin, left field; Muddy Ruel, catcher; and Walter Johnson. Johnson was selected by a landslide as the team's all-time best player.

Bucky may have been one of the best Senators in 100 years, but at that point he still wasn't fit for Cooperstown. When the all-time Senators team was announced, *Post* writer Bob Addie made the case for Bucky to be selected to the Baseball Hall of Fame. "Harris is a senior trouble shooter and scout for the Senators these days. It's fitting he should be where he belongs — home. Harris always prided himself that he never finished last, no mean feat when you consider he managed the Senators for 18 years. As a player Bucky was aggressive. These days he would probably be known as a human credit card — he charged everything."

Addie listed Bucky's second base records for putouts in a season, 479, in 1922; most chances in one World Series game, 13; and most putouts in one series, 26.

"He belongs in Hall of Fame. Of all his qualities he was loyal and unflappable. A golden anniversary for a man with a heart of gold."[12]

In 1974, when Bucky was passed up for the hall once again, he, for probably the first time in his life, talked himself up. He told Addie, who visited him on his 76th birthday, "If you get down to brass tacks, I ought to be in. I never saw myself play, but I know I liked to come up to the plate in a pinch. If I were picking I'd have to select Bucky Harris on his record and I don't say that because I happen to be Bucky Harris.

"When I was passed up again last year, I got an awful lot of mail and some of the sweetest letters. They gave me great enjoyment. Imagine anybody remembering me."

He said he missed baseball in D.C. a lot and that a friend took him to Baltimore to see the Orioles eight or 10 times that summer, but it wasn't the same. He loved watching sports on TV. Talking about the 1974 World Series, he said, "Remember that so-called intentional walk when Rollie Fingers struck out Johnny Bench on a 3–2 pitch? I smelled that one. I saw a lot of that in my time."[13]

While Bucky got old, he didn't get old-fashioned about baseball. Though he never completely warmed up to the obsession with the home run, believing it detracted from the art of pure hitting, he wasn't one who believed the good old days and good old players were better. He predicted further expansion, divisional play and even inter-league play.[14]

In a *Post* column, after Selkirk, who had been a lifetime .290 hitter in nine seasons with the Yankees in the 1930s and 1940s, joked to Bucky that if they could roll back the clock they could play as well as modern players, Bucky said, "I'm not supposed to say this but they play better today. They are faster and better on defense. I know I'm supposed to protect the old player by saying they were better."

Bucky said if it was true, as a lot of old-timers liked to say, that there weren't as many good players in the minors as there used to be, it was because so many young men were going to college and into other careers.[15]

In 1956 Bucky had been taken to task by Ty Cobb and others for quotes in an article in the *Saturday Evening Post* entitled "Ball Players Are as Good as Ever."

"There are more first class ball players today than ever before," Bucky said. "I'm convinced the old stars in the Hall of Fame would have conniption fits and considerably lower averages had they faced the variety of trick stuff the pitchers throw today. The slickest fielders and double play combinations of my time couldn't match the brilliance of the defensive artists on all clubs now.

"Nowadays rookies fresh out of the minors have three or four different pitches. I believe the boys play harder today because there is more incentive for winning. Anyway you look at it the fielding has improved enormously. All this yapping about the scarcity of talented rookies is hogwash."

After the Senators moved to Texas, Bucky was out of a job in baseball of any kind for the first time. He stayed in the news periodically, especially on his birthdays, when writers would visit him and chat, mining column ideas. Addie did on Bucky's 80th birthday in 1976.

> There's a tremor in his hands now — big, gnarled hands; infielder's hands, hand veined in the way of old age. The left foot beats a quiet endless tap on the blue-green rug.
>
> The tremor and the beat tell you something: Parkinson's disease. Six, maybe seven years ago it had Bucky near helplessness. Then came a drug called L-Dopa. He's gotten older, but he's gotten better. The chin is firm. There's a fold in the cheek where there used to be a dimple. But the mind is clear and strong.
>
> He likes two things to do. "Television and walking."
>
> Looking out at the parking lot he said, "That parking lot goes way back up there. I go up and back, up and back. No curbs. No traffic." He paused and patted the leg that was trembling oh so slightly. "My legs are in good shape now. They are the best part of me that's left."

On the wall next to his bed was a reproduction of a page from the *Washington Post* of September 28, 1924. "They put Washington on the baseball map" it says. There are pictures of Joe Judge, Walter Johnson, Muddy Ruel and Goose Goslin. There's a picture of Bucky, too, 27, and manager. Fifty years have gone by and we've seen the tightfisted glumness of the Griffiths, the easy glib attitude of Bob Short. We've seen the tightlipped purpose of George Allen and the ebullient swagger of Edward Bennett Williams and here is the one man who gave Washington a World Championship.

Bucky told Addie he signed with Washington for $375 a month in 1920, but only for the season. Addie calculated that was $2,275 a year "or less than Catfish Hunter gets for two innings." Bucky talked to Addie about the old days. "I used to walk down 7th Street and take the streetcar out to Griffith Stadium. No laundry money in those days. Got $3.50 for meals. Today the players get $22.50 and they always try to eat for free. Of course, steak only cost 75 cents in those days."

"No air-conditioning on the trains. You had the windows open all the time. You'd wake up in the morning and start by spitting the coal dust out of your mouth."

He recalled how after the 1924 Series Griffith gave him a $5,000 bonus. Bucky went home for a visit and when he came back, he said he wanted a $10,000 bonus.

Griffith screamed and squawked. And Bucky said, "You know, he was a little close with his money."[16]

On his 80th birthday Bucky's other visitors were players from the Redskins Alumni Association, including Andy Farkas, a fullback from the pre–World War II days, and Joe Tereshinski, an end from 1947 to 1954. They talked about the Redskins, and Bucky said, "I got all excited Sunday watching the Redskins beat San Francisco. That boy Joe Theismann has quite an arm. He would have made a great baseball pitcher."[17]

Bucky touched one writer in a far-out way. Bob Arnebeck wrote Richard Nixon might have been saved had he been a Bucky Harris fan.

> With Bucky we learned to savor the exquisiteness of being the eternal underdog. We learned to wait with patient dignity. How seldom we booed Bucky and with good reason. Did Bucky spy on the opposition, hide when things got tough, trade what wasn't his to trade? Bucky never said that losing is like death.
>
> The mayor is probably impatiently waiting for a big parade if the Redskins win the Super Bowl. He should have had a parade when Bucky made the Hall of Fame. That's the parade Washington needs, one for the old saw — it's not if you win or lose, it's how you play the game.
>
> Remember what Bucky was like. Slouched easily in the dugout walking slowly to the mound to aid a boy in distress, saving his wrath for that moment when the ump's call was even too much for Job to bear.

I got Bucky's autograph once after a big loss in his last year. The kids still called him "Mister Harris." When anyone told me "keep your eyes on the ball," I saw the tired old eyes of Bucky Harris carefully guiding his scrawl across my dirty scorecard.

What if Bucky Harris had been Nixon's idol and not Allen and Lombardi? A president reminded daily by the lesson of the Washington Senators, interned in the living tradition that you couldn't win them all would not have fallen into the trap of Watergate.[18]

Chapter 24
Bucky as Dad

On March 20, 2009, Bucky's sons, Stanley, a retired federal judge, and Dick Harris, a broker, met in Stanley's Bethesda apartment to talk about their father, who was to them, as he was to inside baseball people, two men. To baseball men Bucky the player was the fighting, fiery, take-no-prisoners, never-back-down competitor between the lines and the mild-mannered, low-key, non-confrontational manager in the dugout.

To Bucky's sons, he was the baseball manager who was consumed with baseball at work and the father at home to whom the work was just another day at the office.

Stanley laughed when he recounted a story of a cocktail party Bucky went to in New York. "When Dad was managing the Yankees, probably in '48, he had not yet married his second wife. They went to a cocktail party in New York. They left the party and Dad said, 'Who was the skinny kid talking baseball all the time?' His wife-to-be said, 'You're probably the only person in the United States who doesn't know who Frank Sinatra is.' That was indicative of Dad's single-mindedness about baseball. He just didn't have outside interests."

Except for family when his kids were young. "His job was a different job than other people had," Stanley said. "But like everybody else, he went to work and he came back. His basic theory was you win some, you lose some, and some are rained out. We didn't have any sense that he was a celebrity, that he was a big deal. It all seemed like ordinary stuff. Griffith Stadium was my summer camp. Dad took me to the park. I had a little uniform. The ballplayers were good to me. They treated me great, like big brothers, when I was growing up. But it seemed like just ordinary stuff."

It seemed like ordinary stuff in the Harris family, but to people on the outside, it sounds like a fantasy childhood, what with Mickey Vernon passing his first baseman's mitts on to Stanley when he got a new ones and Dutch Leonard teaching Dick how to throw a knuckleball.

After games it took a while to get home. "Bucky was last to leave," Stanley said. "He was nonstop signing. People around the stadium just worshipped him."

But for all his celebrity, Bucky didn't have a sense of himself as such. He wasn't a collector. He didn't save or display mementoes of his career.

"Earl Weaver apparently had a room in his house that was a shrine to himself," Stanley said. "Dad never did that. When the Hall of Fame called our house asking if we had anything we could send them for his slot, we didn't have a damn thing except one old glove."

One piece of memorabilia did survive. Stanley still has a handwritten letter from First Lady Grace Coolidge accepting an invitation to Bucky's wedding to Elizabeth Sutherland in 1926.

The brothers' biggest perk as Bucky's sons was a road trip with the Yankees when Bucky was the manager in 1947 and 1948 when Stanley was 16 or 17 and Dick was 12 or 13. Bucky took them along on a western swing. They rode alongside Yankees on the trains, worked out at practices, hung out in the locker rooms, and watched the games from the dugouts and bullpens. Dick said two stories from those trips stand out in his memory. In one, Joe Page nearly freezes Dick's arm off.

"Two things happened that I'll never forget. We were down in the clubhouse and Joe Page was hollering at me to get him a Coke. They had these big containers that were full of ice. So I take my arm and the water is up to here with the ice and I can't feel any Cokes and my arm is freezing. Page said they were way down at the bottom. So I'm told where they are and I'm told to get one. Page was sitting on the trunk laughing when somebody said, 'Joe, that's Buck's son.' He came flying off that trunk so fast there were sparks flying off his spikes. He reaches his hand down there and grabs two Cokes and says, 'Here, have one on me.'

"I remember when we took the '48 trip we were banished to the bullpen. We were in Cleveland. The bullpen was in left field on the other side of a chain-link fence. Joe Page said, 'Let's play Mother-May-I.' Like, 'Mother, may I take two giant steps?' and we're playing in full view of a sold-out crowd. The bullpen phone rang and Dad said, 'Will you guys stop that foolishness out there.'"

Stanley was befriended by Joe DiMaggio. "Joe didn't like the attention. We were on the train, just the two of us, seated together. The train stopped in Pittsburgh. DiMaggio went into the station to get a paper. In five minutes there must have been 15 people wanting to get his autograph. When he came back, he asked me about what I was doing. When I told him I was playing ball at Virginia and wanted to go to law school, he said he'd do anything to trade places with me.

"One night I met a beautiful young girl. I thought I'd impress her and introduce her to Joe and I did and she walked off with Joe.

"When I asked Dad how DiMaggio kept his sanity and played so well all the time with all the women and people wanting to buy him drinks and dinner, Dad said, 'It's like eating bananas. Eat one, okay. If you eat a dozen, you'll get sick. He limited himself.'"

The brothers took infield with the Yankees. "Stan would take McQuinn's place at first base and I would take Rizzuto's place for second infield," Dick said. "I considered Phil Rizzuto my idol. I wore number 10, or tried to, in high school, college and professionally. I even have it on my license plate.

"One time Dad was hitting me ground balls and he was hitting some hard ground balls. One of them hit me in the leg and I ran after it into right field and I'm afraid to limp so nobody would know it hurt. Rizzuto said, 'Bucky, why don't you take it easy on him?' and Dad said, 'If you can catch it, so can he.'

"In order to develop quicker hands he got a sponge and put it in my glove and said, 'Don't close your hand.' So the ball would hit the sponge and come banging out so you learned to get a quicker right hand," Dick said.

Bucky was a handsome man, an impeccable dresser and attractive to women. Perhaps it was inevitable given the lifestyle that Bucky's marriage to the brothers' mother, Elizabeth Sutherland, didn't survive.

As Stanley described it, "They reached buddy-buddy point as lots of marriages do and they broke up." They were divorced in 1951. There was an irony to the situation, given Bucky was estranged from his father who left his mother and divorced, though the situations were quite different. Bucky's father apparently walked away when Bucky and Merle were little. Bucky stayed with his family until Stanley and Dick were out of high school and he stayed connected. "I have vivid memories of Dad coming to the house for Christmas and leaving with tears in his eyes," Stanley said.

Stanley also has a theory that Bucky's Parkinson's may have inadvertently delayed Bucky's entrance into the Baseball Hall of Fame. "He had a lot of contact with Joe Cronin. Cronin and Dad would have a cup of coffee and Dad's hands were shaking. Cronin came to the conclusion that Dad had a serious drinking problem. Years later, when I was in my first judgeship, I was told by either Maury Segal or Shirley Povich that Cronin was blocking Dad from getting in the Hall of Fame because he had a drinking problem. I wrote a letter to the committee explaining he had Parkinson's, not a drinking problem."

Bucky made a lot of money in his career. The $100,000 he got from the Senators for 1926, 1927, and 1928 had the buying power equivalent to $2,000,000 today. But in later years, though Bucky worked for salaries ranging

Drew Smith, Bucky's grandnephew, at the dedication of Bucky Harris field in Pittston, Pennsylvania, in 2008.

from roughly $20,000 to $60,000, he never came close to making money equivalent to what he made with that 1920s contract. At the end, he had little left. His sons said he always picked up the check. He was a free spender and a poor investor, passing on a chance to become part-owner of the Redskins and losing a fortune buying some of the proverbial swampland in Florida. In the end he lived mostly on a $700-a-month baseball pension and he almost didn't have that. When the pension fund was created, managers were excluded. When managers were voted into the pension plan in 1962, Bucky paid a $250 fee to be eligible for $700 a month for life.

Until very late in his life Bucky stayed connected to his old Pennsylvania stomping grounds, where he was widely hailed whenever he came home. Drew Smith, Merle's grandson and Bucky's grandnephew, said he visited every winter for years. Merle had a son known as "Pee Wee" Harris who had a restaurant by that name and Bucky would often hold court there. On at least one occasion he was feted by the exclusive local country club, Fox Hill. But his real joy was visiting with Merle, playing cards and drinking well into the wee hours.

"Bucky was competitive about everything, including cards," Smith said. "If he was losing he'd keep my grandfather up all night. I was in high school and had to get up in the morning for school. I used to beg my mother to let me stay up and listen to the stories. I was enthralled."

Bucky Harris died on November 13, 1977, on his 81st birthday. He is buried in St. Peter's Lutheran Church cemetery in Hughestown, Pennsylvania. He is next to the church where he got his first baseball job as shortstop for the Sunday school team. He is across the street from the house where he grew up, a two-minute walk from the site of the no. 9 colliery of the Pennsylvania Coal Company where he had his first job, and a five-minute walk from the baseball diamond where he learned the ropes from his brother Merle, a field that now bears his name — Stanley R. "Bucky" Harris Field.

In the end it was to Hughestown where Bucky returned. "His wish was he wanted to be buried with Mother and Merle," Stanley said. When Dad would come to our house when he was in assisted living, I'd pick him up, and he'd have candy for my three sons. When I left for Pittston to bury his ashes, my seven-year-old came up to me with a handful of M&Ms and said 'Dad could you put these in there.' At the service I dropped the M&Ms in the grave."

Epilogue

In 1975, when Stanley Raymond "Bucky" Harris was elected to the Baseball Hall of Fame as a manager, he was third on the all-time wins list with 2,157. Only Connie Mack and John McGraw had more managerial victories. But Bucky wasn't a winning manager. He was second in losses to Mack with 2,218, giving him a .493 winning percentage. In 29 seasons he managed three league championship teams and won two of three World Series. He never finished last, an accomplishment of which he was justifiably proud given he managed the Senators for 18 years and the 1943 Phillies, but he never finished second and finished third and fourth only six times combined. That means he finished fifth, sixth or seventh, in eight-team leagues in 20 of his 29 seasons.

So, was Bucky's election to the Baseball Hall of Fame justified? Though Harris had a losing record, so did Mack, and Mack's winning percentage was lower than Bucky's. But Mack is Mack. He was inducted with the Hall's second class, in 1937, 40 years before Bucky. If Bucky's won-lost record and his 20 second-division finishes in 29 seasons don't sound like Hall-of-Fame credentials, maybe Bill James can improve Bucky's case. James, in his book *Bill James Guide to Baseball Managers*, ranked Bucky 26th in his top 50 managers, up to 1996. According to the James formula, Bucky, though 61 games under .500 on his lifetime record, was 52 games better than expectation. And James ranks Bucky's 1924 performance, when the Senators upset the Yankees in the American League pennant race and the Giants in the World Series, as the 12th-best managerial debut season of all-time, with the team improving by 16 wins over the previous season. As discussed in Chapters 6 and 16, James believes Bucky had a huge impact on the way baseball strategy evolved by practically inventing the closer concept in relief pitching with Marberry in 1924 and 1925 and Joe Page in 1947 and 1948.

In his analysis of Bucky as a manager, James cites Bucky's bold strategy in the seventh game of the 1924 Series. Bill Terry, a rookie left-handed batter for the Giants, was 6-for-12 in the first six games, all against right-handed pitchers. McGraw benched him against lefties. As discussed in Chapter 9, Bucky feared Terry and used a gambit called the "beard" or "cover" pitcher to get Terry out of the game. It had been used before, but never in such a high-stakes, high-profile game. Bucky was elected to the Baseball Hall of Fame 20 years before the James *Guide to Baseball Managers* was published. The men on the Baseball Hall of Fame Veterans Committee who elected him weren't thinking about Bill James, relief pitching or beard pitchers when they elected Bucky to the hall at their annual meeting at the Americana Hotel in New York on February 3, 1975. They were thinking about Bucky Harris the man, a man they admired as much as any in baseball.

Veterans Committee executives that year were former National League president Warren Giles, who, like Bucky, was 78 years old; Bill DeWitt, a former executive with the Browns, Yankees and Tigers who was 72; and Hall president Paul Kerr, also in his 70s. The writers were Charley Segar, Bob Broeg, Dan Daniel and Fred Lieb. The latter two were in their 80s and had written many flattering pieces about Bucky in their heydays, as had Broeg. The Veterans Committee consisted of five players. Two, Bill Terry and Stan Musial, who was the youngest at 54, did not attend the meeting. Musial's mother had died and Terry was sick. The other three players — Joe Cronin, Charley Gehringer and Waite Hoyt — voted for Bucky and then called him to give him the news. "It's funny," Bucky admitted, "because the three men that called me, I managed them all."[1]

Broeg wrote a column about Bucky a month after voting for his induction wherein he quoted Cronin and Gehringer. In the Broeg column Gehringer said when Bucky came to Detroit in 1929, his plan was to play second base and have Gehringer play short. When it didn't work, in part because Gehringer couldn't get used to runners on second dancing in front of him, Bucky, then 33, moved Gehringer back to second, took himself out of the lineup and became a full-time manager.

Gehringer: "He was the nicest manager I ever played for. The nicest and most intelligent and I say that even though I remember fondly the pennant winning seasons under Mickey Cochrane."

Joe Cronin played under Bucky at Washington in 1928 and they flip-flopped managerial jobs in 1935, with Bucky going from Boston to Washington while Cronin went the opposite way.

"I learned a lot from Bucky," Cronin said. "The very fact that he managed almost 30 years in the majors shows he was respected for doing better than could be expected most of the time with the material he had. You don't get the jobs Bucky did on the strength of friendship."

Cronin's assertion that Bucky didn't get baseball jobs for almost 30 years out of friendship is debatable. Bucky was hired eight times as a major league manager, but five of those times were by the same two teams, Washington and Detroit, where combined he spent 23 of his 29 seasons as a manager and where he was revered by the Griffith and Briggs families, respective owners of the teams. With the other three major league teams, he managed one (Boston), two (New York), and one-half (Philadelphia) seasons.

Throughout his career Bucky was described in newspaper and magazine stories as "easy-going" and "mild-mannered." He was considered a player's manager because he let players play. His style endeared him to many.

Gil Coan, a 6'1", 180-pound left-handed hitting outfielder from North Carolina, was the *Sporting News* Minor League Player of the Year in 1945, but Coan was a bust during his first four years as a Senator, from 1946 to 1953. He shuttled between the Senators and the minor leagues, and when he did play for the Senators, he didn't hit. He batted .232 and .218 in 1948 and 1949 and everyone had a theory. Bucky came back to manage the Senators for his third term in 1950. Suddenly in 1950 and 1951, Coan became a .300 hitter, batting .303 in both seasons. Coan credited Bucky and his laissez faire style.

"When Bucky Harris became manager, he told me, 'I'm leaving you strictly alone.' That did me more good than all the advice I ever got," Coan said.

Jackie Jensen came up with the Yankees the same time as Mantle. Yankee manager Casey Stengel played him in 101 games in 1950 and 1951 combined and he hit only .260 with nine home runs. Early in 1952 Bucky acquired him for the Senators as the principal in a five-player deal in which the Yankees got Irv Noren. Jensen's first game with Washington was May 4. Bucky sought him out and said, "You're our right fielder and you're batting third."

Jensen was impressed. "No pep talk, no nothing, but he made it sound like I was the right fielder and third place hitter for a long time to come. It made me feel good."

Jensen declined to be part of a *Baseball Digest* story in 1950 called, "It's Great to Be an Ex-Yankee," but he did say, "It's nicer with Washington. Bucky Harris doesn't panic if you go hitless or lose a ball game. He doesn't single out individuals. With Stengel it was always watch that curve ball or watch for that changeup. Bucky let you on your own up there."

Frank "Spec" Shea was a pitcher who came over from the Yankees to the Senators in the Jensen deal. "Ask any ballplayer who he'd like to play for and he'd say Bucky Harris," Shea said. "I won't mention names, but some of the Yankee regulars said they wish they were going with me. Bucky never goes crazy in the clubhouse. If you make a mistake, he doesn't rant and rave in front of the team and embarrass you. He'll get you aside quickly and make his point."[2]

When Bucky went to the Phillies in 1943, his only time in the National League, Philadelphia sports columnist Ed Rumill wrote: "He leaves a pile of memories behind him in the A.L., particularly among the baseball writers. There have been few managers or players more popular with the press. Of course, he has not gone very far. The Phils are still in the big leagues despite rumors to the contrary. The fellows in the press row will still get to see him and that is a break for them."[3]

Babe Dahlgren, who played for Bucky with the Phillies in 1943, liked Bucky's style and honesty. "Bucky was quiet, but you could always tell the old mental wheels were spinning. He made the most out of his material. I led the N.L. for two months because he had me believing in myself."

It's not that Bucky never criticized players, but he never did it publicly or loudly and he did it with a wry sense of humor.

George Case played for Bucky for six years, from 1937 to 1945. When Bucky died on his 81st birthday in 1977, Case, then 62, said, "I guess I'm the oldest of his ex-players. I remember my first year, I made a lot of mistakes. I threw to the wrong base several times. The third time it cost us a game. I sat on the bench by the water cooler as far away from Bucky as I could. He came over casually like he was getting a drink and said out of the side of his mouth, 'Got an outfield job in Chattanooga.' That's all that was needed to straighten me out."

Eddie Robinson, who played for Bucky with the 1950 Senators, came in after curfew and Bucky spotted him. Bucky didn't say anything until Robinson struck out four times the next day.

After the game Bucky stopped by his locker and said softly, "I've tried it Eddie and it won't work."

Bucky often had little jabs for players. He was known to say things like he said to Roy Johnson, after the Tiger outfielder dropped a fly ball. "Forget it. It hit you in a bad spot — right in the middle of your glove."

Mickey Harris, a pitcher for the Senators in 1950, was seated across the aisle from Bucky with a couple of writers on a train when Mickey ordered a double scotch on the rocks. Mickey asked, "You don't mind if your pitchers drink?"

"I don't care if or how much you drink as long as you can pitch. If you can't, your fanny will be back in Chattanooga before the ice in your drink melts."[4]

Some players didn't like him for the same reason many others did — he was hands off.

George Case once said Bucky never gave him a sign unless it was for a hit and run. That worked for most players but not all. In Fay Vincent's book, *The Only Game in Town*, Tommy Henrich said,

I played for three prominent managers, Bucky Harris, Casey Stengel and Joe McCarthy. I'll just plain put Joe McCarthy number one. That's all there is to it and Casey Stengel is very smart, never mind his way of talking. He knew the game of baseball as well as anybody, but his personality didn't fit in. The attitude changes, of course, when you lose a McCarthy. Then we went through two years of Bucky Harris. Now Bucky's a nice guy, but he didn't command the respect that McCarthy did. Harris was fired after the '48 season. Weiss fired Bucky for being too lax. That's what they said. Now I liked Bucky, but I'll give you one for instance.

I'm coming up in the eighth inning against Washington. Mickey Vernon is playing first base and there is a situation where there is a man on first and second, nobody out. I don't want to bunt. I went back to Harris and asked him if I should bunt or not. He says, "Do what you want."

McCarthy never would've said that. He would have told me what he wanted done.

Wayne Terwilliger was an infielder during Bucky's last term in Washington and held a grudge for a slight from Bucky: "Late in the '54 season I was really struggling. I had been batting eighth every day. One day the starting pitcher Mickey McDermott batted ahead of me in batting practice. 'I'm batting eighth today, see ya,' he said."

Terwilliger didn't believe it, and when McDermott stayed in the cage, they got in a shoving match. When another player said McDermott was right, Terwilliger looked at the lineup posted in the dugout and saw he was batting ninth.

"I never forgave Bucky Harris for that. I thought about it when I started managing — why would a manager do that to a player who was struggling? He should have talked to me"[5]

While most scribes and inside baseball people thought Bucky was a Hall of Fame-caliber manager, there was an undercurrent of criticism. In some circles he was considered a proven loser who was hired and rehired only because of good-old-boy cronyism.

If the legitimacy of his place in the Baseball Hall if Fame were to be argued on his record, the case could be made he's not deserving.

By any other measure, Cooperstown is where Bucky Harris belongs.

Appendix: Career
Statistics and Highlights

*Bold indicates led league

Batting Record

Year	Team	G	AB	R	H	2B	3B	HR	RBI	BB	SO	HBP	SH	SB	CS	AVG	OBP	SLG
1919	WAS	8	28	0	6	2	0	0	4	1	3	1	1	0		.214	.267	.286
1920	WAS	136	506	76	152	26	6	1	68	41	36	**21**	24	16	17	.300	.377	.381
1921	WAS	154	584	82	169	22	8	0	54	54	39	**18**	27	29	9	.289	.367	.354
1922	WAS	154	602	95	162	24	8	2	40	52	38	**14**	17	25	11	.269	.341	.346
1923	WAS	145	532	60	150	21	13	2	70	50	29	13	25	23	16	.282	.358	.382
1924	WAS	143	544	88	146	28	9	1	58	56	41	7	**46**	20	10	.268	.344	.358
1925	WAS	144	551	91	158	30	3	1	66	64	21	9	**41**	14	12	.287	.370	.358
1926	WAS	141	537	94	152	39	9	1	63	58	41	9	27	16	11	.283	.363	.395
1927	WAS	128	475	98	127	20	3	1	55	66	33	5	**30**	18	3	.267	.363	.328
1928	WAS	99	358	34	73	11	5	0	28	27	26	2	10	5	2	.204	.264	.263
1929	DET	7	11	3	1	0	0	0	0	2	2	0	1	1	0	.091	.231	.091
1931	DET	4	8	1	1	1	0	0	0	1	1	0	0	0	0	.125	.222	.250
(12 Years)		1263	4736	722	1297	224	64	9	506	472	310	99	249	167	91	.274	.352	.354

World Series Batting Record

Year	Team	G	AB	R	H	2B	3B	HR	RBI	BB	SO	HBP	SH	SF	SB	CS	AVG	OBP	SLG
1924	WAS	7	33	5	11	0	0	2	7	1	4	0	0	0	0	1	.333	.353	.515
1925	WAS	7	23	2	2	0	0	0	0	1	3	1	4	0	0	0	.087	.160	.087
(2 Years)		14	56	7	13	0	0	2	7	2	7	1	4	0	0	1	.232	.271	.339

Fielding Record

Year	Team	POS	G	GS	CG	INN	PO	A	ERR	DP	TP	AVG
1919	WAS A	2B				8	21	28	4	4	0	.925
1920	WAS A	2B	134	134	132	1189	345	401	33	59	0	.958
1921	WAS A	2B	154	154	**153**	1372.2	417	481	38	**91**	1	.959
1922	WAS A	2B	**154**	**154**	152	1348.1	**483**	483	30	**116**	1	.970
1923	WAS A	2B	144	144	138	1239.2	**418**	449	**35**	120	0	.961
1923	WAS A	SS	2	1	1	9	0	2	1	0	0	.667
1924	WAS A	2B	143	143	141	1252	393	386	26	**100**	0	.968
1925	WAS A	2B	144	143	135	1208.1	402	429	26	**107**	0	.970
1926	WAS A	2B	141	138	126	1113.1	**356**	427	30	74	0	.963
1927	WAS A	2B	128	128	117	1047	**316**	413	21	68	0	**.972**
1928	WAS A	2B	95	90	87	772	251	326	18	61	0	.970
1928	WAS A	RF	1	0	0	0	0	0	0	0	-	
1928	WAS A	3B	1	1	1	9	3	0	0	0	0	1.000
1928	WAS A	OF	1	0	0	0	0	0	0	0	-	
1929	DET A	2B	4	3	1	9	5	13	2	0	0	.900
1929	DET A	SS	1	0	0	0	0	0	0	0	-	
1931	DET A	2B	3	3	3	24	5	6	0	1	0	1.000
(12 Years)		2B	1252	1234	1185	1057	5.1	3412	3842	263	801	2.965

World Series Fielding Record

Year	Team	POS	G	GS	CG	INN	PO	A	ERR	DP	TP	AVG
1924	WAS A	2B	7	7	7	67	27	27	2	8	0	.964
1925	WAS A	2B	7	7	6	59	23	18	0	5	0	1.00
(2 Years)		2B	14	14	13	126	50	45	2	13	0	.979

Managerial Record

Year	Team	G	W	L	PCT	STANDING
1924	WAS A	156	92	62	.597	1
1925	WAS A	152	96	55	.636	1
1926	WAS A	152	81	69	.540	4
1927	WAS A	157	85	69	.552	3
1928	WAS A	155	75	79	.487	4
1929	DET A	155	70	84	.455	6
1930	DET A	154	75	79	.487	5
1931	DET A	154	61	93	.396	7
1932	DET A	153	76	75	.503	5
1933	DET A	153	73	79	.480	5
1934	BOS A	153	76	76	.500	4

Year	Team	G	W	L	PCT	STANDING
1935	WAS A	154	67	86	.438	6
1936	WAS A	153	82	71	.536	4
1937	WAS A	158	73	80	.477	6
1938	WAS A	152	75	76	.497	5
1939	WAS A	153	65	87	.428	6
1940	WAS A	154	64	90	.416	7
1941	WAS A	156	70	84	.455	6
1942	WAS A	151	62	89	.411	7
1943	PHI N	94	39	53	.424	7
1947	NY A	155	97	57	.630	1
1948	NY A	154	94	60	.610	3
1950	WAS A	155	67	87	.435	5
1951	WAS A	154	62	92	.403	7
1952	WAS A	157	78	76	.506	5
1953	WAS A	152	76	76	.500	5
1954	WAS A	155	66	88	.429	6
1955	DET A	154	79	75	.513	5
1956	DET A	155	82	72	.532	5
Total (29 Years)		4410	2158	2219	.493	

World Series Managerial Record

Year	Team	G	W	L	PCT
1924	WAS A	7	4	3	.571
1925	WAS A	7	3	4	.429
1947	NY A	7	4	3	.571
Total (3 Years)		21	11	10	.524

Records

- Most seasons leading the American League in double plays, 5 (tied with Eddie Collins, Nellie Fox, Bobby Doerr, and Nap Lajoie)
- Chances accepted in a World Series game, 13, October 11, 1925 (tied with Davey Lopes and C.C. Ritchey)
- Putouts in a World Series game, 8, October 8, 1924 (tied with Davey Lopes, extra innings)
- Assists in a World Series game, 8, October 7, 1924 (tied with Eddie Collins, H.A. Schaefer, H.C. Janvrin, C.C. Ritchey, Joe Gordon and Bobby Doerr)
- First manager to win a World Series with two different franchises (Washington Senators, New York Yankees)
- Longest span of seasons between World Series titles, manager, 23 (1924, Washington; 1947, New York)

Chapter Notes

Chapter 1

1. *Wilkes-Barre Times Leader*, "Harris Fined," December 26, 1917.
2. James Naismith, *Basketball: Its Origin and Development* (New York: Associated Press, 1941), 29–60.
3. *Wilkes-Barre Times Leader*, December 5, 1892.
4. Robert W. Peterson, *Cages to Jump Shots: Pro Basketball's Early Years* (Lincoln: University of Nebraska Press, 2002), 15–31.
5. Irving Vaughn, *Chicago Tribune*, October 14, 1924, p. 21.
6. Joseph Gorman, *Washington Post*, September 21, 1924.
7. *Mine Boy to Manager*, a series of newspaper articles syndicated in 1925 by the North American Newspaper Alliance. The quotes and anecdotes about Bucky's early life and baseball education in Hughestown were taken from Chapters one and two. The series was later published in a hardcover book, *Playing the Game*.

Chapter 2

1. *The Christian Science Monitor*, October 11, 1919, p. 13.
2. *Boston Daily Globe*, October 14, 1920, p. 1.
3. *Mine Boy to Manager*, Chapter 1.
4. *Mine Boy to Manager*, Chapter 2.
5. *Wilkes-Barre Times Leader*, August 6, 1916.
6. *Wilkes-Barre Times Leader*, August 8, 1916.
7. *Wilkes-Barre Times Leader*, August 16, 1916.
8. *Mine Boy to Manager*, Chapter 2.
9. Peterson, *Cages to Jump Shots*, pp. 32–45.
10. Regarding Schmeelk's swimming, *New York Times*, August 22, 1915.
11. Interview with Bucky's sons, Stanley and Dick Harris, Bethesda, Maryland, March 20, 2009.
12. http://sportsillustrated.cnn.com/vault/article/magazine/.../index.htm.
13. Peterson, *Cages to Jump Shots*, p. 82.
14. *Wilkes-Barre Times Leader*, December 13, 1916.
15. *Wilkes-Barre Times Leader*, February 26, 1916.
16. *Wilkes-Barre Times Leader*, September 26, 1916.
17. Accounts of the PSL games were found in the *Wilkes-Barre Times Leader*, February 1917.
18. APBR.org (American Professional Basketball Research).

19. http://hoopedia.nba.com/index.php?search=beckman&go=Go.
20. http://www.jewishsports.net/BioP.s/BarneySedran.htm.
21. Red Smith, "Red Smith's Views," *Washington Post*, August 28, 1966.
22. *Wilkes-Barre Times Leader*, December 22, 1917.
23. *Wilkes-Barre Times Leader*, December 26, 1917.
24. Playoff game accounts found in the *Wilkes-Barre Times Leader*, March 20–29, 1918.
25. Playoff game accounts found in the *Wilkes-Barre Times Leader*, March 21 to April 12, 1919.
26. *Wilkes-Barre Times Leader*, April 14, 1919.
27. *Wilkes-Barre Times Leader*, November 11, 1919.
28. *Wilkes-Barre Times Leader*, January 14 and 29, 1920.
29. *Wilkes-Barre Times Leader*, February 2, 1920.
30. *Wilkes-Barre Times Leader*, April 23, 1921.

Chapter 3

1. Bob Addie, "Harris Dies," *Washington Post*, November 10, 1977.
2. *Mine Boy to Manager*, Chapter 15.
3. *Washington Post*, "Bisons Cash In," May 22, 1944.
4. *Wilkes-Barre Sunday Independent*, February 10, 1924.
5. *Mine Boy to Manager*, Chapter 17.
6. *Wilkes-Barre Times Leader*, "Harris to Go South," October 6, 1919.
7. *Wilkes-Barre Times Leader*, August 6, 1918.
8. *Mine Boy to Manager*, Chapter 17.
9. Mark Gauvreau Judge, *Damn Senators: My Grandfather and the Story of Washington's Only World Series Championship* (San Francisco: Encounter Books, 2003), 45.
10. *Mine Boy to Manager*, Chapter 19, details of Bucky's being scouted and signed.
11. *Wilkes-Barre Times Leader*, August 27, 1919.
12. J.V. Fitz Gerald, *Washington Post*, August 27, 1919, p. 12.
13. J.V. Fitz Gerald, *Washington Post*, August 29, 1919, p. 12.
14. *Ibid.*
15. *Mine Boy to Manager*, Chapters 20 and 21, details Bucky's major league debut.

Chapter 4

1. *Wilkes-Barre Times Leader*, October 15, 1919.
2. *Wilkes-Barre Times Leader*, "Babe Ruth to Play," October 16, 1919.
3. *Wilkes-Barre Times Leader*, January 1, 1920.
4. *Mine Boy to Manager*, Chapter 24.
5. *The Sporting News*, February 29, 1920.
6. *Washington Post* story was reprinted in the *Wilkes-Barre Times Leader*, February 23, 1920.
7. *Mine Boy to Manager*, Chapter 24.
8. *Wilkes-Barre Times Leader*, "Washington Out for Harris," March 29, 1920.
9. *Washington Post*, March 21, 1920, p. 14.
10. Fitz Gerald, *Washington Post*, March 21, 1920.
11. Shirley Povich, "This Morning," *Washington Post*, December 19, 1934, p. 19.
12. *Wilkes-Barre Times Leader*, April 2, 1920.
13. *Washington Post*, March 11, 1920, p. 5.
14. *Wilkes-Barre Times Leader*, April 13, 1920.

15. *Wilkes-Barre Times Leader*, June 2, 1920.

16. *Mine Boy to Manager*, Chapter 28.

17. Fitz Gerald, *Washington Post*, July 13, 1920; reprinted in the *Wilkes-Barre Times Leader*, July 15, 1920.

18. John Dugan, *Washington Post*, August 30, 1920, p. 8.

19. *Mine Boy to Manager*, Chapter 28.

20. John Dugan, *Washington Post*, October 4, 1920, p. 8.

Chapter 5

1. *Wilkes-Barre Times Leader*, "Cage Shots," September 24, 1920.

2. *Wilkes-Barre Times Leader*, "Cage Shots," November 13, 1920.

3. *Wilkes-Barre Times Leader*, "Cage Shots," November 14, 1920.

4. *Wilkes-Barre Times Leader*, "Cage Shots," November 14, 1920.

5. *Wilkes-Barre Times Leader*, "Cage Shots," February 20, 1921.

6. *Washington Post*, February 25, 1921, p. 11.

7. *Washington Post*, March 12, 1921, p. 10.

8. John Dugan, "Senators Shutout Florida," *Washington Post*, March 30, 1921.

9. *Washington Post*, April 14, 1921, p. 1.

10. *The Sporting News*, April 28, 1921.

11. *New York Times*, "Curves and Bingles," June 26, 1921.

12. Stephen Able, SABR Biography project, http://bioproj.sabr.org., http://bioproj.sabr.org.

13. Cort Vitty, SABR Biography project, http://bioproj.sabr.org., http://bioproj.sabr.org.

14. *Wilkes-Barre Times Leader*, "Harris May Be Traded," December 31, 1921.

15. *Washington Post*, December 30, 1921, p. 12.

16. Tom Simon, SABR Biography project, http://bioproj.sabr.org., http://bioproj.sabr.org.

17. *Wilkes-Barre Times Leader*, February 7, 1922.

18. John Dugan, *Washington Post*, March 4, 1921, p. 14.

19. *Washington Post*, March 1, 1922, p. 21.

20. Robert Maxwell, *Washington Post*, March 29, 1922, p. 18.

21. *Hartford Courant*, March 29, 1922, p. 18.

22. Robert Maxwell, *Washington Post*, March 29, 1922, p. 18.

23. *Washington Post*, April 14, 1922, p. 1.

24. *Wilkes-Barre Times Leader*, "Clark Griffith Turns Down Offer," June 20, 1922.

25. Effie Welsh, "In the Sporting World," *Wilkes-Barre Times Leader*, September 11, 1922.

26. *Mine Boy to Manager*, Chapter 30.

27. *New York Times*, July 4, 1923, p. 10.

28. Frank Young, *Washington Post*, September 26, 1921, p. 17.

29. Frank Young, *Washington Post*, September 22, 1921, p. 19.

Chapter 6

1. Leonard Koppett, *The Man in the Dugout* (New York: Crown, 1993), 208–209.

2. Francis Stann, *Washington Times-Star*, reprinted in *Baseball Digest*, January 1954.

3. Frank Young, *Washington Post*, January 27, 1924, p. S1.

4. Frank H. Young, *Washington Post*, February 8 1924, S1.

5. *Washington Post*, February 1, 1924, p. 17.
6. *Washington Post*, February 5, 1924, p. S1.
7. *Washington Post*, February 7, 1924, p. S1.
8. Frank H. Young, *Washington Post*, February 10, 1924, p. S1.
9. *Ibid.*
10. *Mine Boy to Manager*, Chapter 31.
11. N.W. Baxter, "From the Press Box," *Washington Post*, February 11, 1924.
12. *The Sporting News*, February 21, 1924, p. 3.
13. N.W. Baxter, "From the Press Box," *Washington Post*, February 12, 1924, p. S3.
14. *Washington Post*, "Harris Says," February 10, 1924.
15. *Mine Boy to Manager*, Chapter 32.
16. Bob Addie, *Washington Post*, April 4, 1962.
17. Frank H. Young, *Washington Post*, February 24 1924, p. S1.
18. *Mine Boy to Manager*, Chapter 32.
19. *Mine Boy to Manager*, Chapter 32.
20. *Washington Post*, April 10, 1924.
21. *Mine Boy to Manager*, Chapter 32.
22. Frank H. Young, *Washington Post*, April 10 1924, p. S1.
23. Frank H. Young, "No Better Than '23," *Washington Post*, April 1 1924.
24. Reed Browning, *Baseball's Greatest Season, 1924* (Boston: University of Massachusetts Press), p. 15.
25. *Washington Post*, April 16, 1924, p. 1.
26. Browning, *Baseball's Greatest Season*, 23.
27. Frank H. Young, *Washington Post*, May 5, 1924, p. S1.
28. *Washington Post*, "Baseball Comedy Pair," June 2, 1924.
29. Mark Amour, SABR Baseball biography project, http://bioproj.sabr.org.
30. *Washington Post*, October 8, 1924, p. 2.
31. Bill James, *The Bill James Guide to Baseball Managers from 1870 to Today* (New York: Scribner's, 1997), 329–331.
32. Judge, *Damn Senators*, 82–83.
33. Frank Young, *Washington Post*, "Double Bill Today," June 28, 1924.
34. N.W. Baxter, *Washington Post*, June 26, 1924, p. S1.
35. Shirley Povich, "This Morning," *Washington Post*, June 26, 1924.

Chapter 7

1. http://www.whitehouse.gov/about/presidents/calvincoolidge.
2. Harry Stringer, *Washington Post*, June 27, 1924, p. S1.
3. *New York Times*, July 6, 1924, p. 23.
4. Frank Young, *Washington Post*, July 7, 1924, p. S1.
5. *Washington Post*, July 10, 1924, p. S3.
6. Frank Young, "Senators Recover," *Washington Post*, July 13, 1924, p. S1.
7. *Washington Post*, July 13, 1924, p. S2.
8. Frank Young, *Washington Post*, July 14, 1924, p. S1.
9. Frank Young, *Washington Post*, July 15, 1924, p. S1.
10. *Philadelphia Evening Public Ledger*, July 25, 1924.
11. Frank Young, *Washington Post*, August 22, 1924, p. S1.
12. Frank Young, *Washington Post*, August 23, 1924, p. S1.
13. Henry W. Thomas, *Walter Johnson: Baseball's Big Train* (Lincoln: University of Nebraska Press, 1995), 207.
14. *Washington Post*, "Hundreds of Fans," August 27, 1924.
15. *Washington Post*, August 30, 1924, p. 5.

16. Frank Young, *Washington Post*, August 30, 1924, p. S1.
17. George Sisler, *Washington Post*, August 31, 1924, p. S1.
18. Frank Young, *Washington Post*, September 1, 1924, p. 1.
19. *Washington Post*, September 1, 1924, p. 1.
20. *Washington Post*, September 3, 1924, p. 1.
21. *Washington Post*, "Notes of the Senators," September 5, 1924.
22. Frank Young, *Washington Post*, September 6, 1924, p. S1.
23. Frank Young, *Washington Post*, September 13, p. S1. This was yet another story about the origin of Bucky's nickname.
24. Thomas, *Walter Johnson*, 208.
25. *Washington Post*, September 17, 1924, p. S4.
26. Thomas, *Walter Johnson*, 242.
27. *Washington Post*, September 18, 1924, p. S1.
28. *Washington Post*, September 25, 1924, p. 2.
29. H.I. Phillips, *Boston Globe*, September 27, 1924.
30. Frank Young, *Washington Post*, September 29, p. S1.
31. Frank Young, *Washington Post*, September 30, p. S1.
32. Thomas, *Walter Johnson*, 212.

Chapter 8

1. *New York Times*, September 30, p. 1.
2. *Ibid.*
3. *Washington Post*, September 30, p. S3.
4. *New York Times*, October 1, 1924, p. 15.
5. *Hartford Courant*, October 1, 1924, p. 13.
6. *New York Times*, September 30, 1924, p. 1.
7. James O'Leary, *Boston Globe*, October 1, 1924, p. 11.
8. *Washington Post*, September 28, 1924, p. S1.
9. *Washington Post*, October 1, 1924, p. 1.
10. N.W. Baxter, "In the Press Box," *Washington Post*, September 30, 1924.
11. *New York Times*, September 30, p. 19.
12. Frank Young, *Washington Post*, September 30, 1924, p. 1.
13. Frank Young, *Washington Post*, October 1, 1924, S1.
14. Wil Rogers, *Hartford Courant*, September 27, 1924, p. 12.
15. *Washington Post*, September 30, 1924, p. 1.
16. *New York Times*, "Coolidge Welcomes," and *Washington Post*, October 2, 1924, pp. 1–2.
17. *Washington Post*, October 2, 1924, p. 2.
18. *Boston Daily Globe*, October 3, 1924, p. 24.
19. *Washington Post*, October 4, 1924, p. 2.
20. *Washington Post*, October 3, 1924, p. 1.
21. *Washington Post*, October 3, 1924, p. 10.
22. Judge, *Damn Senators*, 104.
23. Details of quotes of the scandal: *Los Angeles Times*, October 3, 1924, p. B2; *Boston Globe*, October 2, 1924, p. 24; Irving Vaughn, *Chicago Tribune*, October 2, 1924, p. 1; N.W. Baxter, *Washington Post*, October 3, 1924, p. 1; *Washington Post*, October 3, 1924, p. 1; Judge, *Damn Senators*, 105.
24. *New York Times*, October 3, 1924, p. 24.
25. Stanley Harris, *Washington Post*, October 2, 1924, p. S1.
26. Stanley Harris, *Washington Post*, October 3, 1924, p. S1.
27. *New York Times*, October 4, 1924, p. 8.

Chapter 9

1. Descriptions and quotes of the World Series Game 1 pre-game activities: Francis P. Daley, *Washington Post*, p. 4; *Washington Post*, p. S3; *Washington Post*, "Sidelights," p. S3; *New York Times*, October 5, 1924, p. 1.
2. Francis P. Daley, *Washington Post*, p. 4.
3. *Mine Boy to Manager*, Chapter 35.
4. *New York Times*, October 5, 1924, p. 29.
5. Bucky Harris, *Washington Post*, October 5, 1924, p. 1.
6. *New York Times*, October 5, 1924, p. 1.
7. W.O. McGeehan, *Washington Post*, October 5, 1924, p. 3.
8. *Washington Post*, October 6, 1924, p. S2.
9. Bucky Harris, *Washington Post*, October 6, 1924, p. 1.
10. *New York Times*, October 7, 1924, p. 1.
11. *New York Times*, October 8, 1924, p. 13.
12. N.W. Baxter, "Crippled Nats Win," *Washington Post*, October 8, 1924.
13. *New York Times*, October 8, 1924.
14. Browning, *Baseball's Greatest Season, 1924*, p. 140.
15. N.W. Baxter, *Washington Post*, October 8, 1924, p. 1.
16. *New York Times*, October 8, 1924, p. 13.
17. N.W. Baxter, *Washington Post*, October 9, 1924, p. 1.
18. *New York Times*, October 9, 1924, p. 18.
19. Frank Young, *Washington Post*, October 9, 1924, S1.
20. Bucky Harris, *Washington Post*, October 9, 1924, p. 2.
21. *New York Times*, October 9, 1924, p. 18.
22. Francis Daily, *Washington Post*, October 10, 1924, p. 4.
23. *New York Times*, October 10, 1924, p. 15.
24. N.W. Baxter, *Washington Post*, October 10, 1924, p. 1.
25. Jerome P. Carmichael, *My Greatest Day in Baseball* (New Haven, CT: A.S. Barnes, 1945), 58.
26. Arthur Knapp, *Washington Post*, October 11, p. 15.
27. Judge, *Damn Senators*, 126.
28. *Ibid.*, 132.
29. Francis P. Dailey, *Washington Post*, October 11, 1924, p. 2.
30. *Boston Globe*, October 11, 1924, p. 9.
31. N.W. Baxter, *Washington Post*, October 11, 1924, p. 1.
32. *New York Times*, October 11, 1924, p. 10.

Chapter 10

1. Westbrook Pegler, *New York Times*, March 27, 1929, p. 19.
2. *Washington Post*, October 12, 1924, p. 2.
3. *Boston Globe*, October 12, 1924, p. 9.
4. *Washington Post*, October 13, 1924, p. S1.
5. *Washington Post*, October 30, 1924, p. S1.
6. *Washington Post*, November 2, 1924, p. 15.
7. Frank Young, *Washington Post*, November 11, 1924, p. S1.
8. *Washington Post*, December 31, 1924, p. S1.
9. *Washington Post*, December 2, 1924, p. S1.
10. David Jones, editor, *Deadball Stars of the American League* (Dulles, VA: Potomac, 2006), 690.
11. Frank Young, *Washington Post*, December 14, 1924, p. S4.
12. Frank Young, *Washington Post*, December 15, 1924, p. S1.

13. *Washington Post*, December 31, 1924, p. S1.

14. *Boston Globe*, February 16, 1925, p. 6.

15. *New York Times*, March 4, 1925, p. 13.

16. *Boston Globe*, March 5, 1925, p. A26.

17. Leonard Koppett, *The Man in the Dugout: Baseball's Top Managers and How They Got That Way* (New York: Crown, 1993), 180.

18. *New York Times*, February 24, 1925.

19. Davis Walsh, International News Service, March 10, 1925.

20. Billy Evans, syndicated column, *Fredrick News Post*, March 27, 1925.

21. *New York Times*, "Giants Lose Final," April 13, 1925.

22. *Boston Globe*, April 29, 1925, p. A22.

23. *Washington Post*, May 2, 1925, p. 18.

24. Young, *Washington Post*, September 14, 1925, p. 13.

25. Young, *Washington Post*, September 20, 1925, p. 21.

26. *Washington Post*, September 23, 1925, p. 13.

27. Thomas, *Walter Johnson*, 275.

28. Walter Johnson, *Los Angeles Times*, October 6, 1925, B2.

29. *Ibid.*

30. Harry Cross, *New York Times*, October 6, 1925, p. 23.

31. *New York Times*, October 7, 1925, p. 23.

32. *Washington Post*, October 7, 1925, p. 20.

33. *New York Times*, October 8, 1925, p. 1.

34. Thomas, *Walter Johnson*, 275.

35. *Brooklyn Eagle*, October 8, 1925, p. 2A.

36. Judge, *Damn Senators*, 136–137.

37. James R. Harrison, *New York Times*, October 16, 1925, p. 1.

38. Judge, *Damn Senators*, 136–138.

39. *Baseball Digest*, "Walter Johnson's Toughest Defeat," February 1963.

40. James Dawson, *New York Times*, October 16, 1925, p. 14.

41. N.W. Baxter, "Second Guessers Say," *Washington Post*, October 17, 1925.

42. *Washington Post*, October 16, 1925, p. 1.

43. *New York Times*, October 17, 1925, p. 12.

Chapter 11

1. *Washington Post*, June 20, 1926, p. SM3.

2. This story comes up in various forms. It was told to Larry Amman in an interview with Al Schacht (Baseball Research Journal Archive/BRJ —1982) where Schacht said it happened in the 1925 pennant race and Red Ruffing was the pitcher. No matching game could be found.

3. Shirley Povich, *Baseball Digest*, May 1952.

4. Interview with Bucky's sons, Stanley and Dick Harris, Bethesda, Maryland, March 20, 2009.

5. *Washington Post*, November 26, 1925, p. 1.

6. Frank Young, *Washington Post*, January 17, 1926, p. M21.

7. Shirley Povich, *Washington Post*, October 11, 1928, p. 16.

8. Frank Young, *Washington Post*, February 2, 1926.

9. Ron Anderson, SABR Biography project, http://bioproj.sabr.org., http://bioproj.sabr.org.

10. Ralph Berger, SABR Biography project, http://bioproj.sabr.org., http://bioproj.sabr.org.

11. *Washington Post*, October 2, 1926, p. 1.

12. Frank Young, *Washington Post*, December 13, 1925, p. 1.
13. Frank Young, *Washington Post*, December 16, 1925, p. 17.
14. Frank Young, *Washington Post*, October 16, 1927, p. 1.
15. *Washington Post*, October 16, 1927, p. 23.
16. Frank Young, *Washington Post*, March 5, 1928, p. 11. Quotes and description of new discipline.
17. *Washington Post*, "Harris Sees Long Rest," April 27 1928.
18. Shirley Povich, *Washington Post*, January 18, 1961, p. D1.
19. Frank Young, *Washington Post*, October 7, 1928.
20. Frank Young, *Washington Post*, October 1, 1928, p. 1.
21. Shirley Povich, *Washington Post*, October 11, 1928, p. 16.
22. Joseph D. Kaufman, *Washington Post*, Letter to the Editor, October 16, 1928.

Chapter 12

1. *Washington Post*, October 16, 1928, p. 13.
2. *Chicago Tribune*, October 20, 1928, p. 25.
3. *Washington Post*, October 25, 1928, p. 13.
4. *Los Angeles Times*, December 13, 1928, p. B1.
5. *Los Angeles Times*, March 24, 1929, p. A1.
6. *New York Times*, March 27, 1929, p. 33.
7. *Hartford Courant*, March 24, 1929, p. C11.
8. *Washington Post*, March 29, 1929, p. 17.
9. *Washington Post*, April 14, 1929, p. A4.
10. Frank Young, *Washington Post*, June 6, 1929, p. 13.
11. Rory Costello, SABR Biography project, http://bioproj.sabr.org., http://bioproj.sabr.org.
12. *Washington Post*, "Baseball Briefs," March 8, 1933.
13. Frank Stan, *Baseball Magazine*, January 1953, p. 25.
14. *Los Angeles Times*, March 14, 1933, p. A10.
15. *Chicago Tribune*, September 24, 1933, p. A1.
16. http://www.thedeadballera.com/NiceGuys_Yawkey_Tom.htm.
17. *Washington Post*, "New Deal," October 30, 1933.
18. *Hartford Courant*, December 14, 1933, p. 17.
19. *Christian Science Monitor*, January 10, 1934, p. 6.
20. *Washington Post*, January 21, 1934, p. M19.
21. *Christian Science Monitor*, January 10, 1934, p. 6.
22. *Washington Post*, February 4, 1934, p. M19.
23. *Dallas Morning News*, March 8, 1934.
24. John Kieran, *New York Times*, March 16, 1934, p. 29.
25. John Kieran, *New York Times*, March 20, 1934.
26. *Ibid.*
27. *Hartford Courant*, April 10, 1934.
28. John Kieran, *New York Times*, April 28, 1934, p. 20.
29. *Hartford Courant*, July 13, 1934, p. 15.
30. Alan Gould, *Los Angeles Times*, August 3, 1934, p. A11.
31. *Washington Post*, October 27, 1934, p. 19.

Chapter 13

1. *Washington Post*, October 27, 1934, p. 19.
2. *Hartford Courant*, October 27, 1934, p. 11.

3. Shirley Povich, *Washington Post*, February 4, 1934, p. M19.
4. *Washington Post*, October 28, 1934, p. 18.
5. *New York Times*, October 28, 1934, S1.
6. *Washington Post*, November 14, 1934, p. 18.
7. *Christian Science Monitor*, November 14, 1934, p. 8.
8. *Roscoe McGowen, New York Times*, December 13, 1934, p. 31.
9. Shirley Povich, *Washington Post*, December 20, 1934, p. 21.
10. Shirley Povich, *Washington Post*, Dec 19, 1934, p. 19.
11. Shirley Povich, *Washington Post*, January 3,1935, p. 15.
12. *Washington Post*, January 21, 1935, p. 17.
13. Shirley Povich, *Washington Post*, January 27, 1935, p. 17.
14. Katherine Smith, "On the Air," *Washington Post*, February 7, 1935.
15. Shirley Povich, "This Morning," *Washington Post*, February 9, 1935.
16. Atchinson, *Washington Post*, January 18, 1935, p. 19.
17. Shirley Povich, *Washington Post*, February 27, 1935, p. 17.
18. Shirley Povich, *Washington Post*, March 1, 1935, p. 21.
19. Shirley Povich, Washington *Post*, "Harris Plans Revamping," June 23, 1935.
20. *Baseball Digest*, April 1970.
21. Shirley Povich, *Washington Post*, April 19, 1935, p. 19.
22. *Washington Post* April 24, 1935, p. 22.
23. *Washington Post*, September 27, 1942, SP1.
24. Shirley Povich, "This Morning," *Washington Post*, October 2, 1942.

Chapter 14

1. Shirley Povich, *Washington Post*, October 2, 1942, p. 12.
2. Harris's sons interview.
3. Addie, *Washington Post*, November 9, 1971, p. D1.
4. *Washington Post*, September 23, 1942, p. 28.
5. *Hartford Courant*, February 28, 1943, p. C4.
6. Roscoe McGowen, *New York Times*, March 2, 1943, p. 24.
7. *New York Times*, February 26, 1943.
8. *New York Times*, February 25 1943, p. 29.
9. Shirley Povich, *Washington Post*, February 25, 1943, p. 12.
10. *Christian Science Monitor*, February 26, 1943, p. 15.
11. *Washington Post*, February 25, 1943, p. 12.
12. *The Sporting News*, March 23, 1943, p. 3.
13. Judson Bailey, *Gettysburg Times*, March 24, 1943.
14. James Dawson, *New York Times*, Mar 26, 1943, p. 23.
15. *Lebanon Daily News*, July 28, 1943.
16. Harris's sons interview.
17. *New York Times*, August 2, 1943, p. 8.
18. *Washington Post*, August 3, 1943, p. 10.
19. *New York Times*, November 24, 1943, p. 24.

Chapter 15

1. Whitney Martin, *Hartford Courant*, December 13, 1943, p. 9.
2. *Buffalo Evening News*, October 14, 1943.
3. *New York Times*, October 15, 1943, p. 23.

4. Shirley Povich, "This Morning," *Washington Post*, January 22, 1944.

5. Rory Costello, SABR Biography project, http://bioproj.sabr.org.

6. Joe Overfield, *The 100 Seasons of Buffalo Baseball* (Kenmore, NY: Partners Press, 1985), 87–88.

7. *Hartford Courant*, September 18, 1944, p. 9.

8. *Washington Post*, June 3, 1945, p. R1.

9. Overfield, *Buffalo Baseball*, 87–88.

Chapter 16

1. Allen Barra, *Yogi Berra, Eternal Yankee* (New York: W.W. Norton, 2009), 55–57.

2. Roscoe McGowen, *New York Times*, September 10, 1946, p. 10.

3. *Washington Post*, September 11, 1946, p. 10.

4. *New York Times*, May 25, 1946, p. 23.

5. *The Sporting News*, "Open Criticism," June 5, 1946.

6. *New York Times*, September 14, 1946, p. 10.

7. *Washington Post*, "MacPhail Won't Say," October 26, 1946.

8. *New York Times*, October 27, 1946, p. 15.

9. John Drebinger, "Dressen Top Aide," *New York Times*, November 6, 1946.

10. Barra, *Yogi Berra*, 57.

11. *Baseball Digest*, April 1962.

12. *New York Times*, "Ex-Brown to Join," June 26, 1947.

13. Carlo DeVito, *Yogi: The Life and Times of an American Original* (Chicago: Triumph, 2008), 80.

14. James, *Bill James Guide*, 329–331.

15. *Baseball Digest*, July 1957.

16. Barra, *Yogi Berra*, 85–86.

17. Drebinger, "Jubilant Bombers," *New York Times*, September 16, 1947.

18. DeVito, *American Original*, 113.

19. Roscoe McGowen, *New York Times*, October 3, 1947.

20. Roscoe McGowen, *New York Times*, October 4, 1947, p. 11.

21. James P. Dawson, *New York Times*, October 4, 1947, p. 12.

22. James P. Dawson, *New York Times*, October 7, 1947, p. 34.

Chapter 17

1. Yogi Berra with Dave Kaplan, *Ten Rings: My Championship Seasons* (New York: HarperCollins, 2003), 8.

2. DeVito, *American Original*, 68.

3. *Ibid.*, 61–62.

4. Berra, *Ten Rings*, 21–22.

5. Barra, *Yogi Berra*, 68.

6. Joe Trimble in the *Daily News Book of American Originals* (Champaign, IL: Sports Publishing, 1998), 75.

7. Barra, *Yogi Berra*, 71–72.

8. *Ibid.*, 75.

9. *Ibid.*, 79.

10. Berra, *Ten Rings*, 88–89.

11. Shirley Povich, *Washington Post*, October 3, 1947, p. B6.

12. Richard Cramer, *Joe DiMaggio: The Hero's Life* (New York: Simon & Schuster, 2000), 256–257.

13. *Ibid.*

14. *Baseball Digest*, January 1951.

15. David E. Kaiser, *Epic Season: The 1948 American League Pennant Race* (Amherst: University of Massachusetts Press, 1998), 141–142.

16. *Ibid.*, 143–144.

17. *Ibid.*, 145–148.

18. *Ibid.*, 145.

19. Louis Effrat, *New York Times*, October 5, 1948, p. 33.

20. Shirley Povich, *Washington Post*, October 6, 1948, p. 21.

21. Milton Gross, *Baseball Digest*, August 1951, p. 87.

22. Shirley Povich, *Washington Post*, October 3, 1947, p. B6.

23. Milton Gross, *Baseball Digest*, August 1951, p. 87.

24. *Ibid.*

25. Roger Kahn, *The Era, 1947–1957* (New York: Ticknor & Fields, 1993), 87.

26. DeVito, *American Original*, 67.

27. Neil J. Sullivan, *A Diamond in the Bronx: Yankee Stadium and the Politics of New York* (New York: Oxford University, 2002), 79.

28. Arthur Daley, *New York Times*, October 20, 1948, p. 41.

29. Berra, *Ten Rings*, 32.

Chapter 18

1. *New York Times*, October 7, 1948, p. 41.

2. *Chicago Daily Tribune*, October 16, 1948, A2.

3. Dan Daniel, *The Sporting News*, February 2, 1949, p. 18.

4. *San Diego Daily Journal*, December 15, 1948, p. 1.

5. Shirley Povich, *Washington Post*, January 4, 1949, p. 14.

6. *Washington Post*, July 12, 1948, p. 10.

7. Al Wolf, *Los Angeles Times*, February 1, 1949, p. C1.

8. *The Sporting News*, February 6, 1949, p. 18.

9. Al Wolf, *Los Angeles Times*, February 8, 1949, p. C1.

10. *Los Angeles Times*, March 5, 1949, p. B3.

11. Bob Addie, *Washington Post*, November 10, 1972, p. D4.

12. *The Sporting News*, April 13, 1949.

13. Al Wolf, *Los Angeles Times*, April 16, 1949, p. B2.

14. Justin Murphy, SABR Biography project, http://bioproj.sabr.org.

15. Frank Finch, *The Sporting News*, March 30, 1949, p. 2.

16. *San Diego Union*, March 20, 1949, p. A23.

17. Frank Finch, *The Sporting News*, March 30, 1949, p. 2.

18. *Los Angeles Times*, May 10, 1949, p. C1.

19. Frank Finch, *The Sporting News*, March 30, 1949, p. 2.

20. *San Diego Union*, March 20, 1949, p. A23.

21. *The Sporting News*, April 6, 1949, p. 29.

22. *San Diego Union*, March 30, 1949, p. 1.

23. *San Diego Union*, April 1–5, 1949, p. 3B, 5B.

24. *Los Angeles Times*, May 16, 1949, p. C1.

25. Mark Stewart, SABR Biography project, http://bioproj.sabr.org.

26. *Los Angeles Times*, August 12, 1949, p. C3.

27. Justin Murphy, SABR Biography project, http://bioproj.sabr.org.

28. *San Diego Union*, September 27, 1949, p. 5.

29. *Los Angeles Times*, October 10, 1949, p. C1.

30. *The Sporting News*, October 19, 1949, p. 23.

Chapter 19

1. Morris Siegel, *Washington Post*, October 17, 1949, p. 14.
2. Shirley Povich, *Washington Post*, October 18, 1949, p. 17.
3. Morris Siegel, *Washington Post*, October 17, 1949, p. 14.
4. Shirley Povich, *Washington Post*, October 18, 1949, p. 17.
5. Shirley Povich, *Washington Post*, October 23, 1949.
6. Al Wolf, *Los Angeles Times*, October 31, 1949, p. C2.
7. Shirley Povich, *Washington Post*, October 23, 1949.

Chapter 20

1. Arthur Richman, *Baseball Digest*, August 1951.
2. *Washington Post*, November 22, 1949, B6.
3. Shirley Povich, *Washington Post*, December 14, 1949, p. 19.
4. Charles Dexter, *Baseball Digest*, July 1951, pp. 13–18.
5. *Ibid.*
6. Shirley Povich, *Washington Post*, February 26, 1949, p. 10.
7. Joe Trimble, *Baseball Digest*, January 1951, p. 60.
8. Shirley Povich, *Washington Post*, May 10, 1951, p. 19.
9. Marshall Smith, *Baseball Digest*, September 1951, pp. 39–45. This is the source of the Marrero quotes and descriptions.
10. Shirley Povich, *Washington Post*, April 21, 1951, p. 1.
11. Marshall Smith, *Baseball Digest*, September 1951, p. 39–45.
12. *Ibid.*
13. Shirley Povich, *Washington Post*, February 29, 1952, p. B5.
14. *Baseball Digest*, April 1953, p. 14.
15. *Ibid.*
16. Shirley Povich, *Washington Post*, February 17, 1952, p. C1.
17. *Baseball Digest*, May 1956.
18. Shirley Povich, *Baseball Digest*, September 1952. p. 6–9.
19. Shirley Povich, *Washington Post*, May 25, 1952, p. C1.
20. Shirley Povich, *Washington Post*, July 4, 1952, p. 10.
21. *Baseball Digest*, October 22, 1952, p. 12.
22. *The Sporting News*, March 11, 1953, p. 26.
23. Bob Addie, *Washington Post*, January 15, 1957, p. A17.
24. *Washington Post*, September 25, 1954, pp. 1 and 12.

Chapter 21

1. Francis Stann, *Baseball Digest*, July 1959, p. 5.
2. *Baseball Digest*, March 1959.
3. *The Sporting News*, June 16, 1954, p. 37.
4. Harris's sons interview.
5. Koppett, *The Man in the Dugout*, 267.
6. *New York Times*, September 7, 1954, p. 29.
7. *New York Times*, September 8, 1954, p. 41.
8. *Washington Post*, September 9, 1954, p. 19.
9. Shirley Povich, *The Sporting News*, March 17, 1954, p. 13.
10. Shirley Povich, *The Sporting News*, March 10, 1954, p. 14.

11. Shirley Povich, *The Sporting News*, March 17, 1954, p. 13.

12. *Baseball Digest*, November 1954, p. 77.

13. Hal Middlesworth, *Baseball Digest*, January 1956, p. 39.

14. Bob Addie, *Baseball Digest*, October 1955, p. 15.

15. Telephone interview with Paul Foytack, June 23, 2009.

16. Telephone interview with Frank Lary, June 23, 2009.

17. *Baseball Digest*, March, 1956, p. 77.

18. *Chicago Tribune*, June 27, 1956, p. C3.

19. Patrick Joseph Harrigan, *The Detroit Tigers: Club and Community* (Toronto, Canada: University of Toronto Press, 1997), 58–61.

20. *The Sporting News*, September 5, 1956, p. 25.

21. *Washington Post*, September 28, 1956, p. 61.

22. Watson Spoelstra, *The Sporting News*, October 3, 1956, p. 20.

Chapter 22

1. *Boston Globe*, "Boston Red Sox and Racism," June 18, 2001.

2. http://www.npr.org/programs/morning/features/2002/oct/redsox/.

3. Clark Booth, *Dorchester Reporter*, July 23, 2009.

4. *Jet* magazine, May 7, 1959, p. 53.

5. http://www.npr.org/programs/morning/features/2002/oct/redsox/.

6. Clark Booth, *Dorchester Reporter*, July 23, 2009.

7. Will McDonough, *Boston Globe*, December 2, 2000.

8. Chuck Davis, *Chicago Defender*, August 27, 1950.

9. Scott Ostler, *San Francisco Chronicle*, July 21, 2009.

10. Paul Harber, *Boston Globe*, April 26, 2005.

11. Ed Linn, *Hitter: The Life and Turmoils of Ted Williams* (Boston: Mariner Books, 1994), 222.

12. *Ibid.*, 313.

13. Howard Bryant, *Shut Out: A Story of Race and Baseball in Boston* (Boston: Beacon Press, 2002), 52.

14. Clark Booth, *Dorchester Reporter*, July 23, 2009.

15. *Jet* magazine, "Do the Red Sox Practice Jim Crow?" May 7, 1959.

16. *The Sporting News*, July 15, 1959.

17. Linn, *Hitter*, 302.

18. *The Sporting News*, July 8, 1959, p. 16.

19. Shirley Povich, "This Morning," *Washington Post*, September 8, 1960.

20. *Christian Science Monitor*, June 11, 1959.

21. *Jet* magazine, August 6, 1959.

22. Juan Williams' radio report, http://www.npr.org/programs/morning/features/2002/oct/redsox/, October 11, 2002.

Chapter 23

1. William Barry Furlong, *Washington Post*, August 19, 1975, p. D1.

2. Harris's sons interview.

3. Bob Addie, *Washington Post*, August 18, 1975, p. D1.

4. Interview with Drew Smith, October 9, 2009.

5. Harris's sons interview.

6. Furlong, *Washington Post*, August 19, 1975, p. D1.

7. Bob Addie, *Washington Post*, April 4, 1962, p. C1.

8. Associated Press syndicated story, including *San Antonio Express and News*, January 26, 1963.

9. Dave Brady, *Washington Post*, January 26, 1962, p. D19.

10. Bob Addie, *Washington Post*, November 9, 1971, p. D9.

11. *Washington Post*, January 20, 1970, p. D1.

12. Bob Addie, *Washington Post*, August 19, 1975.

13. Bob Addie, Washington Post, November 10, 1972, p. D4.

14. *Christian Science Monitor*, August 3, 1960.

15. Dave Brady, *Washington Post*, January 26, 1962, p. D19.

16. Bob Addie, *Washington Post*, August 19, 1975.

17. Bob Addie, *Washington Post*, November 9, 1976, D8.

18. Bob Arnebeck, *Washington Post*, April 27, 1975, p. 250.

Epilogue

1. Bill Broeg, *The Sporting News*, March 22, 1975, page 34.

2. *Baseball Digest*, March, 1951.

3. Ed Rumill, "In the Dugout," *Christian Science Monitor*, February 25, 1943.

4. *Baseball Digest*, March 1953.

5. Fay Vincent, *The Only Game in Town* (New York: Simon & Schuster, 2006) 66.

Bibliography

Books

Barra, Allen. *Yogi Berra, Eternal Yankee*. New York: W.W. Norton, 2009.

Berra, Yogi, with Dave Kaplar. *Ten Rings: My Championship Seasons*. New York: Harper-Collins, 2003.

Browning, Reed. *Baseball's Greatest Season, 1924*. Boston: University of Massachusetts Press, 2003.

Bryant, Howard. *Shut Out: A Story of Race and Baseball in Boston*. Boston: Beacon Press, 2002.

Carmichael, Jerome P. *My Greatest Day in Baseball*. New Haven, CT: A.S. Barnes,1945.

Cramer, Richard. *Joe DiMaggio: The Hero's Life*. New York: Simon & Schuster, 2000.

DeVito, Carlo. *Yogi: The Life and Times of an American Original*. Chicago: Triumph, 2008.

Harrigan, Patrick Joseph. *The Detroit Tigers: Club and Community, 1945–1995*. Toronto: University of Toronto Press, 1997.

Harris, Bucky. *Playing the Game: From Mine Boy to Manager*. New York: Frederick A. Stokes, 1925.

James, Bill. *The Bill James Guide to Baseball Managers from 1870 to Today*. New York: Scribner's, 1997.

Jones, David, editor. *Deadball Stars of the American League*. Dulles, VA: Potomac, 2006.

Judge, Mark Gauvreau. *Damn Senators: My Grandfather and the Story of Washington's Only World Series Championship*. San Francisco: Encounter, 2003.

Kaiser, David. *Epic Season: The 1948 American League Pennant Race*. Amherst: University of Massachusetts Press, 1998.

Koppett, Leonard. *The Man in the Dugout: Baseball's Top Managers and How They Got That Way*. New York: Crown, 1993.

Linn, Ed. *Hitter: The Life and Turmoils of Ted Williams*. Boston: Mariner Books, 1994.

Naismith, James. *Basketball: Its Origin and Development*. New York: Associated Press, 1941.

Overfield, Joe. *The 100 Seasons of Buffalo Baseball*. Kenmore, NY: Partners Press, 1985.

Peterson, Robert W. *Cages to Jump Shots: Pro Basketball's Early Years*. Lincoln: University of Nebraska Press, 2002.

Sullivan, Neil J. *The Diamond in the Bronx: Yankee Stadium and the Politics of New York*. New York: Oxford University, 2002.

Thomas, Henry W. *Walter Johnson: Baseball's Big Train*. Lincoln: University of Nebraska Press, 1995.

Thorn, John. *The Relief Pitcher: Baseball's New Hero*. New York: Dutton, 1979.

Trimble, Joe, in Bannon, Joseph L., Jr., and Wright, Joanna L., coordinating eds. *Yogi Berra: An American Original*. Champaign, IL: Sports Publishing, 1998.

Vincent, Fay. *The Only Game in Town: Baseball Stars of the 1930s and 1940s Talk About the Game They Loved*. New York: Simon & Schuster, 2006.

Newspapers

Boston Daily Globe, 1920–2005
Brooklyn Eagle, 1925
Buffalo Evening News, 1943
Chicago Defender, 1950
Chicago Tribune, 1924–1954
Christian Science Monitor, 1919–1959
Dallas Morning News, 1934
Dorchester Reporter, 2009
Fredrick News Post, 1925
Gettysburg Times, 1943
Hartford Courant, 1922–1944
Lebanon Daily News, 1943
Los Angeles Times, 1924–1949
New York Times, 1921–1977
Philadelphia Evening Public Ledger, 1924
San Antonio Express and News, 1963
San Francisco Chronicle, 2009
San Diego Daily Journal, 1948–1949
San Diego Union, 1948–1949
Washington Post, 1919–1977
Wilkes-Barre Sunday Independent, 1924
Wilkes-Barre Times Leader, 1892–1922

Magazines

The Sporting News, 1920–1975
Baseball Digest, 1951–1964
Baseball Magazine, 1953–1970
Jet, 1959

On-line sources

http://www.bioproj.sabr.org.http://sportsillustrated.cnn.com
http://www.hoopedia.nba.com
http://www.jewishsports.net
http://www.npr.org/programs/morning/features
http://www.retrosheet.org
http://www.sabr.org
http://www.thedeadballera.com
http://www.whitehouse.gov/about/presidents

Index